BOLLINGEN SERIES XLVII

ISIS
Tomb of Thutmosis IV, Thebes, XVIII *Dynasty*

THE
GREAT MOTHER

AN ANALYSIS OF THE ARCHETYPE

BY

ERICH NEUMANN

Translated from the German by
RALPH MANHEIM

BOLLINGEN SERIES XLVII

PRINCETON UNIVERSITY PRESS

COPYRIGHT 1955, © 1963 BY BOLLINGEN FOUNDATION INC., NEW YORK, N. Y.;
COPYRIGHT © RENEWED 1983 BY PRINCETON UNIVERSITY PRESS
Published by Princeton University Press, Princeton, N. J.
ALL RIGHTS RESERVED

Second Edition, 1963

First Princeton / Bollingen Paperback Edition, 1972
Second Printing, 1974

Seventh paperback printing, for the Princeton / Bollingen Mythos series, 1991

THIS IS THE FORTY-SEVENTH IN A SERIES OF WORKS
SPONSORED BY
BOLLINGEN FOUNDATION

Library of Congress Catalogue Card No.: 55–10026
ISBN 0–691–01780–8 (paperback edn.)
ISBN 0–691–09742–9 (hardcover edn.)

12   11   10   9   8

PRINTED IN THE UNITED STATES OF AMERICA
BY PRINCETON UNIVERSITY PRESS, PRINCETON, NEW JERSEY

TEXT DESIGNED BY ANDOR BRAUN

To C. G. Jung

FRIEND AND MASTER
IN HIS EIGHTIETH YEAR

FOREWORD

SOME years ago Professor C. G. Jung and Mrs. Olga Froebe-Kapteyn suggested that I write an introduction to the first publication of material from the Eranos Archive for Symbolic Research in Ascona, Switzerland—a volume devoted to the manifestations, in art and culture, of the Great Mother archetype.

In founding the Eranos Archive Mrs. Froebe has taken the lead in the important task of tracking down, collecting, and arranging examples of archetypal material that has found its creative expression in art.

I am deeply grateful not only for the original suggestion but also for Mrs. Froebe's generous consent to my enlargement of her original plan. For it soon became clear that the work was undergoing a transformation in my hands, and that for me the written text, an exposition of the Archetypal Feminine, was assuming paramount importance. The reproductions from the Eranos Archive had become illustrations to this text. These represent perhaps half the pictorial material of the present volume, having been supplemented by many more examples.

Yet it should not be thought that the pictures merely provided the first spark of inspiration; throughout my work on this book they held the center of my interest and determined the whole content and rhythm of my thinking. In this sense the book, even in its present form, may be regarded wholly as a presentation of the Eranos Archive.

I wish to thank the Bollingen Foundation for making possible not only the writing of this book but also its translation into English. I owe personal thanks to the editorial staff of Bollingen Series, particularly for supplying most of the picture sources and other reference apparatus. To Mr. Ralph Manheim I owe special thanks for his care and skill in making the translation. A number of persons who have helped me in composing and revising my text have wished to remain unnamed. I should like here to express my thanks to them all.

E. N.

Tel Aviv, 1952; October, 1954

NOTE OF ACKNOWLEDGMENT

Acknowledgment of the sources of the plates is made as fully as possible in the List of Plates. Every effort has been made by the publishers to locate the source of each photograph reproduced and to give due credit, but in a number of in-stances this has not been possible. The publishers and the author wish to express their appreciation for the use of all of the illustrative material. Grateful acknowl-edgment is made to the following publishers and others for the reproduction of illustrations or for permission to quote:

Allen and Unwin, London, for passages from Briffault, *The Mothers;* American-Scandinavian Foundation, New York, for passages from *The Poetic Edda;* British School of Archaeology at Athens, for a figure from its *Annual,* Vol. VII; Cahiers d'Art, Paris, for plates from Zervos, *La Civilization de la Sar-daigne* and *L'Art en Grèce;* Cambridge University Press for a figure from Harrison, *Themis;* Chatto and Windus, London, for passages and a figure from Layard, *The Stone Men of Malekula;* Dodd, Mead and Co., New York, for a figure from Fergusson, *History of Indian and Eastern Architecture;* Faber and Faber, London, and the Czechoslovak Theatrical and Literary Agency, Prague, for a passage from Karel Čapek; Folkwang-Verlag, Hagen, Germany, for illustrations from Danzel, *Mexiko,* and Fuhrmann, *Peru II;* W. de Gruyter and Co., Berlin, for figures from Ermann, *Die Religion der Ägypter;* Harvard University Press, for passages from the Homeric Hymns in the Loeb Classical Library; J. C. Hinrichs Verlag, Leipzig, for an illustration from *Der Alte Orient;* H. Keller Verlag, Berlin, for an illustration from Deubner, *Attische Feste;* Alfred A. Knopf, New York, for a figure from Glotz, *The Aegean Civilization;* Kungliga Vitterhetshistorieoch Antikvites Akademia, Stockholm, for a plate from Roosval, *Die Steinmeister Gotlands;* Macmillan and Co., London, for figures from various works of Sir Arthur J. Evans; Thomas Nelson and Sons, Edinburgh, for extracts from the Rouse translations of the Iliad and the Odyssey; Orell Füssli Verlag, Zurich, for illustrations from Leicht, *Indianische Kunst,* and for our plate 82a; Penguin

NOTE OF ACKNOWLEDGMENT

Books, Harmondsworth, for passages and figures from Piggott, *Prehistoric India;* E. Pfeiffer Verlag, Leipzig, for a plate from Benzinger, *Hebräische Archäologie;* Presses Universitaires de France, Paris, for an illustration from Sarzec's work on Chaldea; Princeton University Press, for passages from *Ancient Near Eastern Texts;* Putnam and Co., London, for a passage and a plate from Oppenheim, *Tell Halaf;* Anton Schroll and Co., Vienna, for figures from Hoernes, *Urgeschichte der bildenden Kunst;* B. Schwabe and Co., Basel, for figures from Mode, *Indische Frühkulturen;* Charles Scribner's Sons, New York, and Macmillan, London, for a poem by George Meredith; Society of Antiquaries of Scotland, for a figure from Allen, *The Early Christian Monuments of Scotland;* J. Springer Verlag, Berlin, for illustrations from Prinzhorn, *Bildnerei der Geisteskranken;* Stanford University Press and Geoffrey Cumberlege, Oxford University Press, London, for figures from Morley, *The Ancient Maya;* Editions "Tel," Paris, for our plates 136, 137, and 160, from the *Encyclopedie photographique;* Thames and Hudson, New York and London, for an illustration from Leenhardt, *Arts of the Oceanic Peoples;* Verlag Ullstein (Propyläen-Verlag), Berlin, for illustrations from Glaser, *Gotische Holzschnitte,* Holländer, *Aeskulap und Venus,* and Schäfer and Andrae, *Die Kunst des Alten Orients;* Mr. Philip Wayne, for a passage translated from Goethe.

NOTE TO THE SECOND EDITION

For the present edition, the references and bibliography as well as some of the quotations have been revised in order to bring them into accord with the English translations of works by Erich Neumann and by C. G. Jung which have been issued since 1955. Other corrections of a minor nature have been made in the text and captions. It was the author's wish that the motto from J. J. Bachofen be added at the beginning of Part I.

CONTENTS

xii

Contents

xiii

LIST OF PLATES

While about half of the plates were originally chosen from the pictures in the Eranos Archive, many have been replaced by technically more satisfactory photographs obtained from museums, professional photographers, etc. (The abbreviation P means "photograph.") Where original Eranos Archive pictures have been reproduced, the actual photographic source is given if known; every effort has been made to trace the original source and to make proper acknowledgment. Full references to books and articles are given in the Bibliography of this volume.

xv

xvi

List of Plates

xix

48. Baubo figures
Terra cotta, Priene, Asia Minor, v century B.C.
Museum für Völkerkunde, Berlin. P: Unknown source

49. Goddess
Alabaster, Parthian, c. I–II century A.D.
Louvre. P: Giraudon

50. The earth goddess Tlazolteotl
Aztec, Codex Borbonicus, fol. 13, date unknown
Chambre des Députés, Paris. Drawing from Danzel, *Mexiko*, Vol. I, Pl. 37b

51. Hecate-Artemis as whelping bitch
Black stone scaraboid seal, archaic Ionian style
Collection of Dr. Rudolph Reitler, Haifa. P: Courtesy of the owner

52. Winged goddess
Terra cotta, Mexico (Colima complex), pre-Columbian
Collection of Mrs. Henry Moore. P: Courtesy of Mrs. Moore and Curt Valentin

53. Female figure
Red clay, Ixtlán de Rio, near Tepic, Mexico, pre-Columbian
Museum für Völkerkunde und Vorgeschichte, Hamburg. P: Museum

54. The nude goddess
Impressions of cylinder seals, hematite (except c, green jasper). a–c, Babylon, I Dynasty; d–g, Syria, c. 1450 B.C.
Pierpont Morgan Library, New York. (Cf. Porada and Buchanan, *Corpus of Ancient Near Eastern Seals*, Vol. I, resp. figs. 504, 503, 505, 944 [here reversed], 945 [here reversed], 946, 937.)
P: Library

55a. Enthroned nude figure
Terra cotta, Sanctuary of Delphi, perhaps prehistoric
Delphi Museum. P: From *Fouilles de Delphe*, Vol. V (Paris, 1908), fig. 60, p. 14

55b. Vessel: female figure with snake
Terra cotta, red glaze, from a tomb at Kournasa, Crete, early Minoan II period
P: From Evans, *Palace of Minos*, Vol. IV, Pt. 1, fig. 121, p. 163

56. Snake goddess
Faïence, Palace at Knossos, Crete, middle Minoan III period
Candia Museum. P: British Museum, from a restored cast in its possession

57. Alchemical vessel
Codex Pluto 89, sup. 35, fol. 20b, XIII century
Biblioteca Medicea Laurentiana, Florence. P: Unknown source

58. Snake goddess
Terra cotta, Greece, VI century B.C.
Museum Antiker Kleinkunst, Munich. P: Unknown source

59. Atargatis, or Dea Syria
Bronze, Rome
Museo Nazionale delle Terme, Rome. P: Alinari

List of Plates

xxi

List of Plates

82*b*. Snail god
Clay vessel, Peru, Chimu culture, pre-Columbian
Museum für Völkerkunde und Vorgeschichte, Hamburg. P: Museum

83*a*. Sea crab with star god
Clay vessel, Peru, Chimu culture, pre-Columbian
Museum für Völkerkunde, Berlin. P: Museum

83*b*. Sea crab with star god
Clay vessel, Peru, Chimu culture, pre-Columbian
Formerly in Museum für Völkerkunde, Frankfort on the Main (destroyed during the Second World War). P: Unknown source

84*a*. Serpents strangling (?) the star god
Clay vessel, Peru, Chimu culture, pre-Columbian
Museum für Völkerkunde und Vorgeschichte, Hamburg. P: From Fuhrmann, *Peru II*, Pl. 74

84*b*. Gorgon goddess with snakes
Clay pitcher, Peru, Chimu-influenced culture, pre-Columbian
Ethnological Collection, Zurich University. P: From Leicht, *Indianische Kunst*, p. 243, fig. 6

84*c*. Crab goddess giving birth
Painted clay vessel, Peru, Chimu culture, pre-Columbian
Formerly in the Museum für Völkerkunde, Frankfort on the Main (destroyed in the Second World War). P: From Fuhrmann, *Peru II*, Pl. 95

85. The solar barge passing into the mountain of the west
Detail from an Egyptian papyrus (?)
P: Drawing from Maspero, *The Dawn of Civilization*, p. 197

86. Female figurines
Clay, Aztec, central Mexico, lower middle culture
American Museum of Natural History, New York. P: Courtesy of the Museum

THE GREAT ROUND

87. Goddess
Alabaster figure with shell and lapis-lazuli eyes, Temple of Ishtar, Mari, Syria, c. 3000 B.C.
Aleppo Museum. P: From *Syria, Revue d'Art Oriental et d'Archéologie*, 1935, Pl. 10, fig. 1, following p. 26

88. Funerary figure
Basalt, Tell Halaf, Mesopotamia, IX century B.C.
Institut für Vorderasiatische Altertumskunde, Freie Universität, Berlin. P: F. Paul Mann, Berlin

89. Veiled sphinx
Stone, Tell Halaf, Mesopotamia, IX century B.C.
Institut für Vorderasiatische Altertumskunde, Freie Universität, Berlin. P: From Oppenheim, *Tell Halaf*, Pl. XI

List of Plates

List of Plates

164. Theodorus Poulakis, of Crete: *Madonna*
Detail of painting, second half XVII *century*
P: Em. Seraf, Athens

165. Philosophia-Sophia
From manuscript of Herrad of Landsberg, Hortus deliciarum, XII *century*
Formerly in Bibliothèque nationale, Strasbourg (destroyed 1870). Reconstructed drawing from Keller and Straub (eds.), *Hortus deliciarum*

166. Philosophia with the World Disk
Miniature from a manuscript of St. Augustine's De civitate Dei *(MS. 9005/06). Flanders, c. 1420*
Bibliothèque royale, Brussels. P: Staatliche Bildstelle, Berlin

167. Madonna as Paradise
From MS. 665, fol. 191, XIV *century*
Universitätsbibliothek, Leipzig. P: Bibliothek

168. Baptism
Miniature from Les Grandes Heures du duc de Berry *(MS. Lat. 919), 1413 or earlier*
Bibliothèque nationale, Paris. P: Bibliothèque

169. Paradise as vessel
Page from Wynandus de Stega, Adamas colluctancium aquilarum *(Codex Palatinus Latinus 412),* XV *century*
Vatican Library. P: Library

170. Alchemical egg vessel
Page from the De lapide Philosophorum *(MS. Sloane 1171),* XVI *century*
British Museum. P: Museum

171. Alchemical vessel with tree
From Abraham the Jew, Livre des figures hieroglifiques *(MS. Français 14765, fol. 317),* XVI *century*
Bibliothèque nationale. P: Bibliothèque

172. Bartel Bruyn (*c.* 1493–1555): *The Annunciation*
Painting, Cologne
Rheinisches Landesmuseum, Bonn. P: Museum

173. The Outpouring of the Holy Spirit
Miniature from Beatus' Commentary on the Apocalypse (MS. Lat. nouv. acq. 1366, fol. 120), XII *century*
Bibliothèque nationale, Paris. P: Bibliothèque

174. Sophia-Sapientia
Detail from MS. Pal. Lat. 1066.
Vatican Library. P: Library

175. Ecclesia
Single-leaf drawing from a German XII-*century manuscript*
Collection Forrer, Strasbourg. P: Unknown source

xxxi

LIST OF TEXT FIGURES

See Bibliography for full references to publications.

List of Text Figures

List of Text Figures

PREFACE

I N THIS work we have attempted a structural analysis of an archetype; we have striven to show its inner growth and dynamic, and its
manifestation in the myths and symbols of mankind. Such an undertaking is one of the central needs of analytical psychology. For, in both a
theoretical and a practical sense, it is very hard for those who have not
experienced the reality of the archetype by undergoing analysis to
understand what depth psychology means by an archetype.

Throughout, we have cited an abundance of aesthetic and mythological material, but even so, selectivity has been necessary. Our choice
may be arbitrary in the sense that every work of art and every myth
might be replaced by similar or corresponding examples. But we believe
that the work of arrangement, development, and classification of this
material attempted in Part II is not arbitrary, inasmuch as it is based
on the psychology and structural analysis of the archetype provided in
Part I.

The reader who is not interested in our inherently difficult theoretical analysis of the archetype may prefer to begin by reading Part II,
which, with its abundance of literary and pictorial illustrations, may
alone provide a considerable insight into the archetypal world. Those
who wish to obtain a fundamental orientation will require Part I.

By this we do not wish to imply that Part I is addressed only to a
restricted circle of scientific psychologists. On the contrary, our aim has
been to provide anyone who is seriously interested with an introduction
to the world of the archetypes, and to make this introduction as simple
as possible. For this reason we have included in Part I a number of
schemas, or diagrams, which, as experience has shown, make things
much easier for most people, though by no means for all.

Our exposition does not deal with the archetype in general, but with a specific archetype, namely, that of the Feminine or, in a more restricted sense, of the Great Mother.

This book, which was preceded by a small volume of short works on the same theme and by a commentary on Apuleius' tale of Eros and Psyche,[1] is the first part of a "depth psychology of the Feminine." The investigation of the special character of the feminine psyche is one of the most necessary and important tasks of depth psychology in its preoccupation with the creative health and development of the individual.

But this problem of the Feminine has equal importance for the psychologist of culture, who recognizes that the peril of present-day mankind springs in large part from the one-sidedly patriarchal development of the male intellectual consciousness, which is no longer kept in balance by the matriarchal world of the psyche. In this sense the exposition of the archetypal-psychical world of the Feminine that we have attempted in our work is also a contribution to a future therapy of culture.

Western mankind must arrive at a synthesis that includes the feminine world—which is also one-sided in its isolation. Only then will the individual human being be able to develop the psychic wholeness that is urgently needed if Western man is to face the dangers that threaten his existence from within and without.

The development of a psychic wholeness, in which the consciousness of every individual is creatively allied with the contents of the unconscious, is the depth psychologist's pedagogical ideal for the future. Only this wholeness of the individual can make possible a fertile and living community. Just as in a certain sense a sound body is the foundation for a sound spirit and psyche, so a sound individual is the basis for a sound community. It is this basic fact of human collective life, so often ignored, that gives psychological work with the individual its social significance and its significance for the therapy of human culture. Not

[1] My *Zur Psychologie des Weiblichen* and *Amor and Psyche*. [For full references, see the Bibliography.]

only does our concern with the archaic world of the archetypes—though they are seemingly anachronistic and far removed from the everyday reality of modern man—provide the foundation for all psychotherapy; it opens up to man a view of the world that not only enriches his own personality but also gives him a new perspective on life and on mankind as a whole. The experience of the archetypal world leads to an inner form of humanization that, because it is not a knowledge of consciousness but an experience of the whole man, will perhaps one day prove more reliable than the form of humanism known to us up to now, which is not grounded in depth psychology. One of the decisive symptoms of this new humanization is the development of the psychological conscience in the individual and in the community, without which any future development of imperiled humanity seems unthinkable.

I

Wir sind ja alle genötigt, unsere Ziele weiter zu stecken, als unsere Kräfte
reichen, um am Ende nicht weniger zu leisten, als sie erlauben.
                           —Bachofen, *Die Sage von Tanaquil*

Chapter One

THE STRUCTURE OF THE
ARCHETYPE

W HEN analytical psychology speaks of the primordial image or archetype of the Great Mother, it is referring, not to any concrete image existing in space and time, but to an inward image at work in the human psyche. The symbolic expression of this psychic phenomenon is to be found in the figures of the Great Goddess represented in the myths and artistic creations of mankind.

The effect of this archetype may be followed through the whole of history, for we can demonstrate its workings in the rites, myths, symbols of early man and also in the dreams, fantasies, and creative works of the sound as well as the sick man of our own day.

In order to explain what analytical psychology means by an "archetype," [1] we must distinguish its emotional-dynamic components, its symbolism, its material component, and its structure.

The dynamic, the effect of the archetype, is manifested in energetic processes within the psyche, processes that take place both in the unconscious and between the unconscious and consciousness. This effect appears, for example, in positive and negative emotions, in fascinations and projections, and also in anxiety, in manic and depressive states, and in the feeling that the ego is being overpowered. Every

[1] Jolande Jacobi, *Complex/Archetype/Symbol*. [For full references, see the Bibliography.]

3

mood that takes hold of the entire personality is an expression of the dynamic effect of an archetype, regardless whether this effect is accepted or rejected by the human consciousness; whether it remains unconscious or grips the consciousness.

The symbolism of the archetype is its manifestation in specific psychic images, which are perceived by consciousness and which are different for each archetype. The different aspects of an archetype are also manifested in different images. Thus, for example, the terrible aspect and the life-giving, "kindly" aspect of an archetype appear in diverging images. But on the other hand, the terribleness of one archetype, e.g., the Terrible Mother, is expressed in other symbols than that of another archetype, e.g., the Terrible Father.

By the material component of an archetype we mean the sense content that is apprehended by consciousness. When, however, we say that an archetypal content of the unconscious is assimilated, this assimilation—if we disregard the emotional character of the archetype— refers to the material component.

The structure of the archetype is the complex network of psychic organization, which includes dynamism, symbolism, and sense content, and whose center and intangible unifier is the archetype itself.

The archetype is manifested principally in the fact that it determines human behavior unconsciously but in accordance with laws and independently of the experience of the individual. "As *a priori* conditioning factors, [the archetypes] represent a special, psychological instance of the biological 'pattern of behaviour,' which gives all living creatures their specific qualities." [2] This dynamic component of the unconscious has a compelling character for the individual who is directed by it, and it is always accompanied by a strong emotional component.

In other words, a state of biopsychical seizure is always connected with the constellation of an archetype. This latter may bring about a change in the instincts and drives as well as in the passion, affectivity, and, on a higher plane, in the feeling tone of the personality on which the archetype works. But the dynamic action of the archetype extends

[2] C. G. Jung, "Trinity," p. 149 n.

beyond unconscious instinct and continues to operate as an unconscious will that determines the personality, exerting a decisive influence on the mood, inclinations, and tendencies of the personality, and ultimately on its conceptions, intentions, interests, on consciousness and the specific direction of the mind.[3]

When the unconscious content is perceived, it confronts consciousness in the symbolic form of an image. For "A psychic entity can be a conscious content, that is, it can be represented, only if it has the quality of an image and is thus representable." [4] For this reason, even the instincts, the psychic dominants, which of all unconscious contents are most important for the psychological totality, seem to be linked with representations of images. The function of the image symbol in the psyche is always to produce a compelling effect on consciousness. Thus, for example, a psychic image whose purpose it is to attract the attention of consciousness, in order, let us say, to provoke flight, must be so striking that it cannot possibly fail to make an impression. The archetypal image symbol corresponds, then, in its impressiveness, significance, energetic charge, and numinosity, to the original importance of instinct for man's existence. The term "numinous" [5] applies to the action of beings and forces that the consciousness of primitive man experienced as fascinating, terrible, overpowering, and that it therefore attributed to an indefinite transpersonal and divine source.

The representation of the instincts in consciousness, that is to say, their manifestation in images, is one of the essential conditions of consciousness in general,[6] and the genesis of consciousness as a vital psychic organ is decisively bound up with this reflection of the unconscious psychic process in it. This fundamental constellation is itself a *product* of the unconscious, which thus constellates consciousness, and not merely an "activity" of consciousness itself. For this reason Jung

---

[3] Here we cannot concern ourselves with the fact that this dynamic effect of the archetype plays a crucial role in psychic disorder, particularly in psychosis, but also in neurosis. Jung, "On the Nature of the Psyche," section on "Patterns of Behaviour and the Archetypes," pp. 200 ff.

[4] Jung, "Spirit and Life," p. 322.

[5] Rudolf Otto, *The Idea of the Holy.*

[6] My *Origins and History of Consciousness.*

says: "The primordial image might suitably be described as the *instinct's perception of itself*, or as the self-portrait of the instinct." [7]

Thus, despite the seeming contrast between them, the instinctual plane of the drive and the pictorial plane of consciousness belong together, for "man finds himself simultaneously driven to act and free to reflect." [8] "As well as being an image in its own right, [the archetype] is at the same time a dynamism." [9]

But the pictorial plane, on which the archetype becomes visible to consciousness, is the plane of the symbol, and it is here that the activity of the unconscious manifests itself in so far as it is capable of reaching consciousness. [10]

Symbolic images, as archetypal representations, must be distinguished from the "archetype *an sich*." [11] "The archetype *an sich* is an 'irrepresentable' factor, a 'disposition' which starts functioning at a given moment in the development of the human mind and arranges the material of consciousness into definite patterns." [12]

For this reason Jung says that "[the archetypes] exist preconsciously, and presumably they form the structural dominants of the psyche in general. They may be compared to the invisible presence of the crystal lattice in a saturated solution." [13] In other words, the "archetype *an sich*" is a nuclear phenomenon transcending consciousness, and its "eternal presence" [14] is nonvisible. But not only does it act as a magnetic field, directing the unconscious behavior of the personality through the pattern of behavior set up by the instincts; it also operates as a pattern of vision in the consciousness, ordering the psychic material into symbolic images.

We designate the symbols belonging to an archetype as its symbol group or symbol canon. A difficulty arises, however, from the fact that this co-ordination is not unequivocal. For "the single archetypes are not

---

[7] "Instinct and the Unconscious," p. 136.
[8] Jung, "On the Nature of the Psyche," p. 206.
[9] Ibid., p. 211.
[10] Jung, *Psychological Types*, Def. "symbol"; Jacobi, *Complex*.

[11] Jung, "On the Nature of the Psyche," p. 213 (where tr. as "archetype as such").
[12] Jung, "Trinity," p. 148 f.
[13] Ibid., p. 149 n.
[14] Jung, *Psychology and Alchemy*, p. 211.

isolated from each other in the unconscious, but are in a state of contamination, of the most complete, mutual interpenetration and interfusion." [15] This contamination is proportionately greater as the differentiating consciousness is weaker; it diminishes as consciousness develops and—what amounts to the same thing—learns to make clearer differentiations.

Thus to the differentiation of consciousness corresponds a more differentiated manifestation of the unconscious, its archetypes and symbols.[16] As consciousness unfolds, the unconscious manifests itself in a series of forms, ranging from the absolute numinosity of the "archetype *an sich*," through the scarcely definable image paradox of its first emergence—in which images that would seem to be mutually exclusive appear side by side—to the primordial archetype.

The term "primordial archetype" is a seeming pleonasm and requires explanation. We employ the concept of the archetype as Jung has clearly defined it in his most recent writings [17]—as a structural concept signifying "eternal presence." But since for an understanding of the history of consciousness and for psychotherapeutic practice it has proved essential to differentiate the archetype from the standpoint of its "development" within the psyche, we employ the term primordial archetype to stress the genetic aspect: by it we define the archetype as manifested in the early phase of human consciousness before differentiation into the particular archetypes. The process of the differentiation of archetypal phenomena, which I have designated in my *Origins and History of Consciousness* as the "fragmentation of archetypes," leads to the emergence of individual archetypes from a great complex mass, and to the formation of coherent archetypal groups.

Parallel to this development, the symbols are differentiated and ordered. The symbols are the manifest visibility of the archetype, corresponding to its latent invisibility. While, for example, the primordial archetype may contain the most diverse and contradictory symbols,

---

[15] Jung, "Archetypes of the Collective Unconscious" (1939–40 edn.), p. 91.

[16] My *Origins*, pp. 325 f.

[17] Especially "On the Nature of the Psyche."

which for consciousness are mutually exclusive—e.g., positive and negative, male and female—these symbols later split apart and order themselves according to the principle of opposites.

The symbols, like the archetype itself, possess a dynamic and a material component. They take hold of the human personality as a whole, arouse it and fascinate it, and attract consciousness, which strives to interpret them.

The material component of the symbol sets consciousness in motion; aroused by the symbol, consciousness directs its interest toward it and seeks to understand it. That is to say, the symbol, aside from its dynamic effect as an "energy transformer," [18] is also a "molder of consciousness," impelling the psyche to assimilate the unconscious content or contents contained in the symbol.[19] This assimilation culminates in the formation of views, orientations, and concepts by consciousness; although these have their origin in the sense content of the symbol and hence in the collective unconscious, of which the archetype is a part, they now, independent of their origin, claim an existence and validity of their own.[20]

Let us take as an example the archetype of the "way." As far as we know, this archetype first appeared among the prehistoric men of the ice age. In a ritual that was still in large part unconscious, the way led these early men into mountain caves, in whose hidden and almost inaccessible recesses they established "temples" adorned with representations of animals on the killing of which their existence depended.

The magical and sacral significance of these paintings and of the caves in which they are found is today unquestioned. But it is also evident that the "hard and dangerous way," by which alone these caves could often be reached, formed a part of the ritual reality of the mountain temples that we now see in them.[21]

At a later cultural stage, when consciousness was more highly developed, this archetype of the way became a conscious ritual. In the

[18] Jung, "On Psychic Energy," pp. 41 f.
[19] My *Origins*, pp. 367 ff.
[20] Cassirer, *The Philosophy of Symbolic Forms*, Vol. III: *The Phenomenology of Knowledge*.

[21] My "Zur psychologischen Bedeutung des Ritus," in *Kulturentwicklung und Religion*, pp. 9 f.

temple precinct, for example—from the temples of Egypt to the Boro-budur of Java—the worshiper is compelled to follow a ritual way from the periphery to the center, the shrine. Christ's Calvary is another, more highly developed form of this archetype: here the way of destiny becomes the way of redemption; and with Christ's conscious utterance, "I am the way," this archetype attains to a new, wholly inward, and symbolic level, which has determined the attitudes of all the ensuing generations that have re-enacted this inward Christian way. Moreover, this symbol of the archetypal way has taken a universal place in the consciousness and orientation of modern man. We take for granted such expressions as "inner ways of development"; and the companion symbols of "orientation" and "disorientation," as well as references to philosophical, political, artistic "trends," belong to the same context. All these linguistic formulations are based on the archetype of the way, whose pattern determines the originally unconscious behavior of man moving toward a sacral goal.

The difficulty of describing the structure of an individual archetype arises in part from the fact that the archetype and the symbol erupt on a number of planes, often at the same time. The phenomenology of the workings of the archetype extends from the unconscious instinctive drive of the primitive individual, contained in the group, to the formulation of concepts and beliefs in the philosophical systems of the modern individual. In other words, a vast number of forms, symbols, and images, of views, aspects, and concepts, which exclude one another and overlap, which complement one another and apparently emerge independently of one another, but all of which are connected with *one* archetype, e.g., that of the Great Mother, pour in on the observer who takes it on himself to describe, or even to understand, what an archetype, or what this archetype, is. Although all these many forms are ultimately "variations on a ground theme," [22] their diversity is so great, the contradictory elements united in them so multifarious, that in addition to speaking of the "eternal presence" of the archetype, we must also speak of its symbolic polyvalence.

[22] Jung, "On the Nature of the Psyche," p. 213.

The manifestation of the archetype as a symbolic expression of the unconscious can, in its relation to man, be formulated from two points of view, which seem contradictory but actually complement one another. The archetype may manifest itself "spontaneously," or else it may stand in a compensatory relation to the consciousness of the man in whom it appears. When the archetype appears as a spontaneous expression of the unconscious, it operates independently of the psychic situation of the individual and of the group, as an autonomous force that determines the actual situation. This is most evident in phenomena of irruption, e.g., psychosis, in which the archetypal phenomenon irrupts unpredictably and with the strangeness of something "totally other," and in which it is impossible to establish adequate relations between whatever it is that irrupts and the victim of the irruption. But even here partly intelligible connections can be demonstrated between the type and content of the psychosis and the personality of the affected individual.

This means, however, that the archetypal manifestation is not isolated but—this must be said to round out the picture—is determined by the total constellation of the collective unconscious. It depends not only on the race, people, and group, the historical epoch and actual situation, but also on the situation of the individual in whom it appears.

When we say that the archetype and the symbol are spontaneous and independent of consciousness, we mean that the ego as the center of consciousness does not actively and knowingly participate in the genesis and emergence of the symbol or the archetype, or, in other words, that consciousness cannot "make" [23] a symbol or "choose" to experience an archetype. This by no means precludes a relation of the archetype or the symbol to the totality of the personality and consciousness; for the manifestations of the unconscious are not only a spontaneous expression of unconscious processes but also reactions to the conscious situation of the individual, and these reactions, as we see

[23] Even in such exceptional cases as the genesis of the "uniting symbol" (Jung, *Psychological Types*, Def. 51), there is, to be sure, an activity of the ego and consciousness; yet here again the ego "makes" nothing, but merely plays a part in the constellation of the unconscious.

most commonly with dreams, are usually of a compensatory nature. This means that the appearance of archetypal images and symbols is in part determined by a man's individual typological structure, by the situation of the individual, his conscious attitude, his age, and so on.

As man becomes individualized, we must, for an understanding of the archetypal reaction, bear in mind the uniqueness of the individual situation, e.g., the relation of such an artist as Leonardo da Vinci to the archetype; [24] but the more we have to do with a spontaneous expression of the collective unconscious, and the more collective the constellation of the unconscious is—as, for example, in early mankind—the more we can dispense with a knowledge of the situation of the individual in seeking an understanding of an archetypal structure.

Because certain constant relations are demonstrable in the depth psychology of mankind, and because to a certain extent a co-ordination is possible between psychic phenomena and the historical stages in the development of the human consciousness, the structural analysis of a particular archetype is not impossible.

The term Great Mother, as a partial aspect of the Archetypal Feminine, is a late abstraction, presupposing a highly developed speculative consciousness. And indeed, it is only relatively late in the history of mankind that we find the Archetypal Feminine designated as Magna Mater. But it was worshiped and portrayed many thousands of years before the appearance of the term. Yet even in this relatively late term it is evident that the combination of the words "mother" and "great" is not a combination of concepts but of emotionally colored symbols. "Mother" in this connection does not refer merely to a relationship of filiation but also to a complex psychic situation of the ego, and similarly the term "Great" expresses the symbolic character of superiority that the archetypal figure possesses in comparison with everything human and with created nature in general. If in Egypt the Goddess Ta-urt is called "The Great," this is consequently a symbolic expression for the impersonal anonymity of the archetype, analogous to the plural form of Goethe's "Mothers."

[24] Cf. my "Leonardo da Vinci and the Mother Archetype."

Before the comprehensive human *figure* of the Great Mother appeared, innumerable symbols belonging to her still-unformed image arose spontaneously. These symbols—particularly nature symbols from every realm of nature—are in a sense signed with the image of the Great Mother, which, whether they be stone or tree, pool, fruit, or animal, lives in them and is identified with them. Gradually, they become linked with the figure of the Great Mother as attributes and form the wreath of symbols that surrounds the archetypal figure and manifests itself in rite and myth.

This wreath of symbolic images, however, surrounds not only *one* figure but a great number of figures, of Great Mothers who, as goddesses and fairies, female demons and nymphs, friendly and unfriendly, manifest the one Great Unknown, the Great Mother as the central aspect of the Archetypal Feminine, in the rites and myths, the religions and legends, of mankind.

It is an essential feature of the primordial archetype that it combines positive and negative attributes and groups of attributes. This union of opposites in the primordial archetype, its ambivalence, is characteristic of the original situation of the unconscious, which consciousness has not yet dissected into its antitheses. Early man experienced this paradoxical simultaneity of good and evil, friendly and terrible, in the godhead as a unity; while as consciousness developed, the good goddess and the bad goddess, for example, usually came to be worshiped as different beings.

The primordial archetype belongs to a consciousness and an ego that are still incapable of differentiation. The more contradictions that are combined in it, the more confounding and overwhelming are its actions and manifestation. Because so many contradictory motifs and symbols are joined in the archetype, its nature is paradoxical: it can neither be visualized nor represented.

In the early phase of consciousness, the numinosity of the archetype consequently exceeds man's power of representation, so much so that at first no form can be given to it. And when later the primordial archetype takes form in the imagination of man, its representations are often monstrous and inhuman. This is the phase of the chimerical creatures composed of different animals or of animal and man—the griffins, sphinxes, harpies, for example—and also of such monstrosities as phallic and bearded mothers. It is only when consciousness learns to look at phenomena from a certain distance, to react more subtly, to differentiate and distinguish, that the mixture of symbols prevailing in the primordial archetype separates into the groups of symbols characteristic of a single archetype or of a group of related archetypes; in short, that they became recognizable.

In the course of a long period of development, the inward and outward forces of tradition become so strong that the archetypal images attain a degree of form that enables man to fashion sacral images.

In our attempt to describe the structure of the archetype of the Great Mother or the Feminine on the basis of numerous reproductions of art works, we shall have to take a very broad view of the scope of our undertaking. For only through "amplification"—the method of comparative morphological psychology, which interprets analogous material from the most varied spheres of religious history, archaeology, prehistoric studies, ethnology, and so on—can we reach an understanding of the archetypes and the individual symbols. However, the true object of our inquiry is the symbolic self-representation of the archetype that has passed through the medium of man, and that speaks to us from images fashioned sometimes unconsciously and sometimes consciously.

The archetypes of the collective unconscious are manifested, as Jung discovered many years ago,[25] in the "mythological motifs" that appear among all peoples at all times in identical or analogous manner and can arise just as spontaneously—i.e., without any conscious knowledge—from the unconscious of modern man.

Since we cannot presuppose a knowledge of this basic discovery, crucial for modern depth psychology, we shall illustrate it by one example, and otherwise refer the reader to Jung's extensive work, in which the discovery of the collective unconscious assumes a central position.

[25] *Wandlungen und Symbole der Libido* (1911–12; tr. 1916 as *Psychology of the Unconscious*).

For the sake of simplicity, we shall quote our example directly from him.[26]

Jung relates how one day in an insane asylum he saw a patient standing in the corridor, peering out the window at the sun and moving his head strangely from side to side:

> He took me by the arm and said he wanted to show me something. He said I must look at the sun with eyes half shut, and then I could see the sun's phallus. If I moved my head from side to side the sun-phallus would move too, and that was the origin of the wind.
>
> I made this observation about 1906. In the course of the year 1910, when I was engrossed in mythological studies, a book of Dieterich's came into my hands. It was part of the so-called Paris magic papyrus and was thought by Dieterich to be a liturgy of the Mithraic cult.* It consisted of a series of instructions, invocations, and visions. One of these visions is described in the following words: "And likewise the so-called tube, the origin of the ministering wind. For you will see hanging down from the disc of the sun something that looks like a tube. And towards the regions westward it is as though there were an infinite east wind. But if the other wind should prevail towards the regions of the east, you will in like manner see the vision veering in that direction." The Greek word for 'tube,' αὐλός, means a wind-instrument, and the combination αὐλός παχύς in Homer means 'a thick jet of blood.' So evidently a stream of wind is blowing through the tube out of the sun.
>
> The vision of my patient in 1906, and the Greek text first edited in 1910, should be sufficiently far apart to rule out the possibility of cryptomnesia on his side and of thought-transference on mine. The obvious parallelism of the two visions cannot be disputed, though one might object that the similarity is purely fortuitous. In that case we should expect the vision to have no connections with analogous ideas, nor any inner meaning. But this expectation is not fulfilled, for in certain medieval paintings this tube is actually depicted as a sort of hose-pipe reaching down from heaven under the robe of Mary. In it the Holy Ghost flies down in the form of a dove to impregnate the Virgin. As we know from the miracle of Pentecost, the Holy Ghost was originally conceived as a mighty rushing wind, the πνεῦμα, "the wind that bloweth where it listeth." In a Latin

---

[26] "The Structure of the Psyche," pp. 150 f.
*Ed. Note in 1960 edn.: "Eine Mithrasliturgie, pp. 6–7. As the author subsequently learned, the 1910 edition was actually the second, there having been a first edition in 1903. The patient had, however, been committed some years before 1903."

text we read: "Animo descensus per orbem solis tribuitur" (They say that the spirit descends through the disc of the sun). This conception is common to the whole of late classical and medieval philosophy.[27]

This example may suffice to show that the archetype is a mythological motif and that, as an "eternally present" content of the collective—i.e., universal human—unconscious, it can appear equally well in the theology of Egypt or the Hellenistic mysteries of Mithras, in the Christian symbolism of the Middle Ages or the visions of a modern psychotic.

The archetype is not only a *dynamis*, a directing force, which influences the human psyche, as in religion, for example, but corresponds to an unconscious "conception," a content. In the symbol, i.e., image of the archetype, a meaning is communicated that can be apprehended conceptually only by a highly developed consciousness, and then only with great pains. For this reason the following remark of Jung's is still applicable to the modern consciousness: "Myth is the primordial language natural to these psychic processes, and no intellectual formulation comes anywhere near the richness and expressiveness of mythical imagery. Such processes deal with the primordial images, and these are best and most succinctly reproduced by figurative speech."[28] This "figurative speech" is the language of the symbol, the original language of the unconscious and of mankind.

As we have elsewhere shown,[29] early man—like the child—perceives the world "mythologically." That is, he experiences the world predominantly by forming archetypal images that he projects upon it. The child, for example, first experiences in his mother the archetype of the Great Mother, that is, the reality of an all-powerful numinous woman, on whom he is dependent in all things, and not the objective reality of his personal mother, this particular historical woman which his mother becomes for him later when his ego and consciousness are more developed. Similarly, early man does not, like modern man,

---

[27] The earliest form of this archetypal conception known to us is found—as so often—in Egypt, in the union of the sun god Ra, who here appears as a creator figure par excellence, with Ammon, the "breath of life," to form the divine figure "Ammon-Ra." Cf. especially Frankfort, *Kingship and the Gods*, pp. 160 f.

[28] *Psychology and Alchemy*, p. 25.

[29] My *Origins*, pp. 40 ff.

experience states of weather, but divine or godlike powers on whom his fate depends, and whose behavior is connected with his own in a magical or religious-ethical way. We need only consider, for example, the rain and its significance for fertility, often carrying a decision as to life and death. Prayers for rain, processions for rain, are even today an expression of this mythologically apperceptive mentality, which guided early cultural life almost exclusively. Human life in the beginning is determined to a far higher degree by the unconscious than by consciousness; it is directed more by archetypal images than by concepts, by instincts than by the voluntary decisions of the ego; and man is more a part of his group than an individual. And similarly, his world is not a world seen by consciousness, but one experienced by the unconscious.[30] In other words, he perceives the world not through the functions of consciousness, as an objective world presupposing the separation of subject and object, but experiences it mythologically, in archetypal images, in symbols that are a spontaneous expression of the unconscious, that help the psyche orient itself in the world, and that, as mythological motifs, configure the mythologies of all peoples.

This means that the symbols do not, like the functions of consciousness, relate to the individual ego, but to the whole of the psychic system, which embraces consciousness and the unconscious. For this reason, the symbol contains both conscious and unconscious elements, and, in addition to symbols and symbolic elements that consciousness can assimilate relatively quickly, we find others that can only be assimilated in the course of long developments or not at all, which remain irrational and beyond the scope of consciousness.[31]

Another indication of the natural symbol's independence of consciousness is that its very structure represents the character of the unconscious from which it arises. Whereas the division into I and thou, subject and object, is a characteristic of consciousness, the fundamental characteristics of the "original situation" of the unconscious recur in the symbol. Not only are rational and irrational, conscious and unconscious, elements—elements arising from both inner and outward worlds—

[30] All this still applies, in somewhat attenuated form, to modern man, in whom this manner of functioning, though less prominent than before, has not ceased to exist.

[31] Jung, *Psychological Types*, Def. 51.

joined in the symbol, as the term "symbol" indicates; in it, moreover, they appear as an original and natural unity.

The symbolic imagery of the unconscious is the creative source of the human spirit in all its realizations. Not only have consciousness and the concepts of its philosophical understanding of the world arisen from the symbol but also religion, rite and cult, art and customs. And because the symbol-forming process of the unconscious is the source of the human spirit, language, whose history is almost identical with the genesis and development of human consciousness, always starts out as a symbolic language. Thus Jung writes: "An archetypal content expresses itself, first and foremost, in metaphors. If such a content should speak of the sun and identify it with the lion, the king, the hoard of gold guarded by the dragon, or the power that makes for the life and health of man, it is neither the one thing nor the other, but the unknown third thing that finds more or less adequate expression in all these similes, yet—to the perpetual vexation of the intellect—remains unknown and not to be fitted into a formula." [32]

This example shows once again what we mean by mythological apperception, but it also illustrates the tendency of the symbol to combine contradictory elements, to bring the most diverse provinces of life into contact with one another, by crossing, blending, and weaving them together. The symbol intimates, suggests, excites. Consciousness is set in motion and must employ all its functions to assimilate the symbol, for a merely conceptual assimilation proves totally inadequate. The symbol also acts with greater or less force upon feeling, intuition, and sensation.

The action of the symbol takes a different direction in primitive man and in the man of today. In modern Western man, it compensates for overemphasis on consciousness; in early man, however, it not only strengthens, but positively forms consciousness. Through the symbol, mankind rises from the early phase of formlessness, from a blind, purely unconscious psyche without images, to the formative phase whose image making is an essential premise for the genesis and development of consciousness.[33]

[32] "The Psychology of the Child Archetype," p. 157. [33] My *Origins*, p. 366.

Chapter Two

THE ARCHETYPAL FEMININE
AND THE GREAT MOTHER

W E SHALL attempt to clarify the process just described by means of Schema I (facing page 19), showing the development from the uroboros through the Archetypal Feminine to the Great Mother and further differentiations.

First we must define certain basic concepts necessary to the understanding of this schema. As I have elsewhere set forth in detail,[1] the uroboros, the circular snake biting its tail, is the symbol of the psychic state of the beginning, of the original situation, in which man's consciousness and ego were still small and undeveloped. As symbol of the origin and of the opposites contained in it, the uroboros is the "Great Round," in which positive and negative, male and female, elements of consciousness, elements hostile to consciousness, and unconscious elements are intermingled. In this sense the uroboros is also a symbol of a state in which chaos, the unconscious, and the psyche as a whole were undifferentiated—and which is experienced by the ego as a borderline state.

The uroboric totality also appears as a symbol of the united primordial parents from whom the figures of the Great Father and the Great Mother later crystallized out. Thus it is the most perfect example of the still undifferentiated primordial archetype. Although its paradoxical

[1] My *Origins and History of Consciousness:* "The Great Mother," pp. 39 ff.

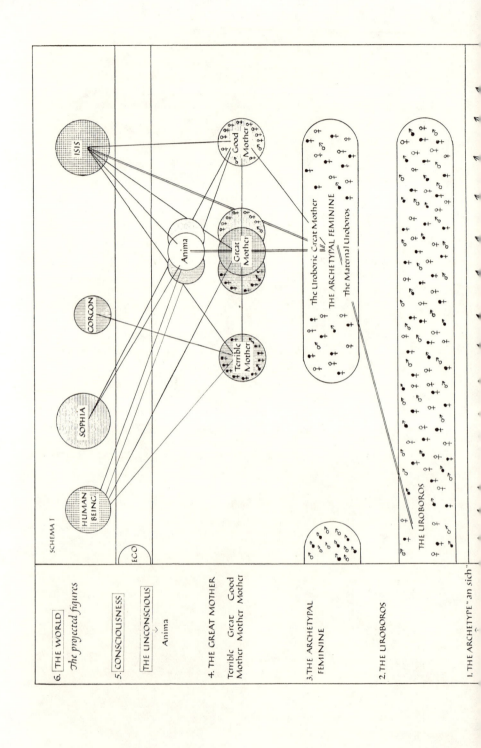

SCHEMA I

6. THE WORLD
The projected figures

5. CONSCIOUSNESS

THE UNCONSCIOUS
Anima

4. THE GREAT MOTHER

Terrible   Great   Good
Mother   Mother   Mother

3. THE ARCHETYPAL
FEMININE

2. THE UROBOROS

1. THE ARCHETYPE "an sich"

and polyvalent character is not evident in the seemingly simple symbol of the circular snake, it becomes evident as soon as we attempt to differentiate all the inexhaustible meanings contained in this symbol.[2]

As symbol of the beginning, the uroboros stands between the formless, purely effective phenomenon of the "archetype *an sich*" and such already specified figures of the primordial archetype as the Archetypal Feminine or the Archetypal Masculine. But the transitions between the uroboros and the primordial archetype of the Feminine, and between the latter and the archetype of the Great Mother, are fluid. For the degree of mixture between the archetypes and the difficulty of distinguishing the still almost formless figures from one another increase as we penetrate more deeply into the collective unconscious—that is to say, the older the symbol and the less developed the consciousness of the personality in whose psyche it appears. When we speak of a "maternal uroboros," we mean that in the Archetypal Feminine of this phase the accent is on the uroboric element, while the maternal element is secondary. On the other hand, we speak of a "uroboric Great Mother" when the archetypal figure of the uroboros shines through the figure of the Great Mother, revealing its peculiar symbolism and mode of action, but the configured reality of the Great Mother is dominant.

In order to make our representation of the primordial archetype as "unconceptual" as its psychic reality, we avoid specifying symbols, qualities, behavior patterns, and so on in our schema, but merely differentiate "male" and "female," "positive" and "negative," attributes: "positive" attributes are shown in white, "negative" in black, and the usual signs are employed for male and female.[3]

[2] The earliest symbols to emerge are the simplest, which we usually designate as "abstract," e.g., the circle and the cross. They are closest to the nonvisual character of the "archetype *an sich*," and are to be understood as the preconcrete and prepictorial form of the beginning, whose simplicity is elementary and not abstract. In the course of psychic development their schematic structure is filled more and more with sense content, but in the further development of consciousness they are progressively de-emotionalized and finally experienced as abstract signs of consciousness. The spirit aspect of the archetype seems to embrace the first depths and ultimate heights of man's conscious development, since it uses the same signs in the beginning as symbols for a still inarticulate multiplicity preceding form, and in the end for an abstract conceptuality succeeding form.

[3] Since the symbolism of what is to be designated as "female" is an essential theme of our whole book, we cannot define it at the outset.

Our first schema requires an understanding of the concept of projection.[4] Just as in the motion picture an image situated behind the observer appears before him on the "projection" plane of the screen, so contents of the unconscious are primarily "projected" indirectly as contents of the "outside world" and not directly experienced as contents of the unconscious. Thus, for example, a "demon" is not regarded as a part of the man to whom he appears, but as a being who is present and active in the outside world.

In addition to the "outward plane of projection" there is an "inward" one, upon which the contents of the unconscious are mirrored. As inward phenomena they are not assigned to any outside world, but they retain, as in the case of dreams, their character of projections. Thus the dream world appears to the dream ego as something outside, and the contents of the inward projection plane are *de facto* "psychic contents" that are experienced by the dream ego in projection as outside contents.

Schema I falls into three strata: the unconscious, consciousness, and the world. We first turn to the unconscious, which is represented in four planes.

1. This plane is the nonvisual reality and action of the "archetype *an sich*."

2. The uroboros. Only the right half of it is represented, for we are here interested only in the development of its feminine aspect. It contains as examples of its symbolic polyvalence four symbolic elements, through which our schema strives to represent the development: male positive ♂, female positive ♀, male negative ♂, and female negative ♀. They all work together without order or arrangement. In other words, the little ego belonging to the primordial situation experiences female maternal protection ♀ and at the same time killing aggression ♂. Through the same "object" that is the vehicle of the uroboros symbol, regardless whether it be a godhead or a person, it can experience both a devouring female force ♀ and a force that actively supports conscious-

---

[4] Jung, *Psychological Types*, Def. 43.

ness and the ego ♂. The mixture of all these elements makes for the nonvisual character of the situation, which cannot be adequately apprehended by consciousness and is expressed in the image paradoxy of symbols. (The number of the elements is unimportant.)

3. The Archetypal Feminine and Archetypal Masculine have been differentiated.[5] The Archetypal Feminine has features of the maternal uroboros and of the uroboric Great Mother. It contains essential elements of the Feminine ♀ ♀, but they are without order and hence impossible for the ego that experiences them to predict and apprehend. This primordial archetype of the Feminine contains positive and negative male determinants ♂ ♂ aside from the predominant female elements.

4. A configured form of the Great Mother has emerged from the primordial archetype. Now an order is discernible in the elements. She has three forms: the good, the terrible, and the good-bad mother. The good feminine (and masculine) elements configure the Good Mother, who, like the Terrible Mother containing the negative elements, can also emerge independently from the unity of the Great Mother. The third form is that of the Great Mother who is good-bad and makes possible a union of positive and negative attributes.

Great Mother, Good Mother, and Terrible Mother form a cohesive archetypal group.[6]

5. The fifth plane of our schema is the stratum of consciousness intercalated between the world and the unconscious. To it belongs the ego as the center of the system of consciousness. The ego can see and experience the archetypal constellations of the unconscious directly or indirectly—directly by perceiving them on the inner projection plane as psychic images, indirectly by experiencing them in their projection into the world. Modern man with his reflective consciousness speaks of a direct psychic experience when a content of the psyche, e.g., an archetype, appears in a dream, a vision, or in the imagination. We call it an

---

[5] Here we shall not follow the development of the Archetypal Masculine to the Great Father, and so on.

[6] The plane of the *anima* will be discussed below, p. 37.

indirect psychic experience when an intrinsically psychic content is experienced as belonging to the outside world, e.g., a demon as the living spirit of a stone or a tree.[7]

6. The sixth plane of our schema is the extrapsychic stratum, since we designate it as "world." Our diagram, however, relates to the world only in so far as it offers an outward plane of projection on which projected inner images are experienced.

The indirect experience of the archetypal images by consciousness occurs in the world, particularly through figures or persons. (Experience through situations, objects, symbols, and so forth is here disregarded.) By experience through "figures" we mean eminently the experience of gods. This we have represented by the example of three female deities: the Egyptian Isis, the pre-Hellenic Gorgon, and the Hellenistic-Jewish-Christian Sophia, or Wisdom.

The figures of gods are experienced by the personality as outside, i.e., as what the normal ego designates as "real." Thus for the Greeks Olympus and its gods are outside and world, and not, as for us, the inner psychic reality of the Hellenes. That from a psychological point of view the figures are projections of the inner world is indicated in the schema by the lines connecting them with the archetypal structures of the unconscious. Thus the terrifying figure of the Gorgon with the snakes writhing round her head—the sight of whom turns men to stone—is a projection of the Terrible Mother, while Sophia is a projection of the Good Mother. The figure of Isis, however, combining features of the Terrible and of the Good Mother, corresponds to the archetype of the Great Mother and also discloses suggestions of the primordial archetype of the Feminine and of the uroboros.[8]

The archetype is experienced indirectly also through individuals upon whom it is projected. In the schema, the examples corresponding to the "figures" are indicated in the zone of the world. But here the

[7] For the more naïve and less reflective consciousness of early man, either this distinction does not prevail or it has the exact opposite significance. For the distinctly extraverted attitude of primitive man the appearance, for example, of a god in "outside reality" passes as a direct experience. But his appearance in a dream or vision is evaluated as a lesser, indirect experience if the god appears "only" in the dream but not "face to face."
Cf. my *Origins*, index, s.v. "Isis."

Gorgon is projected into a woman who, for example, transfixes one with terror in an anxiety neurosis. Similarly there are individuals in whom the projector unconsciously experiences the figures of Sophia or of Isis. Such projection phenomena, as modern depth psychology discovered, are of crucial importance not only for the genesis of psychoneuroses and for their therapy but also for normal development.

The structural analysis of the archetype of the Great Mother must of course be a central concern of any psychology of the Feminine in general. But before we attempt to trace the development of the archetype, it will be necessary to explain what we mean by Feminine.

Chapter Three

THE TWO CHARACTERS
OF THE FEMININE

IT IS necessary to distinguish two characters of the Feminine, which, in their interpenetration, coexistence, and antagonism, are an essential part of the Feminine as a whole. These are the elementary and the transformative characters of the Feminine.

This representation of the Feminine on the basis of these two characters is an attempt to give a unitary interpretation both of woman's experience of herself and of man's experience of woman.

The personal equation—the proposition that every statement is contingent on the personal psychology of the speaker, on his unconscious conditioning, his prejudices, and so on—applies particularly to statements on the opposite sex. Here the projection phenomenon plays a special role because the elements of the opposite sex in the speaker's own psyche, the anima in the man and the animus in the woman,[1] are experienced as the reality of the opposite sex.

The presence, however, in all structures of essential contrasexual components, this hermaphroditic quality, makes possible an inner "independent" experience of the opposite sex. In other words, the man possesses an inner, though primarily unconscious, experience of woman, and the woman of man.[2] This experience of the other sex is further ob-

[1] Jung, "The Relations between the Ego and the Unconscious," pp. 186 ff.

[2] This becomes clear when the cultural situation is determined by the psychological dominance of *one* sex, as in matriarchy or patriarchy. In patriarchy, for example, as I have

24

jectivized through the living relation with this sex that has become usual in the modern world, and that makes it possible, particularly for the psychologist, to gain an insight into the unconscious structure of the opposite sex.

Statements on the opposite sex become much less questionable when, as in the structural analysis of the Archetypal Feminine, the material on which they are based stems in large part from the collective unconscious. The objectivity of this profound stratum, its imperviousness to human influence, are so great as to leave relatively little room for distortion through the inadequacy of the observer. And this means that even if our interpretation is open to all the objections that can be raised against a subjective view, the abundance of the material presented guarantees at least a relative objectivity.

As *elementary character* [3] we designate the aspect of the Feminine that as the Great Round, the Great Container, tends to hold fast to everything that springs from it and to surround it like an eternal substance. Everything born of it belongs to it and remains subject to it; and even if the individual becomes independent, the Archetypal Feminine relativizes this independence into a nonessential variant of her own perpetual being.

Bachofen has brilliantly shown this elementary character to be typical of matriarchy; and if understood psychologically rather than sociologically, his discoveries have lasting value.

The elementary character of the Feminine becomes evident wherever the ego and consciousness are still small and undeveloped and the unconscious is dominant. Consequently, the elementary char-

---

elsewhere shown, we find that, despite the difference in the psychology of man and woman, the male position of consciousness and its development apply also to the modern woman, who has developed and must develop a contemporary consciousness. It is conversely true that in a situation dominated by a matriarchal psychology, the feminine "matriarchal consciousness" is effective also for the man.

[3] When we speak of a "character" of the Feminine we mean two things. First, we mean the Feminine as it is experienced in its projection, for example, through the godhead, the world, and life. At the same time the character is an attribute of the psyche, corresponding to psychic structures and processes that we interpret and that we must invoke for an understanding of the symbolic facts of mythology. In exposition these two aspects cannot always be kept apart, particularly because the autonomy of the character operates with the autonomy of a complex or of a person and must be described in this way.

acter almost always has a "maternal" determinant. The ego, conscious-ness, the individual, regardless whether male or female, are childlike and dependent in their relation to it.

The elementary character, although intrinsically as ambiguous and relative as the transformative character, i.e., although it too has a "good" and a "bad" aspect, is the foundation of that conservative, stable, and unchanging part of the feminine which predominates in motherhood.

In the relation between the ego and the unconscious, a "psychic gravitation" may be observed, a tendency of the ego to return to its original unconscious state.[4] This tendency is inversely proportional to the strength of the ego and consciousness. In other words, the stronger the energetic charge of consciousness, the more free libido is available to the ego as will and interest and the smaller is the inertia expressive of psychic gravitation. And the weaker the consciousness and the ego, the stronger becomes the psychic gravitation tending to restore the unconscious state. And here the ego and consciousness may be in-sufficiently developed to resist the gravitation—as in early man and the child—or else they may have been impaired by sickness, fatigue, or other constellations.

We are dealing with tensions between the energetic charges of the two systems—consciousness and the unconscious—and between their contents. Here again we encounter the principle of attraction by the greater mass, which in the psyche is manifested as the greater charge of energy. As consciousness develops, it tends to form an independent and relatively self-contained system with the ego complex at its center. When consciousness is sufficiently charged, a content remains in it; that is to say, the content is conscious and open to consciousness. But when the charge in the conscious system diminishes and the tension of its field is reduced, its contents respond to attraction by the more highly charged contents of the unconscious, the complexes and arche-types; in other words, the content becomes once again unconscious. Thus we have a situation in which certain contents move as complexes

[4] My *Origins and History of Consciousness,* p. 280.

in a psychic field that is determined by the energetic charge of the contents and their direction. Such relations, however, are manifested in the psyche not only as a dynamic but also as a symbolic process. The plane of images and symbols is closer to the unconscious than is the plane of consciousness, but often the process that takes place on the symbolic plane has an anticipatory character and makes possible the later conscious process.

A psychic depression, for example, is characterized by an *abaissement du niveau mental*, by a loss of libido in the consciousness, expressed in lack of enthusiasm and initiative, weakness of will, fatigue, incapacity for concentration and work, and in "negative" contents, such as thoughts of death and failure, weariness of life, suicidal leanings, and so on. Often, however, this psychic process also becomes visible; that is to say, it appears in the familiar symbolism of the light, the sun, the moon, or the hero being swallowed up by darkness in the form of night, the abyss, hell, monsters. A deep psychological analysis then reveals the irruption of an archetype, e.g., the Terrible Devouring Mother, whose psychic attraction is so great because of its energetic charge that the charge of the ego complex, unable to withstand it, "sinks" and is "swallowed up."

A contrary movement may be represented symbolically as follows: the hero devoured by the monster cuts off a piece of its heart and so slays it. This symbolic process corresponds, on the image plane, to a conscious realization. A corresponding process takes place on the plane of consciousness when, through the "splitting up of the archetype," [5] the ego achieves a rise to consciousness; that is, consciousness comes to "understand" parts of the archetypal contents and incorporates them in itself. When this happens, the ego is strengthened and consciousness broadened. Consciousness not only recovers from the archetype the libido it had lost to it, but in addition takes new libido from the "split-off" or "cut-off" part of the archetype by "assimilating," i.e., digesting, it.

It is no accident that in the symbols we have cited as examples

[5] Ibid., pp. 320 ff.

27

consciousness is identified with the figure of the male hero, while the devouring unconscious is identified with the figure of the female monster. As we have elsewhere shown at length,[6] this co-ordination is general; that is, in both sexes the active ego consciousness is characterized by a male symbolism, the unconscious as a whole by a female symbolism.

The phenomenon of psychic gravitation, i.e., the natural inertia that causes certain contents of the unconscious to remain unconscious and certain contents of consciousness to become unconscious—taken together with the symbolic phenomenon of the predominant femininity of the unconscious in its relation to consciousness—forms the foundation of what we call the "elementary character of the Feminine."

In terms of psychological energy the elementary character of the Feminine and its symbolism express the original situation of the psyche, which we therefore designate as matriarchal. In it the unconscious as a whole is dominant over all individual contents and tendencies. In this phase the unity of the unconscious determines all psychic processes in so high degree that the ego, which is a particular complex of the psyche, can as yet achieve no independence; again and again, responding to psychic gravitation, it sinks back into the unconscious or circles as a satellite around the Archetypal Feminine.

We may most readily understand this constellation if we bear in mind how relatively close early man was to the animal in the psychological sense. (We cannot date this phase historically, but we know beyond any doubt that it existed.) The determining role of instincts and drives in the creatures of this stage signifies that they exist essentially as parts of the species or, in our terminology, that they are still wholly dominated by the Great Mother. Only gradually does an individuality emerge, an ego bound up with an initially feeble and intermittent consciousness.

But since the ego is the center of consciousness, consciousness in this phase is in very high degree dependent on the guidance of the unconscious. The conflict, as well as the living tension between the unconscious and the ego consciousness, can begin only when this ego consciousness has become relatively strong and independent.

The *transformative character* of the Feminine is the expression of a

[6] Ibid., p. 42.

28

different fundamental psychic constellation, which is also connected with feminine symbolism. In the transformative character, the accent is on the dynamic element of the psyche, which, in contrast to the conservative tendency of the elementary character, drives toward motion, change, and, in a word, transformation.[7] In psychic development the transformative character is at first "dominated" by the elementary character and only gradually throws off this domination to assume its own independent form. The transformative character is already clearly at work in the basic function of the Maternal-Feminine, in the gestation as well as the bearing of children. The function of feeding may be ascribed either to the elementary or the transformative character, according to whether the accent lies on the tendency to preserve what exists or on the tendency toward amplification and change. In other words, the two characters are not antithetical from the very start but interpenetrate and combine with one another in many ways, and it is only in unusual and extreme constellations that we find one or the other character isolated. But although both are usually present at once, one of them is almost always dominant.

The total domination of the Great Round in the elementary character implies that in the beginning the Great Round also integrates the transformative character with itself. Even where transformation occurs—and from the very first life is bound up with transformation—the elementary character bends everything that changes or is changed back into its own eternal sameness.

When, in the elementary character, there is a relationship to the offspring, this relationship is retained as an indissoluble bond between mother and child. This *participation mystique* between mother and child is the original situation of container and contained. It is the beginning of the relation of the Archetypal Feminine to the child, and it likewise determines the relation of the maternal unconscious to the child's ego and consciousness as long as these two systems are not separated from one another.[8]

---

[7] A distinction between the transformative character and those unconscious forces that are expressed by a masculine symbolism must be reserved for a later chapter.

[8] In a purely psychological sense this means that psychic life is predominantly static and constant and that all processes of variation and transformation keep leading back to the original

The life feeling of every ego consciousness that feels small in relation to the powers is dominated by the preponderance of the Great Round that encompasses all change. This archetype may be experienced outwardly as world or nature or inwardly as fate and the unconscious. In this phase the elementary feminine character, which still contains the transformative character within it, is "worldly"; natural existence with all its regular changes is subservient to it. The central symbol of this constellation is the unity of life amid the change of the seasons and the concurrent transformation of living things. What Bachofen described as the death character of the material-maternal is an expression of this archetypal domination of nature and the unconscious over life, and likewise over the undeveloped childlike, or youthfully helpless, ego consciousness. In this phase the Archetypal Feminine not only bears and directs life as a whole, and the ego in particular, but also takes everything that is born of it back into its womb of origination and death.

The dynamic movement within this Great Round belongs to the transformative character of the Feminine, but in this first phase does not yet assume a form and shape of its own. It merely creates change within the circular snake of the uroboros, for the uroboros of the beginning is not only the Round but also the wheel rolling upon itself and the serpent which at once bears, begets, and devours.

In psychological terms, this means that where the elementary character is dominant, all processes of change still take place within the unconscious; and that even where an ego-consciousness quality has begun to form, it possesses an existence of its own for a brief time only and is then redissolved in the unconscious.[9]

But as the personality is differentiated and emerges from pure unconsciousness, the transformative character also becomes independent and is experienced as such. The transformative character drives toward

situation from which they arose. We therefore find the elementary character of the feminine, e.g., as dogma or as church, at work in the background of all tradition-bound psychic states.

[9] Mythologically this constellation is manifested, for example, in the dominance of the seasons, in the fixed and predestined course of the stars, or in numinous powers and gods, on which human life depends in a fatalistic and almost invariable way. In contrast, active magic, as an exertion of the human ego, consciousness, and will, represents a decisive attempt to break through this ring of determinacy and to establish the independent existence of man, and particularly of the human ego consciousness.

development; that is to say, it brings movement and unrest. Consequently, it is not experienced by consciousness as purely positive any more than the elementary character is experienced as purely negative. Both characters are vehicles of the ambivalence that is typical of the Archetypal Feminine as well as the Great Mother, and that moreover is an original characteristic of every archetype.

Although the elementary character, like the transformative character, is experienced also in projection as a quality of the world, it appears predominantly as a psychic quality, precisely, of the Feminine. We must distinguish, however, between the man's experience of this transformative character and the woman's experience of herself. First and foremost the woman experiences her transformative character naturally and unreflectingly in pregnancy, in her relation to the growth of her child, and in childbearing. Here woman is the organ and instrument of the transformation of both her own structure and that of the child within her and outside her. Hence for the woman the transformative character—even that of her own transformation—is from the beginning connected with the problem of the *thou* relationship.

The transformation mysteries of the woman are primarily blood-transformation mysteries that lead her to the experience of her own creativity and produce a numinous impression on the man.[10] This phenomenon has its roots in psychobiological development. The transformation from girl to woman is far more accentuated than the corresponding development from boy to man. Menstruation, the first blood-transformation mystery in woman, is in every respect a more important incident that the first emission of sperm in the male. The latter is seldom remembered, while the beginning of menstruation is everywhere rightly regarded as a fateful moment in the life of woman.

Pregnancy is the second blood mystery. According to the primitive view, the embryo is built up from the blood, which, as the cessation of menstruation indicates, does not flow outward in the period of pregnancy.[11] In pregnancy woman experiences a combination of the elementary and transformative characters.

The growth of the foetus already brings about a change of the

[10] My "Über den Mond."   [11] Briffault, *The Mothers*, Vol. II, p. 444.

woman's personality. But although the woman's transformation to motherhood is completed with birth, birth sets in motion a new archetypal constellation that reshapes the woman's life down to its very depths.

To nourish and protect, to keep warm and hold fast—these are the functions in which the elementary character of the feminine operates in relation to the child, and here again this relation is the basis of the woman's own transformation. Briffault [12] looked upon the mother-child relationship and the female group behavior built upon it as the foundation of social life and hence of human culture. This well-supported hypothesis gains further cogency from the biological observation that the human species is the only one in which the infant, during the first year of life, may be regarded as an "embryo outside the womb." [13] This implies that it completes its extrauterine embryonic life in a social environment essentially determined by the mother. The circumstance enhances the importance of the mother for the child and strengthens the mother's attachment to the child, whose embryonic dependency becomes a basis for her unconscious and conscious maternal solicitude.

After childbirth the woman's third blood mystery occurs: the transformation of blood into milk, which is the foundation for the primordial mysteries of food transformation. [14]

In addition to these situations in which woman experiences the transformative character in her own body, there are others where it operates in her relation to a *thou.* The male experiences this aspect of the Feminine directly and indirectly as provocative, as a force that sets him in motion and impels him toward change. Here it is a matter of indifference whether the transformation of the male is caused by a positive or negative fascination, by attraction or repulsion on the part of the woman. Sleeping Beauty and the captive princess, as well as the active inspiration of the Feminine presiding over the birth of the new, are exponents of the transformative character that achieves its purest form in the figure of the anima. The anima, [15] the "soul image," which

[12] Ibid., Vol. I, pp. 195 f.
[13] Portmann, *Biologische Fragmente zu einer Lehre vom Menschen*, pp. 68 ff.

[14] See below, pp. 282 f.
[15] Cf. Jung, "Relations," pp. 186 ff.; *Psychological Types*, Def. 48.

the male experiences in the female, is his own inner femininity and soulfulness, an element in his own psyche. But the anima—as Jung pointed out from the very first—is formed in part by the male's personal as well as archetypal experience of the Feminine. For this reason, the man's anima figure, which has found its expression in the myth and art of all times, is a product of genuine experience of the nature of the Feminine, and not a mere manifestation of male projections upon the woman.

We have already referred to the co-ordination between the growing independence of the ego consciousness and the process in which the archetypal figures become clear and are differentiated from one another. There is also a correspondence between the detachment of the anima figure from the mother archetype (elsewhere described) and the detachment of the transformative character from the elementary character.

If in the following we cite the relation of the male to the anima as a prototype of the relation of consciousness to the transformative character of the Feminine, this by no means implies that the relation is relevant only to the male. The specifically different relation of the woman to the transformative character will be discussed in the final chapter.

The anima is the vehicle par excellence of the transformative character.[16] It is the mover, the instigator of change, whose fascination drives, lures, and encourages the male to all the adventures of the soul and spirit, of action and creation in the inner and the outward world.

With the emergence of something soullike—the anima—from the Archetypal Feminine, the unconscious, not only does a change occur in the relations of ego to unconscious and of man to woman, but the action of the unconscious within the psyche also assumes new and creative forms.[17] While the elementary character of the Feminine tends to dissolve the ego and consciousness in the unconscious, the transformative character of the anima fascinates but does not obliterate; it sets the personality in motion, produces change and ultimately trans-

---

[16] We choose the designation "anima character" for the transformative character because the figure and function of the anima have been frequently described in analytical psychology and the understanding of the trans- formative character can be enriched by its findings.

[17] My *Origins:* "The Captive and the Treasure," pp. 195 ff., and my *Amor and Psyche.*

formation. This process is also fraught with danger, often with mortal peril, but when it actually leads to the destruction of the ego, it is because the Great Mother or even the maternal uroboros is preponderant over the anima; i.e., the detachment of the anima from the mother archetype is incomplete.[18]

The anima figure has also a positive and a negative aspect; it preserves the ambivalent structure of the archetype and, like the Great Mother, forms a unity in which positive, negative, and ambivalently balanced constellations stand side by side.

When a personality is assailed by the transformative character of the Feminine and comes into conflict with it, this means psychologically that its ego consciousness has already achieved a certain independence. A constellation of this sort is no longer merely "natural," but already specifically human. As long as the ego and consciousness are dependent, the transformative character is contained in the elementary character, and the transformative process—like that of embryonic life—flows on without conflict as though decreed by nature or fate. But when the personality comes into conflict with the transformative character of the Feminine, it would seem—mythologically speaking—as though the Feminine were determined to retain the ego as a mate. The anima, as in countless fairy tales, confronts the ego hero with a "trial" that he must withstand.

But even where the transformative character of the Feminine appears as a negative, hostile, and provocative element, it compels tension, change, and an intensification of the personality. In this way an extreme exertion of the ego is provoked and its capacity for creative transformation is directly and indirectly "stimulated." [19] But of course the transformative character is not to be understood as a conscious intention of woman, as it appears in the mythological image; it attains to this awareness only late, and in the highest form of femininity. But

[18] For reasons that cannot be gone into here, such mixed situations are often characteristic for a certain type of creative man. The Romantics, for example, were wholly dominated by this constellation in which the mother archetype of the collective unconscious overpowers the anima and by its fascination leads to the uroboric incest of the death urge or to madness.

[19] All this is equally true of the male personality and of the female, whose conscious ego usually takes a male form in confronting the unconscious.

even the unconscious workings of the feminine transformative character spur the male on to achievement and transformation. Even where the trial by the Feminine is not, as in many myths and tales, consciously planned, it is immanent in the male relation to the feminine transformative character.

This means that the anima figure, despite the great danger that is bound up with it, is not terrible in the same way as the Great Mother, who is not at all concerned with the independence of the individual and the ego. Even when the anima is seemingly negative and "intends," for example, to poison the male consciousness, to endanger it by intoxication, and so on—even then a positive reversal is possible, for the anima figure is always subject to defeat. When Circe, the enchantress who turns men into beasts, meets the superior figure of Odysseus, she does not kill herself like the Sphinx, whose riddle Oedipus has solved, but invites him to share her bed.

The numerous princesses who present riddles to be solved do indeed kill their unsuccessful suitors. But they do so only in order to give themselves willingly to the victor, whose superiority, shown by his solving of the riddle, redeems the princess herself, who is this riddle. In other words, even the seemingly "deadly" anima contains the positive potentiality of the transformative character.

The unconscious as the elementary character of the Archetypal Feminine is entirely independent and self-contained, as, for example, in the spontaneous processes of the collective unconscious, which are demonstrable also in mental disorder. This means that the processes of the unconscious are here unrelated to the human personality in which they operate. The affected individual does not in reality "have" the visions; rather, they occur within him as an autonomous natural process. The structure of the transformative character already relates to a personality embracing the spontaneity of consciousness. It relates to a possible future constellation of the total personality and communicates a content or an experience that is of vital importance for the future development of the personality. That is to say, in the transformative character of the anima the prospective, anticipatory function of the unconscious has become personified and configured; confronting the ego as the nonego, it attracts it and exerts a spell upon it. The ego, however, does not at first experience this fascination directly in relation to its psyche, but in indirect projection as a demand or stimulus from outside, which for the man is usually represented by an anima figure. The soul-guiding animus figure plays a corresponding role for the woman.

The anonymity of the unconscious, characteristic for the matriarchal situation and the Archetypal Feminine, is surpassed as the anima becomes independent. The Feminine as configured in the anima character has moved far away from uroboric formlessness and unhumanity, which are the early manifestations of this archetype. It is closest to consciousness and the ego of all the forms that the feminine can assume in the male psyche.

Those women in whom the elementary character is dominant are related only collectively to their mate; they have no individual relation to him and experience only an archetypal situation in him. In a patriarchate, for example, the woman sees man as the archetypal father who begets children, who provides security—preferably also in the economic sense—for herself and her brood, and lends her a social persona position in the community.

The woman in whom the transformative character is dominant represents a higher, or rather later, stage of development. In her the matriarchal character of the Feminine, in which the relation to the mate as well as the ego and the individual is still undeveloped,[20] is surpassed. For if the transformative character of the Feminine is consciously experienced by the woman, if she has ceased to be merely its unconscious vehicle but has realized it in herself, then her relation to the individual personality of her mate has become predominant—she has become capable of a genuine relationship.

In Schema I we further attempt to represent the subsequent psy-

[20] That in the development of modern woman this phase must be relatively surpassed, and at what stage, is shown in my *Amor and Psyche.*

chological development. The development from the uroboros to the appearance of the figure groups of the Great Mother is now carried one step farther. But at the same time it is differentiated by the introduction of two characters of the Feminine: the elementary character indicated in vertical shading, the transformative character in horizontal shading.

The Great Mother stands between the Archetypal Feminine, which itself as maternal uroboros is close to the primordial, and the anima, which is already a part of the personality and thus occupies the middle position between the collective unconscious and the uniqueness of the individual.

For simplicity's sake, we have disregarded the projection of the anima upon figures and persons. (We have indicated that the transformative character is a fundamental characteristic of the Feminine by showing it to be contained not only in the Great Mother but also in the Archetypal Feminine.)

The entire schema then corresponds psychologically to the differentiation of psychic structures, which are present and effective from the very beginning but only become visible in the course of development. Their differentiation goes hand in hand with a shift in dominance from the elementary to the transformative character, to which in turn corresponds an intensified structuring of the personality as ego and consciousness.[21] In the beginning the undifferentiated unconscious as Archetypal Feminine (uroboros) corresponds to the undifferentiated personality; but as the human psyche takes form and develops authorities,[22] the two characters of the Feminine become discernible. Here it is evident that the characters are conceptions of the reflecting consciousness, which have their foundation in the symbolism of the Archetypal Feminine, but are not, like the psychical authorities—the self, the old

---

[21] For this reason we find the psychology of the feminine transformative character realized predominantly in Western development. Here the male relation to the anima becomes the force of destiny (cf. my "Leonardo da Vinci"). In purely patriarchal cultures, as in India, the maternal elementary character of the feminine remains dominant.

[22] See, e.g., Jung, "Relations," and my *Origins*, pp. 349–51.

wise man, the shadow, for example—present as "structural" elements. The authorities are personally colored partial structures of the psyche, while the characters are ordering principles of consciousness, corresponding to psychic trends.

We now possess a broader foundation for our characterization of the Archetypal Feminine. In addition to saying that a figure or person has a uroboric character, that it reveals features of the Terrible or the Good Great Mother, we can now show that sometimes the elementary and sometimes the transformative character is predominant.

Thus, for example, a goddess can be a Good Mother in whom the elementary character is predominant, or she may reveal traits of the Terrible Mother with a predominance of the transformative character. Both characteristics are significant for the situation of the ego and consciousness. The Good Mother can, for example, be associated with an infantile ego and then be typical for a negative-development situation. An example is the witch in the fairy tale of Hänsel and Gretel, whose house, i.e., exterior, is made of gingerbread and candy, but who in reality eats little children. Conversely, the Terrible Mother may be associated with a tendency toward the transformative character, i.e., toward the anima; her appearance may introduce a positive development in which the ego is driven toward masculinization and the fight with the dragon, i.e., positive development and transformation. For this constellation the myth of Perseus is typical: Perseus must kill the Terrible Mother before he can win Andromeda.[23]

The opposition and coexistence of the two fundamental characters, as well as their shifts in dominance, can be demonstrated at every stage in the development of the Archetypal Feminine. At its center stands one image that appears in ever new variations and embraces both characters.

[23] My *Origins*, pp. 213 ff.

Chapter Four

THE CENTRAL SYMBOLISM
OF THE FEMININE

THIS central symbol is the *vessel*. From the very beginning down to the latest stages of development we find this archetypal symbol as essence of the feminine. The basic symbolic equation woman = body = vessel corresponds to what is perhaps mankind's—man's as well as woman's—most elementary experience of the Feminine.

The experience of the body as a vessel is universally human and not limited to woman. What we have designated as "metabolic symbolism" [1] is an expression of this phenomenon of the body as vessel.

All the basic vital functions occur in this vessel-body schema, whose "inside" is an unknown. Its entrance and exit zones are of special significance. Food and drink are put into this unknown vessel, while in all creative functions, from the elimination of waste and the emission of seed to the giving forth of breath and the word, something is "born" out of it. *All* body openings—eyes, ears, nose, mouth (navel), rectum, genital zone—as well as the skin, have, as places of exchange between inside and outside, a numinous accent for early man. They are therefore distinguished as "ornamental" and protected zones, and in man's artistic self-representation they play a special role as idols. [2]

The concrete corporeity of the body-vessel whose inside always

<hr />

[1] My *Origins and History of Consciousness*, pp. 28 ff., 290 ff.

[2] Klages, *Der Geist als Widersacher der Seele*, Vol. III.

remains dark and unknown is the reality in which the individual experiences the whole unconscious world of instinct. This begins with the infant's elementary experience of hunger and thirst, which, like every urge and every pain and every instinct, comes from inside, from the body-vessel, to disturb him. And the ego consciousness is typically situated in the head, by which the foreign effects stemming from the inside of the body-vessel are perceived.

The archetypal body-vessel equation is of fundamental importance for the understanding of myth and symbolism, and also of early man's world view. Its significance is not limited to the exit zones that make whatever issues from the body into something "born"—whether it be hair-vegetation or breath-wind. The inside of this vessel-body also has its central symbolism.

The inside of the body is archetypally identical with the unconscious, the "seat" of the psychic processes that for man take place "in" him and "in the darkness"—which last, like the night, is a typical symbol of the unconscious.

The vessel symbolism of the body containing the psyche is also alive in modern man. We too speak of our "inwardness," of the world of "inner" values, and so on, when we mean psychic or spiritual contents, as though they were contained "in" us, in our body-vessel, and as though they came "out" of it. In reality, however, the contents of the collective unconscious, for example, are in the same sense "outside" as the world of objects; we can situate them equally well "outside," "above," "below," or "inside" us. Thus from time immemorial mankind has projected one part of the archetypal "inner" world into "heaven," and another part into "hell." But despite these projections the characteristic relatedness to the image of the body-vessel "in" which the content lives is clearly preserved.

This relation to the body-vessel is manifested especially in two forms. In the first, the outside is experienced as world-body-vessel—as, for example, when an "unconscious content," experienced by mythological apperception as a cosmic entity, a god, a star, is seen "in the belly" of the celestial woman. Then the content, e.g., the warlike-affective

Nergal-Mars,[3] which we designate as an aggression drive, is at the same time "outside," a star and cosmic entity, and "inside," in the belly of the celestial mother. This symbolically paradoxical, twofold nature of the projection corresponds exactly to the psychological reality that our consciousness formulates when it speaks of a "collective," i.e., trans-personal content, which is also *inside* the psyche, namely, the collective unconscious.

Early man, who, without being aware of it, occupies a position in the center of the world, whence he relates everything to himself and himself to everything, fills the world around him with images of his unconscious. In so doing, he projects himself into three regions on the inner surface of the world-vessel that encompasses him. These three regions, in which the images of his own unconscious become visible as images of the world, are the heavens above him, the earth on which he lives along with all living things, and the realm that he experiences as the dark space "under" him, the underworld, the inside of the earth.

While the first relation consists in the body-vessel symbol in its cosmic projection upon the world as a world-body-vessel, the second, which is no less important, is expressed in the correlation of certain cosmic bodies, directions, constellations, gods, demons, with the zones and organs of the body. This correlation is so universal for primitive man that the world-body correspondence may be looked upon as a law of the primitive world view.

This early magical-psychic image of the body and the outside world is correlated not only with certain powers but also with colors, regions, plants, elements, and so forth. The resulting *participation mystique* of the world in certain zones and organs of the body is manifested by a mutual magical dependency, in which influences pass from the mythical universe to man and the zones of his body, and conversely from the zones of man's body and the substances connected with them to the mythical universe.[4]

In Egypt and Mexico, in India and China, in the writings of the

[3] Nergal is the Babylonian and Mars the Roman war god, corresponding to the Greek Ares.

[4] This accounts in part for the effect of magical substances such as spittle, urine, feces, hair, and sweat.

Gnostics as in the cabala, we find the body schema as archetype of the first man, in whose image the world was created.[5] Modern consciousness interprets these processes as projections, i.e., as an outside experience of archetypal images. But early man lived in the middle of this psychophysical space in which outside and inside, world and man, powers and things, are bound together in an indissoluble unity.

The symbol of this original psychic situation is the circular snake, the uroboros,[6] which as the Great Round, or sphere, is a still-undifferentiated whole, the great vault and vessel of the world, which contains in itself the entire existence of early man and so becomes the Archetypal Feminine, in which the elementary vessel character predominates.[7]

Thus in many mythologies we encounter the egg as the archetypal symbol of world creation. As the container of opposites it may, for example, be divided into two halves, white and black, with heaven above and the earth below. This is the Orphic egg, whose symbolic significance has been elucidated by Bachofen.[8]

For obvious reasons woman is experienced as the vessel par excellence. Woman as body-vessel is the natural expression of the human experience of woman bearing the child "within" her and of man entering "into" her in the sexual act. Because the identity of the female personality with the encompassing body-vessel in which the child is sheltered belongs to the foundation of feminine existence, woman is not only the vessel that like every body contains something within itself, but, both for herself and the male, is the "life-vessel as such," in which life forms, and which bears all living things and discharges them out of itself and into the world.

Of course it is particularly the elementary character of the Feminine that is experienced in the symbol of the vessel. For as the Great Round it is the vessel that preserves and holds fast. But, in addition, it is the nourishing vessel that provides the unborn as well as the born with food and drink.

[5] Cf. my *Origins*, p. 25; the concept of "magical anatomy" in Danzel, *Magie und Geheimwissenschaft;* and Cassirer, *Philosophy of Symbolic Forms.*

[6] My *Origins*, pp. 5 ff.

[7] The masculine components which are also contained in the uroboros, and with which we shall concern ourselves below, stand in no symbolic relation to the vessel character of the Great Round.

[8] *Versuch über die Gräbersymbolik der Alten*, index, s. v. "Ei."

Only when we have considered the whole scope of the basic feminine functions—the giving of life, nourishment, warmth, and protection
—can we understand why the Feminine occupies so central a position in
human symbolism and from the very beginning bears the character of
"greatness." The Feminine appears as great because that which is
contained, sheltered, nourished, is dependent on it and utterly at its
mercy. Nowhere perhaps is it so evident that a human being must be
experienced as "great" as in the case of the mother. A glance at the
infant or child confirms her position as Great Mother. Her numinous
superiority constellates the characteristic situation of the human infant
in contrast to the newborn animal, which is far more independent at
birth.

While in animals a kind of sensory consciousness sets in immedi-
ately after birth, the consciousness of man arises in the course of the first
years of life, and is in part molded by the social bond of the infant with
the group, but particularly with its most prominent representative, the
mother.[9]

If we combine this body-world equation of early man in its first
unspecific form with the fundamental symbolic equation of the feminine,
woman = body = vessel, we arrive at a universal symbolic formula for
the early period of mankind:

$$Woman = body = vessel = world$$

This is the basic formula of the matriarchal stage, i.e., of a human phase
in which the Feminine is preponderant over the Masculine, the unconscious over the ego and consciousness.

We shall first attempt to represent the world-filling matriarchal
symbolism of the Great Round on the basis of the vessel-symbol and its
numerous ramifications. A survey of this sort will better enable us to
understand the fateful importance of the Archetypal Feminine in its
concrete reality as it confronts us in the myths and rites, the images and
religious attitudes, of early mankind.

Here it should not be forgotten that "early mankind" and "matriarchal stage" are no archaeological or historical entities, but psychological

[9] See above. Ch. 3.

realities whose fateful power is still alive in the psychic depths of present-day man. The health and creativity of every man depend very largely on whether his consciousness can live at peace with this stratum of the unconscious or consumes itself in strife with it.

Once again we shall seek to orient ourselves by a general schema (Schema II, page 45). In Part II, in which we describe the unfolding of the Archetypal Feminine and illustrate it with pictorial representations, we shall fill in and complement this basic schematic orientation.[10]

At the center of the schema is the great vessel of the female body, which we do in fact know as a real vessel.[11] Its principal symbolic elements are the mouth, the breasts, and the womb. For, for the sake of simplicity, we have emphasized the "belly" zone symbolizing the totality of the body-vessel, and as symbol of the "inside" we have inscribed the appropriate organ, the heart.

We begin with the territory of the belly, which most strikingly represents the elementary containing character of the vessel; to it belongs the womb as symbol of the entrance into this region. The lowest level of this belly zone is the underworld that is contained in the "belly" or "womb" of the earth. To this world belong not only the subterranean darkness as hell and night but also such symbols as chasm, cave, abyss, valley, depths, which in innumerable rites and myths play the part of the earth womb that demands to be fructified.[12]

The cave, in its relation to the mountain that unites the character of vessel, belly, and earth, also belongs to the dark territory of the underworld. Rock and stone have the same significance as mountain and earth.[13] Accordingly, it is not only the mountain that is worshiped as the Great Mother but also rocks representing it—and her.

[10] Since the symbolism we have sketched is archetypal, it can be demonstrated in the myths and rites, the legends and art, of all times, and also in the religion and folklore of the whole world, though of course this lies beyond the scope of the present work.

[11] Cf. figs. 16–18, 21, and 28; Pls. 27–28, 31, 33a, 40–41, and 55b.

[12] Cf. Part II.

[13] Rock and stone are "the same" as mountain by virtue of the law of *pars pro toto* governing all entities related to one another in *participation mystique*. Wherever an identity is established between persons and objects, it applies—according to this law—also to their parts. Since every part contains the totality to which it belongs, since the whole acts or is acted upon in the part, a man can be bewitched, for example, by an enemy who has acquired his fingernail cuttings, and a hunter can exert a magic influence on an animal whose image he possesses.

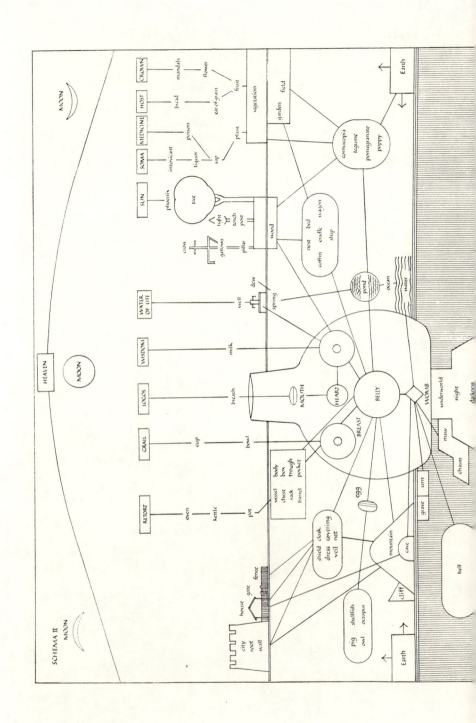

But the elementary character of the Archetypal Feminine is far from containing only positive features. Just as the Great Mother can be terrible as well as good, so the Archetypal Feminine is not only a giver and protector of life but, as container, also holds fast and takes back; she is the goddess of life and death at once. As the symbol of the black-and-white egg indicates, the Feminine contains opposites, and the world actually lives because it combines earth and heaven, night and day, death and life.

Not only as underworld and hell does the earth belong to the elementary vessel character but also as tomb and cave. The cave is a dwelling as well as a tomb; the vessel character of the Feminine not only shelters the unborn in the vessel of the body, and not only the born in the vessel of the world, but also takes back the dead into the vessel of death, the cave or coffin, the tomb or urn.

As we pursue this symbolism of the belly-vessel, we must distinguish between symbols in which the function of containing is dominant and those in which the protective function holds the foreground. The symbolism of containing dominates in the vegetative symbol of the fruit, e.g., the pomegranate and poppy in which the abundance of seeds stresses containment. The pod and—in an abstract sense—the cornucopia are also characteristic of this, and in the animal world such creatures as the pig, the squid, the shellfish, and the owl. In the pig the accent is on fertility, in the shellfish on the form of the womb, in the squid and owl on the uterine form of their bodies. Among the culture symbols of this province we may mention containers of various sorts, particularly the barrel, but also the box, basket, chest, trough, sack, and so on.

Another symbolic sphere in which the maternal character of containing is stressed includes nest, cradle, bed, ship, wagon, and coffin. Aside from its connection with wood, which we shall discuss below, this group represents a transition to the symbols in which the function of protection outweighs that of containing. The function of protection, which still belongs to the elementary character of the vessel, is particularly evident in the mountain, which in German (*Berg*) is symbolically related to *sich bergen*, 'taking refuge'; *sich verbergen*, 'hiding'; *Geborgen-*

heit, 'safety'; and *Burg,* 'castle.' Mountain as mound or tumulus also embraces this function of protection and safeguarding.

The sheltering cave as part of the mountain represents historically the natural form of such culture symbols as temple and *temenos,* hut and house, village and city, lattice, fence, and wall, signifying what protects and closes off. (Here gate and door are the entrance to the womb of the maternal vessel.)

Subordinate but no less important are the culture symbols of protection, which likewise belong to the feminine vessel character, namely such coverings as shirt, dress, coat and veil, net, and finally shield. (Characteristically, such German words as *Höhle,* 'cave'; Hel, the Germanic goddess of death; *hohl,* 'hollow'; *Halle,* 'hall'; *Hülle,* 'covering'; *Hülse,* 'husk' or 'pod'; and *Helm,* 'helmet,' derive from the root *hel,* 'shelter.')

In the two following symbol groups, the transformative character is more pronounced, although the elementary character is still paramount. Its typical intermediary position between the groups in which the elementary or the transformative character clearly predominates is evident in the fact that the one group is situated close to the belly-center of the female vessel, while the other derives from the region of the breasts. In both groups we have to do not with nature symbols but with culture symbols, every one of which can be followed through the entire history of mankind.

The first group that belongs to the vessel character of the belly includes jar and kettle, oven and retort. Here the elementary formal character of the Great Round predominates, but the creative aspect of the uterus and the potentiality of transformation also play a part.[14] If the suggestion of what goes on "inside" them did not include the secret of transformation, these symbols would be no more than containing vessels and would not go beyond the elementary character.

The other series, deriving from the breasts of the woman-vessel,

[14] Concerning the connection between these symbols and the primordial mysteries of the Feminine and the earliest human culture, see Part II.

consists of the symbols vessel, bowl, goblet, chalice, grail. It combines the elementary character of containing with that of nourishing. The fact that these symbols are open in character and form, just as those of the other series are closed, accents the motif of giving, donating. The transformative character of these symbols relates to the nurturing of an already-born ego, either in the childhood stage or already independent. For this reason, and also by virtue of its formal quality, this series belongs to the symbol group of the breast. Thus the transformative character is correlated, symbolically as otherwise, with a region of the body-vessel "higher" than that of the elementary character,[15] namely, with the breasts, heart, and mouth.

But also the symbols of the transformative character almost always retain a connection with the elementary character of the Feminine and with the symbols of the womb and belly region. In direct correspondence with the symbolism of the body-vessel, the upper is built on the lower and is inconceivable except in connection with it. The transformation starts at the lower level and encompasses it. In the matriarchal world, it is never a free-floating, rootless, "upper" process, as the abstract male intellect typically imagines.

The natural elements that are essentially connected with vessel symbolism include both earth and water. This containing water is the primordial womb of life, from which in innumerable myths life is born. It is the water "below," the water of the depths, ground water and ocean, lake and pond.

But the maternal water not only contains; it also nourishes and transforms, since all living things build up and preserve their existence with the water or milk of the earth. Since the water can be symbolically related to the breast as well as the womb, the rain can appear as the milk of the celestial cow and the earth water as the milk of the earth

---

[15] The accentuation of the breasts for the transformative character can also be expressed in a pronounced diminution of the breasts, for example, when the elementary character of the nourished is rejected in favor of the transformative character of the "little breasts." It is interesting to note that we find something of this sort in the earliest figures of the primordial mother. *Pl. 6*

body, for the milk-giving animals, especially the cow and goat as central symbols of the nourishing, exist as cosmic entities both above and upon the earth.

Since water is undifferentiated and elementary and is often uroboric, containing male elements side by side with the maternal, flowing and moving waters, such as streams, are bisexual and male and are worshiped as fructifiers and movers.

Where the matriarchal Feminine is predominant, we often find, side by side with the child symbolism of that which is born from it, a hermaphroditic symbolism preserving an undifferentiated uroboric character. But even where the born water is looked upon as masculine, that which is born from the depths of the earth-mother vessel has the significance of a son; it is typical for the matriarchal sphere that the son is dominated by the Great Mother who holds him fast even in his masculine movement and activity.

To the realm of the earth water belong not only the pond and lake but also the spring. While in the well the elementary character of the Feminine is still evident—it is no accident that in fairy tales a well is often the gate to the underworld and specifically to the domain of the earth mother [16]—in the spring the rising, erupting motif of "being born" and of creative movement is more strongly accented than that of being contained. Yet symbolically the spring's connection with the maternal earth nevertheless remains the determining factor.

This "child" character—to sum up a number of similar attitudes— belongs to a great number of symbols from the province of the Feminine. Everything that issues from the darkness within its vessel is looked upon as its offspring and child, and the domination of the Archetypal Feminine over all this constellates the unity and fateful power of the matriarchal world.

The Great Earth Mother who brings forth all life from herself is eminently the mother of all vegetation. The fertility rituals and myths of the whole world are based upon this archetypal context. The center of this vegetative symbolism is the tree. As fruit-bearing tree of life it is

[16] E.g., in Grimm's fairy tale (No. 24), "Mother Holle."

female: it bears, transforms, nourishes; its leaves, branches, twigs are "contained" in it and dependent on it. The protective character is evident in the treetop that shelters nests and birds. But in addition the tree trunk is a container, "in" which dwells its spirit, as the soul dwells in the body. The female nature of the tree is demonstrated in the fact that treetops and trunk can give birth, as in the case of Adonis and many others.

But the tree is also the earth phallus, the male principle jutting out of the earth, in which the procreative character outweighs that of sheltering and containing. This applies particularly to such trees as the cypress, which, in contrast to the feminine forms of the fruit trees and leafy trees, are phallic in the accentuation of their trunks. The phallic nature of the tree, which does not exclude the character of containing vessel, is clearly expressed in such words as *Stammbaum*, 'family tree'; *ent-stammen*, 'stem from'; *ab-stammen*, 'descend from'; *Stammhalter*, 'first-born son,' derived from *Stamm*, 'tree trunk.' In this sense the post and pillar are phallic-masculine but also containing-feminine. A fine example of this is the Egyptian *djed* pillar of Osiris.[17]

Here again the uroboric nature can shine through [18] when the pillar, as in the case of the asherah, is a symbol of the Great Mother. Thus the *djed* pillar of Osiris as coffin, as chest containing the dead, is also maternal-feminine. The symbolism of tree, trunk, pillar, and stake is also determined by the nature of wood, the ὔλη, which is not only a product of growth but is also the matter, the *materia*, from which all things arise, and as such possesses an elementary character.

The accent of a symbol depends in large measure on the matriarchal or patriarchal culture situation in which it is embedded. In a patriarchate, for example, the *mater* character of the symbol *materia* is devaluated; matter is regarded as something of small value in contrast to the ideal—which is assigned to the male-paternal side. Similarly, the symbol ὔλη is not revered as the foundation of the world of growth but, as, for example, in all gnosticizing religions from Christianity to Islam,

---

[17] See my *Origins*, index, s.v. "*djed* pillar."
[18] A fine example of this "double symbolism" is the Indian sculpture of the phallus "in" which Shiva or Shakti is contained.

Pls. 106-7

becomes inert, negatively demonized "matter," as opposed to the divine spirit aspect of the male νοῦς.

Whereas under matriarchy even the male-phallic tree retains its character of dependence on the earth, the patriarchal world of India, as of the cabala and Christianity, knows of a tree whose roots are "above," in the patriarchal heaven. The "antinatural" symbolism of this spiritual tree is, of course, distinctly patriarchal in meaning. But here we encounter a paradox: unless the male spirit is able—as in mathematics—to construct a purely abstract world, it must make use of the nature symbols originating in the unconscious. But this brings it into contradiction with the natural character of the symbols, which it distorts and perverts. Unnatural symbols and hostility to the nature symbol—e.g., Eve taken out of Adam—are characteristic of the patriarchal spirit. But even this attempt at revaluation usually fails, as an analysis of this symbolism might show, because the matriarchal character of the nature symbol asserts itself again and again.[19]

But the tree as house or bearer of fruit is not only evaluated positively as a place of birth; in accordance with the ambivalent structure of the Archetypal Feminine from which it arises, it can also be an abode of death. Into the treetops the dead are hoisted; the tree trunk embraces the corpse as the cedar tree [20] embraced Osiris; the wooden coffin is laid in the earth—here the character of the earth-womb taking the body back into itself is combined with that of the encompassing wood. To this symbolic group belong the variants of the death tree as gallows, as cross, and as stake.

The ambivalence of the archetype that is so evident in the elementary character of the Feminine is preserved in the transformative character. It recedes only at the level that we designate as spiritual transformation, the new factor in which is a synthesis surpassing the original principle of opposites.

Transformative symbolism is in high degree determined by the

[19] It would be highly interesting, and fruitful for the history of psychology, to attempt to trace the archetypal symbolism underlying philosophy and investigate the process in which the original symbolism was replaced in philosophy by an accentuated conceptual world in opposition to it.
[20] The "erica tree"—now thought to have been cedar.

most numinous of all the transformation mysteries: growth. In the blood-transformation mystery [21] the secret of the Feminine seems to lie on the animal plane, but Plato's words also apply: "In fertility and generation, woman does not set an example to the earth, but the earth sets an example to woman." [22] Because the earth, as creative aspect of the Feminine, rules over vegetative life, it holds the secret of the deeper and original form of "conception and generation" upon which all animal life is based. For this reason the highest and most essential mysteries of the Feminine are symbolized by the earth and its transformation.[23]

The phenomenon of growth unfolds in such a wealth of colors and forms that we are still overwhelmed by the archetypal numen of vegetation, although today its effect on us is more aesthetic than sacral.

In perpetual transformation, the humble "rotting" seed lengthens into stalk and sprouting leaves, long stem grows into dense bud, whence the blossom bursts forth in all its diversity and color. And this transformation of form and color, in which the colorless seed unfolds into the green and gold of leaves and thence into the radiant colors of the flower, culminates in the reversal by which the scented fragility of the blossom becomes the concentrated mature fruit, again with its infinite variety of form, color, consistency, taste, and smell. This mysterious process begins under the earth and is completed with the help of water in the air, beneath the fire of the sun; it is subject to the influence of invisible forces that early man experienced in earth and water, in the heavenly powers of night and day, in the stars, the moon, the sun, and their seasonal changes.

Man is bathed in this abundance of vegetative life in forest and steppe, in mountain and valley. Everywhere it grows: roots and tubers under the earth, a sea of fruit on trees attainable and unattainable,

---

[21] See above, pp. 31 f.

[22] *Menexenus.*

[23] In the agrarian cultures, with their emphasis on growth, the image of the Great Mother and the sociological matriarchate occupy the foreground. But this only means that here the Archetypal Feminine achieves greater clarity than elsewhere—and also a certain one-sidedness. Actually, this archetype is at work both in lower and higher strata. The archetypal structure of the Great Mother can be demonstrated among the hunters of the Stone Age as well as in the modern world—quite independently of the social structure, which, in far higher degree than is realized in our era of highly developed consciousness, is conditioned by the psychic-archetypal constellations within the group.

herbs and berries, nuts and mushrooms, leaves and grains, in field and forest. And this primordial world is also a world of the Great Round and the Great Mother; she is the protectress, the good mother, who feeds man with fruits and tubers and grains, but also poisons him and lets him hunger and thirst in times of drought, when she withdraws from living things.

In this primordial world of vegetation, dependent on it and hidden in it, lives the animal world, bringing danger and salvation; under the ground the snakes and worms, uncanny and dangerous; in the water fishes, reptiles, and aquatic monsters; birds flying through the air and beasts scurrying over the earth. Roaring and hissing, milk-giving and voracious, the animals fill the vegetative world, nestling in it like birds in a tree.

And this world, too, is in transformation, bursting eggs and crawling young, corpses decomposing into earth, and life arising from swamp and muck. Everywhere mothers and suckling cubs, being born, growing, changing, devouring and devoured, killing and dying. But all this destroying, wild, terrifying animal world is overshadowed by the Great Mother as the Great World Tree, which shelters, protects, nourishes this animal world to which man feels he belongs. Mysterious in its truthfulness, the myth makes the vegetative world engender the animal world and also the world of men, which thus appears merely as a part of the World Tree of all living things.

> The generations of men are like the leaves of the forest. Leaves fall when the breezes blow, in the springtime others grow; as they go and come again so upon the earth do men.[24]

Bachofen repeatedly cited this metaphor of Glaucus as characteristic of the life feeling, the natural wisdom and natural sadness, of the matriarchate: "The leaves of the tree do not rise from one another but all alike from the branch. So also the generations of man in the matriarchal view. . . . The engendered belongs to the maternal matter, which has harbored it, brought it to light, and which now nurtures it. But this

[24] *Iliad*, VI, 145–49 (tr. Rouse).

mother is always the same; she is ultimately the earth, represented by earthly woman down through the endless generations of mothers and daughters."[25]

The archetypal character of this relationship may be seen from the fact that in the poetry of all ages the same images recur in the same context; indeed, the poetry of the world might be classified according to the archetypes it expresses. We shall cite here an example from nineteenth-century poetry, disclosing the same fundamental matriarchal situation as in the lines from Homer. It would be a simple matter to quote examples from the poetry of all peoples.

> A wind sways the pines,
> And below
> Not a breath of wild air;
> Still as the mosses that glow
> On the flooring and over the lines
> Of the roots here and there.
> The pinetree drops its dead;
> They are quiet, as under the sea.
> Overhead, overhead
> Rushes life in a race,
> As the clouds the clouds chase;
> And we go,
> And we drop like the fruits of the tree,
> Even we,
> Even so.[26]

Where growth and transformation are governed by the Feminine, they often appear in the tragic aspect of transience. The individual passes and his death is as nothing in view of the unchanging abundance

[25] Bachofen, *Mutterrecht*, Vol. 1, p. 95. Modern scientists unfamiliar with Bachofen have confirmed this connection between Glaucus and the matriarchate. See Persson, *The Religion of Greece in Prehistoric Times*, index, s.v. "Glaucus."

[26] George Meredith, "Dirge in Woods," from *A Reading of Earth* (1888). In citing the poem in the anthology *The Limits of Art*,

Huntington Cairns quotes Frank Harris (*Contemporary Portraits* [First Series], p. 215) as having said, "it is almost a rendering of the magical verse beginning: Ueber allen Gipfeln ist Ruh" (Goethe, "Wanderers Nachtlied"). It could be shown that a great part of all nature poetry, particularly that of the Romantics, is an expression of the archetype we have been discussing.

of renascent life. But this tragic aspect, this expression of the predominance of the Great Round over what is born of it and, psychologically speaking, of the unconscious over consciousness, is only one side, the dark earthly side, of the cosmic egg. In addition to its earthly half, the Great Round has also a heavenly half; [27] it embodies not only a transformation downward to mortality and the earth, but a transformation upward toward immortality and the luminous heavens.

[27] In this point Bachofen's understanding remains strangely limited by patriarchal-Christian conceptions. Dazzled by his fundamental discovery of the development from the matriarchal to the patriarchal and from the lunar to the solar, he never arrived at a full understanding of the matriarchal spirit, which he devaluates as material and lunar. This view is just as understandable and just as much to be rejected as the corresponding psychological view that subordinates the unconscious to consciousness. In both cases, which are essentially identical, we have before us two systems, the later of which (sun, patriarchate, consciousness) cannot exist without the earlier (moon, matriarchate, unconscious) and neither of which exhausts the ultimate possibilities of transformation.

Chapter Five

THE TRANSFORMATION
MYSTERIES

THE transformation mysteries of the Feminine [1] are grounded in a material or natural element to which, however, they bring not only a quantitative change but also a qualitative transformation. Something new and supreme is achieved, which is manifested in connection with the symbol of the "spirit."

The matriarchate's experience of itself is, as we have said, subsumed under the equation woman = body = vessel = world. The mystery of transformation, in which the "spirit" comes into being, is also a product of this Great Round; it is its luminous essence, its fruit, and its son. For the matriarchal spirit does not deny the native maternal soil from which it stems. It does not, like the Apollonian-solar-patriarchal spirit, present itself as "sheer being," as pure existence in absolute eternity, but remains "sonlike." Apprehending itself as historically generated, as a creature, it does not negate its bond with the Earth Mother.

For this reason, the favored spiritual symbol of the matriarchal sphere is the moon in its relation to the night and the Great Mother of the night sky. The moon, as the luminous aspect of the night, belongs to

[1] In contrast to the feminine mysteries, the transformation mysteries of the Archetypal Masculine have the character of a surprise attack, and sudden irruptions are the decisive factor. Consequently lightning is the characteristic symbol for them. In regard to the combination of features of male and female mystery transformation and the transition from the matriarchal to the patriarchal accent on transformation, see the chapter "Transformation, or Osiris" in my *Origins and History of Consciousness*, pp. 220 ff.

her; it is her fruit, her sublimation as light, as expression of her essential spirit.[2]

Day and sun are seen in the matriarchate as children of the Feminine, which as dark night and as morning is the mother of the bright aspect. Thus in Egypt, for example, the same sign signifies day and sun, but the hours are reckoned according to the stars and the months according to the moon;[3] in other words, time as an entity embracing day and night is not related to the sun. But although in the matriarchal sphere day and sun are the opposite of night, it is not they which represent the spiritual side of the darkness. The Great Round embraces in itself light and dark, day and night, but priority is given to the night, as Bachofen has convincingly shown. Throughout the world, lunar mythology seems to have preceded solar mythology. But we also know that in the human psyche the experience of totality always precedes the experience of particulars. "The night sky and the daytime sky," writes Preuss, "were apprehended earlier than the heavenly bodies, because the whole was seen as a unitary being and the religious intuition of the heavenly bodies often confounded them with the sky as a whole; that is to say, it could not free itself from the total view." [4]

Thus the totality of the diurnal sky was originally regarded as the primary entity, of which the sun was a part. Here again we must free ourselves from the scientific and by no means self-evident knowledge of the modern consciousness that the sun "makes" the day and the daylight. This assertion stands in evident contradiction to the naïve experience that it is light even when the sky is cloudy, for example. The sun was originally looked upon as the luminary of the daytime sky, just as the moon was the luminary of the dark night sky. Thus early man spoke no more of *the* sun than he did of *the* moon. Just as he knew a new moon, a full moon, a waning, and a dark moon, he looked upon the eastern sun of the morning, the meridian sun of noon, and the western sun of evening

---

[2] Here it should be recalled that man was not originally in possession of the scientific fact that the moon "merely reflects" the light of the sun, but acquired it only at a relatively late date. On this and the following, see my "Über den

Mond und das matriarchale Bewusstsein."

[3] Kees, *Der Götterglaube im alten Aegypten*, p. 225.

[4] Preuss, *Die geistige Kultur der Naturvölker*, p. 9.

as different suns. But because of its contrast with the darkness, the light side of the moon and of the stars makes a far deeper impression on man than do the daylight and the sun. For this reason the moon is experienced as forming a totality with the background against which it stands out. It is the light fruit of the night tree and the night, just as the flame is the fruit of the wooden torch and the apple is the luminous fruit of the seed germinating in the darkness of the earth.

Archetypally the luminous bodies are always symbols of consciousness, of the spiritual side of the human psyche. Therefore their position in the mythologies, religions, and rites is characteristic of the psychic constellations predominant in the group that has projected these mythologies, etc., upon the heavens out of their unconscious. It is in this sense that by way of simplification we correlate the sun with the patriarchal consciousness and the moon with the matriarchal consciousness.

The lunar spirit of matriarchy is not the "immaterial and invisible spirit" of which the patriarchate boasts: "While the feminine is by nature unable to cast off materiality, the man becomes wholly removed from it and rises to the incorporeality of the sunlight." [5]

This patriarchal consciousness that says, "The victory of the male lies in the spiritual principle," [6] devaluates the moon and the feminine element to which it belongs. It is "merely of the soul," "merely" the highest form of an earthly and material development that stands in opposition to the "pure spirit" that in its Apollonian-Platonic and Jewish-Christian form has led to the abstract conceptuality of modern consciousness. But this modern consciousness is threatening the existence of Western mankind, for the one-sidedness of masculine development has led to a hypertrophy of consciousness at the expense of the whole man. Consequently the knowledge distilled by the abstracting collective consciousness of man—the knowledge of matter, for example —resides in the hands of earthly representatives of masculinity who seem by no means suited to incarnate the "pure incorporeal solar principle." And, on the other hand, the character of wisdom and light

[5] Bachofen, *Mutterrecht*, Vol. 1, p. 412. [6] Ibid., Vol. 2, p. 600.

belonging to the Archetypal Feminine ought not to be designated as "merely of the soul."

The patriarchal consciousness starts from the standpoint that the spirit is eternal *a priori;* that the spirit was in the beginning. After describing the three stages of development—the tellurian-material, the lunar-psychic, and the solar-spiritual—Bachofen declares: "Now the third stage can be looked upon as the first and original one. What came last to consciousness now becomes first; the sun becomes the primordial power, from which the two lower stages issued by emanation. What Aristotle [7] stated to be the law of all development is fulfilled. What comes last appears by no means as the last, but as the first and original. 'For that which genetically follows is by nature first and that which is genetically last is first.' " [8]

Here we are not concerned with the philosophical aspect of this statement but with its psychological foundation. Starting from the final product of this process of development, from consciousness, with which he identifies himself, the male proceeds to deny the genetic principle, which is precisely the basic principle of the matriarchal world. Or, mythologically speaking, he murders his mother and undertakes the patriarchal revaluation by which the son identified with the father makes himself the source from which the Feminine—like Eve arising from Adam's rib—originated in a spiritual and antinatural way.

The necessity and relative inner justification of this standpoint for consciousness, and particularly for a male consciousness, cannot be contested,[9] but in its radical one-sidedness it can only be understood against the background of the fundamentally antithetical, equally necessary, and equally justified principle of the matriarchal world.

In this matriarchal world, the spirit world of the moon, corresponding to the basic symbolism of the Archetypal Feminine, appears

---

[7] *De partibus animalium*, 2, 1. [In the Peck (Loeb) tr.: "Now the order of things in the process of formation is the reverse of their real and essential order; I mean that the later a thing comes in the formative process the earlier it comes in the order of Nature, and that which comes at the end of the process is at the beginning in the order of Nature."—ED.]

[8] Bachofen, *Mutterrecht*, Vol. 1, p. 412.

[9] My *Origins*, pp. 402-3.

as a birth—and indeed as rebirth. Wherever we encounter the symbol of rebirth, we have to do with a matriarchal transformation mystery, and this is true even when its symbolism or interpretation bears a patriarchal disguise.

Since in the second part of this work we shall discuss the symbolism of spiritual transformation, we shall here content ourselves with a few general remarks based on our schema (Schema II) and specifically on its upper zone.

Transformation symbolism always becomes sacral where, over and above the purely natural transformative process, there is an intervention by man; where it ceases to be a process only of nature or the unconscious and the human personality enters into it and heightens it.

Although the highest form of this sublimated natural transformation is the integration process of the creative human personality, the more partial forms of cultural transformation also belong to it. Such processes are the primordial mysteries of the Feminine, which in our opinion stand at the beginning of human culture. In all such forms of mystery as, for example, the preparation of food and drink, the fashioning of garments, vessels, the house, natural things and things transformed by nature are subjected to a higher mode of transformation by human intervention.

A transformation of this kind is not originally a "technical" process, as our secularized consciousness sees it, but a mystery. For this reason the symbolism connected with these primordial mysteries always has a spiritual character transcending the merely real.

Thus, for example, a transformation sequence leads from the fruit to the juice, thence by fermentation to the intoxicant, whose lunar-spirit character appears in such potions of immortality as soma, nectar, mead, and so on. Another sequence rises from the natural realm of plants to the essences of poison and medicine, in which the spiritual side of creation triumphs, and which is likewise governed by the moon and in the last analysis by the Great Mother. Medicines as well as poisons are numinous contents that have been acquired and communicated in mysterious wise. The communicators and administrators of this aspect of the Feminine—originally almost always women—are sacral figures, i.e., priestesses.

The character of spiritual transformation is most evident in connection with intoxicants, poison, and medicine. The feeling that he is transformed when he imbibes them is one of the deepest experiences of man. It is significant, however, that such a transformation is experienced not as corporeal but as spiritual. Sickness and poisoning, drunkenness and cure, are psychic processes that all mankind relates to an invisible spiritual principle, by whose action the personality is changed.

The experiences of hunger and satiety, thirst and the appeasement, refreshment, and pleasure that come of quenching it, are indeed more commonplace than the experiences of intoxicants, poison, and medicine; but they form the foundation of the mystery experience of transformation by food, which underlies all these phenomena. To this sphere belong also the modification of natural food by fire and the corresponding processes of boiling, baking, roasting, and so on. They are all crucial cultural achievements of mankind; indeed they are the presupposition of all human culture.

But this cultural development is also set in motion by mysteries that belong to the secret province of the Feminine. The conspicuous and characteristic factor of the matriarchal transformation mysteries is that they always remain "incorporate," i.e., in some way connected with matter. In this transformation, to be sure, matter becomes a sublimated, essential matter, a "quintessence," but it does not go beyond the sphere of the Great Female.

This transformation of matter becomes most evident in the alchemistic transformation of the human personality. But before it appears in the mysteries as an independent psychic experience, it is perceived in projection upon animated nature. Consequently a great number of these spiritual transformation symbols of nature enter into the mysteries. Grass becomes grain and is transformed into bread and into the Host; wood is transformed into flame and light. The blossom becomes a crown and a mandala and a place of "higher," spiritual birth

—like tree, rock and mountain, ear, flank, and head—and the vessel in which this spiritual birth takes place appears as a magic vessel and as a vessel of transformation, as baptismal font, as grail, and finally as alchemistic retort.

Even the most abstract matriarchal symbols preserve their relation to the vessel-body symbolism of the Feminine. Wisdom becomes the milk of wisdom, and thus retains not only its blood-milk transformation character but also its character as food and its connection with creative birth through the Feminine. Similarly, the elixir preserves the character of the nature symbol, and the *summum bonum* appears as herb or fruit of immortality, as liquor or *aqua vitae*, as diamond or pearl, as flower or kernel.

Finally, the world of the spirit as something born, as a product of creative nature itself, has its most abstract symbol in the form that leads from mouth to breath, and from breath to word, the logos, the spiritual symbol, whose son character became a historical force in the logos of Philo and subsequently of Christianity.

In our schema, accordingly, we have related this symbol group to the center of the great woman-body-vessel, the heart. True, the breath-logos sequence, like many other symbols and symbol groups, was later appropriated by the patriarchate, but it everywhere reveals its matriarchal origin. Thus an Egyptian myth, recorded at a time when the patriarchate had completely revaluated the original matriarchal situation, contains the words: "The Demiurge who created all the Gods and their Kas is in his heart and in his tongue." [10] Here we already discern the masculine trend toward an abstract spirit that has found its clearest expression in the Mosaic doctrine of creation by the word, but beneath it we still perceive the primordial situation in which the word is "born" as essence of the divine corporeal totality, the Great Round—the situation in which it is said: "My heart, my mother; my heart, my mother! My heart of transformations." [11]

The matriarchal world is far from being, as Bachofen supposed,

[10] Moret, *The Nile and Egyptian Civilization*, p. 376.

[11] Book of the Dead, Ch. XXX (Budge, p. 147).

merely that of the lower level, of earthly transience and darkness. In the mysteries of rebirth the individual is also raised to the light and immortalized. But this individual is initiated by the spirit mother, as remains evident down to the Eleusinian mysteries, and his rebirth takes the form of a luminous birth in the nocturnal sky. As immortal star or hero, he becomes a star in the night and so remains united with the Great Nocturnal Mother, whether as a luminous infant glittering in her dark belly, or as a point of light sparkling on her nocturnal cloak, or as a part of her tree of light illumining her nocturnal world. Even in his immortality she does not release him—any more than does the Great Father, who gathers his immortals round him in the heavenly mandala.

If we survey the whole of the symbolic sphere determined by the vessel character of the Archetypal Feminine, we find that in its elementary and transformative character the Feminine as "creative principle" encompasses the whole world. This is the totality of nature in its original unity, from which all life arises and unfolds, assuming, in its highest transformation, the form of the spirit.

The matriarchal world is geocentric in the comprehensive sense that tangible, visible reality is the source even of its highest manifestations, namely, the spiritual phenomena that arise in it. In the matriarchal world the woman as vessel is not made by man or out of man or used for his procreative purposes; rather, the reverse is true: it is this vessel with its mysterious creative character that brings forth the male in itself and from out of itself. Bachofen rightly pointed out that in the matriarchate man is looked upon as a sower, but he did not perceive the radical meaning of this image, in which the man is only an instrument of the earth and the seed he sows is not "his" seed but earth seed. This situation still prevails in an African usage reported by Frobenius:

> Arriving at the broken field, the man advances with a long planting stick and pierces one seed hole after another in the earth. His woman goes behind him. From the calabash bowl supported on her hip she takes one handful after another and throws them into the openings in the earth realm. But she does not throw the first grains with her own hand. She presses them into the child's little fist and thence lets them drop into the plowed field. During this

time the man does not look around. In silence and almost in awe, he lets the woman act.[12]

The Great Vessel engenders its own seed in itself; it is parthogenetic and requires the man only as opener, plower, and spreader of the seed that originates in the female earth. But this seed is born of the earth; it is at once ear of grain and child, in Africa as in the Eleusinian mysteries. (Later the patriarchate postulates the reverse just as one-sidedly; namely, that the male seed is the creative element while the woman as vessel is only its temporary abode and feeding place.)

Let us now, with the help of our three schemata, sum up what we have attempted to say of the structure of the Archetypal Feminine. Schema I shows the genetic aspect of an archetypal development, which it traces up to the differentiation of the Great Mother figure, and introduces the anima figure. In Schema II the comprehensive significance of vessel is sketched, as the central symbol of the matriarchal world.

Our next task, which will be to combine these findings in a dynamic and living general view, will again require a schema for orientation amid the inexhaustible wealth of data, symbols, images, and figures.

Precisely because we do not wish to arrange the material in Part II systematically, we must here provide a certain abstract groundwork. It is with this in mind that we shall now describe the "functional spheres" of the Archetypal Feminine.

[12] Frobenius, *Das sterbende Afrika*, p. 290.

Chapter Six

THE FUNCTIONAL SPHERES
OF THE FEMININE

THE structural diagram (Schema III, facing page 82) of the Archetypal Feminine is built around two axes and four circles. The two axes correspond to the characters of the Feminine: the axis designated as M, to the elementary character—here the accent is on the maternal—while the other axis, designated as A, corresponds to the transformative character in which the accent is on the anima.

Both axes have an upper, positive pole and a lower, negative pole. Axis M thus indicates the range of the elementary character, whose lower, negative pole is the Terrible Mother (M−), and whose upper, positive pole is the Good Mother (M+). Analogously, the other axis shows the range of the transformative character from the negative, lower (A−) to the upper, positive (A+).

The purpose of the schema is, of course, not to provide a dead system of co-ordinates but rather to translate the numinous dynamic of the archetypal development into quasivisual terms.

To this end we have combined the axial schema of the characters of the Feminine with a circular schema of its manifestations. The functions, concepts, and conceptual symbols, which we situate at certain "points" in the schema, are all to be taken as "concentration zones" of psychic processes, for which, as it were, they merely provide group headings. To each such function there actually corresponds a whole sphere of symbols, phenomena, modes of acting and being acted upon, which here can only be hinted at.

The circle in the center represents the *elementary character of the Feminine*. And in this area, as we have shown, the maternal elementary character predominates over the transformative character. For the sake of clarity, we have drawn in the functions of the Archetypal Feminine. The center of the elementary circle fulfills the function of *containing*. Along the rising axis indicating the elementary M character, the function of *bearing* and *releasing* as basis of growth and development takes the direction toward the positive M pole. Opposite it, tending toward the negative pole, lies the function of *holding fast, fixating*, and *ensnaring*, which indicates the dangerous and deadly aspect of the Great Mother, just as the opposite pole shows her aspect of life and growth.

This arrangement of opposites is in itself symptomatic of the ambivalent character of the archetype. Bearing and releasing belong to the positive side of the elementary character; their typical symbol is the vegetation symbol, in which the plant bursts out of the dark womb of the earth and sees "the light of the world." This release from the darkness to the light characterizes the way of life and also the way of consciousness. Both ways lead always and essentially from darkness to light. This is *one* of the reasons for the archetypal connection between growth symbolism and consciousness—while earth, night, darkness, and unconscious belong together, in opposition to light and consciousness. In so far as the Feminine releases what is contained in it to life and light, it is the Great and Good Mother of all life.

On the other hand, the Great Mother in her function of fixation and not releasing what aspires toward independence and freedom is dangerous. This situation constellates essential phases in the history of consciousness and its conflict with the Archetypal Feminine. To this context belongs a symbol that plays an important role in myth and fairy tale, namely, captivity. This term indicates that the individual who is no longer in the original and natural situation of childlike containment experiences the attitude of the Feminine as restricting and hostile. Moreover, the function of ensnaring implies an aggressive tendency, which, like the symbolism of captivity, belongs to the witch character of the negative mother. Net and noose, spider, and the octopus with its ensnaring arms are here the appropriate symbols. The victims of this constellation have always acquired some element of independence, which is endangered; to them containment in the Great Mother is no longer a self-evident situation; rather, they have already become "strugglers." [1]

Perpendicular to this section of Axis M runs the corresponding section of Axis A. Axis A also intersects the central circle of the elementary character at two points. At the intersection of the positive segment leading to Pole A+, we have inscribed the function of *giving*, differentiated into the functions of protecting, warming, and nourishing. The elementary character is most distinct in the function of protecting; in those of warming and nourishing the transformative character plays a part.

At the opposite intersection of the elementary circle with the segment of Axis A leading to Pole A−, we have inscribed the functions of *rejection* and *deprivation*. These functions, like those of holding fast and ensnaring, belong to the dark aspect of the Great Female, which in the schema extends from the center downward to the negative Feminine (F−) with its differentiation into Poles M− and A−.

In a positive sense rejection is a basic function of the elementary maternal that releases the grown young, particularly the males, and at a certain stage—as among the animals—drives them away. Consequently, rejection also expresses a part of the transformative character that permits living creatures to arrive at their natural development—and this is why we place it at the intersection with Axis A. (In a certain sense, this is the negative form of "release" by the Archetypal Feminine, which begins with birth and leads to growth.)

Rejection begins in the experience of the individual when containment ceases; i.e., it is always present where the *necessary* development puts an end to containment in the uroboros, in the Great Mother, and so on. This constellation is the foundation of what has been personalistically designated as the "birth trauma" and interpreted as the cause of

[1] My *Origins and History of Consciousness*, index, s.v.

all evil. In reality we are dealing with the existential fact that the ego and individual that emerge from a phase of containment, whether in a gradual and imperceptible process of development or in sudden "birth," experience the situation as rejection. Consequently, we find a subjective experience of distress, suffering, and helplessness in every crucial transition to a new sphere of existence. Wherever an old situation of containment ends or is ended, the ego experiences this revolution, in which an old shell of existence is burst, as rejection by the mother.[2]

The function of rejection is closely related to that of deprivation, which in the elementary sphere forms the counterpart to the function of giving. Deprivation is a basic function of the elementary character because the "withdrawal of love" determines the relation of all creatures to the Archetypal Feminine from the very first. But it is only at a conscious stage that withdrawal of love and deprivation appear as a voluntary negative activity of the Archetypal Feminine or the Great Mother. But since all positive elements of existence, such as nourishment, food, warmth, protection, safety, are associated with the image of the Great Mother—which in its relation to the small individual, the child and the childlike, actually does communicate all these positive contents—man imputes all interruptions and disturbances in the positive stream flowing from the mother to living things, all distress and all privation, to the same Great Mother in her aspect of "bad" and Terrible Mother. But it will be seen that here again the transformative character of the Feminine plays a part.

The Great Mother is the giver not only of life but also of death. Withdrawal of love can appear as a withdrawal of all the functions constituting the positive side of the elementary character. Thus hunger and thirst may take the place of food, cold of warmth, defenselessness of protection, nakedness of shelter and clothing, and distress of contentment. But stronger than these is often loneliness, the *principium individuationis*, the contrary of the containment that is the basic principle of *participation mystique*, of the bond in which there is no loneliness.[3]

[2] My *Origins*, index, s.v. "dragon fight."
[3] Excellent examples of this may be found in the documents of the great religions and among the mystics, whose aim is dissolution into the containment of the godhead.

Characteristic of this relationship is the German word *Elend*, which means both misery and exile. Consequently, the symbols of exile and desert also belong to the present context.

This existential privation can also assume a universal and symbolic form. Birth is experienced not only as release into life but also as a rejection from the uterine paradise; consciousness not only as a progressive and affirmative development toward the light but as expulsion from the nocturnal bliss of sleep in the unconscious and—as, for example, in all world views of Gnostic coloration—as loss of the original home.

But there are situations in which the role of the Archetypal Feminine is more actively negative. Then it uses the "withdrawal of love" as an instrument of power, as a means of perpetuating the rule of the Great Mother, of preventing her offspring from achieving independence. At this point, rejection and deprivation change into the clinging and even ensnaring that we have encountered as negative functions of the elementary character. (In other words, we find here a connection between the lower left-hand end of Axis A and the corresponding lower right-hand end of Axis M.) We have now described the first sphere, that of the elementary functions.

Following Axis M to the second circle, the circle of *transformation*, we assign the function of *development* to the positive pole, and that of *diminution* and *devouring* to the negative pole. These functions are continuations of the basic trends in the elementary circle. Development corresponds to the point below it on the axis, bearing-releasing; while diminution and devouring correspond to the holding fast and ensnaring of the elementary circle. However, these two points no longer belong to the elementary circle, but lie at the intersection of Axis A with the second circle, the circle of the transformative character, which corresponds to Axis A, just as the first circle corresponds to Axis M.

The transformative character is built upon the elementary character; it not only represents another character of the Archetypal Feminine but also in a certain sense a higher level. Or, in other words, the elementary character (M) is recessive in this second circle and the transformative character (A) is dominant.

Thus the intersection of Axis A with the elementary circle and the function of giving corresponds to the intersection of the rising Axis A with the second circle and the function of *transformation* and *sublimation*. Similarly, in the negative lower side of the schema, the descending Axis A intersects the second circle; here we have the function of *transformation* and *dissolution*, corresponding to the deprivation of the preceding intersection.

The schema as a whole, and the combination of the two axes with the circles, reveal the correspondences between the positive and negative side of each character as well as the mixtures and combinations of the two characters. In this way we can perceive the changes and direction of change of the various functions; that is to say, we have gained some intimation of the inner dynamic of the archetype.

Thus, for example, in the clinging, ensnaring function of the woman we already discern a will to release nothing from her dominion, but in the function of diminution and devouring this will is still stronger and is seen to be aggressively negative. But here, on the other hand, the transformative character of the feminine plays a part, though the transformation is toward death and dissolution. Consequently, there is a correspondence between this point in the second circle, on the one hand, and the intersection with Axis A and the functions of transformation and dissolution, on the other.

Nevertheless, the difference between the two characters is preserved, since Axis M of the elementary character indicates more the corporeal-material "lower" efficacy of the Feminine, while Axis A signifies more its psychic-spiritual "upper" side. In other words, the development of negative Axis M leads from diminution and devouring to *extinction* and *death*, which is precisely physical death, while the negative continuation along Axis A from transformation-dissolution leads to *madness* as a psychic-spiritual death and a psychic-spiritual extinction.

We find analogous relations on the upper half of the schema. The function of development along Axis M, to which all vegetation symbolism belongs, rises above the elementary functions of bearing and releasing. Although it stands in the closest relation to the function of transformation and sublimation on Axis A—for all growth presupposes transformation and sublimation of the elementary—here again the direction of Axis M is more material and corporeal, that of Axis A more psychic and spiritual.

Above the two circles we have so far been discussing—those of the elementary and the transformative character—we have drawn a third circle, that of *spiritual transformation*. In this third circle of spiritual transformation we find, as culmination of Axis M—birth-development—the *fruit* as the highest transformation form of the seed, as the place of its physical rebirth. The seed, buried in the womb of the earth and rising out of the darkness of the vessel containing it, unfolds in growth and finally attains "to itself" in the fruit as sublimated seed. This mystery of development is eminently bound up with the symbolism of the ear of grain. Here the transformative character plays a part; but although the development along Axis M overcomes its material character in the sphere of spiritual transformation, its tie with the elementary character is stronger than in the development along Axis A.

The development along Axis A leads, at the intersection with the circle of spiritual transformation, to *inspiration*. In this term we have summed up everything mantic, religious, prophetic, and poetic, which in the male, always and everywhere, is imputed to the anima or transformative character of the Feminine in its immaterial, spiritual aspect.

That the anima or transformative character is not merely a projection of the male upon the female, but corresponds to an authentic experience of the Feminine, follows from Briffault's demonstration [4] that women were everywhere the original repositories of mantism.

A comparison of the symbol of the spirit as fruit with the symbol of inspiration will show why we have assigned the two to different axes of the feminine structure. The slow processes of growth that carry the fruit to its end and culmination are psychologically different from the inspirations that belong to the transformative character of the Feminine, and are characterized by the sudden and overwhelming intervention of a spiritual factor. Here begins the relation of the Feminine to a

[4] *The Mothers*, Vol. II, Ch. XIX, "The Witch and the Priestess."

spiritual-male principle that we designate as the "paternal uroboros" —its nature cannot concern us here,[5] since it belongs to the province of the Masculine rather than that of the Feminine.

We have characterized the intersections of axes M and A with the third circle [6] as *fruit-birth, death, inspiration,* and *madness.* The upper part of the axes, leading from development (M) and transformation-sublimation (A) to fruit-birth and inspiration, are distinctly progressive and positive, both in a physical and a psychic sense. On the other hand, the lower parts of the axes, leading from diminution-devouring (M) and transformation-dissolution (A) to death and madness, are regressive and negative. While the upper part leads to the birth of the individual and to the formation, broadening, and transformation of consciousness, the lower part tends toward the dissolution of the individual and of consciousness.

To the four intersections of the axes with the circle of spiritual transformation we assign four categories of feminine mystery. As mysteries we designate not only the concrete and historical enactment of a mystery festival, as, for example, the Eleusinian mysteries, but, more generally, a psychic sphere common to all mankind; centered on an archetype, it consists of rites, mysteries, conceptions, usages, and embraces a whole network of unconsciously related symbols.

To the *death mysteries* at the lower right-hand intersection belong not only the rites of the goddesses of death and the dead, but all mortuary usages and symbols having to do with the burial and care of the dead, all sacrifices leading to death—e.g., the fertilization of the earth by blood—and hence innumerable conceptions through which, for example, the goddesses of war and of the hunt are drawn into this province.

The mysteries of death as mysteries of the Terrible Mother are based on her devouring-ensnaring function, in which she draws the life of the individual back into herself. Here the womb becomes a devouring

[5] My "Über den Mond und das matriarchale Bewusstsein."

[6] The schema shows the "conceptual symbols" (see pp. 76 ff.) on either side of each of the four axes. All these relationships determine not only myth, the phylogenetic childhood of mankind, but also the mythology of childhood, i.e., the ontogenetic childhood of the individual.

maw and the conceptual symbols of diminution, rending, hacking to pieces, and annihilation, of rot and decay, have here their place, which is associated with graves, cemeteries, and negative death magic. Here belongs also the blood-drinking goddess of death, whose hunger can be appeased only through the slaying of innumerable living creatures, whether like Kali in India she must be satisfied by the killing of men and animals; whether as goddess of war she perpetually demands the blood of men, or as goddess of death destroys all living things without distinction.

To the opposite upper left-hand point M+, indicating development or growth, are assigned the *vegetation mysteries*, a few of which we have already mentioned. They are all closely connected with the fertility rituals of the Great Mother, which have to do with growth and the increase of life.

To the upper right-hand point A+, designated as *inspiration*, belong all spiritual-psychic spheres of manticism, prophecy, and so forth. The mantically inspired, not inspiring, quality of the Feminine is almost always bound up with a male-spiritual power, the paternal uroboros. This figure first appears as transpersonal and anonymous but then, as the lord of woman, becomes a god—most beautifully exemplified in the figure of Dionysus.

The ecstatic, orgiastic nature of the Feminine, which belongs at the positive pole of the transformative character, is manifested most clearly in the relation of women to Dionysus. But its danger, consisting in a tendency to shift to the negative Pole A— of madness, is also unmistakable in this relation.[7]

[7] At first sight the character of vision and inspiration seems, because of its connection with Pythian Apollo, to stand in opposition to Dionysus. But this opposition is superficial, not only because of the historical reconciliation between Dionysus and Apollo that took place at Delphi, but also because in Apollo's Delphi the representative of manticism is Pythia, a woman. That Pythia originally belonged to the matriarchal province of the moon—and not to the solar realm of Apollo—is shown moreover by Plutarch's report that she was inspired only at night and by moonlight ("Sir Galahad," *Mütter und Amazonen*, p. 17). The "historical" connection between the two gods is only the expression of the fact that despite all antagonism there was an essential bond between them. Illuminating in this connection is Nilsson's remark on the seer Melampus, who was "closely connected with the Dionysian movement" and at the same time was known as "Apollo's darling." He tamed the Dionysian movement with "Apollonian methods," and Nilsson remarks: "It looks like a homeopathic remedy when we read that he took the strongest youths and had them chase the raving women from the mountains to Sikya amid cries and enthusiastic dancing." Nilsson, *Geschichte der griechischen Religion*, Vol. I, p. 582.

The positive segment of Axis A, showing the psychic-spiritual development of the Feminine from the functions of giving through transformation-sublimation to their creative climax, the "feminine spirit," culminates in vision and inspiration.

To this province of *inspiration mysteries* belong medicine, intoxicants, and all positive stimulants that make for progression of the personality and consciousness.

The mention of the prophetic phenomena and of the Delphic Pythia suggests the cultural significance of this sphere of the Feminine. The primitive groups and collectives obtained their essential orientation from the intuitive faculty of the feminine nature, which, it is most probable, originally governed all manticism, and which even later, when the patriarchal gods and priesthood had supplanted it, long remained predominant in the field of mantism.

In shamanism, which was the primitive foundation of the higher prophetic-mantic form, vision-inspiration, which we assign to the positive pole, and madness-ecstasy, which we assign to the negative pole, of Axis A, were very close together. An evaluation of these opposites as positive and negative is possible only in relation to the ego consciousness and the individual. In other words, where the personality as individual and consciousness disintegrates or is impaired in madness, as in many cults involving intoxicants, we assign the phenomenon to the negative pole. But where the element that enhances life *and* wholeness is predominant, we relate the phenomena to the positive pole.

This problem of evaluation becomes especially evident when we evaluate the *mysteries of drunkenness*—of drugs, stupor, and reduction of consciousness—which belong to the fourth minus pole of Axis A at the lower left. They are negative in relation to consciousness and often to the personality as a whole. On the other hand, there is hardly any form of positive ecstasy and inspiration that does not make use of these aids. The only question therefore is whether the stimulation of the unconscious, which is involved in every case, ends in a regression of the personality and a loss of consciousness, or whether on the contrary the temporary reduction of consciousness by intoxicant or poison leads to an extension of the consciousness or personality. And this very problem shows why we speak of two poles of one and the same axis; the two poles indicate related phenomena that taken together constitute the transformative character.

The negative pole of Axis A, based on the functions of transformation, dissolution, rejection, and deprivation, pertains more to the character of spiritual-psychic *death* than to that of physical death, which played so significant a role in the death mysteries of the Terrible Mother, the "old witch" of the negative pole of Axis M. The negative intoxicant and poison—in contrast to medicine—and everything that leads to stupor, enchantment, helplessness, and dissolution, belong to this sphere of seduction by the "young witch." In the negative mysteries of drunkenness and stupor the personality and consciousness are "regressively dissolved"; poisoned by negative orgiastic sexuality, narcotics, or magic potions, they succumb to extinction and madness. Here again, ecstasy is produced, but it reduces and disintegrates the personality; and for this reason sickness, considered as "negative enchantment," belongs to this sphere, as does the pain that is inflicted in order to weaken, rather than as a necessary road to recovery. Rejection and deprivation are also a function of this disintegrating force of the negative anima, whose symbols are forsakenness and nakedness, exposure and banishment into the void.

But precisely at this extreme point the negative pole of Axis A can shift into the positive.

Chapter Seven

THE PHENOMENON OF REVERSAL
AND
THE DYNAMIC OF THE ARCHETYPE

THIS paradoxical reversal is of crucial importance. In seemingly negating our schematic orientation, this phenomenon actually confirms the soundness of our arrangement, which shows the dynamic and the polyvalence of the archetypal structure of the Feminine.

The four polar points on the third circle of our schema are no static or conceptual quantities. At each pole an archetypal figure is situated, e.g., the Good Mother, the Terrible Mother, the negative anima (or, more simply, the seductive young witch), and the positive anima (or, more simply, the Sophia-virgin). And this signifies that each pole exerts a strong psychic attraction on the ego and consciousness. Because the archetype fascinates consciousness and is dynamically very much superior to it, the ego consciousness, when it approaches the pole, is not only attracted by it but easily overwhelmed. The outcome is seizure by the archetype, disintegration of consciousness, and loss of the ego.[1] But since this fascination or disintegration of consciousness means that at

---

[1] This is particularly true of the lower poles, which are therefore experienced and characterized as negative. It is less true of the positive poles, because in them, as we have pointed out, a consciousness-promoting component is present, which despite all fascination protects consciousness and the ego. Here again we see that for mankind the positive, the consciousness-promoting, and the progressive belong together, as do the negative, the consciousness-destroying, and the regressive.

the polar points consciousness loses its faculty of differentiation and in this constellation can no longer distinguish between positive and negative, it becomes possible for a phenomenon to shift into its opposite. Helplessness, pain, stupor, sickness, distress, loneliness, nakedness, emptiness, madness, can therefore be the forerunners of inspiration and vision and so manifest themselves as stations on a road leading through danger to salvation, through the extinction of death to rebirth and new birth. Conversely, the positive element of inspiration and the positive rapture of ecstasy may lead to the decline of the ego, to possession and madness.

Particularly *ecstasy*, which with its disintegration of consciousness leaves the way open either for a positive or a negative development of the psychic situation, is typical for the phenomenon of reversal that is possible in both polar situations. The pole is not only an end point but also a "turning point."

When an ego approaches a pole along one of the axes, there is a possibility that it will pass beyond this pole to its opposite. This is to say that in their extremes the opposites coincide or can at least shift into one another. This phenomenon, which is typical for the unfathomably paradoxical character of the archetype, constitutes the foundation of a great number of mysteries, rites of initiation, and occult doctrines, in which this basic psychological situation is realized and in which those undergoing initiation are expected to realize it.[2]

In the first circle of the schema, that of the elementary character of the Feminine, the transformative character was still recessive; but in the second circle, it becomes dominant, though without losing its connection with the elementary character. In the third circle, the oppositions of Axes A and M reach their extreme at the poles, but are at the same time transcended through the appearance of a new quality, the *character of spiritual transformation*, which can no longer be reduced to the M or the A character. Here we no longer find the old "functions," but attributes of the process of spiritual transformations, "conceptual symbols," which represent a mixture of the symbolic and nonconceptual

[2] My "Mystic Man."

with elements that can be apprehended conceptually. With the phenomena of reversal at the poles, which dissolve the oppositions and differences in the functions and axes, the fourth, uroboric circle of the Archetypal Feminine is achieved. The characters of M and A, as well as their positive and negative qualities, are here uroborically combined and interchanged; i.e., through its position in the uroboric fourth circle, *each of the four poles* becomes a *point of indifference.*

Our bidimensional schema now becomes tridimensional when we consider that the axes running from its center, considered as north pole, are prolonged in both directions and become the meridians of a globe. The four poles meet at a given point, which, because the axes form two circles, appears as a point of indifference at the south pole of the sphere. In other words, Poles A+ and A− now coincide as do poles M+ and M−, and, moreover, point of indifference A is identical with point of indifference M. This point of indifference at the south pole of the sphere corresponds to the central point in the elementary circle of our schema, to the north pole, which contains axes M and A, undeveloped, i.e., likewise as a point of indifference. Thus the Archetypal Feminine appears as a sphere; one pole consists in the center of the elementary circle in our schema, the other in the point of indifference at which A+ and A− coincide with M+ and M− (and F+ and F−).

To characterize this "indifferent" Feminine archetype on the basis of its coinciding poles, we have the figures of the Mother (M+), of the Virgin (A+), of the *young witch* (A−), and of the *old witch* (M−). This paradoxical unity corresponds exactly to what we have attempted to represent as Archetypal Feminine in Schema I, and the indifference of its paradoxical polyvalence corresponds to what we have indicated as its uroboric character.

The numerous orientations in our schema may seem confusing at first, but on closer scrutiny the schema makes possible a certain orientation with regard to the structure of the archetype of the Feminine, and at the same time throws light on the *dynamic within this archetype and in the relation of consciousness to it.* The separation into axes, the unfolding into circles, the attraction of the poles, and the shifting of the phenomena in the enclosing uroboric circle communicate different but related aspects.

The movement along the axes represents the movement of the ego and consciousness, which from the elementary stage of containment (first circle) progress to the transformative stage (second circle) and finally arrive at spiritual transformation (third circle). The fourth circle appears to the ego and consciousness as a borderline experience that plays a significant role in the mysteries of religion, in mysticism, but also in the development of the modern individual.[3] The "spiritual transformation" characteristic of the third circle always involves processes that move the whole personality in a direction transcending consciousness. In this sense madness, as well as vision and inspiration, are spiritual phenomena transcending consciousness.

Spiritual transformation, i.e., a fundamental change of the personality and consciousness, occurs only through the crucial emergence of an archetype. Negative spiritual change is also archetypally conditioned, and for that reason madness, in mythology, for example, is not simply a loss of consciousness and spirit, but a "confusion" of the spirit. Yet madness may be regarded as sacred and taken positively as an inspirational initiation because, behind inundation by the spirit, the world of archetypes appears as the power that determines fate.

In the sphere of spiritual transformation, not only does the Archetypal Feminine creatively unite the elementary and the transformative character in itself, but it passes beyond them to the "feminine spirit," the highest phase in the development of the "matriarchal consciousness." [4] The matriarchal consciousness is the original form of consciousness, in which the independence of the ego system is not yet fully developed and still remains open toward the processes of the unconscious. The spontaneity of the unconscious and also the receptivity of consciousness are here greater than in the relation between the relatively detached patriarchal consciousness,[5] typical for Western development,

<hr />

[3] See Jung, *Psychology and Alchemy;* "Psychology and Religion"; *Symbolik des Geistes.*
[4] My "Über den Mond und das matri- archale Bewusstsein."
[5] My *Origins and History of Consciousness,* pp. 403–4.

and the unconscious. The matriarchal consciousness is usually dominant in the woman, and has usually receded in the man, but it is very much at work in the creative individual who is oriented toward the spontaneity of the unconscious. The primordial productivity of the unconscious, which is decisive for the matriarchal consciousness and is a living force in primitive man and in children, belongs to the elementary segment of Axis M. The transformative character of Axis A+ is most active in the creativity of a psyche in which the receptivity of the masculine consciousness to the unconscious has become difficult, and which is therefore dependent on the anima or transformative character.

Those psychic transformative phenomena which belong to Axis A+, as well as those which arise from the unconscious and belong to Axis M+, culminate in extension and change of consciousness and the total personality, which we designate as spiritual transformation.

We have inscribed the conceptual symbols [6] of the upper semicircle of spiritual change between the intersections of the circle of Axes M and A. The symbols of *rebirth* and immortality belong to the "fruit-birth" pole of M, while *vision* and *wisdom* belong to the inspiration pole of Axis A; between them we find the symbols of "the work" and of redemption.

The negative character is so predominant in the "conceptual symbols" of the lower semicircle between Axes A and M that it seems less important to differentiate them.

Death, extinction, rending to pieces, are the core of the negative M pole, which, in accordance with its elementary character, originally took the form of *sacrifice* and ritual execution, and only later assumed a symbolic significance. Pain and *sickness*, as consuming attributes that weaken and kill, also fit into this negative context.

The other pole, *madness, impotence, stupor*, is characterized by its tendency to dissolve the personality, which is also characteristic of enchantment. Like sickness and pain, those components which go to make up distress—emptiness, nakedness, misery, and so on—also have

---

[6] It goes without saying that the selection and arrangement of these conceptual symbols are "arbitrary," representing merely an attempt at orientation.

a distintegrating effect. In this sense their transformative character leads to a "being-beside-oneself," to a loss of self.

Finally we have inscribed in Schema III a number of goddesses, who illustrate the nature and effect of the poles. At the positive M pole, we find the mother figure of Demeter, goddess of the Eleusinian mysteries; but the Greek and non-Greek Artemis as well as Egyptian Isis, Babylonian Ishtar, Buddhist Kwan-yin, and innumerable other goddesses of all ages and nations are configurations of this pole. The Jewish figure of the Shekinah corresponds to a maternal component of this pole, while the Christian Mary also possesses strong components of Pole A+, i.e., of the virgin figure.

The A+ pole of inspiration is the locus of the divine virgins and the Muses, who are aspects of an archetypal, inspirational figure. The virginal Athene and Artemis are related to this pole, but they also have other components. Athene, as a pre-Hellenic, Cretan mother goddess, also belongs to pole M+; Artemis, as Great Goddess, includes the attributes of the other poles. Kore, as daughter and partial figure of Demeter, as well as Maat, the Egyptian goddess of justice, and the later figure of Sophia-Wisdom,[7] should also be correlated with this pole.

At the negative pole M stand all goddesses whose nature is that of the Terrible Mother: Kali of India, Gorgon of the pre-Hellenic age, and Hecate of Greece, as well as terrible Ishtar, Isis, Artemis, and innumerable goddesses of the underworld and the dead. To this group belong such negatively demonic figures as the Erinyes, Furies, and lamias, the Empusae, witches, and so on. Their plurality usually indicates that they belong to a stage of the human consciousness prior to the configurative phase in which they appear as goddesses; or else they may be figures that, superseded by the dominant gods, have regressed to a more primitive and anonymous, preconfigurative state.

At the negative pole of Axis A we find the alluring and seductive figures of fatal enchantment, some of which are goddesses like Astarte,

[7] The "conceptual symbols" are often hypostasized as figures and "deified," only to degenerate later into allegories and concepts.

Aphrodite, and Artemis; some specters like Lilith, the Lorelei, and others; and some, like Circe and Medea, personalized forms of primordial goddesses. In all of them the character of enchantment leading to doom is dominant. To this group belong the preconfigurative pixies, elves, sprites, and so on, which appear in the plural. Characteristically, we find these collective groups predominantly at the lower part of our schema, the seat of the unconscious and of the tendency toward regression into the unconscious. In contrast, the consciousness-promoting powers of the upper half are formed figures.

It is characteristic of the same genetic context, wherein the numinous develops from unconfigured, consciousness-promoting elements, that when one and the same deity appears simultaneously at different poles, its "lower" and negative manifestation is almost always the historically earlier one, while the upper and positive one is the later manifestation.

With this we conclude our exposition of Schema III. The schema will be open to two opposite criticisms. On the one hand, it will be said that because it is a schema it constitutes an oversimplification; and on the other hand, that it is not simple enough because the inner dynamic elements of transformation and reversal burst through the schema. Both objections are justified, and both follow from the actual paradox that we have attempted to encompass in the schema, but which by the very nature of things can only be partially formulated. The most we can hope for is a certain general orientation, not an exhaustive exposition. Even the concepts of the schema are in a certain sense "symbols," each of which embraces a whole area of psychic meanings, and which evade any sharp definition.

We wish to stress once again that the purpose of Part I has been to work out the structure of what analytical psychology calls an archetype, and to explain this structure on the basis of the one archetype of the Feminine. The concrete reality of this archetypal world can be apprehended through its expressions in cult image and rite, in religion and customs, and it is with these expressions that we shall concern ourselves in the second part. But if we look back over the schemata and observe how the archetype of the Feminine has unfolded, how it becomes differentiated in accordance with our circles and axes, how it is concretized in the symbol group of the vessel, how it shifts at the poles of the axes and passes through the point of indifference, we shall perhaps have gained an intimation of the unity and multiplicity of the living archetype.

This structural aspect is rounded out by the genetic-psychological perspective, which distinguishes stages in the development of consciousness and correlates historical material with them. But the development of psychic phases does not coincide with the development of human history since, as we have elsewhere explained, the correlation of psychic phases with one another is not identical with the temporal succession of historical events.

As I have remarked elsewhere, Flinders Petrie established a system of what he called "sequence-dating" [8] for the early history of Egypt, that is, sequences within which one can lay down a "before" and "after" without knowing the temporal correlation. For instance, s.d. 30 comes before s.d. 77, though this does not tell us to what dated period we must assign s.d. 30 or 77, or how great an interval lies between them. Similarly, we have to make do with psychological sequence-dating in dealing with the archetypal stages. The uroboros comes "before" the stage of the Great Mother, and the Great Mother "before" the dragon fight; but an absolute correlation in time is impossible because we have to consider the historical relativity of individual nations and cultures. The Creto-Mycenaean culture was, for the Greeks, the prehistoric Great Mother period since her cult was dominant in that culture. Greek mythology is largely the dragon-fight mythology of a consciousness struggling for independence, and this struggle was decisive for the spiritual importance of Greece. But whereas in Greece this development falls roughly between 1500 and 500 b.c., the corresponding process in Egypt probably took place long before 3300.

In other words, the manifestations illustrating the archetype may belong to the most diverse epochs, times, and cultures; a monument of a

[8] My *Origins*, pp. 264 f.; Petrie, *The Making of Egypt*, p. 8.

82

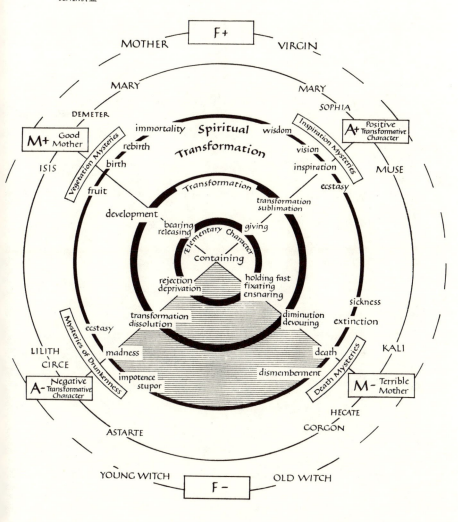

late culture may symbolize an early phase, while a monument of an early culture may symbolize a late phase, of archetypal development. Similarly, in the analysis of a human individual, symbols and symptoms of future and later developments may appear at the very beginning, and conversely infantile and archaic elements may present themselves in stages of relatively fuller psychic development.

Our conscious classifications and schematizations are always attempts to arrive, through abstraction, at an orientation within the reality of life. But this living reality, with its crests and troughs, progressions and regressions, irruptions and anticipations, is at every moment spontaneous and unformulable. Even where living psychic reality follows laws, the laws are so complex and unfathomable that at best we can abstract the most infinitesimal parts of them and test them by experiment in such a way as to be able to predict future development. But in actual fact, e.g., in the reality of an analysis or of an analytical situation, and assuredly in real life, every step is individual, every dream is unpredictable, and it is only in the most general sense that transformations can be correlated with a schema of development. In living reality, every development is surprising; with all its inner causality and purposiveness, it is new and unique for the consciousness that experiences and investigates it, and hence defies schematization.

For this reason, the most that can be achieved by an exposition in the field of depth psychology is a compromise between conscious schematization and the uniqueness of the material that fills and overflows the schema. Thus it will always be possible to criticize the schema for being far from reality, and to criticize the material chosen to illustrate the schema for being accidental. Both criticisms may be true to a certain extent. But they will be powerless to alter the fact that psychic reality evades our desire for schematic exposition. Nor will they prevent such an exposition, inadequate as we know it to be, from helping the whole, living man toward a fruitful orientation in the living reality of the psyche.

II

The Mother of Songs, the mother of our whole seed, bore us in the beginning. She is the mother of all races of men and the mother of all tribes. She is the mother of the thunder, the mother of the rivers, the mother of trees and of all kinds of things. She is the mother of songs and dances. She is the mother of the older brother stones. She is the mother of the grain and the mother of all things. She is the mother of the younger brother Frenchmen and of the strangers. She is the mother of the dance paraphernalia and of all temples, and the only mother we have. She is the mother of the animals, the only one, and the mother of the Milky Way. It was the mother herself who began to baptize. She gave us the limestone coca dish. She is the mother of the rain, the only one we have. She alone is the mother of things, she alone. And the mother has left a memory in all the temples. With her sons, the saviors, she left songs and dances as a reminder. Thus the priests, the fathers, and the older brothers have reported.
—*Song of the Kagaba Indians, Colombia*

A

THE ELEMENTARY CHARACTER

Chapter Eight

INTRODUCTION

IN OUR present attempt to portray the archetype of the Great Female with the help of texts [1] and reproductions, we shall follow the classification and system sketched in Part I. Our illustrations of the timeless archetype will be drawn from all epochs and cultures.

If we offend against "history" by removing documents and representations from their cultural context, we hope to compensate by correlating our archetypal investigation with a "psychohistory," that is to say, with the stages in the development of the human psyche. Taking the development of consciousness as the decisive phenomena of human history, we arrive at an arrangement of the phenomena that does not, to be sure, coincide with the usual sequence of historical events, but makes possible the psychological orientation we require.

The old interpretation of history as a straight line, leading from prehistory through antiquity and the Middle Ages to modern times, is no longer accepted. It has given way to a historical consciousness that looks upon the various coexistent and successive cultures as individualities and not as links in a continuous chain. This view makes it possible to do justice to the individual character of each culture, but it is also a symptom of the decline of the ordering principle that had hitherto

[1] The text on the title page of Part II is tr. from Preuss, *Die Eingeborenen Amerikas*, p. 39. In the original text the phrase "Mother of Songs" reads "Sibilaneuman"; the names Sintana, Seizankua, Aluanuiko, and Kultsavitabauya are here rendered as "saviors."

enabled European, Christian mankind to regard itself as the culmination and climax of human development.

Once the idea of a universal mankind, embracing all the multiplicity of cultures, religions, and historical epochs, came within the scope of men's minds, the naïve Western view of history for which the Near East was quite secondary, while Asia, America, and Africa merited scarcely any attention, became untenable.

With the discovery of the collective unconscious as the common psychic foundation of mankind and with the insight that the relation of consciousness to the unconscious determines the character of a cultural phase or of a culture, modern man has gained a new point of orientation. The development of consciousness, from almost total containment in the unconscious in primitive man to the Western form of consciousness, has been glimpsed as the central factor in human history as a whole. For this orientation, the various cultures are merely phases in this basic trend of psychic life: the development of consciousness, which, without being the *conscious* goal of the individual cultures or of human culture as a whole, can be shown to be operative in every culture and age.

The tendency toward the light, which C. G. Jung once called human heliotropism, has in the long run proved stronger than all the forces of darkness that have striven to extinguish consciousness. In the broad view, epochs seemingly characterized by a regression of consciousness may almost always be recognized as transitional stages necessary to further development.

For the psychological study of human history, the primordial era refers then to the time when the unconscious was predominant and consciousness was weak. The modern era signifies a time of developed consciousness and of a productive bond between consciousness and unconscious. In other words, the normative development of the individual from containment in the unconscious to the development of consciousness presents an analogy to the collective development of mankind. In the system of co-ordinates representing psychohistorical development, later periods may therefore, as we said, represent an early state of consciousness and early epochs a mature level.[2] Thus, for example, the relatively late monuments of the monolithic culture of England and France are psychologically much "earlier" than the Egyptian monuments that preceded them by thousands of years. And in an epoch of modern history, regressive collective tendencies may appear, which threaten to annul the arduously acquired development of the individual and the individual consciousness, and to bring back an earlier stage of human history.

The psychological development that we are following—independently of the historical development of the various nations and cultures —begins with the "matriarchal" stage in which the archetype of the Great Mother dominates and the unconscious directs the psychic process of the individual and the group. The psychic world connected with the archetype of the Great Mother, or in a more general sense of the Feminine, is the object of our investigation. The question whether or not the dominance of this archetypally "feminine" world involves the economic or political domination of the woman is here irrelevant.

Of course, this attempt to distill the archetype from the symbol group related to it and characteristic of it can provide no more than suggestions and intimations. The exposition and interpretation of each single symbol might well fill an entire volume. But since our chief interest here is a synopsis that may disclose the underlying achetype, we must avoid obscuring the total context by an excessive accumulation of material.

The archetypal image of the Great Mother lives in the individual as in the group, in the man as well as the woman. When therefore we say that the matriarchal world precedes the patriarchal world, we are not referring to a sequence of sociological structures, such as that set up by Bachofen.[3]

[2] One of the reasons for such discrepancies is the possibility of thorough differentiation in the small, early group and, conversely, the primitivization and recollectivization of the late group through the entrance into the historical process of great uncivilized and undifferentiated masses.

[3] In his judgment of social phenomena, e.g.,

the position of the woman, Bachofen was unquestionably led astray by his juridical discovery of *Mutterrecht*, 'mother right.' But it is equally important that in spite of this he always kept in mind a total cultural-psychological structure, and never limited himself to social or juridical relations. Precisely because he was oriented toward this totality of the cultural situation and

The dominance of the archetype of the Great Mother constellates the human psyche of the primordial situation in which consciousness develops only slowly and only gradually emancipates itself from the domination of unconscious directing processes.

Although the beginnings of the psychological-matriarchal age are lost in the haze of prehistory, its end at the dawn of our historical era unfolds magnificently before our eyes. Then it is replaced by the patriarchal world, and the archetype of the Great Father or of the Masculine, with its different symbolism, its different values, and its different tendencies, becomes dominant.

The study of archetypes involves an abundance of symbolic material from the most diverse cultural strata and spheres; it compels the psychologist to delve into many different fields in which he is not specialized. In each of these fields the material is so vast that an outsider cannot hope to master it entirely. Errors and faulty interpretations—particularly in matters of detail—are almost inevitable. Actually the goal we have set ourselves could only be fully attained through collaboration between specialists in the science of religion, ethnology, and so on and a depth psychologist. The provisional and problematic nature of such a work is therefore obvious and we can only appeal to the insight and indulgence of the reader who is more concerned with a synthesis of essentials than with the correctness of every single detail. But there is also a positive, compensatory factor that should not be disregarded. The interpretation of the symbolism of the unconscious in modern man—and the symbolism of the unconscious remains unchanged—gives the psychotherapist an empirical-scientific foundation for the interpretation of collective symbolism, a foundation that must needs be lacking in every other scientist who concerns himself with this material.

Our account of the Archetypal Feminine is arranged according to the schematic outline we have sketched in the Part I. We shall follow the unfolding of the archetypal unity of the Feminine from the elementary character through the transformative character down to the mysteries its position within the development of mankind, he was able—in far greater measure than he himself could realize—to discover and follow the psychic stages of human development and their symbolism.

of the spiritual transformation character, in which the development of feminine psychology reaches its culmination.

This artificial arrangement is by no means intended to efface all the merging and crisscrossing relations. On the contrary, one of our tasks will be to account, for example, for the recurrence of the same symbols at the most diverse stages, and for the transformations they undergo in these stages. While the purpose of our arrangement is to indicate the archetypal structure underlying the numerous images and symbols, it is hoped that our many references to cross-connections and overlappings will give an intimation of the radiant diversity of the archetypal reality.

The ubiquity of similar symbols and symbolic contexts has all too frequently led to arbitrary and fantastic theories of influences, migrations, and so forth. As a matter of principle we shall seek to avoid any such explanation by superficial "historical" relations and also the reduction, so popular today, of similar relations to corresponding sociological phenomena. But if we content ourselves with a phenomenological picture and a psychological interpretation of this picture, this does not mean that we shall make no attempt to work out the significant developmental trends. Yet it seems too soon to write the psychic history of mankind; the most we can offer today is certain beginnings and directives. And one of the necessary preliminary tasks is to train the "eye for the archetypal." It must remain for future works to examine the relation of particular cultures to the archetypally conditioned development of consciousness and to the dominance of particular archetypes.

Chapter Nine

THE PRIMORDIAL GODDESS

WITH the Stone Age sculptures of the Great Mother as a Goddess, the Archetypal Feminine suddenly bursts upon the world of men in overwhelming wholeness and perfection. Aside from the cave paintings, these figures of the Great Goddess are the earliest cult works and works of art known to us.[1]

The appearance of these figures in a territory extending from Siberia to the Pyrenees seems to presuppose the presence of a unitary "world view" centering round the Great Goddess. The homogeneity of this Stone Age culture is independent of the origin of the figures, and is in no way affected by the question whether primordial migrations carried this figure outward from a center, or whether these plastics appeared simultaneously at different places.[2]

Pls. 1–2   The first four reproductions represent this widely distributed type of the Great Stone Age Mother most completely. Their cult significance is unquestioned. They exemplify the dominance of the matriarchal, regardless whether and to what extent the male, e.g., the hunter group, seized power over the woman in this epoch.

For our further investigations, therefore, it remains irrelevant whether the female or the male group or—as we believe—both were the psychic vehicles of the archetype. The archetype of the Great Mother Goddess can take form in a patriarchal society, as conversely

---

[1] This is true regardless whether we take them to be twenty thousand or only twelve thousand years old.   [2] Cf. p. 117, n. 41.

94

that of the Father God can take form in a matriarchal society. Similarly, in an individual man (e.g., a male neurotic in whom the mother archetype is dominant) the characteristics of the matriarchal world may be more easily found than in a healthy woman.

Our exposition of the archetypal world is in this sense exemplary. It draws its documentation from the male as well as the female psychology of the group and the individual. Sex and sociological structure may vary the basic archetypal constellation, but not essentially change it.

Of the Stone Age sculptures known to us, there are fifty-five female figures and only five male figures. The male figures, of youths, are atypical and poorly executed,[3] hence it is certain that they had no significance for the cult. This fits in with the secondary character of the male godhead, who appeared only later in the history of religions and derived his divine rank from his mother, the Goddess.

In the figures of the Primordial Mother we find two radically different physical types: one squat and pyknic, the other (not illustrated in our material) slender and asthenic. This contrast is strikingly brought out when one compares a statuette [4] from Gagarino, on the Don River in Russia, with the so-called Venus of Willendorf and with a figure resembling her, which was also found in Gagarino.[5]

Attention has often been called [6] to the lack of correspondence between the skeletal remains and the representational type of the Great Mother. It follows that the different types of Mother Goddess have a symbolic significance, which we must seek to understand.

The present figures were found in France, in the entrances of caves *Pls. 1b, c, 2* devoted to a magical hunt cult; the Goddess, this makes clear, stood at the center of the group life enacted in these caves.

With their emphasis on the impersonal and transpersonal, these figures of the Great Mother Goddess are primordial types of the feminine elementary character. In all of them the symbolism of the rounded vessel predominates. The belly and breasts, the latter often gigantic, are like the central regions of this feminine vessel, the "sole reality." In

[3] Bohmers, *Die Aurignac Gruppe.*
[4] Levy, *The Gate of Horn*, Pl. VI e.
[5] Ibid., Pl. VI d.
[6] Bohmers; Levy, p. 58.

these figures the fertility of the Feminine has found an expression both prehuman and superhuman. The head is sightless, inclined toward the middle of the body; the arms are only suggested, and they too stress the middle of the body. The gigantic thighs and loins taper off into thin legs; the feet have broken off, but there is no doubt that they were frail and by no means conceived as supports of the giant body-vessel. In the

Pl. 1c   magnificent Lespugue figure, whose breasts, belly, thighs, and triangular genital zone form a single cluster, this symbolic fullness of the elementary character is still more evident than in the naturalistic and

Pl. 1a   therefore less symbolic Venus of Willendorf.

The unshapely figures of the Great Mother are representations of the pregnant goddess of fertility, who was looked upon throughout the world as the goddess of pregnancy and childbearing, and who, as a cult object not only of women but also of men, represents the archetypal symbol of fertility and of the sheltering, protecting, and nourishing elementary character.[7]

It is true that there is a broad gap between the Stone Age representations of the Great Mother and those of the Near East; but the discoveries at Tell Halaf have shown that corresponding female figures were fashioned at some time before the fourth millennium B.C. "The latter are almost all plastic representations of nude, painted females, with the head hardly indicated, but with exaggerated portrayal of the breasts, abdomen, buttocks, and vulvar region, in keeping with the earlier Aurignacian practice." [8] The large number of animal figures belonging to these representations shows that this figure of the Great Goddess of birth is the mother of all living things, of animals as well as men.[9]

These figures reveal the static nature of the elementary character by the integration of the arms, the active elements of action and motion,

Pl. 3

Pls. 7b, 3a

[7] Albright, *From the Stone Age to Christianity*, p. 92.

[8] Albright, p. 98.

[9] It is possible and even probable that the original physical type of the Great Mother and of the priestesses who represented her was secularized and sexualized in later patriarchal times; that this "taste" is therefore not original, but a phenomenon of decadence. The "fat woman" as desired sexual object, harem inmate, prostitute, for example, is an archaic remnant of the mother complex in the male (Fuchs and Kind, *Die Weiberherrschaft*, Vol. I.) extending down to modern times. These archaic images of the Great Mother recur also in the psychoses of modern men.

with the block of the torso or vessel, and by the frequent underemphasis on the head, which is small and sightless, a mere appendage, as it were, of the accentuated torso. Another characteristic of these figures is the disproportionate breadth and fullness of the posterior.

It would be a mistake to derive this steatopygia from any racial characteristics.[10] This quality of the Great Primordial Mother is exceedingly widespread and is found in regions where there can be no question of a particular African or Hottentot type. Here again a psychological interpretation carries us deeper and farther.

It has also been repeatedly stressed that these archetypal figures cannot be attributed to the "sexual taste" of the male. There is no doubt that the relationship between "taste" and the figure is just the opposite and far more complex. Actually male sexuality is influenced by the archetypal figure of the Feminine, which is active in the unconscious. Wherever the inordinately stout, unshapely woman is the favored sexual object, we may infer an—unconscious—domination of the mother archetype in the male psyche.[11]

The sexual accent on the posterior may be derived from the fertility rites, which aim at the magical increase of animals. In the paleolithic age, just as today among primitive peoples, there were fertility rituals in which the mating of animals, with coitus from behind, played a central role. Thus we are dealing in these rites, not with a personal sexual component in the man, but with an impersonal symbolic behavior, which becomes understandable in this light. In far higher degree than is generally realized even today, the sexual tendencies of individuals are dependent on unconscious archetypal images, which first determine the spirit and behavior of the collectivity, and later the behavior of deranged individuals with an atavistic fixation.[12] There are strong indications that the matriarchal or patriarchal dominance in the unconscious world view also determines the position of the partners in

[10] Levy, p. 58.
[11] See n. 9.
[12] The tendency that occurs in the modern neurotic to prefer stout, unshapely sexual partners or to assume the sexual posture mentioned often goes back to an archetypal situation, in which the accent is on the impersonal character of the female and the personal unrelatedness of the male to this female.

the sexual act. Whether, for example, the woman lies below as earth and the man above as heaven, or the reverse, depends on the archetypal conditions of the culture in question. The operation of such archetypal phenomena and the dependence of sexual behavior upon them can still be observed in the neuroses, perversions, and psychoses of modern man, but also in his normal and average sexual behavior.[13]

Steatopygia, i.e., emphasis on the posterior, in the art of early cultures must be interpreted symbolically.[14] The Great Mother is often represented sitting on the earth. This "sedentary" character, in which the buttocks form the antithesis to the feet, the symbols of free movement on the earth, represents a close bond with the earth, as can still be seen in the symbolism of language. The symbolic character of sitting is still evident in such terms as *sitzen*, 'to sit'; *besitzen*, 'to possess'; *Besitz ergreifen*, 'to seize possession'; and *besessen sein*, 'to be possessed.' Similarly the *Sitz*, 'seat,' and *Wohnsitz*, 'home' or 'seat,' of a tribe refer to the region whence it came or where it became *ansässig*, 'settled.' In ritual and custom, to sit on something has the significance of "to take possession" of it.

Her very unwieldiness and bulk compel the Great Mother to take a sedentary attitude, in which she belongs like a hill or mountain to the earth of which she is a part and which she embodies. Even where she stands, her center of gravity draws her downward toward the earth, which in its fullness and immobility is the "seat" of the human race. The seated Great Mother is the original form of the "enthroned Goddess," and also of the throne itself.

As mother and earth woman, the Great Mother is the "throne" pure and simple, and, characteristically, the woman's motherliness resides not only in the womb but also in the seated woman's broad expanse of thigh, her lap on which the newborn child sits enthroned. To be taken on the lap is, like being taken to the breast, a symbolic expression for adoption of the child, and also of the man, by the Feminine. It is no accident that the greatest Mother Goddess of the early cults was

[13] Fuchs and Kind.
[14] It goes without saying that such a symbolic accentuation of the Feminine—even when unconscious—may cause such female types to be favored and sometimes even "cultivated."

named Isis, "the seat," "the throne," the symbol of which she bears on her head; and the king who "takes possession" of the earth, the Mother Goddess, does so by sitting on her in the literal sense of the word. *Pl. 4*

The enthroned Mother Goddess lives in the sacral symbol of the throne. The king comes to power by "mounting the throne," and so takes his place on the lap of the Great Goddess, the earth—he becomes her son. In widespread throne cults,[15] the throne, which was originally the godhead itself, was worshiped as the "seat of the godhead."

The original throne was the mountain, which combines the symbols of earth, cave, bulk, and height; the mountain was the immobile, sedentary symbol that visibly rules over the land. First it was the Mountain Mother, a numinous godhead; later it became the seat and the throne of the visible or invisible numen; still later, the "empty throne," on which the godhead "descends." The mountain seat as throne of the Great Goddess, of the Mountain Woman, is a later stage of development; its most beautiful representation is perhaps the well-known Cretan seal showing the Mother Goddess standing on the mountain, *Fig. 62* while a youth worships her.

The symbolism of the female godhead as hill and mountain persists to a late date in the East where the *hieros gamos* between heaven and earth is enacted on a mountaintop or on a tower symbolizing it, as in Babylon and other places. Here the male god of sky, clouds, lightning, thunder, and rain descends and is united with the Earth Goddess, who is the mountain or who has her "seat" on the earth. And the priestess who represents the Goddess also receives the god in the chapel on the mountaintop.

Later the throne becomes the sacral symbol of the Great Mother, who has receded into the background, and it is on this throne that the king sits. In our patriarchal age, the term "to possess" a woman is used for the sexual act in which the man, lying above, believes—for reasons

[15] According to Menghin, in Hoernes, *Urgeschichte*, Reichel (*Über vorhellenische Götterkulte*) derives the throne cult from the Near East; giant thrones are to be found in Lydia and Phrygia, in Greece, Rhodes, and Thera (Santorin); replicas of the great thrones occur in tombs of Tiryns, Mycenae, Menidi, and Nauplia. In addition to the throne cults of the classical era, we find thrones in connection with the cult of the dead in Sicily, Etruria, etc.

that defy rational understanding—that he has made her his possession. But the term still reveals the primordial, pregenital form of possession, in which the male obtains the earth from the female by being taken on her lap as her son. Down to our own day, the throne, originating as it does in matriarchal symbolism, has played a significant role. As Hocart points out: ". . . we speak of a king ascending the throne, meaning that he succeeds to the kingship." [16] Our view of the maternal origin of the throne is further confirmed by Indian coronation rituals: "The king is made to sit on a throne which represents the womb." [17]

FIG. *1*. "ISLAND FIGURE"

Limestone, near Sparta, c. XV (*?*) *century* B.C.

The prestige of the throne or chair was also enhanced by its contrast with the squatting or recumbent position usual for early man. A memory of the human form of the maternally receptive chair has been preserved down to our own time in the terms "arms," "legs," and "back" of a chair. That the primordial images of the mother-throne, the throne as mother, the "enthroned" child, still live in the depths of the *Pl. 5* modern psyche is shown by one of Henry Moore's sculptures that contains all these elements.

Pl. 7a Female figures with exaggerated rump have been found in Peru and
Fig. 1 also in the Balkans. A so-called "island figure" from Greece combines these physical characteristics with tattooing. Analogous figures have
Pl. 24 been found on the Greek islands,[18] and the primitive Stone Age figures

[16] Hocart, *Kingship*, p. 97. [18] Hoernes, *Urgeschichte*, p. 367, n.
[17] Ibid., p. 92.

100

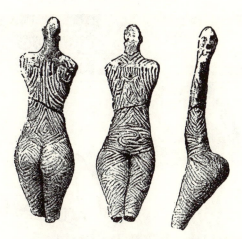

FIG. 2. CLAY FIGURINES

Romania, prehistoric

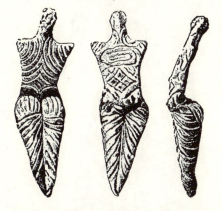

from Romania and Thrace derive from the same psychic stratum. All these figures are related to similar archetypal forms, the distribution of which extends through Syria, Crete,[19] and Mesopotamia, as far as India.[20]

Side by side with these representations, in which the posterior is emphasized, stand others, nude figures of goddesses, in which the genital

Fig. 2; Pl. 6

Fig. 3; Pls. 3–11
Pl. 15

[19] Levy, *The Gate of Horn*, Pl. VIII, a, b.   [20] Mode, *Indische Frühkulturen*, fig. 16a, b.

FIG. *3*. CRETAN WOMAN

Fresco, Greece, late Helladic period

triangle is particularly stressed. Their distribution can be traced from predynastic Egypt through Syria, Mesopotamia, Iran, and Asia Minor to Troy, the Aegean Islands, Cyprus, and Crete, and to southern Europe.

Pls. 6, 8, 9, 10–14
Pls. 16, 17, 23

This group overlaps with another in which the genital triangle is again prominent but which is further characterized by a "holding of the breasts"; that is to say, the character of fertility and sexuality is accented. In late plastics of the Indian Great Mother (whose broad, well-rounded haunches characterize the dominant type in all Indian sculpture), the genital zone is usually covered;[21] but the covering, which is represented from the earliest times and recurs even in the latest Indian idols, lends emphasis to this zone.

Pls. 8, 9, 10, 12a 13, 20

Pl. 15

As early seals show, the nude Great Mother with emphasized genital zone was also known in India as the goddess of sexuality and fertility.[22]

The significance of these representations of the Great Primordial Goddess is by no means limited to their emphasis on particular parts of the body. To be sure, breasts, posterior, genital triangle, carry important symbolic accents, but this must not lead us to forget the figure as a whole and the manner in which these zones are integrated with it. What we have called the "polyvalence of the archetype" is most evident in these early figures, from which the particular types of goddess, with their diverse and conflicting accents on zones and symbols, were differentiated only in the course of development.

Thus in the early period we sense a unity of startlingly conflicting archetypal characteristics. Many figures, it is true, with their exaggeration of genitals and breasts, the symbols of bearing and nourishing, disclose only the elementary character; but we also find others in which accentuation of the vessel character and of the belly, genitals, and posterior is accompanied by a distinct underemphasis of the breasts. Here a contradiction within the Feminine itself is manifested in the paradoxical formal contrast between above and below. The lower,

Pls. 1c, 6

---

[21] Ibid.
[22] Zimmer, *The Art of Indian Asia*, Vol. 1, Pl. A8, above, right.

childbearing and maternal aspect is combined with an almost irreconcilably different prewomanly, virginal aspect above. This contradiction *Pl. 1c* is clearly manifested at a very early stage in the Lespugue "Venus." The upper part of her body has a "soulful" quality very different from the exuberant womanhood below. The delicate upper part and the virginal head are bent over a luxuriant body bursting with the elementary fullness of motherhood, so stressing by purely stylistic means the contrast between the static elementary character of the mother and the dynamic transformative character of the young woman.

It goes without saying that this is an expression of an unconscious stratum at work in the artist, and no conscious artistic solution of a formal problem. Yet, in the connection between the fecund belly and the incorporeal slenderness of the upper body, which seems almost leaflike in the lateral view, the figure of the divine archetype reveals the typical correlation of elementary character with the "lower" and of transformative character with the "upper."

Pl. 16 Correspondingly, we find in representations of the snakeheaded goddesses an exaggeratedly slender figure holding a child and having a strongly accented genital zone; the extreme slenderness is presumably connected with the snake nature of these women.

These examples show how difficult it is to distinguish between a *Pl. 17* "sensuous" style susceptible of sociological derivation and an "imaginative" style.[23] The upper half of the Lespugue goddess is "imaginative" and abstract in trend, as opposed to the "sensuous" and materialistic lower part. The opposition between elementary character and transformative character underlying our exposition is a datum of psychological structure. Such a combination of opposites is typical for an early period, which we designate as uroboric because the uroboros is the symbol of the union of opposites in the psychic situation of origination. *Pl. 6* We find a similar combination of opposites in the figure of the Thracian goddess.

One means by which early man could represent the numinous magnificence and archetypal uniqueness of the Feminine consisted in an

---

[23] Kühn, *Die Kunst der Primitiven*, pp. 11 ff.

expressive "exaggeration" of form, an accentuation of the elementary character. Here the body feeling plays a decisive role. The individual who created and the group which worshiped these works were unquestionably fascinated and attracted by the corporeity, the exuberant fullness and massive warmth, that emanate from such a figure. (This is the justification for applying the term "sensuous" to such works.) The

FIG. 4. A WOMAN

Scratched on ivory, Předmost, Czechoslovakia, late paleolithic

attraction is identical with an unconscious accentuation of the infantile, and for this accent the goddess is an adequate image of the elementary character of containment.

With these figures contrast the "abstract" representations in which we discern an emphasis on the transformative character. The earliest example of this type is probably the Předmost scratched drawing of a female figure. While the elementary character makes for sculpture, the abstracting expression of the transformative character tends toward an ornamental design closely related to the tattooing and body painting whose purpose it is to transform and spiritualize the body.

The primary purpose of body painting is never "ornamentation,"

Fig. 4

but rather a dynamic transformation.[24] The painting gives power to the living or dead object, charges it with mana; and in the primitive phase the red coloring that, it has been proved, was given to many prehistoric goddesses and other plastic works has the same significance.

The transformative import of tattooing is also demonstrated by its use as a sign of initiation. Likewise, the painted vessel was originally sacral. It was distinguished from profane vessels by its ornamentation, consisting of such fundamental and meaningful symbols as the spiral, the cross, the circle, the wave.

Pl. 6   The Thracian figure of a seated goddess is one of a group of neolithic ceramics [25] that have been found in a territory extending from western Russia to the Balkans and central Europe. They originate in a matriarchally accented cultural milieu, related in all probability to Aegean culture and its precursors. The character of this figure is so primitive that, independently of its historical dating, we must assign it to a very early psychological stratum.

This plastic takes some of its uncanny quality from the contradictions contained in it. The vessel form stresses the corporeal elementary character, while the dense, tattooed ornamentation tends toward disembodiment; the body is literally covered by the symbol. The tiny, barely suggested breasts reinforce the—unconscious—tendency to surpass the elementary and corporeal. Here the element of abstraction that brings out the symbolic transformative character of the Feminine is particularly evident: the belly is not vaulted in fertility and fullness; rather, the genital triangle, which is accentuated for this reason, bears the symbol of the spiral, one end rolling upward and the other downward.

This brings us to an essential content of this abstracting tendency.[26] A goddess represented in this way is never a goddess only of fertility but is always at the same time a goddess of death and the dead. She is the Earth Mother, the Mother of Life, ruling over everything that rises up and is born from her and over everything that sinks back into her.

[24] On the painting of vessels and bodies, cf. pp. 107, 114 f.

[25] Hoernes, *Urgeschichte*, p. 204 f.

[26] It goes without saying that this term does not imply a conscious process of abstraction.

For this reason this Thracian goddess—found in a tomb—bears on her belly the continuous rising and descending spiral, showing her to be mistress both of life and death.

"Abstraction" is a symbolic term for minimization of the material element; abstracting representation is a symbolic expression of the conflict between corporeal and incorporeal and of a transformation tending from the corporeal to the incorporeal.

An incorporeal factor operates here in a dynamic that stands in a certain opposition to material reality. But in its otherness, its removal from reality, it can also appear as an abstract, a quintessential extract from this reality. This spiritual, psychic element, which in the primitive phase combines the essential, the symbolic, the ideational, the transpersonal and conceptual, is the effective force in the tendency toward abstraction.

Here it is immaterial whether this spiritual and psychic factor is experienced as something preceding or coming after the corporeal world. The "spiritual" soul that animates the living and departs from the dead belongs just as much to the region of the unworldly and preworldly as to that of the incorporeal and precorporeal.

In so-called primitive and archaic art, especially in masks, we find an abundance of abstract motifs, which possess a "spiritual" character in this primitive sense. The coexistence of naturalistic elements and of abstracting, imaginative elements in the same work of art shows that we have to do with a meaningful tendency of unconscious representation, and not with a "style" dependent on outward determinants.

If we compare the two Benin heads in our illustrations,[27] one, *Pls. 18, 19* despite its stylization, is amazingly realistic; while the other, representing a spirit, is covered with a network of symbols that produce the disembodying effect of tattooing. Despite the plastic character of the symbols, the abstracting tendency is evident.

"Abstracting" representation does not, like the realistic forms of sculpture, seek to express the numinous by expressive exaggeration of real features, but by an imaginative and essentially different inner

[27] Cf. Underwood, *Masks of West Africa*, Pls. 26, 27.

vision. Here we indubitably face the same contradiction as in the psychology of modern man, namely, the opposition between the extraverted and introverted attitudes of consciousness.[28] Of course it would be a fundamental error to infer a corresponding typological structure in the artist or the group. We merely note that such antithetical psychic attitudes and modes of representation existed from the very beginning, and that they not only determine the divergent form of different objects but may also participate in the shaping of one and the same figure.

The opposition between sensuous and imaginative recurs in the distinction between the organic and the geometrical or abstract in art.[29] But to call geometrical art "unsympathetic" and "life-denying" is in a certain sense a misunderstanding. The accentuation of a "spiritual" dynamic, i.e., of a dynamic that *moves* nature but is not *confined* within nature, is not hostile to life, though it is often nonobjective. The proximity of the spirit that is independent of life to the spirits and the dead accounts for the misunderstanding, but for early man the world of the spirits, the dead and the ancestors, though numinous, is not unsympathetic or life-denying. Intercourse with these powers stands at the center of man's cults and rituals precisely because, if properly approached in religion, art, and festivals, they promote and intensify life.

The Great Mother fills the universe and the earth with fertility and abundance, and tends to be characterized by a naturalistic, "sensuous" form, while her aspect as ruler over the spirits and the dead favors forms stressing the unnatural, unreal, and "spiritual." [30] The sensuous fullness of the world is the object of the extraverted attitude, while the abstract character of the spirit world objectifies introversion. (Here, of

---

[28] Jung, *Psychological Types*, Defs. 19 and 34.

[29] Read, *The Meaning of Art*, pp. 58, 88.

[30] At one pole stands the goddess as elementary, material, and natural reality. As we approach the other pole, there is a progressive abstraction from the material; the spirit tends to become "pure" spirit, pure dynamic without material substratum. But this second pole is no longer within the scope of the Archetypal Feminine; it belongs to the specific form of the Masculine, as most fully manifested in the world of the patriarchal spirit.

In line with its anima function, the transformative character of the Feminine mediates between these two extreme poles. The transformative character can mediate between the world of the masculine consciousness and the elementary world of the unconscious; or else, incarnated as prophetess, it may mediate between the spiritual world of the paternal uroboros (Cf. Part I, pp. 71 f.) and the elementary reality of the world.

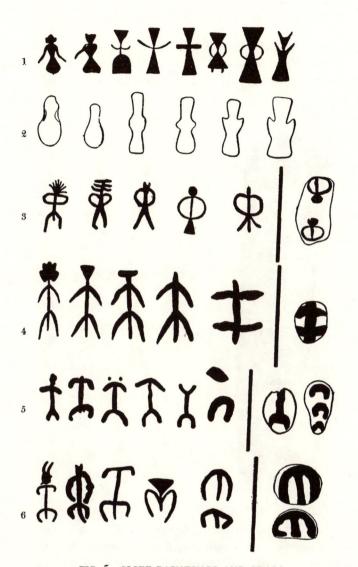

FIG. 5. CLIFF PAINTINGS AND IDOLS

Spain, neolithic. ROW 1: *Cliff paintings of abbreviated human figures.* ROW 2:
Stone idols. ROWS 3–6: *Cliff paintings of abbreviated human figures, compared
with similar designs from painted pebbles of southern France*

course, we have simplified, equating extraversion with sensation, as in the child, and introversion with intuition.) To sum up, the extraverted attitude stresses the experience of the world and its objective reality, while for introversion the accent is on the psychic reaction that the objective world produces upon man. The "abstracting" imaginative atti-

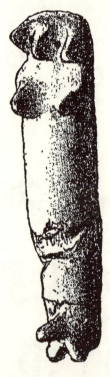

FIG. 6. HERMAPHRODITIC IDOL

Clay, Yugoslavia, Bronze Age

tude is wholly oriented toward an inner process, an experience of the psyche, the spirit, and the spirits. Consequently, the adequate expression of this inward reality consists in a turning away from the outside world, which may take the form of the abstract, symbolic, weird, grotesque, or "fantastic." (It goes without saying that this reality is represented as seen in projection, and that this projection takes the form of abstraction, and so on.)

FIG. 7. CYLINDRICAL "EYE IDOL"

Limestone, Spain, neolithic (three views)

FIG. 8. "EYE IDOLS"

Engraved cow bones, Spain, neolithic

The object of "abstract" representation is something that is "numinous and utterly different." And it is not always possible to distinguish between a schematization leading from the corporeal to the "sign" on the one hand, and an abstract-numinous representation of a figure on

Pl. 32

FIG. 9. DEATH GODDESSES

Reliefs in limestone grottoes, France, neolithic

Fig. 5   the other. For example, in the late paleolithic Spanish cliff paintings and idols collected by Obermaier, the geometrization of the figures is no mere abbreviation and simplification, but also produces a concentration of the symbol.

Fig. 6   The numinous "grotesques" include hermaphroditic figures, whose uroboric nature encompasses the opposites.[31] The very primitive example reproduced here is extremely expressive. To this category belong

Figs. 7–8   also the so-called eye idols.[32] Although it may be formally correct to speak of "disintegrating representation of the face," this approach completely misses the central intention of these marvelously numinous and imaginative works. The intention is similarly missed when an Aegean prototype of the female godhead is said to be "reduced" to the region of the eyes, and "schematized." [33]

Pl. 20   The likelihood that these works, frequently found in tombs, are representations of a primitive "death goddess" supports our thesis on the connection between imaginative abstraction and mortuary rites. Thus the significance of the "reduction" and "schematization" is not formal; they symbolize a "reduction" to the spiritual essentials of the

[31] Cf. Hoernes, *Urgeschichte*, p. 53.   [33] Ibid., p. 214.
[32] Ibid., p. 213.

realm of the dead and the spirits—in contrast to the full-blown character of feminine life.

The imaginative-abstract form of the Cyprian fertility goddess *Pl. 21* from the second half of the second millennium B.C., as well as the much later neolithic cave mother from France, image the goddess of the dead, *Fig. 9; Pl. 22*

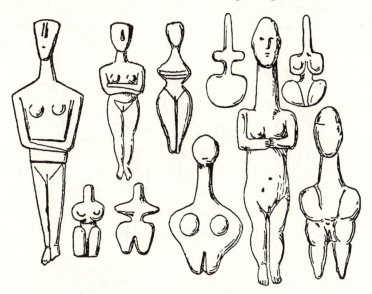

FIG. *10.* SITTING AND STANDING FIGURES OF THE GODDESS

From Amorgos, Naxos, and Crete, pre-Mycenaean

the earth, and fertility, and once more indicate the bond between the numinous-imaginative and the realm of the spirits and the dead. The numinous effect of abstracting form is also evident in the later pre- *Fig. 10* Mycenaean stone sculpture.[34]

Over against these abstracting body forms we find, particularly in predynastic Egypt (i.e., at the dawn of human history), figures closely resembling the Primordial Mother in physical type. A sitting, exag-

[34] The cellolike shape of the Cycladean female idols is so striking that one is tempted to investigate the feminine form of many musical instruments and relate its symbolism to our present contexts. *Pl. 24*

Pl. 25 geratedly broad-hipped sculpture of an Egyptian "maidservant" is one
of a whole group of such works.[35] In contrast to these, the standing
women belong to the group of works representing the "goddess with
Pl. 26 upraised arms." These figures with the exaggerated posterior have been
misinterpreted as African slave women.

Concerning one of them Breasted writes: "Skin decorated with
numerous zigzag, chevron, and animal designs. Feet and hands lacking
(probably from beginning). Scharff [36] thinks such figures are in a danc-

FIG. *11.* STONE DRAWING

Algeria, paleolithic

ing attitude, and as such are the earliest known attempt to represent
the human figure in a specific activity." [37]

The interpretation of such female figures as engaged in prayer is by
no means impossible. The priestesses identified with the Great Mother
as well as the women who worshiped her may well have assumed this
same attitude. But this tells us nothing about the actual significance of
this widely distributed gesture which is characteristic of the archetypal
Feminine.

The "specific activity" of the upraised arms is unquestionably religious, whether we interpret it as prayer, invocation, or magical conjuring. Primary in all probability is the "magical significance" of this

[35] Holländer, *Aeskulap und Venus;* Petrie,   [37] Breasted, *Egyptian Servant Statues,* fig.
The Making of Egypt, Pl. IV, 39, 40; VIII, 55.   82; text, p. 89.
[36] Scharff, "Ägypten," p. 445.

114

posture, which was later retained as an attitude of prayer. And it must be remembered that the original magical intention to move and influence the upper powers is preserved in almost all prayer.

The figure of the goddess with upraised arms is found almost wherever the archetypal figure of the Feminine appears. We find it in the earliest Stone Age "abbreviations." In the paleolithic rock drawing *Fig. 5* showing a male hunter magically connected, from genital to genital, with a female figure with upraised arms, it is a clear expression of the *Fig. 11*

FIG. *12.* VASE DESIGN: WOMEN WITH UPRAISED ARMS

Egypt, perhaps IV *millennium* B.C.

magical function of the Feminine. In all probability the painting on a very early Egyptian vessel also represents hunt magic. Here too the fe- *Fig. 12* male figures are broad-hipped, with accentuated posterior. Moreover, they are much larger than the men standing beside them, and this, as we know, is an expression of "greatness," either for a god or, later, for the Great Individual, the king.

Our interpretation of the figures is confirmed by a remark of Max Raphael: "The clay figure of a woman with upraised arms that played a part in the cult of the dead as far back as Amratian times cannot be regarded as representing a dancer, because in a design on a vase in the Brooklyn Museum (New York) there are two men supporting the upraised arms, holding the woman directly under the armpits, in order to enhance the effectiveness of the posture and to prolong it." [38] Some of

[38] Raphael, *Prehistoric Pottery in Egypt*, pp. 140 f.

115

Raphael's interpretations may be rather too speculative, but he unquestionably succeeds in proving that these figures represent the Great Mother.[39] We find an exact correspondence to the supporting of the arms (see above) in the Bible,[40] where the raising and supporting of Moses' arms determines the victory of the Hebrews over the Amalekites.

Two interpretations of this arm posture are possible, and both ultimately amount to the same thing. The one interpretation stresses the magical character of the attitude, which is accordingly assumed by priests or priestesses of the Great Goddess or by supplicants who wish

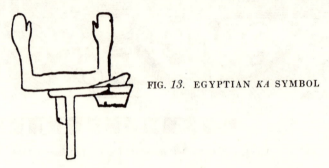

FIG. *13*. EGYPTIAN *KA* SYMBOL

to establish contact with her. In the other interpretation, it is the posture of "epiphany," of the moment in which the godhead appears. Good reasons can be adduced for both interpretations.

Fig. 12   The attitude of the Great Women with upraised arms, with men standing beside them on the Egyptian vessel, is obviously an attitude of supplication, and probably the women had to take this magically effective outward and inner attitude either at the beginning or during the whole course of the men's undertaking, for example, the hunt or battle. We find vestiges of this conception in the numerous taboos that the women must observe while the men are engaged in a hunting or battle expedition, the success of which depends on the magical efficacy of the Feminine.

Often the priestesses of the Great Mother resembled her in physi-

---

Fig. 13   [39] Moreover the posture of the arms is probably related to the protective *ka* symbol, although it is possible that a distinction should   be made between arms lifted to form a circle and merely "upraised arms."
[40] Exodus 17:8–13.

cal type, this being regarded as necessary if they were to "represent" *Pl. 56*
her adequately. This is apparent not only in the figures of the high
Cretan culture but also in Maltese examples. The sleeping woman of
Malta shows that the ideal of a luxuriant body on slender legs was pre- *Pl. 3*
served for thousands of years.[41]

 The frontal position of a figure almost always indicates the numinous, which either "appears" or merely symbolizes an object of wor-

FIG. *14*. CRETAN GODDESS BEFORE HER
WORSHIPERS

Palace, Knossos, ii *millennium*

ship. One of the finest examples of this is a painting of the Cretan god- *Fig. 14*
dess standing before her worshipers. This goddess, with upraised hands,[42]
holding double-edged axes, is known to us from other representations.
Here she has just come down to earth, as the wavy lines of the background indicate.[43]

[41] The question of whether these relatively late (i.e., neolithic) figures were influenced by African or by Cretan-Mycenaean currents is for us unimportant, since the concept of "influence" has no bearing on the archetypal aspect. "Influence" occurs only where a psychic resonance is present, but in this case there are always spontaneous manifestations of the constellation, which brings about a living interaction of influences and often makes for a transformation toward the archetypal (cf. what has been said above about schematization and decadence).

When we attempt to prove influences, migrations, and so on, we must ask why such influences allegedly connect the most distant regions while neighboring cultures and groups of cultures often show no influence upon one another.

[42] Cf. pp. 114 ff., 118.

[43] Persson, in *The Religion of Greece in Prehistoric Times,* pp. 26, 73 f., has pointed out that the wavy line on the rings signifies the delimitation of the heavenly region. Here we must interpret the connection of the wavy line with the descending goddess in the same sense.

We have observed the identity between the goddess and the priestess who represented her. A similar identity prevailed between the posture of the divine epiphany and that of the worshiper of the godhead,[44] so that the worshiped goddess and the worshiper assume the same posture. For this reason we often cannot be certain whether we have to do with a representation of the Goddess, of her priestess, or of a worshiper.

Upraised arms as an attitude of prayer are not only typical for Egypt [45] but are widely distributed elsewhere as well.[46] Often the angular attitude of the arms signifies not worship but a divine epiphany, as is shown by the painting of the Cretan goddess; [47] the primitive figure of the goddess from the shrine of Gournia [48] also shows this attitude, as do many other figures from Mycenae,[49] Troy,[50] Cyprus,[51] and Greece. In the vessel from Troy and a Hallstatt vessel,[52] the handles shaped like upstretched arms are a sure indication of sacral significance.[53] On the basis of this feature Persson proves that the figures represent an epiphany of the Cretan Great Goddess.[54] And the Great Goddess assumes the same posture in India.[55]

This gesture of epiphany is appropriate to the Great Mother when she stands on the earth, as in Egypt; when she descends from heaven, as in Crete; and also when she rises upward from the earth.

The pre-Greek Goddess, whose lower part is undifferentiated like a bell or platform, reminds us of Gaea, the Earth Mother, whose womb coincides with the earth, the lower territory of fertility. The same is true of the Indian "busts" [56] of the Great Mother, the lower part of whose body is in the earth. We find the same archetype almost two thousand years later in a painting showing the earth nourishing monsters—though here a learned knowledge of the ancient figure of Gaea is not precluded.

Frontispiece
Fig. 14

Pls. 27b, 28a
Pl. 27a

Pls. 26, 154–55
Fig. 14
Pls. 24b, 136

Pls. 28a, b
Fig. 15

Pl. 29

---

[44] This is not the case in the many representations of worship where the face is inclined or buried in the folded arms.
[45] Breasted.
[46] Heiler, *Das Gebet*, pp. 101 f.
[47] Nilsson, *Geschichte*, Pl. 14, 4c.
[48] Ibid., Pl. 1.
[49] Kuhn, fig. 81.

[50] Hoernes, p. 361.
[51] Mode, n. 20 to Ch. II.
[52] Hoernes, p. 483.
[53] Cf. p. 132.
[54] Persson, p. 64.
[55] Mode, fig. 36.
[56] Piggott, *Prehistoric India*, p. 108, fig. 9.

A painting by a psychotic shows that the archetype of the Great   *Pl. 30a*
Mother with upraised arms still lives in the unconscious of modern
man.[57] It is an archaic figure of the goddess with archetypal headdress;
the figure is obviously steatopygic and broad-hipped; the genital zone is
surrounded by little black dancing demons; the face is distinctly tattooed. She is standing before a dark-blue night sky; under her feet is a
greenish-yellow something (the moon?).

The abstract, imaginative type of Mother Goddess is found in the

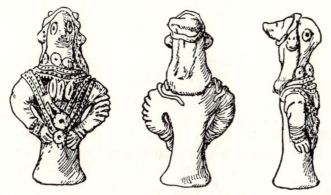

FIG. *15.*   FEMALE FIGURINE

Clay, Baluchistan, prehistoric (three views)

drawings of modern children too. The great figure of the maternal arche-   *Pl. 30b*
type that has appeared in a child's unconscious was conceived as a
picture of a "ship." We shall speak later of the unconscious connection
between ship and mother archetype; in our present picture, as in that of
the psychotic, the expression of the Great Mother is very considerably
affected by the strangely upraised arms.

Thus the Primordial Goddess, combining elementary and transformative character in one, is an "eternal presence"; wherever the
original traits of the elementary or the transformative character appear, her archaic image will be constellated anew, regardless of time
and space.

[57] Prinzhorn, *Bildnerei der Geisteskranken*, Pl. XIV.

119

Chapter Ten

THE POSITIVE ELEMENTARY
CHARACTER

Pl. 2

Figs. 16–17

Pls. 31a, b

A T T H E center of the feminine elementary character in which the woman contains and protects, nourishes and gives birth, stands the vessel,[1] which is both attribute and symbol of the feminine nature. "The clay vessel, and later the vessel in general, is a very characteristic attribute of the woman; in this case it is substituted for her and also given to her. It is one of the primary work implements of the man's water-gathering, fruit-picking, food-preparing household companion, and therefore a symbol of the female deity." [2]

We start with two clay urns, primitive images of the Goddess, from Hissarlik, site of Troy. Of these vessels it has been written: "Beginning in the second city, the whole vessel is formed as a demonic figure, under whose protection the content of the vessel and the well-being of its possessor are placed. And who should this demonic figure be, other than the ruler of the city, the mountain goddess herself?" [3] To this context also belong two products of a different time and country, a "face urn" and a cult figure holding a jar, both from eastern Europe.[4]

Jars that look like forerunners of the numerous pre-Mycenaean face urns of Troy have been found in neolithic settlements in Thessaly

---

[1] Part I, Ch. 4.
[2] Hoernes, *Urgeschichte der bildenden Kunst in Europa*, p. 362.

[3] Ibid, p. 362.
[4] Ibid., p. 531; Sydow, *Die Kunst der Naturvölker und der Vorzeit*.

and Serbia,[5] but, as the corresponding jars from Posen and Branden-
burg, West Prussia, and other parts of the world prove, this form of
representation is archetypal and not determined by tradition and culture.[6] For our purposes it is irrelevant if in the Trojan figures the ac-

FIG. *16.* FACE URN

Red clay, Troy, fourth stratum

centuation of face and sex is more typical, while in the eastern European   *Fig. 20*
works the accent tends to be on the necklace and girdle.[7]

The vessel character of the Feminine is often emphasized by a
duplication of the jar: the woman represented as a jar carries a second
jar. Thus the characteristic head ornament of the goddess and priestess   *Fig. 16*
is probably a development on the jar that was frequently carried on the

[5] Hoernes, p. 359.
[6] According to Hoernes, p. 804, n. 8, Carl   Schuchhardt (in a review of *Urgeschichte*) thinks
this vase "may be apocryphal."
[7] Hoernes, p. 530.

head in the ritual. The vessel held on the head, in front of the body, or *Pl. 33a* sometimes beside it may usually be interpreted as a sacral vessel, which plays a significant part in the ritual of the female godhead.[8]

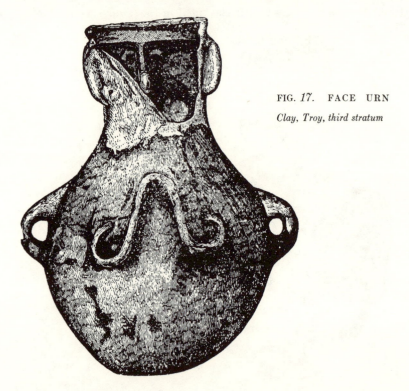

FIG. *17.* FACE URN

Clay, Troy, third stratum

And the vessel character is sometimes represented by "the jar without other symbols (facial features, breasts, etc.) and merely having a small jar beside it as an attribute." [9]

A significant symbolic feature of some of the primitive "woman jars" is the absence of a mouth—which was already typical for the Primordial Goddess. The mouth as rending, devouring symbol of ag-

[8] See the illustrations from Troy, Austria, Germany, Cyprus, Italy, Spain, Romania, Russia, etc. in Hoernes, pp. 198, 361, 451, 497, 507, etc.

[9] Hoernes, p. 362.

gression is characteristic of the dangerous negative elementary character of the Feminine. Consequently, we must ask what bearing its frequent absence has on the elementary character. The character of abundance is one of man's positive, primordial experiences, a part of his experience of the Feminine as a vessel that gives nourishment. For this reason, the breasts are accentuated, while the numinous character is expressed in the dominating eyes, which together with the arch of the eyebrows and nose contribute strongly to the birdlike character of these figures.[10]

The corporeal vessel character of the lower body is offset by the spiritual eye character of the upper body.[11] But an organ of speech, a mouth communicating psychic expression, is lacking. For childlike man, the Archetypal Feminine is still mute existence. The mouth as organ of taking-inward is unnecessary in the Feminine, which possesses everything in the abundance of its vessel, for the Feminine—in so far as it is "good"—is not a devourer but a giver of riches.

The clearest expression of this giving-outward is the breasts, which typify woman as giver of nourishment. According to the Greek tradition, the first *patera*, or bowl, was modeled from Helen's breast.[12] The connection between the mystery of pottery making and the feminine mystery of the miraculous transformation of blood into milk is shown by an example from the primitive world: "The Zuñi women make from old their pitchers in the shape of a female breast. The nipple is left open to the last, and the sealing of it is performed with the solemnity of a religious rite, and with averted eyes. Unless this ritual were observed, the women would be barren or their children would die in infancy." [13] This turning away of the eyes from the completion of the creative woman's work, in which not the human being but the creative numen itself has "the last word," reveals the bond between the feminine and the

---

[10] An indication of the archetypal basis of this feature is that infants, as experiment shows, react positively to the smooth forehead and brow, while the character and expression of the mouth has no effect on them. See Portmann's allusion in "Mythisches in der Naturforschung."

[11] We shall have more to say below of this "upper" character, which from earliest times is clearly accented in the head and its enlargement, e.g., by ornament.

[12] Briffault, *The Mothers*, Vol. I, p. 473.

[13] Cushing, *A Study of Pueblo Pottery*, pp. 512 ff.

Pls. 56, 87

essence of the creative process in which veiling and silence have a special mystery significance.[14]

The archetypal experience of the Feminine as all-nourishing is evident in the multiplication of the breast motif. This multiplication is perhaps most beautifully exemplified in the Peruvian jar, covered with breasts on all sides,[15] but the old European humped ceramics also show the archetypal breast motif.[16]

Pl. 34

Hoernes describes the technical development of these vessels as follows: "As a result of the influence of metalworking technique on pottery making, the flat circular figures became plastic and were raised to form teat-shaped protuberances. A transitional form is the vessel with humps, on which spiral designs were inscribed." [17] He stresses the similarity of a humped jar from Transylvania to another such vessel from Crete.[18] Circular figure, spiral, teat, hump with spiral, hump—this sequence does not only signify a historical development for us, but shows in general what forms the breast motif may take on a vessel. This does not mean that wherever a circle or spiral appears on a jar the breast motif is present, but it does indicate a connection between the hemisphere of the breast and the spiral life motif, and suggests that the double spiral and double circle often symbolize the breasts.[19]

The breast motif involves the symbolism of milk and cow. The Goddess as cow, ruling over the food-giving herd, is one of the earliest historical objects of worship, occurring among the Mesopotamian population after the al 'Ubaid period.

The sacred herd, such as is known to have supplied the temple dairy farm with "the holy milk of Nin-khursag" at Lagash, is returning from

[14] My "Über den Mond und das matriarchale Bewusstsein."

[15] For a similar jar, see Lehmann, *Mexikanische Kunst*, fig. 3.

[16] Sydow, p. 495, below, on Lusatian pottery; likewise Hungarian, Austrian, etc.

[17] Hoernes, p. 415, fig. 2.

[18] Ibid., p. 414.

[19] The Serbian idol of the Mother Goddess, whose mouth and breasts are geometrized and *Pl. 20* represented by a starlike or sunlike symbol, shows how easily what was originally a jar woman may "degenerate" into ornament, so that all we have

left is an ornamented jar, while the female figure it originally symbolizes is no longer recognizable. The vessels of the Mondsee type (see Hoernes, p. 331, from northern, middle, and southern Europe; p. 353, from northern Italy; p. 341, figs. 1 and 6, from Cyprus; p. 307, figs. 4–8, from Transylvania), with "eye" or "sun" ornaments, might also be considered in this context of vessel as woman. But since the ornamentation of these vessels may have developed in any number of ways, a definite decision is hard to reach. On the problem of degeneration, see above, p. 112 f.

pasture, to be met by the young calves who spring from their byre exactly as Homer describes: "At the sight of their mothers the calves skip so wildly that their pens can no longer hold them; they break loose, lowing all the while and gamboling." [20] The religious intention of the scene becomes clearer when it is remembered that all through historic times the infancy of kings and priests was nourished on this milk; that even an Assyrian text refers to it in these words:

> Little wast thou, Ashurbanipal, when I delivered thee
>   to the Queen of Nineveh,
> Weak wast thou . . . when thou didst sit upon her knees,
> Four teats were set in thy mouth . . .[21]

Thus the goddess of the pastures was herself the cow, and is in fact so designated in an incantation for the help of women in travail.[22]

The breast motif appears wherever the archetype of the mother suckling her child is expressed in cult. But the cult is only a focus, where the archetypal image of the Feminine has penetrated the consciousness of men and consciously influenced their life and culture.[23]

The need for a sharper perception of such contexts becomes evident when we see the Cretan idol of Hagia Triada, which unquestionably belongs to one aspect of the Great Mother Goddess, described in terms like the following: "The lower part of the one idol is prominent and covered with warts"![24] There is no doubt that we have to do with a symbol of the "nurturing" Earth Goddess. Usually this Gaea-type of Great Mother is half buried *in* the earth, from which only the bust emerges. An example of this type of Earth Mother is the Cretan urn of Mallia.[25] To the same group belong the Trojan idols, the second of which combines accentuated breasts with upraised handle-arms. In a third example, the breasts are suggested by a curved line. The same ab-

Fig. 18

Pl. 28b
Pl. 27a
Fig. 17

---

[20] *Odyssey*, X, 410–114.
[21] Hall and Woolley, *Ur Excavations*, p. 142.
[22] Levy, *The Gate of Horn*, p. 97.
[23] Even when determinants of other kinds dominate the consciousness and culture of men, the archetype may assert itself. Thus, for example, the so-called humped ceramics were not necessarily connected with a mother cult, yet— for reasons unknown to us—they reveal the symbolism of the breast-vessel with its unconscious emotional ramifications.

[24] Nilsson, *Geschichte der griechischen Religion*, Vol. I, p. 265, n. 2.
[25] In this regard see Picard, "Die Grosse Mutter von Kreta bis Eleusis."

Fig. 19 breviation is reduplicated on the strange pre-Etruscan tombstone near Bologna. "Above stand two rosettes like eyes in a face, under them a cross line and further down, in place of the mouth, an animal figure. Another rosette designates the middle of the body (the navel); the space above is occupied by two pendent double volutes in the middle and on each side two animal figures turned toward the center." [26]

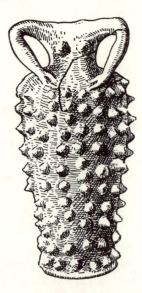

FIG. *18.* FEMALE IDOL

Clay, Hagia Triada, Crete, late Minoan III *period*

This mortuary stele represents a figure whose belly, the "center of life," juts out of the earth; over it two pairs of breasts feed the animals to the left and right. This unquestionably is a representation of the Great Many-Breasted Mother, as ruler and nourisher of the animal *Pl. 35* world. She finds her classical form in the Diana of Ephesus, but in Mexico there is also a representative of this Great Goddess, Mayauel, goddess of the Agave, surnamed "the woman with the four hundred breasts." [27] The Mexican goddess was originally a goddess of heaven,[28] and similarly the upper "eye section" of the Bologna goddess shows her

[26] Hoernes, *Urgeschichte*, p. 462.
[27] See Spence, *The Religion of Ancient* *Mexico*, p. 116.
[28] See below, p. 301.

to be "Queen of Heaven," regardless how we interpret the two cosmic symbols that form her eyes. The one is identical with the life symbol of the womb-navel-center and might be interpreted as the planet Venus. Heavenly "body," sun and moon, as eyes of the heavenly goddess are known to us particularly from Egyptian mythology.

The symbol of the all-knowing, all-seeing, many-eyed god belongs to an archetypal image in which the stars of the night sky appear as the

FIG. *19.* TOMBSTONE IN FEMALE FORM

Vicinity of Bologna, prehistoric Umbrian

eyes of the godhead.[29] The link between the upper and lower regions is characteristic for diverse phases of the Great Mother's rule. As goddess of the tomb, she rules over the world of the dead, but at the same time she governs the celestial world, whose luminaries are her eyes. Similarly the Great Goddess as divine water jar is mistress of the upper waters, the rain; and of the lower waters, the brooks and streams that spring from the womb of the earth. As G. E. Smith has shown, this view is particularly evident in Egypt.[30] In the hieroglyphics, the water jar,

Pl. 33b

[29] Concerning this heavenly luminosity as projection of the luminosity of the unconscious, cf. Jung, "On the Nature of the Psyche," p. 190 ff.

[30] G. E. Smith, *The Evolution of the Dragon.*

symbol of the celestial goddess Nut, is also the symbol of femininity, "female genital," "woman," and the feminine principle.[31]

Pl. 36

As celestial cow, the Great Goddess nourishes the earth with her milky rain, and as uterus she is the vessel that is "broken" at birth, pouring forth water like the earth, the water-bearing goddess of the depths. For this reason, the virgin is a closed well, "a fountain sealed." [32]

Only an appreciation of the "mythological apperception" of early man, who experiences symbolically everything that touches his emotions, can enable us to understand the full significance of these symbolic equations: milk giving = thirst quenching = rain giving = water jar; cow = woman = earth = spring = stream bearing; and woman = heaven = rain bearing. In all these equations the ground water belongs to the belly-womb region of the lower Feminine, and the heavenly rain water to the breast region of the upper Feminine.

The Great Goddess as a whole is a symbol of creative life and the parts of her body are not physical organs but numinous symbolic centers of whole spheres of life. For this reason the "self-representation" of the Great Goddess, her display of her breasts, belly, or entire naked body, is a form of divine epiphany.

Thus in the Cretan cultural sphere, the uncovering of the breasts is a sacred action pertaining to the cult. The goddess and the priests identified with her show their full breasts, the symbols of the nourishing life stream.[33] The widely distributed "Astarte type" of the Great Goddess, pressing or showing her breasts, has the same significance. Where the breasts are beaten in token of mourning, e.g., for Adonis, it means that they are accused as the vital principle that has failed to defeat

Pl. 33a

death. In the Cyprian representations of the Great Mother, dated over a period of several centuries, the identity of the vessel-bearing woman and of the jar woman showing her breasts is evident.

Pl. 37

The nude Hittite goddess, facing forward, standing on a lion and suckling her child, has the numinous power of ceremonial self-display, while the approximately contemporaneous or even earlier group of Isis

[31] F. L. Griffith, *A Collection of Hieroglyphs.*
[32] Song of Solomon 4:12.
[33] The display characteristic of the Amazons

is also to be interpreted as sacral in the same sense; see Picard, "Die Ephesia von Anatolien," p. 62.

with Horus (apart from the Hathor headdress) produces a human and   *Pl. 38*
personal impression. No doubt this impression is enhanced by the non-
frontal perspective of the picture, but the expression of Isis's face, and
the tenderness with which she holds the child's head, stand in the
strongest contrast to the disinterested epiphany of the Hittite goddess.

The archetypal situation of the mother-child relationship is most
apparent in the representations of primitive peoples. The Peruvian jar
of the mother with child strikes us as one of the most outstanding
representations of this archetype. Here the aspect of inhumanity almost
outweighs that of magnificence. The steatopygic component is unmistakable, and again the woman is represented as a vessel, but also as
carrying a vessel and holding her breasts. Somewhere at the side of this
mountainlike mass, in which the impression of fusion with the earth is
intensified by the cloth falling from the head, hangs a human creature,
whose characterization lies somewhere between infant, old man, and
ape. But this gigantic woman, on whom the little one "de-pends" in the
literal sense of the word, stares straight ahead of her, magnificent and
unfeeling, monumentally embodying nature's indifference toward the
living things that depend on her.

Another Peruvian jar shows perhaps even more clearly the little-   *Pl. 41*
ness of the human thing clinging to the mother. Both jars produce a
numinous effect, regardless whether their practical purpose was sacred
or profane.

In our first example of African sculpture the child is again tiny and   *Pl. 39*
dependent; here also the vessel stands beside the woman as companion
symbol, but the expression of the woman is entirely different. It is the
triumph of a wild motherhood, whose proud, overpowering pleasure,
with all its self-satisfaction, is not unrelated to the child. Here we do
not find the tender and personal solicitude of Isis toward her son, but
rather the royal concern of the lusty queen with that which has been
born of her, with that which is dependent on her and nourished by her;
here the Feminine experiences itself—and is experienced—as mother,
nature, earth, and giver of life.

Still different, but no less magnificent, is the representation of the

Pl. 42 nourishing Feminine in the sculpture of the Yoruba. This woman, enthroned in implacable calm amid her children playing round her, shows distinctly phallic breasts. The hanging breasts, artificially induced in Africa, are here exaggerated to produce a phallic form, from which the generative force of life pours into the receiving child. Here the archetypal symbolism of the receiving mouth in relation to the engendering breast is particularly apparent in its authentic and utterly unperverse form.

Pl. 43 In another piece of Yoruba sculpture, the expression of the nurturing woman becomes human and personal despite the sacral accent of the work, which is a priest's staff. Nevertheless, this slender, delicate woman —particularly in front view—is not lacking in grandeur. The pendent, tautly elongated breasts give an impression of fruitfulness; here the woman is like a motionless plant, which bears fruit on all sides: in front the melonlike breasts, on her back the child. The expression and posture of the son are bold and world-conquering; as he rides on the woman and clings to her, he is wholly contained in the protective oval, which rises from the maternal knees to the breasts, profile, and headdress and thence descends to her feet.

These "primitive" African representations of the Great Mother *Pl. 44* bear comparison even to the figure of Isis-Hathor with the king as Horus—which does not belong to the elementary character of the Feminine. The Egyptian figure embodies the symbolic richness of a people into whose consciousness the Archetypal Feminine has entered in myth and ritual and in the historical conception of the kingdom. The king, the Great Individual, the god among men and the intermediary between above and below—he too remains the child of the great Mother Goddess, the mother of all the gods, who bore him and rebore him and through whom alone he is king. The horns of Hathor, the nurturing cow of heaven, tower over her head, which is adorned by the maternal symbols of the snake and the vulture. She is the throne, sitting upon which he possesses the land of Egypt and with it the earth and its center of fertility. All these symbols, it is true, disclose an enrichment, a complication and specification, of the form-giving archetype, but the fundamental situation has remained the same in the personal statue showing the infant Horus, and in the African sculptures, as well as in the pre-Roman Sardinian statues of the Mother Goddess holding her living and her dead son, at once child and man. *Pls. 46, 47*

Thus the Feminine, the giver of nourishment, becomes everywhere a revered principle of nature, on which man is dependent in pleasure and pain. It is from this eternal experience of man, who is as helpless in his dependence on nature as the infant in his dependence on his mother, that the mother-child figure is inspired forever anew. *Pl. 45*

FIG. *20.*   FACE URN WITH NAVEL
Clay, Troy, fifth stratum

This mother-child figure, then, does not betoken a regression to infantilism, in which an "adult" becomes a child, or is moved with nostalgia by the mother's love for her child; rather, man in his genuine identification with the child experiences the Great Mother as a symbol of the life on which he himself, the "grown-up," depends.

With the "royal relief" at Abydos, we find ourselves in a different context. Here there is something new that we can only touch upon in passing. In the figures facing one another, eye to eye, the mother-child relationship is mysteriously transformed. The entrancing face of the young mother is turned toward a male who, it is true, is still a child sitting on her lap, but the tenderness of the Goddess as she holds this face *Pl. 4* in her hands is directed toward a beloved son, and no longer toward an infant.

Pl. 48

Fig. 20

The Feminine consists not only in the nurturing breast, but even more in the belly-vessel that bears all things. Thus the jars in our present reproductions are in every sense "potbellied." Some of them have at their center a circle symbolizing both navel and female genitals. Here, as in representations of the Primordial Goddess, this "generative center" bears a symbol of life.

The navel as center of the world is also archetypal. Characteristically, many shrines are looked upon as navels of the world, as, for example, the Temple [34] at Jerusalem, the sanctuary at Delphi, and so forth. For us it is significant that this symbolism unconsciously "includes" the female symbolism of the earth. The earth in a sense is the womb of a reality seen as feminine, the navel and center from which the universe is nourished.[35] Cf. the shining white Parthian goddess of the luminous moon, who has not only gleaming eyes but also a radiant navel.

Pl. 49

Pl. 27a

The vessel with the life-navel and the handle-arms, situating it in the group of goddesses with upraised arms, is only one example of the world-wide identification of the goddess with the "pot," the belly symbol par excellence.

Fig. 68

Fig. 21

The Great Goddess, e.g., Ishtar, with the branches or ears of grain sprouting from her back,[36] finds a correspondence in the representation on a coin of Phoenicia, minted during the epoch of the Roman emperor Gordianus III, of a large vessel, a pithos, flanked by two sphinxes and having branches or ears of grain sprouting from its "shoulders," i.e., the space between "trunk" and "neck" of the vessel. In Cyprus pots called *kernophorai* [37] were also worshiped as goddesses, but the identification of the Mother Goddess with the pot is not limited to the ancient Mediterranean culture. G. E. Smith has rightly said: "The Mother Pot is really a fundamental conception in all religions, and is almost world-

---

[34] Patai, *Man and Temple*, pp. 85, 132.
[35] The childlike conception of umbilical birth originates in this archetypal symbolism of the navel's identity with the womb as the femi- nine center of life.
[36] Cf. Jeremias, *Handbuch der altorientalischen Geisteskultur*, p. 113, fig. 89.
[37] Briffault, *The Mothers*, Vol. I, p. 474.

wide in its distribution. The pot's identity with the Great Mother is deeply rooted in ancient belief through the greater part of the world."[38] Briffault[39] has also demonstrated the presence of the Mother Goddess as a pot in southern India, where, for example, a group of seven goddesses is worshiped in the shape of seven pots,[40] and in North Borneo and the Philippines as well.

Not only in Eleusis but also among the Vestal Virgins of Rome, in Peru, and in Dahomey, the sacred vessels stand under the specific super-

FIG. *21.* SPROUTING PITHOS

Coin, Phoenicia, III *century* A.D.

vision of the priestesses.[41] This institution is rooted in the fundamental symbolic and sociological significance of the pot. It is one of the original symbols of womanhood, while the making and ornamenting of pottery are among the primordial functions of woman.

In this connection Briffault writes: "The art of pottery is a feminine invention; the original potter was a woman. Among all primitive peoples the ceramic art is found in the hands of women, and only under the influence of advanced culture does it become a man's occupation. In every part of the world where an aboriginal industry of pottery manufacture exists the men have no part in it; as in British Central Africa, it would

[38] G. E. Smith, pp. 182, 199.
[39] Briffault, Vol. I, pp. 474 ff.

[40] Whitehead, *The Village Gods of South India,* p. 36.
[41] Briffault, Vol. I, p. 475.

be little, if at all, short of improper for a man to set about making pots. The art is exclusively in the hands of women throughout North America, Central and South America, and in those parts of the Malay Archipelago and Peninsula, Melanesia, and New Guinea, where the art is practiced as a native industry. In the Nicobar Islands pottery is made by the women only, and in the Andaman Islands it is made exclusively by the women in the northern island, while in the south island men also make pots. In the Pamir highlands of Central Asia the women manufacture all the pottery, and their crockery is admired for its artistic taste. In the Nilgiri Hills, among the Khotas, the pottery is made exclusively by the women; and the same is the case among the wild tribes of Burma. Throughout by far the greater part of Africa pottery is made by the women only. Zulu tradition ascribes the making of the first pot to the first woman. Among certain Hamitic peoples of Uganda the industry has, under Asiatic influence, been taken up by the men, as also in some parts of the Congo. This, however, is quite exceptional. Out of seventy-eight tribes investigated by the ethnologists attached to the Belgian Congo Museum, the men had no hand whatever in the making of pottery in sixty-seven; the others are exceptions arising from special circumstances which in almost every instance it is easy to trace." [42]

Briffault cites further examples and proofs from the Congo, Uganda, New Guinea, Tenerife, Algeria, Tunisia, Nubia, the Pyrenees, the Hebrides, Mexico, and Brazil; from among the Pygmies, the Bushmen, and others. Prehistoric pottery culture also belonged to the domain of the woman, for pottery making is a sacral, creative action, one of the "primordial mysteries of the Feminine." [43]

The sacral relation of the woman to the pot originates in the symbolic significance of the form, which we have already discussed, and also in the symbolic significance of the material from which the pot is made, namely, clay, for clay belongs to the earth, which stands in a relation of *participation* with the Feminine. As one example among many, we cite the Indians of Ecuador, of whom it has been written: "Thus, for instance, the Indian woman has to fabricate clay vessels and manage these

[42] Briffault, Vol. I, pp. 466–70.   [43] See below, pp. 281 ff.

utensils, because the clay, of which they are made, like the earth itself, is female—that is, has a woman's soul." [44]

On this symbolic foundation there arises a sacrally accented division of labor between the sexes, which always has symbolic and mythological, never "practical," grounds. For this reason the domain belonging to the primordial mysteries of the Feminine is taboo and dangerous for men. "In East Africa, among the Nandi, no man may go near the hut where women are engaged in making pottery, or watch a potter at work. If a man should take a woman's pot and place it on the fire he would be sure to die." [45]

The later patriarchal religions and mythologies have accustomed us to look upon the male god as the creator who, like Khmun in Egypt or YHWH in the Old Testament, formed man of clay. Being made of earth (*adamah*), the first man was called Adam, and parallels to this myth may be found in Greece, India, and China.[46] But the original, overlaid stratum knows of a female creative being. At about the year 2000 B.C. there took place in the Mediterranean region a renaissance of the Mother Goddess, who would seem to have been the dominant deity two thousand years before.[47] A Babylonian fragment contains a childbirth incantation in which the primordial traits of Aruru-Ishtar as potter [48] and creatress have been preserved from a much earlier period. In an Assyrian version of it, we read:

> [. . . they kis]sed her feet,
> [saying: "The creatress of mankind] we call thee;
> [The mistr]ess of all the gods be thy name!"
> [They went] to the House of Fate,
> [Nin]igiku-Ea [and] the wise Mama.[49]
> [Fourteen mother]-wombs were assembled
> To tread upon the clay before her.
> [. . .] Ea says, as he recites the incantation.
> Sitting before her, Ea causes her to recite the incantation.

[44] Karsten, "Blood Revenge, War and Victory Feasts among the Jibaro Indians of Eastern Ecuador," p. 12.

[45] Sir Claud Hollis, *The Nandi*, pp. 35 f.

[46] Jeremias, *Handbuch*, pp. 182 f.

[47] Cf. Mode, *Indische Frühkulturen*, esp. p. 60.

[48] Jeremias, p. 253.

[49] Ea: the god of earth and water. Mama or Mami: the Mother Goddess.

[Mama reci]ted the incantation; when she completed
    her incantation,
[. . .] she drew upon her clay.
[Fourteen pie]ces she pinched off; seven pieces she
    placed on the right,
[Seven pie]ces she placed on the left; between them she placed a
    brick.
[Ea] was kneeling on the matting; he opened its navel;
[. . . he c]alled the wise wives.
Of the [seven] and seven mother-wombs, seven brought forth males,
[Seven] brought forth females.
The Mother-Womb,[50] the creatress of destiny,
In pairs she completed them,
In pairs she completed before her.
The forms of the people Mami forms.
In the house of the bearing woman in travail,
    Seven days shall the brick lie.
. . . from the house of Mah, the wise Mami.
The vexed one shall rejoice in the house of the one in travail.
As the Bearing One gives birth,
May the mother of the child bring forth by [her]self.[51]

The making of the pot is just as much a part of the creative activity of the Feminine as the making of the child, i.e., of man, who—like the pot—was so often fashioned mythologically from earth.

There is always a mystery where something puzzling, something that the human consciousness cannot apprehend, moves the whole man to his very depths. In this sense, creation is a numinous mystery, and it is from this mystery that man "turns away," an attitude often misunderstood later as "shame."

In pottery making the woman experiences this primordial creative force; the Feminine experiences itself as shaper of life. Such experiences are most striking when a numinous figure is formed, a cult vessel, for example, and we know how great a role the sacral vessel played in the primordial era, particularly as a vehicle of magical action.[52] In this magical implication the essential features of the feminine transformative

[50] This and (8 li. below) "Bearing One" are references to the Mother Goddess.
[51] Tr. Speiser in Pritchard, *Ancient Near Eastern Texts*, pp. 99 f.
[52] Childe, *New Light on the Most Ancient Near East*, pp. 74 ff.

character are bound up with the vessel as a symbol of transformation. Just this is meant when it is said of those who have been reborn in rites of initiation: "Now the white chick is crawling out of the egg, we are as fresh-baked pots." [53]

The Feminine as the giver of shelter and protection encompasses the life of the family and group in the symbol of the house. This aspect appears in the so-called house urns, vessels formed in the shape of

FIG. *22.* FEMALE TORSO

Relief in a sanctuary, Istria (Yugoslavia), c. *700–300* B.C.

houses.[54] Down to our day, the feminine vessel character, originally of the cave, later of the house (the sense of being inside, of being sheltered, protected, and warmed in the house), has always borne a relation to the original containment in the womb.

In its function of conceiving and bearing, the Feminine is of course largely unconducive to plastic representation. Profane representations of childbirth do not belong to the present context, with the exception of the unique Istrian relief, in which the Feminine is shown as nourishing, protecting, and bearing at once.[55]

Fig. 22

[53] Thurnwald, "Primitive Initiations- und Wiedergeburtsriten."

[54] Hoernes, p. 525; figs., pp. 527, 529.
[55] Ibid., p. 474.

Pl. 50   Unquestionably sacral is the statue of the childbearing Mexican goddess; however, her positive elementary character is overlaid by her terrible aspect—for it is plain that she is wearing the skin of a victim.

Pl. 48   In the Baubo figures of Priene, the belly character of the woman is not symbolically represented by the vessel; rather, the belly of the goddess represents the numinous fertility symbol. Whereas in the frontal position the goddess's whole naked womanhood is permeated by the

FIG. *23*. CYLINDER SEALS

Ur, Babylonia

numinous, which emanates from her as a fascination for good and evil, this limitation to the zone of the belly or womb expresses the *inhuman* gruesome aspect, the radical autonomy of the belly over against the "higher centers" of the heart, breast, and head, and enthrones it as sacred. Here again, the accent is on the numinous power of the childbearing principle and not on that of sexual attraction.

The enthroned nude female figures of the Mycenaean cults,[56] of which the figure from Delphi [57] represents a last offshoot, fit into a group extending from Ur [58] and Lagash,[59] in Babylonia; from Crete [60] and

Pl. 55a

Figs. 23-25

[56] Picard, "Die Grosse Mutter," p. 105.   [59] Ibid., fig. 168b.
[57] Nilsson, Pl. 16, 3.   [60] Ibid., fig. 169.
[58] Mode, fig. 174.

138

Egypt to India,[61] and having an exact correspondence in Central America, with its totally independent development.

Although we have no precise information concerning the figure from Ixtlán de Rio, it unquestionably represents the goddess.[22] The self-display of the childbearing woman or goddess, the spreading of the legs to exhibit the genital region, represent a ritual act, as is proved by the well-known scene in which Baubo bares herself before the grieving Demeter, and also by the ritual baring of Hathor.[63]   *Pl. 53*

The little figure of Isis, with outspread legs, sitting on a pig [64] and   *Fig. 25*

FIG. *24.* CYLINDER SEAL

Lagash, Babylonia

bearing a mystical ladder in her arms, is characteristic for our present context. The pig is a symbol of the Archetypal Feminine and occurs everywhere as the sacrificial beast of the Earth Goddess; it is sacrificed to Demeter in the Thesmophoria,[65] and is also found in this role in Rome. Picard groups our Hellenistic terra cotta with others on which the nude Isis sits in the same attitude on an upturned basket, "the basket of the mysteries," and the clad Demeter sits on the Lovatelli urn (in Alexandria) or the sarcophagus of Torre Nove.[66]

The representation of a whelping bitch on an archaic Greek scarab-   *Pl. 51*
oid seal has been interpreted by its owner as a "theriomorphic represen-

---

[61] Ibid., fig. 171.
[62] The marks on the shoulders connect this figure with our "winged goddess" (Pl. 52). Burland, *Ancient Mexico*, p. 82, Pl. 42.
[63] Cf. Herodotus, *History*, Book II.

[64] Seligmann, *Der böse Blick und Verwandtes*, Vol. II, p. 293.
[65] Picard, p. 105.
[66] Ibid., p. 106

tation of Hecate-Artemis." [67] He showed that the posture, in which the genitals are exposed, is that assumed by many animals of the dog, cat, and horse group in bearing their young and that it is characteristic of numerous representations that it would otherwise be impossible to understand. But "in view of the most obvious feature common to all these pictures," he finally concluded, "the exposure of the genital region, an interpretation as symbolization of fertility is more probable than any

FIG. 25. ISIS SITTING ON PIG

Terra cotta

other one." Here, as in most works characterized as "representations of childbirth," the pregnant womb is conspicuous by its absence; thus the exposure of the genital region and the exaggerated teats lend certainty to the more general interpretation of an animal goddess symbolizing fertility.

Pl. 54   In the case of a nude goddess we find on Syrian cylindrical seals, who is a successor to the nude goddesses of the Euphrates culture,[68] the exposure of the genital region has an unquestionable sacral signifi-

[67] Reitler, "A Theriomorphic Representation of Hecate-Artemis." I am indebted to Dr. Reitler also for the photograph.

[68] Porada and Buchanan, *Corpus of Ancient Near Eastern Seals*, Vol. I, figs. (Syrian) 944, 945, 946, 937; (Babylonian) 504, 503, 505.

cance. While on two of these cylinders the goddess lifts the ends of her *Pl. 54d, g*
robe, displaying her nakedness, on the third she thrusts her garment *Pl. 54e*
back to expose herself. On the fourth, she does not do so, "but the mantle *Pl. 54b*
falling over one leg, far from covering nudity, serves only to accentuate
it." [69]

Of particular importance, however, is the seal showing a worshiper *Pl. 54g*
between the nude goddess and a seated divine figure holding a vessel in
its hand. That the male god with the vessel is a moon god is suggested
both by the offering of the hare, which is an archetypal moon symbol, [70]
and by the sign of the crescent and sphere that is correlated with it.
Whereas the circle in the half-moon is usually interpreted as pointing to
the relation between the sun and the crescent moon, it seems more likely
that it refers to the full moon, i.e., a lunar symbol of wholeness. The
star, on the other hand, belongs to the nude goddess beside whom
stands the fish, the symbol of the fertility goddess, [71] the goddess of the
waters and the seas. (We have several times mentioned the archetypal
character of the moon's fructifying significance for the Feminine. [72])

The vessel held by the divine figure on the seal corresponds to a
Mycenaean gold vessel; [73] both the vessel and the attitude of the holder
correspond to the vessel-holding male god on the millennium-later
Cabirian fragment from Thebes. *Pl. 159c*

The scene on the cylindrical seal probably represents a fecundation
of the Great Goddess by the male moon god, conceived as a conjunction
of the moon and Venus; the event takes place in the domain of the

[69] Ibid., text, p. 124. These cylinder seals reveal archetypal symbols that we shall encounter again and again. The bull on which the goddess stands is the symbol of masculinity; he is the fertilizing male partner god, whose representation as an animal makes him in a sense inferior to the goddess (cf. my *Origins*, pp. 39 ff.). The vultures are well-known symbols of the Mother Goddess, particularly in Egypt (see below, p. 164). Fish and hare (cf. the mythological section in Layard, *The Lady of the Hare*) are fertility symbols, as is the bird, which should probably be interpreted as a dove in view of the corresponding correlation of the dove with the great Love Goddess of Asia Minor, India, Crete, and Greece.

Star, half-moon, and star-in-crescent are astral symbols referring to the Great Goddess as queen of the sky and particularly of the night *Pl. 54d*
sky, with which the planet Venus and the moon are archetypally correlated both in Europe and America. The connection between the nude goddess and the crescent moon is evident in a seal belonging to this group, where this symbol *Pl. 54g*
appears at either end of the goddess's raised mantle (Porada and Buchanan, fig. 938).

[70] Cf. Layard, *The Lady of the Hare.*
[71] Cf. Atargatis, Derceto, the water sprite, etc. (*Origins*, p. 71). *Pl. 54g*
[72] Briffault, *The Mothers*, Vol. II, pp. 582–92; my "Über den Mond."
[73] Porada and Buchanan, text, p. 124.

141

Archetypal Feminine, of the maternal vulture deity who rules over the area. This would confirm the interpretation of the mysteries of the Cabiri begun by Kerényi;[74] these mysteries would then be offshoots of much older matriarchal mysteries of the Great Mother, reinterpreted in patriarchal terms.

It is interesting to note that the nude goddess is accompanied by *Pl. 54g* two clothed little girls,[75] while in another instance a little nude daughter

FIG. *26*. DAUGHTER ON MOTHER'S HEAD

Marble statuette, Aegean Islands, c. XVI *century* B.C.

Pl. 54f goddess stands before the clothed mother goddess. Both examples point to the continuity of the religious relationship, a connection between mother and daughter goddess. Such a connection is evident both here *Pl. 146a, b* and in Crete, where many seals show "handmaidens," or more probably daughters, standing beside the Goddess. This relationship assumed its most significant form in the Demeter-Kore mysteries of Eleusis.[76] The *Fig. 26* Aegean figure [77] showing the mother-daughter genealogy as a female family tree, with the daughter standing on the mother's head, also belongs to this context.

[74] "The Mysteries of the Kabeiroi."
[75] Porada and Buchanan, fig. 937.
[76] See below, pp. 305 ff.
[77] Hoernes, p. 60.

As we may readily understand, the conceiving female often appears as a receiving vessel; the representations of the woman with snake almost always refer to this relation of the female to the procreative male.[78] Among the best-known representations of woman with snake are those found in Crete. Here the Feminine may take the form of a vessel or of a   *Fig. 27*

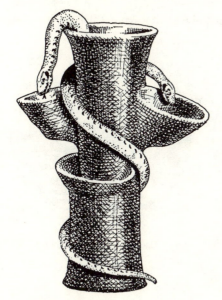

FIG. *27*. SNAKE VESSEL

Clay, Crete, late Minoan II *period*

corresponding female symbol—cist, bowl, and so on—or else it may   *Pl. 55b* appear in human form as goddess or priestess, bearing the snake in her arms or twined round her body. In either case, the snake treats the Feminine with familiarity.[79]

The relation between vessel and snake plays an important role in

[78] The snake as male belongs to the character of the Archetypal Masculine and therefore cannot be treated in this work; but it should be mentioned that the role of the semi-snakelike male divine figure as fecundating lower chthonic power is not limited to the Greek giants, or to the polyform Nereus or Python. Perhaps its oldest representation is to be found on the cylindrical seals of the Akkadian period (Porada and Buchanan, figs. 216–19), where it appears with the goddess of vegetation beneath the crescent moon and also in other symbolic groupings. Also cf. below, pp. 170, 180, 259.

[79] The connection of the Goddess with the snake extends from Crete through Eleusis and Demeter to Athene, whose descent from the pre-Hellenic Cretan pantheon is confirmed by the snake that accompanies her.

Fig. 28
Pl. 57

Pls. 58–61

Fig. 29

the Eleusinian mysteries; it is also illustrated by a Spartan coin and by a late representation of an alchemistic retort, whose feminine vessel character is evident, and which is entwined in a glass snake. The connection between goddess and snake appears in Greek and Roman representations, and also in the Egyptianizing representations of Atargatis and the coin showing Isis.

The snake is so universal and polyvalent a symbol that in this work

FIG. *28*. SNAKE-ENTWINED AMPHORAS

Coin, Sparta

FIG. *29*. ISIS WITH SNAKES

Coin, Egypt, i century B.C.

we cannot go into all its areas of meaning.[80] In line with its uroboric hybrid nature, the snake symbol may also appear as feminine. Because the feminine vessel is creative, the womb is the sacred precinct, the truly numinous feature in body symbolism, and like everything that is numinous it is ambivalent and ambiguous. The snake is associated with it in a subordinate role. Like the male and phallic element, it appears as a part of the Feminine or as its companion. Thus the snake in Crete and India is an attribute of the female deity, and is at the same time her male-phallic companion.

The sexual character of the snake becomes distinct only when the

[80] Cf. Jung, *Symbols of Transformation*, index, s.v. "snake."

uroboric phase is surpassed and the principle of opposites—of snake and vessel, for example—has crystallized out.

For our purposes it suffices to point out the relation of the male fecundation symbolism to the vessel, a relation that may be followed through many symbolic spheres. As lower earth serpent of fertility, the snake is part of the Earth Goddess and as underground water it fecundates her womb; or else it may represent the upper and celestial water, the *nous*-spirit serpent that enters into the feminine soul and guides it (in the manner of the Holy Spirit, for example), or else fecundates it by seduction.

The ambiguous, that is, life-giving and death-dealing, fascination of the belly of the Great Goddess was still alive a thousand years later in a picture where the nude Venus, within a *mandorla* symbolizing the female genitals, appears to a group of men of different periods who were known as great lovers. Pl. 62

The change of the times is evident in the Renaissance picture of Venus. With the development of the patriarchate the Great Goddess has become the Goddess of Love, and the power of the Feminine has been reduced to the power of sexuality. For the men are fascinated by the gleaming belly of the Goddess, whose supernal radiance is visible but ineffectual.[81]

The ambivalence of the whole, which stands symbolically for the Feminine that has now grown ambivalent, is made evident by the strange genii that accompany the Goddess. These winged creatures, late forms of the bird-shaped souls over which the Goddess rules, are Cupids, but they have ugly birds' claws. These feet which were formerly a natural part of the bird's body now produce the effect of an archaic vestige, whose significance is evil. Birds' menacing claws are among the rending attributes of the Archetypal Feminine as siren and harpy;[82] here, as is frequently the case, they have been transferred to the male companion figures.

The birdlike character of woman points primarily to her correlation

[81] Cf. our final chapter.
[82] This feature also goes farther back; its earliest known representation is probably to be found in a winged goddess of the Isin-Larsa period in Mesopotamia.

with the heavens. But this archetypal symbol possesses a positive life-giving and a negative death-dealing aspect. The Egyptian Mother Goddess as vulture gives protection and shelter, but she is at the same time the death-bringing, corpse-devouring goddess of death. Likewise the harpies and sirens have both a positive and a negative significance. In the Renaissance picture, however, the genii bearing weapons and birds' claws are symbols of the voracious impulses revolving around the Golden Aphrodite, who enchants and ruins the men ensnared in her earthly paradise.

Pl. 126   A middle link between the Mesopotamian goddess and the Renaissance Venus, whose negative components have been differentiated, *Pl. 63* is to be found in a Hellenistic relief representing a siren with wings and a bird's claws. This nude female creature appears as an incubus riding on a likewise nude and evidently dreaming man; she belongs, as the Dionysian symbols of the relief show, to the domain of the mysteries. She is an enchanting, seducing, orgiastic, and nightmarish form of the Feminine,[83] whose ambivalent character for man's ego begins where the excessive power and fascination of the numinous becomes a disintegrator of consciousness, and hence is experienced as negative and destructive.

Pl. 64   At first sight, the representation of the fertility goddess of Bali, with its emphasis on the pregnant belly and taut phallic breasts, seems to belong to the group of goddesses representing the positive side of the Feminine. But the expression of the face and particularly of the mouth indubitably has something demonically negative, something lustfully *Pl. 50* cruel, about it. Like the Mexican goddess of childbearing and the *Pl. 70* Gorgon, she is a Terrible Goddess, manifesting the negative elementary character of the Feminine.

[83] Hoernes, p. 60. The Mesopotamian goddess, a Lilith, is of the same negative character.

Chapter Eleven

THE NEGATIVE ELEMENTARY
CHARACTER

BODY-VESSEL and mother-child situation—the positive elementary character of the Feminine—spring from the most intimate personal experience, from an experience that is eternally human; and even when it is projected into the ends of heaven and earth, it preserves its closeness to the central personal phenomenon of feminine life.

The negative elementary character, however, appears in a projective ring of symbols, which do not, like those of the positive elementary character, spring from the visible mother-child relationship. The negative side of the elementary character originates rather in inner experience, and the anguish, horror, and fear of danger that the Archetypal Feminine signifies cannot be derived from any actual and evident attributes of woman. But since we find these negative psychic reactions so often related to the Terrible Mother, we must ask, What is the basis of this primordial human fear and how is it to be interpreted?

We have repeatedly called attention [1] to the basic psychic fact that the human consciousness is experienced as "masculine," and that the masculine has identified itself with consciousness and its growth wherever a patriarchal world has developed.

[1] My *Origins and History of Consciousness*, p. 42.

147

On the other hand, as we have shown, the unconscious, i.e., the psychic stratum from which consciousness arises in the course of human history—and in the course of individual development—is experienced in relation to this consciousness as maternal and feminine. This does not mean that all unconscious contents appear symbolically as feminine. The unconscious contains masculine as well as feminine forces, tendencies, complexes, instincts, and archetypes, just as mythology has male and female gods, demons, spirits, animals, and so on. But in general consciousness sees the unconscious symbolized as feminine and itself as masculine.

The phases in the development of consciousness appear then as embryonic containment in the mother, as childlike dependence on the mother, as the relation of the beloved son to the Great Mother, and finally as the heroic struggle of the male hero against the Great Mother. In other words, the dialectical relation of consciousness to the unconscious takes the symbolic, mythological form of a struggle between the Maternal-Feminine and the male child, and here the growing strength of the male corresponds to the increasing power of consciousness in human development.

Since the liberation of the male consciousness from the feminine-maternal unconscious is a hard and painful struggle for all mankind, it is clear that the negative elementary character of the Feminine does not spring from an anxiety complex of the "men," but expresses an archetypal experience of the whole species, male and female alike. For in so far as the woman participates in this development of consciousness, she too has a symbolically male consciousness and may experience the unconscious as "negatively feminine."

The symbolism of the Terrible Mother draws its images predominantly from the "inside"; that is to say, the negative elementary character of the Feminine expresses itself in fantastic and chimerical images that do not originate in the outside world. The reason for this is that the Terrible Female is a symbol for the unconscious. And the dark side of the Terrible Mother takes the form of monsters, whether in Egypt or India, Mexico or Etruria, Bali or Rome. In the myths and tales of all peoples, ages, and countries—and even in the nightmares of our own nights—witches and vampires, ghouls and specters, assail us, all terrifyingly alike. The dark half of the black-and-white cosmic egg representing the Archetypal Feminine engenders terrible figures that manifest the black, abysmal side of life and the human psyche. Just as world, life, nature, and soul have been experienced as a generative and nourishing, protecting and warming Femininity, so their opposites are also perceived in the image of the Feminine; death and destruction,

FIG. *30.* MAW OF THE EARTH

Aztec, from a codex

danger and distress, hunger and nakedness, appear as helplessness in the presence of the Dark and Terrible Mother.

Thus the womb of the earth becomes the deadly devouring maw *Fig. 30* of the underworld, and beside the fecundated womb and the protecting cave of earth and mountain gapes the abyss of hell, the dark hole of the depths, the devouring womb of the grave and of death, of darkness without light, of nothingness. For this woman who generates life and all living things on earth is the same who takes them back into herself, who pursues her victims and captures them with snare and net. Disease, hunger, hardship, war above all, are her helpers, and among all peoples the goddesses of war and the hunt express man's experience of life as a female exacting blood. This Terrible Mother is the hungry earth, which devours its own children and fattens on their corpses; it is the tiger and *Fig. 31* the vulture, the vulture and the coffin, the flesh-eating sarcophagus voraciously licking up the blood seed of men and beasts and, once fecundated and sated, casting it out again in new birth, hurling it to death, and over and over again to death.[2]

It is in India that the experience of the Terrible Mother has been given its most grandiose form as Kali, "dark, all-devouring time, the bone-wreathed Lady of the place of skulls."[3]

In the very earliest Indian culture, that is, in the temple sites of the

FIG. *31*. ENTRANCE TO THE "TIGER CAVE"

Udayagiri Hill, India

Fig. 32 Zhob River Valley, of northern Baluchistan, we find figures of the Terrible Mother. Concerning them Stuart Piggott writes: ". . . hooded with a coif or shawl, they have high, smooth foreheads above their staring circular eye holes, their owl-beak nose and grim slit mouth. The result is terrifying, even in a tiny model not more than two inches high, and in two from Dabar Kot all pretense is thrown aside and the face is a grinning skull. Whatever may be said of the Kulli figurines, these can hardly be toys, but seem rather to be a grim embodiment of the mother

[2] Concerning the ambivalent character of the Mother Goddess, the relation between fertility rites and blood sacrifice, and the Terrible Mother in Egypt, Canaan, Crete, and Greece, cf. my *Origins:* "The Great Mother."

[3] Zimmer, "The Indian World Mother," p. 81.

goddess who is also the guardian of the dead—an underworld deity concerned alike with the corpse and the seed corn buried beneath the earth." [4]

In this goddess of the dead we have one of the earliest forms of the Goddess who, in India today, as Zimmer tells us, "is worshiped as Durga, the 'Unapproachable' and 'Perilous,' or as Parvati, 'daughter of

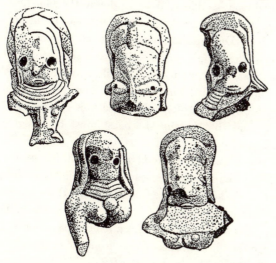

FIG. *32.* FIGURINES OF THE MOTHER GODDESS

Clay, India, c. 3000 B.C.

the mountain,' i.e., of the Himalayas. Her great temple festival in the spring—for the refecundation of nature—is attended by pilgrims from the surrounding plain and from the mountains that enclose it. An Englishman who attended the festival in 1871 reports that each day twenty buffaloes, two hundred and fifty goats, and the same number of pigs were slaughtered in the temple. Under the sacrificial altar there was a deep pit, filled with fresh sand that sucked up the blood of the beheaded beasts; the sand was renewed twice a day, and when drenched with blood it was buried in the earth to create fertility. Everything was

[4] Piggott, *Prehistoric India*, pp. 126-27.

very neat and orderly; there were no bloody remains or evil smell. In preparation for the new agricultural year, the life sap, the blood, was intended to give renewed strength and fertility to the nature goddess, the bestower of all nourishment, the daughter of the mountain, whose gigantic generative strength is embodied in the towering mountains.

"Today the temple of Kali at the Kalighat in Calcutta is famous for its daily blood sacrifices; it is no doubt the bloodiest temple on earth. At the time of the great autumn pilgrimages to the annual festival of Durga or Kali (Durgapuja), some eight hundred goats are slaughtered in three days. The temple serves simply as a slaughterhouse, for those performing the sacrifice retain their animals, leaving only the head in the temple as a symbolic gift, while the blood flows to the Goddess. For to the Goddess is due the life blood of all creatures—since it is she who has bestowed it—and that is why the beast must be slaughtered in her temple; that is why temple and slaughterhouse are one.

"This rite is performed amid gruesome filth; in the mud compounded of blood and earth, the heads of the animals are heaped up like trophies before the statue of the Goddess, while those sacrificing return home for a family banquet of the bodies of their animals. The Goddess desires only the blood of the offerings, hence beheading is the form of sacrifice, since the blood drains quickly from the beheaded beasts. That is why the figures in the tales of the *Hitopadeśa* and *Kathasaritsagara* cut off their heads, though it is also true that the head signifies the whole, the total sacrifice.

Pl. 65   "In her 'hideous aspect' (*ghora-rupa*) the Goddess, as Kali, the 'dark one,' raises the skull full of seething blood to her lips; her devotional image shows her dressed in blood red, standing in a boat floating on a sea of blood: in the midst of the life flood, the sacrificial sap, which she requires that she may, in her gracious manifestation (*sundara-murti*) as the World Mother (*jagad-amba*), bestow existence upon new living forms in a process of unceasing generation, that as world nurse (*jagad-dhatri*) she may suckle them on her breasts and give them the good that is 'full of nourishment' (*anna-purna*)." [5]

[5] Zimmer, "The Indian World Mother," p. 74.

The most terrible of the three images of Kali is not the one with the
inhuman many arms, hideously squatting amid a halo of flames, de-   *Pl. 66*
vouring the entrails that form a deathly umbilical cord between the
corpse's open belly and her own gullet. Nor is it the one that, clad in the
nocturnal black of the earth goddesses and adorned with the hacked-off
hands and heads of her victims, stands on the corpse of Shiva—a barbaric
specter whose exaggeration of horror makes her almost unreal. The
third figure seems far more frightful because it is quieter and less bar-   *Pl. 67*
barous. Here the hands strike us as human. One is extended, the other
strokes the heads of the cobras almost as tenderly as Isis caressing the
head of her child; and though the phallic animal breasts are repellent,
they recall the similar breasts of the African mother goddess. But with
its hooded head, the cobra that is twined round her waist like a girdle
suggests the womb—here in its deadly aspect. This is the snake that
lies coiled in the lap of the Cretan snake goddess, forms the snake robe   *Pl. 56*
of the Mexican goddess Coatlicue, and girds the loins of the Greek   *Pls. 69–70*
Gorgons. And the hideous bloody tiger's tongue of the goddess is the
same as hangs down flame-spewing between the tusks and bestial
striped breasts of the Rangda witch, or darts from between the gnashing   *Pl. 71*
fangs of the Gorgons.

These figures are gruesomely alike. Their sheer frightfulness makes
us hesitate, whether they represent a skull, the head of a snake or hippopotamus, a face showing human likeness, or a head consisting of two
stone knives borne by a body pieced together from parts of snakes,   *Fig. 33*
panthers, lions, crocodiles, and human beings. So great is the inhuman,   *Fig. 34*
extrahuman, and superhuman quality in this experience of dread that
man can visualize it only through phantoms.

But all this—and it should not be forgotten—is an image not only
of the Feminine but particularly and specifically of the Maternal. For in
a profound way life and birth are always bound up with death and
destruction. That is why this Terrible Mother is "Great," and this name
is also given to Ta-urt, the gravid monster, which is hippopotamus and   *Fig. 34; Pl. 72*
crocodile, lioness and woman, in one. She too is deadly and protective.
There is a frightening likeness to Hathor, the good cow goddess, who in   *Fig. 34*

FIG. *33*. THE SOUTHERLY CIRCLE OF HELL

Aztec, page from a codex

the form of a hippopotamus is the goddess of the underworld. She has a positive aspect, and at the same time she is the goddess of war and death. The cow goddess with her, who raises her head out of the burial mountain, at the foot of which is the grave, is Mehurt,[6] the goddess of

[6] Cf. below, p. 213.

154

the beginning. Both bear the same cow's horns, as does Isis pressing the head of Horus to her breast. *Pl. 44*

In the course of the later development of patriarchal values, i.e., of the male deities of the sun and the light, the negative aspect of the

FIG. 34. TA-URT AND HATHOR

From the Papyrus of Ani, Egypt, xvi–xiv *century* b.c.

Feminine was submerged. Today it is discernible only as a content of the primordial age, or of the unconscious. Thus the terrible Ta-urt, as well as the terrible Hathor, Isis, Neith, and others, can be reconstituted from their pictures that have been "painted over," but cannot be viewed directly. Only the monster Am-mit or Amam, which devours the souls *Fig. 35* condemned at the judgment of the dead, points by its parallelism to the terrible aspect of Ta-urt. Am-mit was described as follows: "Her fore-

155

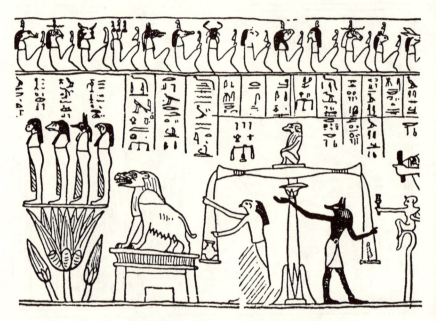

part (is that of) crocodiles, her hinderpart (is that of) hippopotamus, and her middle (is that of a) lion." ⁷ The feminine, animal-mother character of this many-breasted creature is evident as is that of the monster *Fig. 36* wielding the terrible knife, which guards one of the underworld gates through which the souls of the departed must pass.

FIG. *35.* AM-MIT AT THE JUDGMENT OF THE DEAD

From a papyrus, Egypt

Am-mit devours the souls that have not withstood the midnight judgment of the dead in the underworld. But her role has become subordinate, for the religion of Osiris and Horus with its mysteries has now promised rebirth and resurrection to all human souls, and not only,

⁷ As "Api, the Lady who giveth protection in the form of a hippopotamus" (The Book of the Dead [tr. Budge], p. 421), she is the Positive Mother, whose matriarchal form was often represented as a hippopotamus in ancient Egypt. Later, the patriarchal victory of the king was therefore solemnized with the ritual slaughtering of a hippopotamus.

as originally, to the soul of Pharaoh. The certainty of magical success in following the path of the sun, which is communicated to each man after death by the priests, has overlaid the primordial fear represented by Am-mit. But originally she was the terrible ancestral spirit of the matriarchal culture, in which the Feminine takes back what has been born

FIG. *36.* MONSTER GUARDING THE UNDERWORLD GATES

From the Papyrus of Nu, Egypt

of it—just as among the primitive inhabitants of the Melanesian island of Malekula or in the high culture of Mexico.

The underworld, the earth womb, as the perilous land of the dead through which the deceased must pass, either to be judged there and to arrive at a chthonic realm of salvation or doom, or to pass through this territory to a new and higher existence, is one of the archetypal symbols of the Terrible Mother. It is experienced in the archetypal nocturnal sea voyage of the sun or the hero, which the soul of the departed must withstand.

We shall give only the fundamental traits of this frequently analyzed archetype.[8] The sun sinks down in the west, where it dies and enters into the womb of the underworld that devours it. For this reason the west is the place of death, and the hostile and rending "Old Woman in the West" is an image of the Terrible Mother.[9]

Along with the cave and the body-vessel, the gate as entrance and womb is a primordial symbol of the Great Mother. The two pillars of the dolmen, covered with the transverse stone, are one of the earliest representations of the threefold Feminine, to which a fourth part is often added in the lone phallic pillar of the Masculine. The story of this *Pl. 73a, b* megalithic triality as gate-womb, entrance to the underworld, and as sacrificial altar has been described in detail in G. Rachel Levy's book.[10]

In the earliest cults of Mesopotamia we find the winged gate worshiped in connection with the kneeling bull, the goddess with the vessel, and the moon. What this symbol means is unknown. The bull in relation to the fence of the cowpen suggests a fertility ritual. The sacred gate of the Goddess appears as the gate to the enclosure, in which the *Pl. 73c* calves are born and raised. Above the gate stands the pillar of the Great Mother, the emblem of the Great Mother-Cow.[11]

Just as the temple is a late development of the cave, and hence a symbol of the Great Goddess as house and shelter,[12] so the temple gate is the entrance into the goddess; it is her womb, and the innumerable entrance and threshold rites of mankind are an expression of this numinous feminine place. The enclosure, the gate, and the pillars of the temple are symbols of the Great Mother: "The reed bundle and therefore the looped post, both fashioned for the insertion of a closing or *Pl. 124* binding feature to guard the tamed beasts, is the certain symbol of the *Pl. 74* Mother Goddess as the gate of a sanctuary which is in itself (to judge by the hut amulets) conceived as her body ('He the Lamb and I the fold'), an idea already perhaps formed in the mind of paleolithic man." [13]

---

[8] Jung, *Symbols of Transformation*, index, s.v. "night sea journey."
[9] My *Origins*, index, s.v. "Terrible Mother."
[10] *The Gate of Horn*, p. 126.
[11] Ibid., Pl. 10b.

[12] Ibid., pp. 83 f.
[13] Ibid., p. 100, with a reference to enclosures, possibly of sacral significance, on paleolithic wall drawings from La Pasiega, Spain.

The feminine principle of the dolmen and gate is always connected with rebirth through the woman's womb. This is evident from the folklore of the countries where such dolmens occur and where the sick are drawn through them even today, and from still existing Stone Age cultures as well.[14] Consequently the name for the dolmen in Malekula is connected with the root "to come out from, to be born." [15]

The dolmen is also a sacral house; by extension it becomes the temple and the "sacred precinct" in general. The earliest sacred precinct of the primordial age was probably that in which the woman gave birth. It is the place where the Great Goddess rules and from which—as still in the late feminine mysteries—all males are excluded. Not only is the place of childbearing the sacral place of female life in early and primitive cultures; obviously it also stands at the center of all cults that are dedicated to the Great Goddess as the goddess of birth, fertility—and death. In Malekula, for example, the name "birth enclosure" is given both to the fence within which the women give birth and to the one surrounding the site where the male mysteries of rebirth are solemnized.

Thus the primitive fence [16] enclosing the female place of childbearing became a sign for the sacred precinct in general, and the process of birth becomes a prototype for the process of rebirth, of "higher" birth into the heavens as a star or immortal. And the symbolism of rebirth always goes back to the symbolism of birth. Thus it is possible that the "winged gate" of Sumer already meant a rebirth into heaven, which is always symbolically related to the "winged."

When in the mysteries of late antiquity the candidate for initiation must take a dangerous journey through the underworld in order to achieve rebirth, he follows the path of the sun. Thus in Apuleius,[17] the initiate into the mysteries of Isis must pass through the twelve hours of the night, corresponding to the Egyptian conception of the underworld

[14] Layard, *Stone Men of Malekula*, pp. 17, 367, 705.

[15] Ibid., pp. 73, 389, 423.

[16] When later, and especially in the early matrilinear order, the principle of exogamy led the women to take their men "from outside," the childbearing women were always a cohesive group within the community. This institution gave added meaning to the social bond among the childbearing women, to the exclusion of the men.

[17] *Metamorphoses (The Golden Ass)*.

journey of the sun bark, while Ishtar must pass through seven, or some-times fourteen, gates on her journey to hell.[18]

Similarly, in an early Egyptian text, the "Chapters of the Secret Pylons," the soul must pass through twenty-one gates of the under-world.[19] In contrast to the path of the sun, this points to an older moon symbolism connected with Osiris. The underworld of Osiris consists of seven halls, or *arits*, with seven gates,[20] while in an Ishtar text the number is multiplied but retains a relation to the lunar seven, that is to say, the archetypal relation to the earth and fertility goddess. Wherever the number seven plays a dominant role in the journey to the underworld, it relates to the moon hero. The solar journey of the hero, correlated with the number twelve, and, in general, the patriarchal mythology of the sun with its psychology of the day and of conscious-ness, are later than (the matriarchal) lunar mythology and the related psychology of the night.

The seven dwellings of the underworld are seven aspects of the Feminine, to whose sphere belongs Osiris, the moon, as lord, son, and fecundator of the goddess.[21] For this reason Chapter CXLVII of the Book of the Dead, the chapter of the seven houses, is followed by the chapter of the seven cows and their bull on which fertility depends.[22]

At each of the twenty-one gates in the house of Osiris, the female guardian deity is characterized in detail, while the corresponding male god is only mentioned by name. The characterizations of the goddesses of the twenty-one gates offer a unique description of all the manifesta-tions of the Great Goddess in her predominantly terrible aspect.

> Lady of tremblings, with lofty walls, the sovereign lady, the mistress of destruction, who setteth in order the words which drive back the whirlwind and the storm, who delivereth from destruction him that travelleth along the way.
>
> Lady of heaven, the mistress of the world, who devoureth with fire, the lady of mortals, who knoweth mankind.

[18] Roeder, *Die Religion der Babylonier und Assyrer*, p. 142.
[19] Book of the Dead (tr. Budge), pp. 447 ff.
[20] Ibid., Ch. CXLIV.

[21] Cf. my *Origins*: "Transformation, or Osiris."
[22] The seven lean and the seven fat kine in Pharaoh's dream relate to this symbolism.

Lady of the altar, the lady to whom abundant offerings are made, and in whom every god rejoiceth on the day of sailing up to Abtu (i.e., Abydos).

She who prevaileth with knives, the mistress of the world, destroyer of the foes of the Still-Heart, who maketh the decree for the escape of the needy from evil hap.

Fire, the lady of flames, who inhaleth the supplications which are made to her, who permitteth not the . . . to enter in.

Lady of light, the lady to whom abundant supplication is made; the difference between her height and her breadth is unknown; the like of her hath never been found since the beginning. There is a serpent thereupon whose size is not known; it was born in the presence of the Still-Heart.

Robe which doth clothe the divine feeble one, weeping for what it loveth and shrouding the body.

Blazing fire, the flame whereof [cannot] be quenched, provided with tongues of flame which reach afar, the slaughtering one, the irresistible one through whom a man may not pass by reason of the hurt which she doeth.

She who is in the front, the lady of strength, quiet of heart, who giveth birth to her lord; whose girth is three hundred and fifty measures; who sendeth forth rays like the *uatch* stone of the south; who raiseth up the divine form and clotheth the feeble one; who giveth [offerings] to her lord every day.

Thou who art loud of voice, who raisest up those who cry and who make supplication unto her, whose voice is loud, the terrible one, the lady who is to be feared, who destroyeth not that which is in her.

She who slaughtereth always the burner up of fiends, mistress of the every pylon, the lady to whom acclamation is made on the day of darkness. She hath the judgment of the feeble bandaged one.

Thou who invokest thy two lands, who destroyest those who come with flashings and with fire, the lady of splendor, who hearkeneth unto the speech of her lord.

Osiris bringeth his two hands over her and maketh the god Hapi (i.e., the Nile) to send forth splendor out of his hidden places.

Lady of might, who danceth on the blood-red ones, who keepeth the festival of Haker on the day of the hearing of faults.

The fiend, red of hair and eyes, who cometh forth by night, and doth fetter the fiend in his lair; may her hands be given to the Still-Heart in his hour, and may [she] advance and go forward.

Terrible one, the lady of the rainstorm, who planteth ruin (?) in the souls of men, the devourer of the dead bodies of mankind, the orderer, and producer, and creator of slaughter.

Hewer-in-pieces in blood, Ahabit (?), lady of hair.

Lover of the fire, pure of slaughterings which she loveth, cutter off of heads, venerated one (?), lady of the Great House, destroyer of fiends at eventide.

Dispenser of light during her period of life, watcher of flames, the lady of the strength and of the writing of the god Ptah himself.

She who dwelleth within the cavern of her lord, Clother is her name, she hideth what she hath created, she taketh possession of hearts, she swalloweth (?).

Knife which cutteth, when [its name] is uttered, and slayeth those who advance toward its flames. She hath secret plots and counsels.[23]

As we have seen, the Feminine is the belly-vessel as woman and also as earth. She is the vessel of doom, guiding the nocturnal course of the stars through the underworld; she is the belly of the "whale-dragon," which, as in the story of Jonah,[24] swallows the sun hero every night in the west; she is "the destroyer at eventide."

The Great Mother as Terrible Goddess of the earth and of death is herself the earth, in which things rot. The Earth Goddess is "the devourer of the dead bodies of mankind" and the "mistress and lady of the tomb." [25] Like Gaea, the Greek Earth Mother, she is mistress of the vessel and at the same time the great underworld vessel itself, into which *Pl. 75a* the dead souls enter, and out of which they fly up again. The pithos, the great stone jar, served originally for the burial of the dead and thus had the significance of an underworld vessel.[26] According to Jane Harrison every Greek was familiar with the idea "that the pithos was a grave jar, that from such grave jars souls escaped, etc." [27]

The late Eleusinian mysteries are based on this symbolism, which was enriched by the custom of storing grain in subterranean pithoi.

[23] Book of the Dead (tr. Budge), Ch. CXLVI: "The Chapters of the Secret Pylons." Here we quote from each pylon only the text in which the Goddess is evoked.

[24] Cf. the fine picture from the German *Biblia Pauperum* (1471) in Campbell, *The Hero with a Thousand Faces*, fig. 5, in which the casting of Joseph into the well, the swallowing of Jonah by the whale, and the entombment of Christ are placed side by side.

[25] Book of the Dead (tr. Budge), Ch. CLXIV.

[26] Nilsson, *Geschichte der griechischen Religion*, Vol. I, p. 446.

[27] *Prolegomena to the Study of Greek Religion*, pp. 43 f.

The vernal symbolism of the vegetation rising from the earth jar (cf. Adonis and Osiris) and the symbolism of the taking of the seed grain from the "underworld jar" reinforced each other.

The burial of the dead in a jar is pre-Hellenic and examples of it are found in the Aegean cults of the Bronze Age. It probably came from Asia Minor.[28] But the presence of this custom in ancient America and the fact

Fig. 37

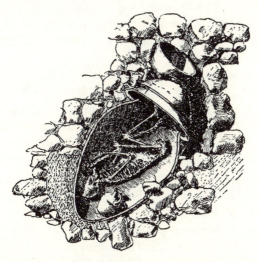

FIG. *37*. CHILD'S SKELETON IN BURIAL URN

Excavated near Nazareth, Palestine

that it is still practiced in South America confirm the view that the jar receiving the dead belongs to the archetypal symbolism of the Feminine.

A form of this jar is the urn in which the dead man is laid as a child in the attitude of an embryo—in Eleusis, for example, and, much earlier, in the Near East; another form is the cinerary urn in which the ashes of buried corpses were kept.

The house urn as a container of ashes occurred in the Bronze Age in Italy [29] and in the north, i.e., in central Germany, Denmark, and south-

[28] Persson, *The Religion of Greece in Prehistoric Times*, pp. 13 ff.; Thomson, *The Prehistoric Aegean*, pp. 249 f.

[29] Cf. van der Leeuw, *Phänomenologie der Religion*, p. 374.

ern Sweden,[30] and also in chalcolithic (Ghassulian) Palestine, whose inhabitants "placed the bones of their deceased in house urns, shaped like the houses of the living. This custom is found also in neolithic Europe." [31] House urns were used also in Crete [32] and in Peru,[33] not, to be sure, for the keeping of ashes, but this by no means precludes a sacral significance.

Pl. 76   A variant of the mortuary jar is the Mexican blood bowl in which the hearts torn out of sacrificial victims were offered up to the sun.[34] It belongs to the Terrible Mother, whose symbol, the land tortoise, is represented on its bottom.

The finest expressions of this relation of the Mother Goddess to the
Pls. 90–91   dead are the Egyptian sarcophagi, on the floors of which a representation of the heaven goddess Nut embraces the dead man. Nut is the goddess of rebirth, but she also has the character of death as Nuit, the black night sky, which is identified with the devouring darkness of
Pl. 91a   the earth and with water.[35] The deathly black garments in this coffin painting with the black Hathor headdress are as striking as the bared breasts, which resemble those of the Indian Kali. She too is the nocturnal West, killing and devouring.

The Terrible Mother is a goddess of death also in her aspect as bird of the dead, vulture and raven. The vulture is the symbol of Nekhbet, one of the oldest mother goddesses of Egypt, who in her good aspect watches over the dead in the underworld, but originally rends bodies in pieces like the corpse-devouring crow, a form of the Celtic enchantress-goddess Morrigan.[36] As Ninck has shown, the Germanic representatives of this feminine stratum of death and doom are the Valkyries, who bring death to heroes.[37] The Valkyrie, says Ninck, "is *waelgrimme* (deadly wrath); and the glosses render the Old English *waelcyrge* (Valkyrie) with the names of ancient demons of war and death (Erinys, Tisiphone, Alecto, Bellona). This wholly corresponds to her dark aspect in the

[30] Hoernes, p. 525; figs., pp. 527, 529.
[31] Albright, *From the Stone Age to Christianity*, p. 102.
[32] Hoernes, p. 525.
[33] Leicht, *Indianische Kunst und Kultur*, fig. 72; Fuhrmann, *Peru*, figs. 2, 3.

[34] See below, p. 186.
[35] Cf. below, pp. 179 ff., and Ch. 12, "The Great Round."
[36] Krause, *Die Kelten*, p. 22.
[37] On the connection of the Archetypal Feminine with "fate," see below, p. 226.

song of the Valkyries and her identification with the raven, the dark bird of the dead, which is called *waelcēasig* (corpse-choosing), a term which exactly accords with *waelcyrge*. In the north we also find the form of a raven in Hliod, Odin's cupbearer in the Volsunga Saga." [38]

But while the Germanic peoples are moved by a strange yearning for death, the Egyptian attitude is the reverse. The Egyptians feared decay more than death; the special striving of their cult of the dead was to preserve, to mummify the corpse, and it is this striving which determined the character of their religious life and their art. Here a chapter from the Book of the Dead gives us a moving insight:

> The Chapter of not letting the body perish. The Osiris Nu, the overseer of the seal, triumphant, saith:—
>
> "Homage to thee, O my divine father Osiris. I came to embalm thee, do thou embalm these my members, for I would not perish and come to an end, [but would be] even like unto my divine father Khepera, the divine type of him that never saw corruption. Come, then, make strong my breath, then, O lord of the winds, who dost magnify those divine beings who are like unto himseh. Stablish me, doubly, then, and fashion me strongly, lord of the funeral chest. Grant thou that I may enter into the land of everlastingness, according to that which was done for thee along with thy father Tem, whose body never saw corruption, and who is the being who never saw corruption. I have never done that which thou hatest, nay, I have cried out among those who love thy *Ka*. Let not my body become worms, but deliver me as thou didst thyself. I pray thee, let me not fall into rottenness even as thou dost permit every god, and every goddess, and every animal, and every reptile to see corruption when the soul hath gone forth from them after their death. And when the soul departeth (or perisheth), a man seeth corruption and the bones of his body rot and become wholly stinkingness, the members decay piecemeal, the bones crumble into a helpless mass, and the flesh becometh foetid liquid, and he becometh a brother unto the decay which cometh upon him, and he turneth into multitudes of worms, and he becometh altogether worms and an end is made of him, and he perisheth in the sight of the god Shu even as doth every god, and every goddess and every feathered fowl, and every fish . . . and every thing whatsoever. . . . Let life [come] from its death [39] and let not decay caused by any reptile make an end [of me], and let them not come against me in their [various] forms. Do not thou give

---

[3] Ninck, *Wodan und germanischer Schicksalsglaube*, pp. 183 f.   [39] I.e., the death of the body.

me over unto that slaughterer who dwelleth in his torture chamber (?), who killeth the members and maketh them rot being [himself] hidden—who worketh destruction upon many dead bodies and liveth by slaughter. Let me live and perform his message, and let me do that which is commanded by him. Give me not over unto his fingers, let him not gain the mastery over me, for I am under thy command, O lord of the gods.

"Homage to thee, O my divine father Osiris, thou hast thy being with thy members. Thou didst not decay, thou didst not become worms, thou didst not diminish, thou didst not become corruption, thou didst not putrefy, and thou didst not turn into worms, I am the god Khepera, and my members shall have an everlasting existence. I shall not decay, and I shall not rot, I shall not putrefy, I shall not turn into worms, and I shall not see corruption before the eye of the god Shu. I shall have my being, I shall have my being; I shall live, I shall live; I shall germinate, I shall germinate, I shall germinate; I shall wake up in peace; I shall not putrefy, my intestines (?) shall not perish; I shall not suffer injury; mine eye shall not decay; the form of my visage (?) shall not disappear; mine ear shall not become deaf; my head shall not be separated from my neck; my tongue shall not be carried away; my hair shall not be cut off; mine eyebrows shall not be shaved off; and no baleful injury shall come upon me. My body shall be stablished, and it shall neither fall into ruin nor be destroyed on this earth." [40]

The figure of the Terrible Mother dominates the pre-Hellenic as well as the early Greek worlds with the same archetypal symbolism.

The petrifying gaze of Medusa belongs to the province of the Terrible Great Goddess, for to be rigid is to be dead. This effect of the terrible stands in opposition to the mobility of the life stream that flows in all organic life; it is a psychic expression for petrifaction and *Pls. 70, 80* sclerosis. The Gorgon is the counterpart of the life womb; she is the womb of death or the night sun.

Pls. 68, 77 The skull is a symbol not only of death but also of the dead sun, which during its life was endowed with the hair rays of power; while when the hero, the night sun, is swallowed up in the belly of the whale, his "hair falls out." The relation between death, bald head, sacrifice, and castration is characteristic for the initiates of the Great Mother,

[40] Book of the Dead (tr. Budge), Ch. CLIV.

166

FIG. *38.* ILAMATECUHTLI, GODDESS OF DEATH

Aztec, from a codex

from the shaven priests of Isis down to the tonsured Catholic monks.[41] The snake hair of the Terrible Goddess corresponds on the other hand to a "negative radiation."

The positive femininity of the womb appears as a mouth; that is why "lips" are attributed to the female genitals, and on the basis of this positive symbolic equation the mouth, as "upper womb," is the birthplace of the breath and the word, the Logos. Similarly, the destructive side of the Feminine, the destructive and deathly womb, appears most frequently in the archetypal form of a mouth bristling with teeth. We

Pl. 78 find this symbolism in an African statuette, where the tooth-studded womb is replaced by a gnashing mask, and in an Aztec likeness of the

Fig. 38 death goddess, furnished with a variety of knives and sharp teeth.[42] This motif of the *vagina dentata* is most distinct in the mythology of the North American Indians. In the mythology of other Indian tribes a meat-eating fish inhabits the vagina of the Terrible Mother;[43] the hero is the man who overcomes the Terrible Mother,[44] breaks the teeth out of her vagina, and so makes her into a woman.[45]

In Egypt too, the correlation of the Feminine with the lips and of the Masculine with the teeth is demonstrable.[46] The negative Masculine as an attribute of the Feminine often takes the form of a destructive

Pl. 75b male companion, a wild boar, for example. And boar's tusks [47] or other animal fangs often appear beside the teeth of the Terrible Female. Like so many alluring and death-dealing female figures, Scylla, the devouring

Fig. 39 whirlpool, has the upper parts of a beautiful woman, while her lower parts consist of three hellhounds.[48] We know the phallic significance of the lone tooth of the Graeae [49]—those female figures whose names are

---

[41] My *Origins*, pp. 59, 159.

[42] See below, 190 f. This archetypal symbol also occurs in the modern world, when the Terrible Mother appears as a castrator, as a womb armed with teeth, in dreams and fantasies. Here too the teeth symbolize the masculine quality of the knife and of the destructive male, which are a part of the negative female.

[43] *Standard Dictionary of Folklore*, s.v. "vagina dentata."

[44] My *Origins*, "The Slaying of the Mother," pp. 159 f.

[45] *Standard Dictionary*, loc. cit.

[46] Kees, *Der Götterglaube im alten Aegypten*, p. 292.

[47] See also, on the cult of the boar's tusks in Malekula, Layard, *Stone Men*.

[48] In contrast to the positive and protecting *Stella Maris* figures of Isis, the Madonna, and Tara, she wields in her hands the helms of wrecked ships.

[49] Jung, *Symbols of Transformation*, index, s.v. "Graeae."

Fear, Dread, and Terror, and who live at the borders of night and death, in the distant west, on the ocean shore.[50] Their sisters are the Gorgons, the daughters of Phorcys, "the Gray," a child of Pontus, the "primordial deep." From all of them terrible mythical monsters are descended. The winged Gorgons with snakes for hair and girdle, with their boar's tusks, beards, and outthrust tongues, are uroboric symbols of the primordial power of the Archetypal Feminine, images of the great pre-Hellenic

FIG. *39*. SCYLLA

Engraved gem, Rome

FIG. *40*. HECATE

Engraved gem, Rome

Mother Goddess in her devouring aspect as earth, night, and under- *Fig. 40* world.[51]

With her outspread legs, the Gorgon throttling an animal takes the *Pl. 80* same posture as the exhibitionistic goddesses. Here to be sure the genitals are clothed and invisible, but they are represented by the terrible face with its gnashing teeth. The uroboric male-female accent of the Gorgon is evident not only from the glaring tusks of her womb-gullet but also from her outstretched tongue, which—in contrast to the feminine lips—always possesses a phallic character. We find this archetypal trait in any number of representations of monsters throughout

[50] My *Origins*, p. 214.
[51] On the Gorgon as night sun, cf. Kaiser Wilhelm II, *Studien zur Gorgo*.

the world.[52] The relationship is fully evident in Oceania. In New Zealand the outstretched tongue is a sign of power, of dynamic energy; [53] and in Lifu, one of the Loyalty Islands, the sexual organ is known as " 'his word,' an expression that gives to this term its complete meaning as the originating force of all action and also of words." [54]

Thus the terrible aspect of the Feminine always includes the uroboric snake woman, the woman with the phallus, the unity of child-bearing and begetting, of life and death. The Gorgon is endowed with every male attribute: the snake, the tooth, the boar's tusks, the out-thrust tongue, and sometimes even with a beard.

Fig. 40

In Greece the Gorgon as Artemis-Hecate is also the mistress of the night road, of fate, and of the world of the dead. As Enodia she is the guardian of crossroads and gates,[55] and as Hecate she is the snake-en-twined moon goddess of ghosts and the dead, surrounded, like Artemis, the wild goddess of the hunt, by a swarm of female demons. Her principal animal is the dog, the howler by night, the finder of tracks, which in Egypt, as in Greece or Mexico, is the companion of the dead. As mistress of the way down and of the lower way, she has for symbol the key, the phallic opening power of the male, the emblem of the Goddess, who is mistress of birth and conception.

Pl. 79

Figs. 30–31

Pl. 81

Thus, when she is angry, the Goddess, as Demeter or Ishtar, as Hathor or Hecate, can close the wombs of living creatures, and all life stands still. As Good Mother, she is mistress of the East Gate, the gate of birth; as Terrible Mother, she is mistress of the West Gate, the gate of death, the engulfing entrance to the underworld. Gate, door, gully, ravine, abyss are the symbols of the feminine earth-womb; they are the numinous places that mark the road into the mythical darkness of the underworld.[56] In its negative aspect the cave, one of the earliest ex-amples of feminine vessel symbolism, is hell and Hel, the Germanic god-dess of the underworld. Characteristically, Hel is the sister of the uroboric Midgard serpent of the ocean that girds the earth, and also of

---

[52] Kohlbrugge, *Tier- und Menschenantlitz als Abwehrzauber.*
[53] Leenhardt, *Arts of the Oceanic Peoples,* pp. 115 f.
[54] Ibid., p. 142.
[55] Nilsson, *Geschichte,* p. 685.
[56] Cf. especially the wealth of material in G. R. Levy, *The Gate of Horn.*

the devouring Fenris-wolf; [57] she is the gaping abyss that untiringly swallows up mortal men.

In Christian myth the Devil is correlated with hell as the devouring maw of the earth; among the Aztecs he has his correspondence in Xiuhtecuhtli, the lord of fire, sitting at the center of the earth. In appearance the Christian Devil has much of the pagan Pan and satyrs about him; his early precursor is the Egyptian Set, enemy of the soul, adversary of Osiris and Horus. In the Book of the Dead, he appears in conjunction with the serpent Apopis as the masculine destroying aspect of the underworld. He is the slaughterer, the destroyer, the render in pieces, partner of the soul-devouring Am-mit. He is called "The fiend, red of hair and eyes, who cometh forth by night, and doth fetter the fiend in his lair." [58] He is the evil one, the adversary, associated with red, which is not only the positive color of fertility but also the color of calamity, evil, blood, death, and the desert, where, thousands of years later, the Devil appeared to tempt the elect.

Hell and the underworld as vessels of death are forms of the negative death-bringing belly-vessel, corresponding exactly to its life-bringing side. The opening of the vessel of doom is the womb, the gate, the gullet, which actively swallows, devours, rends, and kills. Its sucking power is mythologically symbolized by its lure and attraction for man, for life and consciousness and the individual male, who can evade it only if he is a hero, and even then not always.

This is very aptly expressed in Germanic myth and its etymological correspondences. Old Norse *gīna*, 'yawn,' Old High German *ginēn* and *geinōn*, are related to ON. *gin*, 'gullet,' 'cleft'; Old English *giwian*, 'demand'; ON. *gjā*, 'cleft' and 'voluptuous life'; OE. *gipian*, 'to yap,' and *gīpen*, 'to gasp for air, to strive for something.' [59]

The yawning, avid character of the gullet and the cleft represents in mythological apperception the unity of the Feminine, which as avid womb attracts the male and kills the phallus within itself in order to achieve satisfaction and fecundation, and which as the earth-womb of

---

[57] Ninck, *Götter- und Jenseitsglaube der Germanen*, p. 135.

[58] Book of the Dead (tr. Budge), Ch. CXLVI.

[59] Ninck, *Wodan*, pp. 55 f.

the Great Goddess, as womb of death, attracts and draws in all living things, likewise for its own satisfaction and fecundation.

Here the profoundest experience of life combines with human anxiety to form an archetypal unity. A male immature in his development, who experiences himself only as male and phallic,[60] perceives the feminine as a castrator, a murderer of the phallus. The projection of his own masculine desire and, on a still deeper level, of his own trend toward uroboric incest, toward voluptuous self-dissolution in the primordial Feminine and Motherly, intensifies the terrible character of the Feminine. Thus the Terrible Goddess rules over desire and over the seduction that leads to sin and destruction; love and death are aspects of one and the same Goddess. In Egypt as in Greece, in Mesopotamia as in Mexico, the goddesses of love, the hunt, and death are grouped together.[61] In Sparta and Cyprus, Aphrodite is also a goddess of war [62] and Pandora is the fascinating yet deathly vessel of the Feminine.

Even today sexual symbolism is still colored by alimentary symbolism. In the fertility ritual sexuality and nourishment are related; the sexual act, which induces fertility, guarantees the fertility of the earth and hence man's nourishment, and linguistically the two spheres are also connected. Hunger and satiety, desire and satisfaction, thirst and its slaking, are symbolic concepts that are equally valid for both of them.

Similarly magic,[63] which was originally governed by the Feminine, began no doubt as "food magic" and developed by way of fertility magic into sexual or "love magic."

Here again etymological relations indicate an archetypal unity. Ninck continues his development of the stem *gīna:* ON. *geifla,* 'to murmur'; OE. *gifre,* 'lustful'; and finally ON. *ginna,* 'to enchant, allure, stupefy,' *gizki,* 'instrument of magic,' and *gyzki,* 'miracles.' The development of the word meaning from "yawn" to "desire or demand" is easily understood with reference to the hungrily yawning gullet of the wolf.[64] The transition to the signification "enchant" may be elucidated

---

[60] My *Origins*, p. 51.
[61] Cf. ibid., pp. 54 ff., 73 f., for details of the Canaanite and Egyptian war goddesses.
[62] Rose, *Handbook of Greek Mythology*, pp. 122 f.
[63] See below, pp. 287 ff.
[64] Ninck, *Wodan*, p. 56. Of course this explanation is oversimplified.

by a reference to the Norse volvas, or sorceresses. The Hrolf Krakisaga, for example, relates that a volva, before intoning her inner visions from her high magic chair,[65] "opened her jaws and yawned mightily." And again, when the king would not cease plying her with questions: "She yawned mightily and the magic was very painful to her." [66]

We shall have more to say of the yawning depths from which the magic incantation rises up, and of the twilight state of consciousness. For now it will suffice to mention the connection between the fertility of the womb, death, sexuality, and magic in the numinous image of the Terrible Mother.

THE SYMBOLISM OF THE
TERRIBLE GODDESS IN MELANESIA

In a very different place, far removed from the centers of the old Mediterranean and Nordic cultures, in the Melanesian island of Malekula, one of the New Hebrides, we find the same terrible elementary character of the Feminine as in Europe. Here the ritual of an initiation rite fifteen years in the completion has preserved a primordial character that has not yet undergone transformation into a systematized and complicated religion. In Malekula the world of the Western prehistoric and early historic Stone Age culture can still be observed in living rites.

Of the copious material that John Layard [1] has collected and interpreted, we shall cite only what he has to say of the Terrible Goddess and the part she plays in the life of these people. The rite, which has taken on a patriarchal accent, revolves around the group's struggle with a guardian spirit that stands in opposition to the god of light. Today this god of light plays an important role, but it is only in relatively recent years that he has achieved his present significance.[2]

The guardian spirit is either female or of indeterminate sex, but its terrible, female-matriarchal character is in any event clear. Its uroboric bisexuality is explained by mixture with the destructive power of the

---

[65] Cf. our remarks on the throne, pp. 98 ff.
[66] Ninck, *Wodan*, p. 56.

[1] *Stone Men of Malekula.*
[2] Ibid., p. 223.

Feminine, which at a "later" stage is often represented as male. Characteristically, this devouring guardian spirit represents the anger of the ancestors. And these ancestors are precisely "the male representatives of the maternal line . . . mother's brother, mother's mother's brother," [3] and so on; in other words, they are matriarchal ancestors, and the guardian spirit is the evil masculine side of the matriarchal woman, corresponding exactly to the relation of Set, the mother's brother, to Isis, which we have discussed elsewhere.[4] The name of this terrible creature is Le-hev-hev, which means "That which draws us to It so that It may devour us." [5]

This monster belongs to an underworld region, a cave, the symbol of the original land of the dead,[6] and represents "the annihilating influence of the grave." [7] The rites, Layard shows, represent the struggle to assert the masculine principle of light-sun-consciousness, with which the men's group identifies itself, over against the destructive power of this female-negative monster. Here again the male god of light and heaven symbolizes the "conscious striving," "the aspiration . . . to climb ever higher and higher." [8] For this reason the symbol of the ladder belongs to these deities and to the psychic tendencies they represent, and this is true both of Osiris [9] and of the Malekulan god of light.[10] Many lofty monuments, from the graduated towers of Sumer and Mexico to the Borobudur of Java, are related to this heaven-striving trend of the predominantly male spirit.

For the inhabitants of Malekula, the monster Le-hev-hev represents "unconscious fears," "the fear . . . of being devoured by the primeval force from which he [the primitive] has with so much exertion extricated himself and into which he is therefore in constant danger of falling back." [11]

But what concerns us here is not the male group's ritual struggle

[3] Ibid., p. 13.
[4] My *Origins and History of Consciousness*, pp. 65 ff. Layard calls it the "animus" of the woman, which is justified if we extend this term from personal psychology to the archetypal world. But personal and archetypal layers of the animus must be distinguished.

[5] Layard, p. 225.
[6] Ibid., p. 231.
[7] Ibid., p. 13.
[8] Ibid., pp. 223, 256.
[9] My *Origins*, p. 233.
[10] Layard, p. 735.
[11] Ibid., p. 256.

against this danger and not its identification with the celestial power—whose symbol here as in Egypt is the falcon, corresponding to the eagle of the Aztecs and the "red parrot" of the Incas. For our purposes it suffices to recognize here the figure of the Terrible Goddess with her archetypal symbolism. When Layard says that the guardian spirit represents "the reverse side of the social structure," his formulation is far too narrow, particularly in view of his own psychological interpretations. The whole life of mankind and assuredly of primitive mankind—and in what high degree all mankind is primitive!—is involved in the struggle against the suction of the unconscious and its regressive lure; and this is the terrible aspect of the Feminine.

All life in Malekula is filled with the endeavor to overcome the downward pull of psychic gravity [12] through a persistent ritual ascent. Whether or not this process has been successful is manifested in the "journey of the dead"—which is anticipated in the rite of initiation. In this journey, the dead man encounters the devouring monster and finds out whether or not he can stand up to it.

All initiations—those of primitive peoples as well as those described in the Egyptian or the Tibetan Book of the Dead; those of the mystery cults, Gnosis, or the sacramental religions—aim to safeguard the individual against the annihilating power of the grave, of the devouring Feminine. Whether this Feminine is represented as grave or underworld, as hell or Maya, as *heimarmene* or fate, as monster or witch, serpent or darkness, does not matter here. Death is in every case extinction of the individual and of consciousness as light; survival consists in proving that one belongs not to the darkness but to the world of the light.

Layard has shown a connection between the ritual sand tracings of labyrinths and this myth of the devouring monster. The designs are held to represent a way through the underworld and a night sea voyage, that is to say, *the way* that throughout the world forms a primordial component of the earliest rituals.[13] (On the concrete level, the sand tracing we reproduce is said to represent four flying foxes.)

Fig. 41

[12] My *Origins*, p. 16.   [13] Cf. G. R. Levy, *The Gate of Horn.*

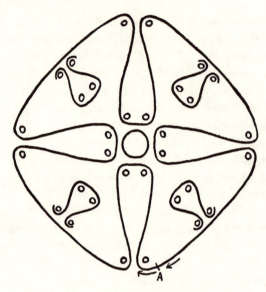

FIG. *41*. SAND TRACING OF A LABYRINTH

Malekula, New Hebrides

According to Layard, the main archetypal traits of the labyrinth are as follows:

1. That it always has to do with death and rebirth relating either to a life after death or to the mysteries of initiation.

2. That it is almost always connected with a cave (or more rarely a constructed dwelling).

3. That in those cases where the ritual has been preserved the labyrinth itself, or a drawing of it, is invariably situated at the entrance to the cave or dwelling.

4. That the presiding personage, either mythical or actual, is always a woman.

5. That the labyrinth itself is walked through, or the labyrinth design walked over, by men.[14]

Whether the labyrinth takes on the infinitely confused and confusing lines of the "way" or the shape of the "guardian spirit," whether

[14] Layard, p. 652. He points to corresponding examples from southern India, Crete, the Celtic sphere, Virgil, and the Christian Middle Ages.

176

the way by which the soul of the dead must pass "through" the intricate devouring labyrinth [15] is traveled or drawn, in every case we have before us "the conception of the divine body as the road traveled by itself and its seeker." [16] Levy seeks to derive these labyrinths and the corresponding earth designs of the Australians from origins in the paleolithic cave religion, whose drawings probably contain symbols of the initiation cave, of the way, and so on.

Here again the essential lies not in a genealogy of usages and interpretations but in an archetypal process. The rite as a way begins always as a "walked" or danced archetype, as labyrinth or spiral, as image of a spirit, or as a way through a gate of death and birth.[17]

The labyrinthine way is always the first part of the night sea voyage, the descent of the male following the sun into the devouring underworld, into the deathly womb of the Terrible Mother. This labyrinthine way, which leads to the center of danger, where at the midnight hour, in the land of the dead, in the middle of the night sea voyage, the decision falls, occurs in the judgment of the dead [18] in Egypt,[19] in the mysteries both classical and primitive, and in the corresponding processes of psychic development in modern man.[20] Because of its dangerous character, the labyrinth is also frequently symbolized by a net, its center as a spider.[21]

In the rites of Malekula, the monster Le-hev-hev, as negative power of the Feminine,[22] is also associated with the spider; [23] with the man-devouring "mythical ogress," "the crab woman" [24] with two immense claws; [25] with the underworld animal, the rat; and with a giant bivalve that when opened resembles the female genital organ, and in shutting endangers man and beast.[26]

This group of archetypal symbols is completed by "the moon." Layard tells us that this ritual figure consists of two moons turned to-

---

[15] Layard, pp. 649 ff.
[16] Cf. Levy, p. 159.
[17] Cf. my "Zur psychologischen Bedeutung des Ritus."
[18] Budge, *Guide to the Egyptian Collection in the British Museum*, p. 212.
[19] The symbolism of judgment, death, and rebirth is correlated with the twelfth hour of the night, with midnight, and also with the midnight of the year, the winter solstice, when the sun reaches the lowest point in its path.
[20] Cf. Jung's works on individuation.
[21] Cf. Jung, *Psychology and Alchemy*, p. 207 f. and fig. 108.
[22] Layard, p. 728.
[23] Ibid., p. 221.
[24] Ibid., p. 730.
[25] Ibid., p. 221, citing Speiser.
[26] Layard, "The Making of Man in Malekula."

ward one another like the lips of a mouth and is identical with the figure of the "way," which the devouring female draws as a test for the dead man. In other words, the terrible gullet of death or the devouring womb that he must pass through consists of the two crescent moons that are everywhere connected with the great dark Goddess of the night and are identical with the shears of the crab monster.[27]

The fact that in Malekula the female dolmens belong to the old matriarchal stratum of cult and ritual,[28] while the erect male megaliths belong to the later patriarchal stratum, confirms the ubiquity of the archetypal symbolism. The designation of the highest stage of female initiation as the "stone altar" brings us back to the bloody, sacrifice-exacting nature of the Great Goddess, who in Mexico, for example, ap-

Pl. 76 pears as a sacrificial blood bowl in the same function.

Let us consider once again the profound psychological meaning of the male's initiation into the dangers constituted by the Feminine. The archetypal roles are distributed by the identification of the upward-striving consciousness with the male and of the regressive, devouring, dangerous unconscious with the female. It is the projection of this symbolic sexual quality upon the men or the women that determines the social and religious position of the sexes until the psychological significance of the symbols has become conscious.

Consequently, the sex of the monster, of the world of the dead, and so on, cannot be socially derived, and it is not, as Layard assumes, complementary to a patriarchal or matriarchal social structure. The underworld, like the unconscious, is always "symbolically feminine" as the vessel that sucks in and destroys, and builds up, transforms, and bears; it is always bisexual. Moreover, the devouring Feminine is connected in various ways with the destructive Masculine. Even when the matriarchal stratum is repressed, it can appear in male form; for example, as a mother's brother, who represents the authority and punishment complex of matriarchal society, like the Malekulan Le-hev-hev representing the male side of the matriarchate. In patriarchal Chris-

[27] The boar's tusks of the Gorgons, etc., may also be negative forms of the moon, and such symbols of danger as cliffs that clash together may belong to the same group of the Terrible Feminine.
[28] Layard, *Stone Men*, p. 731.

tianity, on the other hand, the underworld is feminine as hell and masculine as the Devil, who—like Mephisto in Goethe's *Faust*—stands in a sonlike dependency to the "Devil's grandmother," whose matriarchal shape is still barely visible in the background.

THE MATRIARCHAL WORLD OF AMERICA

If we once again survey the archetypal symbolism of the Terrible Goddess, this time chiefly on the basis of Central American and South American material, it is because the most recent research makes it quite certain that the American cultures developed independently from

FIG. *42.* MOON BIRD GOD

Pottery design, Chimu Indians, Peru

those of the Old World. The striking correspondences between the symbolisms of the two worlds must then rest on an archetypal foundation. While in Mexico a solar mythology almost completely overlaid the original matriarchal stratum and the related lunar mythology, the latter retained its dominance in the coastal regions of South America and particularly in Peru.[1] There the Feminine is the "Woman of the Moon" and the "Woman of the Sea," and once again it becomes evident that sea, night sea, and night sky are one and the same; for the night is the Great

[1] Krickeberg, *Märchen der Azteken und Inkaperuaner, Maya und Muisca*, p. 380; Leicht, *Indianische Kunst und Kultur*, pp. 79 f.

Round, a unity of underworld, night sea, and night sky encompassing
all living things.

Thus in the matriarchal culture of the Chimus, we find a lunar
Fig. 42 mythology with the moon as hero and lord of the night, and we also find
men and heroes originating in the egg, the symbol of the moon.[2] In the
Fig. 43 dragon fight represented on a Chimu jar, the monster is a sea dragon,
but also a dragon of night and death. The hero is characterized as a
moon hero by the sign of the crescent moon on the snakes that he bears

FIG. *43*. DRAGON FIGHT

Pottery design, Chimu Indians, Peru

Fig. 42 in his hands. This sign in connection with the steps is characteristic of
the moon god; we find it in Egypt and in the double-ax symbol of Crete.
Pl. 82a It is impossible for us to decide whether the night owl is a feminine
symbol of the night sky or whether it is the moon itself.

A corresponding figure from the same cultural sphere, also relating
Pl. 83a, b to the Terrible Mother, is the crab with the Gorgon's head on its shell;
it too is a devouring monster of the sea depths. On another jar the devouring shears have become devouring animal mouths, and the Gorgon-
Pl. 84b crab appears as the body or womb of a human figure. The being whom
Pl. 83a, b the crab draws into the depths is interpreted as a star god.[3] The figure
being attacked also seems to be crablike.[4] Here, as so often in Mexican
mythology, we probably have to do with a celestial battle enacted in the
night sea. The assailed and defeated figure might be a moon god.

Crab, snail, and tortoise are frequent symbols of the backward-

[2] Krickeberg, pp. 38, 40 f.   *Peru*, p. 18.
[3] Regarding this picture, cf. Fuhrmann,   [4] Cf. illus. in Fuhrmann, *Inka*, p. 33.

180

moving moon, hiding in the darkness, which when devoured is often associated with negative symbols. Thus the snail god in Peru is a lunar deity in the negative phase. The feelers of the snail god, who shows a similarity to the figure attacked by the crab monster on another jar, are visibly moving a moon; i.e., they are drawing it into the snail's shell or standing it up.   *Pl. 82b*

Our interpretation of the crab-Gorgon as the goddess of the night is confirmed by the fact that—like the night in all mythologies—she is represented as giving birth to the sun. To complete the picture, we call attention to another Peruvian jar with two snakes, symbols of the earth and the night sky, on which the Gorgon is painted as a belly with snakes. (Their mouths are the devouring force that swallows up the luminous bodies in the east and west.) Just as the sun hero is devoured by the Mexican earth goddess with the two snakes' heads corresponding to the land tortoise, so the luminous hero, whether sun or moon, is strangled (?) by the two snakes of the Earth Mother on a Peruvian jar.   *Pl. 84c*   *Pl. 84b*   *Pl. 84a*

But whereas the matriarchal moon-night psychology is predominant in Peru and was overlaid only at a late period by the patriarchal Inca culture, the patriarchal dominance in the culture of Mexico is far more evident and the matriarchal undercurrent much less discernible.

The vast number of Aztec goddesses manifesting the Archetypal Feminine seems at first to make orientation impossible; but nevertheless the unitary archetype underlying them can be disclosed by an analysis of the identifications subsisting between them.[5]

At the beginning stands the divine pair, "Lord and Mistress of Our Flesh,"[6] whose origin and abode are in the thirteenth and highest heaven, "of whose origins no one has ever learned anything." They are the primal creator gods; they are also known as "Lord and Mistress of the Two,"[7] a term presumably meaning "masters of generative duality."[8] They have the first place in the calendar because they are the creative quality of the beginning and of the primordial age; the male

---

[5] The transcription of the names in the following is according to Danzel, *Mexiko*.

[6] Tonacatecuhtli and Tonacacihuatl.

[7] Ometecuhtli and Ometecihuatl.

[8] Danzel, p. 36; Krickeberg, p. 3.

part is identified with heaven and fire, the female part with earth and water.[9] The primordial Mayan gods corresponding to these uroboric figures were regarded as bisexual,[10] which is also suggested in the Aztec designation "Lord and Mistress of the Two." These epithets of the supreme divine pair indicate "that each of them alone embodies the creative force of procreation." [11] The conception of the original divine pair dwelling in the supreme, most remote heaven is mixed with that of Father Sky lying on Mother Earth, which we also encounter in North American myths.[12] The two primeval gods are a uroboric "supreme deity"; despite their central significance they possess no temple and no cult and are not connected with specific things in nature; despite their transcendence they are also the "alimentary uroboros." Their name, "Lord and Mistress of Our Flesh," [13] means not only "Lords of Our Living Substance" but at the same time "Lords of the Corn"; that is to say, they are a deity both of the beginning and of vegetation.

The Terrible Great Mother with her youthful son [14] also plays a prominent role in Mexico. Chicomecoatl, the corn mother with the seven snakes, is regarded as a deity of the oldest aboriginal population [15] with which the Earth Mother, "Heart of the Earth," the mother of the gods,[16] and the grandmother [17] were identified; she was the Demeter of old Mexico, the Mother Goddess.[18]

The "ancient goddess," as may be readily understood, is identified with the primordial goddess [19] and with the earth goddess,[20] who also bears the name "Our Ancestress and Heart of the Earth." She is the goddess of voluptuousness and sin, but also the great genetrix and renewer of vegetation through the sexual act; as moon and earth goddess, she is the goddess of the west, of death and the underworld.[21] She bears

[9] Spence, *The Myths of Mexico and Peru,* pp. 104, 118.
[10] Ibid., p. 236.
[11] Krickeberg, p. 336.
[12] Spence, *The Myths of Mexico and Peru,* p. 119.
[13] The names are paraphrased likewise according to Danzel.
[14] It is possible that an originally matriarchal Toltec culture was here overlaid by the patriarchal culture of immigrating Nahuatlan peoples.

We find an analogous situation in ancient Egypt and probably in India, which might account for the cultural analogies.
[15] Spence, p. 85.
[16] Teteoinnan.
[17] Toçi.
[18] Spence, *The Outlines of Mythology,* p. 101.
[19] Tonacacihuatl.
[20] Tlazolteotl.
[21] Danzel, Vol. I, p. 47.

the death's head, and the female sacrifice offered up to her is beheaded. As wintry aspect of the deathly earth, she stands in opposition to the childbearing earth that is bound up with the east and the spring. She is the primordial goddess of matter, whose terrible character with its eyes and voracious gullets bursts forth from all her joints. Clad in a mantle of snakes, she holds the deadly flint knife and has the claws of the jaguar. *Fig. 38* This animal is the archetypal enemy of the light, the negative male attribute and companion of the Terrible Goddess [22] who, also as the Great Mother, wears the night mantle with the moons. As symbol of the beast of prey, the jaguar is the goa of the cavern and the earth, of the devouring darkness and of the night sky. There is a myth in which the unity of earth and night sky, signifying the original unity of the beginning, is differentiated: the Earth Goddess is brought down from the primordial heavens and torn asunder; from the two halves heaven and earth are made, as in the case of the Babylonian Tiamat.[23] Precisely by this rending she becomes the source of all foodstuffs, but—as compensation for her good character—she then becomes the Terrible Mother: "Sometimes the Earth Goddess cried out in the night, demanding human hearts. And then she would not be comforted until they were brought her and would not bear fruit until she had been given human blood to drink." [24] The jaguar as a power of darkness is the enemy of the eagle, the sun symbol, and the mythical struggles between light and darkness, which stand at the center of the Aztec world view, take the form of battles between the jaguar warriors and the eagle warriors. Every evening the sun god in the west is swallowed up by the earth monster, for the "conception of earth as a tortoiselike devouring monster dominates Mexican art," and "the earth is the insatiable monster that not only devours the dead but also the sun and the stars when they set." [25]

[22] The terrible nature of the Feminine may take either of two forms: either the Goddess herself may become the terrifying animal or her terrible aspect may become the animal that accompanies and dominates her. Thus she may be a lioness (cf. the lion goddess of Egypt), or else she may be enthroned on a lion or ride on a lion; in India she may be a tigress, or else she may ride on a tigress or a lioness; as Artemis she may be a she-bear, or the bear may be her companion animal, just as the bear may be the male principle correlated with her in her sow aspect. *Pl. 130*

[23] See below, pp. 213 f.

[24] Krickeberg, p. 5.

[25] Ibid., p. 312.

Pl. 85   In Mexico, too, the western hole into which the sun descends is the archetypal womb of death destroying what has been born. But for the Aztecs and related peoples the west is more: it is the "place of the women," the primeval home, where mankind once crawled from the primordial hole of the earth.[26] For before the earth and human consciousness existed, everything was contained in the realm of the dead in the west.

This place of the women is not only the dark cave from which mankind issued; it is also "the house from which one descends." For underworld, night sky, and unconscious are one and the same: the west is the seat of the primordial gods, the home of the corn, and the original mythical home of the tribes.[27] In the west there stands the "Temple of Foodstuffs" and the corn tree with the hummingbird, which as symbol of awakened vegetation [28] is connected with the sun hero.

The union of positive and negative symbols at the place of origin and their relation to food are typical for man's original uroboric nature.[29] Thus the west is the place of the world before the world, the uroboric existence of unconscious perfection.[30] Only after the world is created, after light has been made, after the sun has started on its course and the antithetical principle of hostile powers has gone into effect [31]— i.e., after the symbolic tree of the original home has been shattered [32]— does the west become a place of death.

The souls of women who, having died in childbirth, become demons combining death and birth also belong to the symbolism of the west. As spiders,[33] hostile particularly to men, they dangle from the heavens; and as the demonic powers of primordial darkness, they escort the sun down from the zenith to its place of death in the west. They are the powers of the time before time, that is to say, "before the birth of the sun." But these demons of the early matriarchal age are also those of

---

[26] Danzel, Vol. I, p. 23.
[27] Preuss, *Die Nayarit-Expedition*, Vol. I, *Die Religion der Cora-Indianer*, pp. xxxviii–xlii, cited in Krickeberg, p. 317.
[28] Danzel, Vol. I, p. 35.
[29] Cf. my *Origins*, index, s.v. "alimentary uroboros."

[30] Ibid., p. 15.
[31] Ibid., pp. 106 f.
[32] Cf. especially the Codex Borgia 19, according to Danzel, Vol. I.
[33] Seler, *Codex Borgia*, Vol. I, p. 286, cited in Krickeberg, p. 338.

the last days that will swallow up mankind when the end of the world approaches and sun, moon, and stars all clash together.[34]

It is characteristic of the Aztec view of the world that the night of doom hangs over all living things. Not only does each of the four ages of the world end with a terrible catastrophe, but the end of each calendar division of fifty-two years is a time of doom, when the end of the world is expected with terror and chastisements, and the continuation of life is celebrated as a miracle and rebirth. This fifty-two-year interval has its correspondence in the midnight of the full day and the winter solstice of the year. At this time all vessels are destroyed; all fire is extinguished. It is a "time of judgment" like the Jewish New Year, for example, and, as in many of the world's New Year's feasts, the surpassing of this danger point is celebrated with orgiastic rejoicing, rekindling of the fire, and so on.

The conscious world view of the Aztecs is "patriarchal"; the power of the Goddess has grown almost invisible, and the male principle of the light and the sun is dominant. But a closer analysis yields a very different psychological picture. Side by side with the king there governs a figure that, though always represented by a man, bears the name of the terrible Earth Mother: the "Snake Woman." She "was the executive peak of the internal affairs of the tribe, where civil custom and religious demand governed almost every act. . . ." [35] "In Tenochtitlan the Chief of Men and the Snake Woman had double duties in respect of civil and religious affairs, the former actively leading the services and the latter supervising the temples, the form of the rites, and the internal affairs of the priesthood." [36]

Here there is no doubt that an originally matriarchal constellation was overlaid by patriarchal institutions. Among the tribes of North America, we often find that the old women, without official power, govern the internal affairs of the tribe, while the warrior chiefs govern the outward affairs. This corresponds to the original matriarchal situation, in which the group of the women and children is governed by the

---

[34] Danzel, Vol. I, p. 54.

[35] Vaillant, *The Aztecs of Mexico*, p. 122.
[36] Ibid., p. 182.

Old Woman, while the fighting and hunting men's society is ruled by the warrior chieftain or democratically by the male group.

An analysis of this Aztec constellation with its matriarchal traits overlaid by patriarchal features is highly instructive for the history of human development. Originally, the men as warriors stood in the service of the female godhead, to whom they offered blood sacrifices; and thus it remained in the Aztec culture, although the political-social-extraverted dominance had already been taken over by the male group and although the patriarchal solar principle had—seemingly—replaced the matriarchal lunar principle.[37] All Aztec policies were subordinated to the wars that were waged for the purpose of taking prisoners to be sacrificed in the cult of the Snake Woman, who yielded fertility only when satiated by terrible blood sacrifices.

The cruelty of the Mexican rites, which were thought to guarantee the fertility of the earth but also to reinforce masculine, solar, conscious life, expressed the masculine consciousness' dread fear of being swallowed up by the feminine dark aspect of the unconscious.

The characteristic Aztec form of sacrifice was to tear the heart out of the living body and offer it up to the sun; this gave assurance of the fructifying rain that made the earth fertile. In another form of sacrifice, the victim was flayed and the priest was "invested" in the skin—a typical form of transformation symbolism. This was evidently preceded by another type of sacrifice: beheading. As in Egypt, beheading and dismemberment originated in a surpassed matriarchal stratum, vestiges of which are still discernible in the myth and rites of the Aztecs, as, for example, in the conception of the "southern circle of hell," the circle of decapitation and dismemberment.

The beheading of the evil moon-sister goddess was the first deed of the hero-god Huitzilopochtli. The beheading of the female victim was the central rite in the spring festival of the snake-underworld goddess,[38] and the battle-sacrifice festival of the gladiators ended in a dance with the heads of the victims.[39]

[37] Here it must again be stressed that in this connection "matriarchal" signifies a psychic situation and should not be taken as a dominant social position of the woman.
[38] See below, page 194.
[39] Preuss, *Die Eingeborenen Amerikas*, p. 49.

In Mexico, too, the west, as its symbolism shows, is associated with the unconscious; it is the "Great Sea." And because, among the Mexicans and the Cora Indians investigated by Preuss, the night and the night sky are also the nocturnal ocean of heaven,[40] the moon is the night snake that walks in the water,[41] and the deadly western menace of the Terrible Mother is also represented as the danger of flood. "The Cora Indians believe that in the west of the world there lives a mighty snake, the night conceived as water, which the rising morning star [42] kills and the eagle, the daytime sky, devours. If this did not happen, the world would fill with water." [43]

In the westerly symbol group of the Terrible Mother—night, abyss, sea, watery depths, snake, dragon, whale—all the symbols color one another and merge with one another. Devouring water, rending earth-womb, abyss of death, hostile snake of night and death, whale, sea, and whale in the sea—all are aspects of the negative unconscious, the "water of the depths," which lives in the nocturnal darkness beneath the world of men and threatens to fill the world with water.

Consequently, the Feminine, as the Mayan goddess Ixchel, goddess of disastrous floods and of the moon,[44] is the fatal water jar. Her symbol is the overturned vessel of doom, on her head rests the deadly snake, on her hands and feet she bears sharp animal claws, and her mantle is adorned with crossed bones, the emblem of death.

Figs. 44–45

The catastrophe of the flood can be averted only by the sun hero of consciousness, who over and over again defeats the serpent of the abyss. This victory of the hero occurs in the east, where the sun rises, or, as in Mexico, at the noonday zenith,[45] and this corresponds exactly to the worship of the moon hero as new moon or full moon.

Since the Aztecs, as the extraordinary vitality of the archetype of the Terrible Mother among them reveals, were afflicted with a terror of

[40] Preuss, *Nayarit-Expedition*, Vol. I: *Die Religion der Cora-Indianer*, p. xxvii, according to Krickeberg, p. 341.

[41] Krickeberg, p. 360.

[42] Here the morning star plays the role of the sun hero.

[43] Preuss, *Nayarit-Expedition*, Vol. I, pp. 50 f., from Preuss, *Die Eingeborenen Amerikas*,

p. 41. As in Mexico the sun is devoured by the earth in the west, so in Egypt the sun bark bearing the sun, now old and sick to death, descends into the western mountain, which stands in the sign of the nocturnal ocean and of the western Hathor, the nocturnal mother of death.

[44] Morley, *The Ancient Maya*, pp. 230–31.

[45] See above, p. 183.

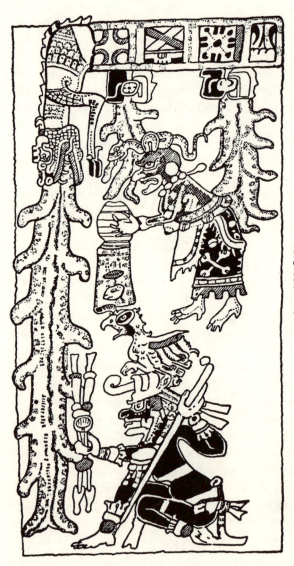

FIG. 44. THE OLD
GODDESS IXCHEL
DESTROYING THE
WORLD BY WATER

Mayan, from a codex

death resembling that of the Egyptians, the archetype of the hero's underworld journey, transformation, and rebirth plays a central role here too.

Blood sacrifice and dismemberment belong to the fertility ritual of the Great Mother. Both fecundate the womb of the earth, as can be seen from a number of rites in which the pieces of the victim—whether

FIG. *45.* IXCHEL
Mayan, from a codex

man or animal—are solemnly spread over the fields. The Greek Thesmophoria, in which little pigs, symbolizing the children of the earth sow, and phallic symbols are thrown into a ravine supposed to be swarming with snakes, also belongs to this context.[46] The ravine is the womb of the earth; taken together, snake and ravine here again represent the fertility of the earth. The decayed flesh of the sacrifices was later recovered from the ravine and distributed over the fields as fertility magic.

The need for fecundating and reviving the feminine earth with blood, death, and corpses—this conception, perpetually reinforced by

[46] My *Origins and History of Consciousness*, pp. 81–82.

the flow of life and death in nature, constellates the Great Mother as terrible, killing, and dismembering. That is why the great goddesses are goddesses of the hunt and of war, dealers in life and blood. That is why the great Aztec Mother Goddess is also the goddess of the obsidian knife with which bodies are dismembered,[47] and why in her aspect of moon goddess she is called the "white stone knife." [48] Correspondingly Set, the male companion of the terrible Isis,[49] has as an attribute the primeval flint knife, the "knife of Set." [50] In America, obsidian as spear point, hunting knife, sacrificial knife, and sword is an instrument of death. The obsidian goddess,[51] related to the goddess of the hunt, was originally a dragonlike figure. Later she herself became a goddess of the hunt.[52] Her butterfly wings were tipped with obsidian. The cult of the magical weapon was connected with her as it is with all primordial goddesses of death and the hunt.

Tezcatlipoca, one of the most important gods of the Aztec pantheon, is also an obsidian god and plays the sacral role of the obsidian knife.[53] The moon as sicklelike weapon, sword, and knife is an archetypal symbol of the fight of the youthful hero against the dragon of darkness, which preceded the solar mythology.

"Mexican tradition reveals very clearly that obsidian, because of its original food-producing properties, came to be regarded as the source of all life, indeed as the very principle of existence. The creative goddess Tonacacihuatl (Lady of Our Subsistence) was said to have given birth to an obsidian knife from which sprang sixteen hundred demigods who peopled the earth. As the Aztec picture manuscripts show, maize is frequently depicted in the form of a sacrificial knife of obsidian." [54]

Spence has expressed the opinion that the original faith of the Aztecs was an "obsidian religion" [55] and with good reason derives it from a preagricultural hunting phase. Thus obsidian is the magical weapon descended from heaven, the life-and-death-bringing central

[47] Obsidian is volcanic glass that chips or flakes to a razorlike sharpness.
[48] Krickeberg, p. 330.
[49] My *Origins*, pp. 64 ff.
[50] Book of the Dead (tr. Budge), Ch. CLIII.
[51] Itzpapalotl (obsidian butterfly).
[52] Spence, *The Religion of Ancient Mexico*, p. 26.
[53] Ibid., p. 27.
[54] Ibid., p. 27.
[55] Ibid., p. 25.

symbol [56] of the bloody primeval Great Mother, who is herself dismembered (see above) and thereupon becomes the source of all life. Later, as hunting gave way to agriculture—regardless whether this took place before or after the conquest of Mexico by the Aztecs—the aspects changed. As an old hymn tells us, the obsidian goddess of the hunt, the obsidian butterfly, became "a goddess of the melon cactus," [57] and the Great Goddess changed from a goddess of the hunt, of blood and the night, to an earth goddess. The son of her fertility now became the corn, which was identical with the obsidian knife—and she herself became the fertility goddess of the corn. But her old terrible nature persisted, for fertility, death, and sacrifice belong together, and the husking of the corn is identical with the tearing out of the heart from the victim with the help of the obsidian knife.

The Great Goddess bears life, the corn, which may appear as the phallic corn god or as the son of the corn, and she also bears death, the obsidian knife. This twofold aspect, in which life becomes death and death life, and in which one depends on the other, recurs again and again in Aztec myth and ritual. It is evident in the sacrifice of the blood, "which by a divine alchemy came to be transformed into rain," [58] and in the sacrifice of living things in general.[59]

[56] Ibid., p. 26.
[57] Ibid., p. 26.
[58] Ibid., p. 27.
[59] It has been calculated that twenty to fifty thousand persons were sacrificed annually; 130,000 skulls have been counted in a single site.

The sacrificial blood bowl is an attribute of the Terrible Mother in her aspect as vessel of death. In connection with the hearts sacrificed to the eagle of the heavens and the sun, she is also the "Eagle Woman"; and the bowl, which bears a picture of the land tortoise on its underside, is called "eagle's bowl." The terrible symbol of the blood bowl still inhabits the unconscious; it occurs in the fantasies and dreams of the sane as well as the insane. An English mass murderer, whose crimes, despite their very conscious refinement, probably followed from an inner compulsion, told of a recurring dream that a bowl of blood was offered him and that he drank from it (Lord Dunboyne [ed.], *The Trial of John George Haigh*, pp. 165 f.). "Blood thirst" is not a mere figure of speech but, as we know, was a feature of primordial cannibalistic orgies and has been preserved in man's unconscious tendency to wage war.

It was the "gods" who impelled early mankind to blood sacrifice; modern man is driven to war and the satisfaction of unconscious blood thirst by transpersonal factors that he tends to project upon such economic demons as "capitalism" and "bolshevism." But in either case he feels "innocent." In the same sense, the mass murderer Haigh said that he had no pangs of conscience after his crimes, for he felt that he knew he was led by a higher power—a higher thing that was outside him and dominated him. He considered that he lived in two worlds that were equally alive but had nothing to do with each other; the deeds were always done by him but the part of his brain that guided his hand did not plan them. Seldom has the gruesome blood thirst of the unconscious been so clearly formulated as in the pathological structure of this modern man.

191

Everywhere the Great Mother is connected with the duality of moon and earth, and the secret of the earth's fecundation is bound up with the moon [60] and its dismemberment: here the moon is the fructifying as well as the dismembered son.

Because ritual killing and dismemberment are a necessary transition toward rebirth and new fertility, the destruction of the luminous gods in the journey through the underworld appears as a cosmic equivalent of the birth of the new day. In the Aztec myth of the journey through hell,[61] the realm of the dead is a blood-framed skull, the center of the world. It is the deathly side of the life-giving world navel.[62] The underworld vessels of death and transformation have the shape of devouring skulls, with eyes and bared teeth. In Mexico the southerly region of decapitation and dismemberment corresponds to the terrible realm of the subterranean gates in Egypt. At its center is a terrible figure with two obsidian knives for a head and deadly blades protruding from its joints; its domain is fenced in with rows of knives.

Fig. 46

Fig. 33

As goddess of death, the Great Mother bears the obsidian knife; the youthful moon god Xipe-totec with the obsidian knife mask is associated with her and enters into her ritual, in which the youthful son is dismembered or castrated. This is the typical self-sacrifice of the moon, leading to its rebirth.

If now, on the basis of the Aztec material, we once again attempt to describe the relationship between the cult of the Great Mother and the sacrifice of her youthful son, who is both her beloved and her fecundator, it is because here the earliest matriarchal ritual of the Terrible Goddess, though overlaid by patriarchal elements, is still clearly discernible. There is reason to suppose that the mother's sacrifice of the male, her son, was preceded in earlier times by a sacrifice of the daughter, or at least that both occurred simultaneously.[63]

We do actually find accounts of the sacrifice of women or girls, i.e., of goddesses, for in Mexico the sacrificial victims were always identical with the gods. But even the sacrifice of a warrior, which plays a promi-

[60] My "Über den Mond und das matriarchale Bewusstsein."
[61] Danzel, *Mexiko*, Vol. I.
[62] See above, p. 132.
[63] Cf. Lord Raglan, *Jocasta's Crime*.

FIG. 46.   THE UNDERWORLD VESSEL OF DEATH
AND TRANSFORMATION

Aztec, from a codex

nent part in the Aztec ritual, does not necessarily imply the sacrifice of a male principle. We know, for example, that in the cult of Xipe, the flayed god, prisoners were shot with arrows, symbolizing sexual union with the earth.[64] In other words, mating and killing are identical, and death represents fecundation.

We have already pointed to the lunar and "westerly" character of Xipe. Concerning his identification with the Feminine, Preuss writes: "Xipe is the male parallel to the earth and moon goddess, to the mother of the gods or the goddess of sensual pleasure, who also personifies the corn plant and the corn or foodstuff. In the present case, Xipe replaces the earth and moon goddess as representative of the earth. This is most apparent from the short skirt of zapote leaves that she wears and from the fact that she is attached to a hole in the middle of the round stone, this hole representing the center and entrance—in the sexual as in other respects." [65]

The identification of the male god Xipe with the Earth Goddess recurs in different form in the broom harvest festival of the same Earth Mother. The victim is a woman and on another day a young girl, playing the part of earth goddess; she is beheaded, and her blood is sprinkled on fruit, seeds, and so on, to guarantee their increase. The rites of this festival, which involve dancing and sham battles, show obvious analogies to marriage rites.[66] Evidently the marriage of mother and son provides the background of the festival and accounts for features that were not formerly understood: "The acts of sex and childbearing are symbolized by phallus bearers and by the outspread legs of the goddess before the image of Huitzilopochtli in certain phases. It is the birth of the corn that is represented in these strange rites." [67]

The essential elements in this fertility ritual are the beheading of the woman as goddess, the fructifying sacrifice of her blood, the flaying of her body, and the investment of the son-god-priest [68] in her skin. Of this Frazer says: "Rather we should expect that as one woman acted

[64] Krickeberg, p. 343.
[65] Preuss, *Die Eingeborenen Amerikas*, p. 44.
[66] Frazer, *The Golden Bough* (abridged edn., 1951), pp. 680–86; and his *The Worship of* *Nature*, pp. 434 f.
[67] Danzel, Vol. I, p. 44.
[68] Cinteotl; see Spence, *The Religion of Ancient Mexico*, p. 65 f.

the divine death so another woman should act the divine resurrection." [69]

The explanation consists in the central content of the transformation mystery: the death of the mother of corn and earth leads to the birth of the corn, her son.[70] The corn son bearing the skin of the sacrificed Earth Mother is the image of his mother's living pregnancy whereby the feminine is transformed into the masculine, which is built from the blood of the sacrificed woman. This blood of transformation is fortified by the sacrifice. The corn-god son [71] wears a mask made from the skin of the victim's thighs, and this is a repetition of the same symbolism of transformation and birth or rebirth.

The identity of mother and son in this fertility mystery is intensified by the fact that before being sacrificed the woman representing the corn goddess wears the mantle of maguey [72] characteristic of the corn-son. The principal ceremony of the flaying festival is the sword-fight sacrifice, a battle between selected prisoners equipped with sham weapons and fully armed warriors—ending, of course, in the death and sacrifice of the prisoners.

The prisoners whose death in battle forms the contents of the sword fight stand on a large stone some ten feet in diameter. They are bound with a rope, the "foodstuff rope," which starts at the center of the stone "representing the center and entrance of the earth—in the sexual as in other respects," and which has the evident character of the umbilical cord.[73] The prisoner who is weary or simply unable to fight is killed in a position that Danzel designates as the receiving position, but it might equally well be characterized as a position of birth.

In this connection, it should be mentioned that a mother who has given birth to a child is said to have "made a prisoner," and that a woman who dies in childbirth is called a "sacrificed prisoner." To understand the ritual it is important to note that a goddess of the oldest

---

[69] Frazer, *Worship*, p. 440.
[70] Cf. below, "Spiritual Transformation,"
pp. 309 ff.

[71] Cinteotl.
[72] Frazer, *Worship*, p. 435; Spence, *The Myths of Mexico and Peru*, p. 90.
[73] Danzel, Vol. I, Pl. 12.

Chichimecs,[74] the "goddess who died in childbed," is known as the "old hero" and as the "sacrificed goddess." [75] Associated with her are the female demons of the west, the souls of the women who have died in childbirth.

The slain prisoner is female and male, mother and son, earth and god of light, soil, and corn in one. He is the dying feminine principle and the renewed male principle, which is represented by the heart and is symbolically identical with the sun and the ear of corn. The sacrificial action, typical for the Aztecs, in which the heart, the gem, the eagle's fruit, is torn from the breast of the victim and held up to the sun, corresponds to the "husking of the corn." The sun as fruit of the daytime sky, as "turquoise prince" and "ascending eagle," is fed on the sacrificed hearts and their blood. The existence of the world depends on its ascending flight.

The corn is a phallic fertility symbol; [76] corn and corn god correspond to the wheat god of the western European cultural sphere. The tearing out and lifting up of the heart are a magical aid for the rising sun and also for the growth of the corn; its rising must be helped; "lifting" as well as "jumping" are magical abettors of growth.

A final confirmation of the relation between the sun god as youthful lover and the Great Mother is found in the figure of Xochipilli-Cinteotl. Xochipilli is the young god of life, of the morning, of procreation, and of foodstuffs, a typical god of the sun, of love, and of vegetation. He is a phallic god [77] standing between night and day, like the youthful Eros-Amor; he is also the butterfly and the "flower prince."

As in Egypt, the youthful morning sun belongs to the maternal night sky; and like the phallic young lovers of European and Asiatic mythology, he is the beautiful prince of flowers, related to the earth.[78] He is the beloved of the Aztec madonna,[79] who also bears him in her arms as her child.

Xochiquetzal, the moon virgin, is the goddess of love's pleasures

---

[74] Itzpapalotl.
[75] Danzel, Vol. I, p. 54.
[76] Cf. Fuhrmann, *Mexiko*, Vol. III, fig. 65.

[77] Danzel, Vol. I, Pl. X.
[78] My *Origins*, pp. 49 f.
[79] Xochiquetzal.

and of sins; of amusements, dances, songs, and art; of spinning and weaving. She is goddess of the marriage bond, and the patroness of harlots.

The identity of the virgin with the uroboric primordial mother points back to the figure of the great primordial mother as virgin. In line with this archetypal identity, she is also regarded as the "first woman to have borne twins"; [80] hence, like all primordial mother figures, as the primordial mother of the principle of opposites, of life and death, death and resurrection. [81]

The archetypal marriage of the Great Mother with the son who appears as god of the light, of the maize and the flowers, is celebrated also in Mexico, and here again a rejuvenated daughter goddess appears beside the terrible mother goddess, with whom she is identical. [82] For this reason the youthful moon-virgin goddess of love and of harlots [83] "is with remarkable frequency 'equated' with the female uroboric goddess of the beginning." [84] Spence rightly believes [85] that the corn goddess [86] stands in the same relation to the corn mother [87] as Persephone to Demeter. The goddesses, like the gods, are all "variations on a theme."

The mother-daughter biunity of the Great Goddess is demonstrable for a very early period. Thus the pre-Aztec clay figures "were usually female, and may have represented a mother goddess, symbolizing growth and fertility—a conception common among the religious ideas of mankind." [88] "Behind these figurines must have existed an austere realization of the complex rhythms of birth, growth, and death in nature, epitomized in the miracle of woman in her bearing of children." [89]

Pl. 86, above

And regarding another group of figures, Vaillant writes: "These figurines, in contrast to the matronly bearing of the local images, have something of a girlish grace." [90] Unquestionably this young goddess is Xochiquetzal, whose son-lover Xochipilli is also the young corn god

Pl. 86, below

[80] Danzel, Vol. I, p. 49.
[81] My *Origins*, pp. 95 ff.
[82] Cf. below, p. 208.
[83] Xochiquetzal.
[84] Tonacacihuatl. Cf. Danzel, Vol. I, p. 49.
[85] Spence, *The Myths of Mexico and Peru*, p. 69.
[86] Tlazolteotl.
[87] Chicomecoatl.
[88] Vaillant, p. 50.
[89] Ibid., p. 51.
[90] Ibid., p. 52.

Cinteotl. It is for this reason that in the festival of Cinteotl, Xochipilli appears in the form of the corn god.[91]

A further confirmation of the young corn god's relation to his mother may be found in the feast of the vernal equinox, where the youthful Xochipilli-Cinteotl takes part in the sacral ball game as the opponent of the terrible old Earth Goddess of the winter solstice.[92]

The import of this festival is cosmic, the victory of the rising young god of spring over the old aspect of the Earth Mother. But this cosmic significance is bound up with fertility, for the growth of the grain forms an archetypal unit with the sun, the light, and consciousness.

The aim of the ball game was to drive the ball by complicated maneuvers through a stone ring, and Danzel rightly equates the flight of the ball with the sexual act: "An indication of this is the cry that the onlookers address to the successful thrower: 'He is a great adulterer.' To judge by this, the ball game had originally the partial significance of a fertility ritual." [93] This interpretation is supported by the circumstance that the ring was called a "spring" and that water was poured through it.[94] The union of son and mother results in the flowing fertility of the maternal womb, the spring, which is also a uroboric, bisexual symbol of creation. The flowing, fecundating water is masculine, but the spring as a whole is a uterine symbol of the childbearing feminine earth that generates brooks and streams.[95]

In incest with his mother, the hero begets himself.[96] But since the son-lover succumbs to the Great Mother in "matriarchal incest," [97] an early death is prophesied for the "great adulterer," the victorious "bull of his mother."

Aztec mythology differs in one important point from the familiar Old World myths of the dying male principle: [98] in the Aztec myth it is not only the young phallic "Adonis-son" who is slain by the Terrible Mother but also his mature form, the warrior.

[91] Danzel, Vol. I, Pl. XXII.
[92] Cihuacoatl-Ilamatecuhtli; see Danzel, Vol. I, pp. 32, 55.
[93] Ibid., p. 32.
[94] Ibid., p. 32.
[95] Cf. Part I, p. 48.
[96] Cf. my *Origins*, index, s.v. "incest, heroic."
[97] Ibid., s.v. "incest, matriarchal."
[98] Ibid., pp. 46 f.

Thus it becomes understandable that the warrior sacrificed on the round stone should also be regarded as Huitzilopochtli.[99] His symbol is the hummingbird, "symbol of the vegetation of the beginning of the rainy season." [100] As a spirit of fertility, the god bears a leg of this hummingbird, which is associated with the maize tree in the west, the realm of the Great Mother.[101] He is a god of the sun and of war; he is born of the virgin mother, who is impregnated by a shuttlecock from heaven, a variant of the motif of "supernatural birth" or fecundation by the sun phallus as source of the wind.[102] As son of the snake-mantled mother, he is entwined in snakes; his scepter is a snake; his drum is a snakeskin.[103] As in the sun phallus, the relationship of sun, snake, and wind recurs in the figure of Huitzilopochtli. He symbolizes the generative luminous aspect, which is also the dominant element in the other hero god of the Aztecs, Quetzalcoatl, the plumed serpent.[104]

As war god, Huitzilopochtli was also the fecundator, for to wage war meant to take prisoners, whose blood was essential to the fertility both of the gods and the world. At one of his festivals an image of him was kneaded of dough moistened with the blood of sacrificed children and pierced with an arrow as a sign of his death up to the time of his resurrection in the following year.[105] The sacred fifty-two-year rhythm of the Aztecs and the ritual drilling of new fire were also connected with the piercing and sacramental eating of this dough image.[106] The sacral existence of Huitzilopochtli was symbolically equated with the vital essence of the fire-sun-blood-grain, for he was not only a fecundator but in his character of corn god was also killed, sacrificed,[107] eaten, and resurrected. He too, like all other male deities of the light, must "become bones," i.e., die.[108]

The coexistence of male-accented and female-accented symbolisms —for even where the Masculine is masculine, it is identified with the

[99] Spence, *Myths*, p. 73.
[100] Danzel, Vol. I, p. 35.
[101] Ibid., Pls. 25, 53.
[102] Cf. Part I, pp. 14 f.
[103] Spence, *Myths*, pp. 73 f.
[104] See below, p. 203.

[105] Spence, *Myths*, pp. 73 f.
[106] Danzel, Vol. I, p. 36.
[107] His designation as "Hare of the Aloes" (Spence, *Myths*, p. 74) points to his sacrifice, for the hare is an archetypal symbol of self-sacrifice (Layard, *The Lady of the Hare*).
[108] Krickeberg, pp. 311 f.

Feminine through the symbolism of sacrifice—is most evident in connection with the corn god, in whose rite the cutting out of the heart is identical with the husking of the corn. For there is an identity between the cutting out of the heart and birth, as is evident from a picture in *Fig. 47* the Codex Borgia.[109] In the lower rectangle, representing the eastern region of the underworld, sits a black goddess with outspread legs. As her color and the stars on her indicate, she is the goddess of night, identical with the earth goddess.[110] Her body consists of a luminary, sun or moon, and her ankles, knees, wrists, and shoulders are also luminous points, from which priests cut the heart with their knives.

The opening at the lower end of the central belly-luminary represents the act of childbearing; the animal's head at the center with the open mouth symbolizes the uterus.[111]

Now the upper part of the picture also becomes intelligible; it represents a mandala bordered by twelve goddesses, presumably earth deities, adorned with moon symbols. Its center represents the descent of light and dark moon (or sun and moon) [112] into the tooth-studded maw of the earth, in which the scene of sacrifice and birth takes place. The scene no doubt represents the devouring, sacrifice, and rebirth of the luminous hero.[113]

The subordination of all heroes of light to the regenerative power of the Great and Terrible Mother constellates the conflict between the Terrible Mother lurking in the background and the patriarchal consciousness of the Aztecs. These two worlds continuously clash and merge. For the Aztec warrior the supreme distinction was to take prisoners to be sacrificed, or himself to be taken prisoner and sacrificed. But "to take a prisoner," "to bear a child," "to be sacrificed as a

[109] Danzel, Vol. I, Pl. 63.

[110] The symbolic contexts we have described make it understandable that she should also be identical with the quasi-masculine nocturnal sun, which has vanished at night, i.e., has returned into her.

[111] The birth scene below the black goddess —representing the earth goddess adorned with death's head, giving birth to the sun over the eastern ocean, the jeweled bowl—confirms our interpretation.

[112] Danzel, text with Pl. 63.

[113] In another picture in the Codex Borgia, representing the southern region, a god has the moon in his body; around him are four destructive animals: bat, jaguar, quetzal, and eagle. But here the moon vessel is open at the top and a heart is brought to it and to the god to feed on, in order that the moon may be renewed. Cf. Danzel, text with Pl. 63.

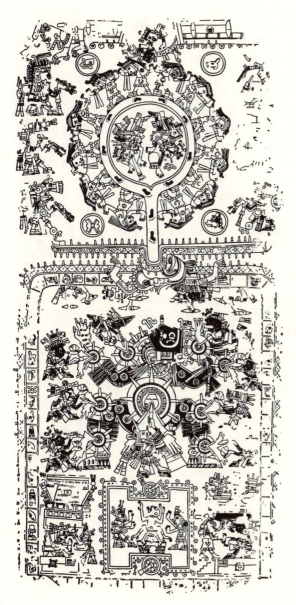

FIG. 47. THE
WAY THROUGH
THE MAW OF
THE EARTH TO
THE EASTERN
REGION OF THE
UNDERWORLD

*Aztec, damaged page
from the Codex Borgia*

prisoner," and "to die in childbed" are identical. Thus we must ask whether the strange mode of expressing feminine life was taken over from the male ritual of sacrifice, or whether the male ritual of sacrifice imitates the fundamental situation of feminine life.

The archetypal relationship between death and birth is intensified by their symbolic connection with loss and sacrifice, and fertility forms a unit with sacrifice of the phallus, castration, and blood.[114]

The warrior who as son is related to the woman, and half identical with her, also represents the masculine, heroic principle and its renewal. Originally the woman was warlike and generative, she was the Amazonian "old hero," and now the same is true of the male. Every man is a warrior, but as such he is also a sacrifice. And just as the woman who gives birth "takes a prisoner," that is to say, gives birth to a future sacrificial victim, so the prisoner's captor is not only his "mother" (for childbearing and taking a prisoner are the same) but is also said to be his father.

When finally the flesh of the slain prisoners is ritually eaten, the captor and owner of the prisoner may not eat of his prisoner's flesh. "He says: 'Shall I then eat myself?' for when he captures him, he says: 'It is as though he were my own son.' And the prisoner says: 'That is my father.' " [115]

According to the same text, the captor is called "sun," "white color," and "feathers," [116] "because he is like one painted white and covered with feathers (one adorned for the sacrifice). The captor was covered with feathers because he had not yet died in battle but would perhaps later and so pay his debt (i.e., be sacrificed). For this reason, his relatives greeted him with tears and words of encouragement." [117]

Thus the dying prisoner was the generative feminine earth prin-

---

[114] In the psychology of the child and the modern psychotic, we find a correspondence to this relationship. Defecation, for example, may be unconsciously experienced either as birth or as loss or castration. The foundation of this archetypal situation is the unity of a male-female, i.e., uroboric, totality, in which the anal zone may be experienced either as childbearing or as conceiving. See my *Origins*, pp. 25 ff., 291.

[115] Preuss, *Die Eingeborenen Amerikas*, p. 46.
[116] These symbols obviously belong to the symbolism of the light (sun) and of the wind and spirit, with which birds and feathers are always associated. But since among the Aztecs white is a symbol of the night or dusk, the allusion is to the dying sun. See Krickeberg, "Das mittelamerikanische Ballspiel."
[117] Preuss, p. 46.

ciple, the woman dying in childbirth; in dying he engendered his heart, the sun. But as the captor who kills, the male warrior is the sun; he is the father of the son who in dying bears the heart-sun principle and thus reinforces the sun of the fathers.

The husking of the corn, the heart, is castration, mutilation, and sacrifice of the essential male part; but at the same time it is birth and a life-giving deed for the benefit of the world or mankind. It is the death and downfall of the earthly principle; but by virtue of its transpersonal relation to the gods and the powers, with which it is identical as sun and godhead, this earthly principle is uroborically whole and immortal and "lives" in the land of the sun, i.e., in the luminous world of the east.

The climax of this development occurs—as in Malekula and in Egypt—in the sacral formula "I and the Father are one," by which the individual emancipates himself from the domination of the Great Mother.

The progress to the male consciousness and the autonomy of the spirit-sun principle requires the "symbolic slaying" of the Great Mother and the heavenly father's support of the son principle that has grown independent of the Earth Mother. Wherever the night sea voyage in pursuit of the sun is undertaken, by the gods or the human soul, it signifies this development toward the relative independence of an ego endowed with such attributes as free will. This tendency, which we have found in the Old World and in Malekula, can also be demonstrated in Aztec Mexico.

It achieves its highest form in the myth of Quetzalcoatl, the Mexican hero figure. He is not a hero who transforms the outside world, but one who transforms himself by atonement. He is the dying and resurrected god, but he is also the hero king and the culture bringer, the earthly and divine representative of the principle of light and humanity. In his dual nature, he combines the western, deathly aspect and the *Fig. 48* eastern aspect of life: he is the evening star and the morning star. As morning star, he is the positive symbol of the ascending power belonging to the male-spiritual aspect of heaven and the sun. For this reason he is associated with the symbol of the east, the plumed serpent, i.e., the wind-ruach-spirit aspect. He is the god of knowledge and the ascending spiral tower is one of his attributes.[118]

The eagle, the luminous sky, devours the serpent of night. The luminous fire of consciousness vanquishes the waters of the unconscious, and, as the Cora Indians say, the "eagle who appears at night naked and small in the middle of the world, as the fire is kindled in the thicket, vanquishes the Old Ones as they sleep, for he wakes.

"Then his feathers grew," and he flew straight away to heaven. "He rose up and stopped in the middle of the sky. There he established himself, turned, and looked down. His feet were a lovely yellow as he stood there. . . . Brightly he looked round him, a lovely yellow is his beak, his eyes shine gloriously. There he remained and looked brightly upon his world." [119]

The cosmic significance of Quetzalcoatl is complex. He is identical with the morning star; he is also a god of the winds and, as a son deity, he differentiates the primordial parents.[120] The same god combines lunar, solar, and astral significance. He is no conceptual entity, but an archetype whose figure can only be suggested by numerous and diverse symbols; he is a fructifying wind god but also the fertility king of the old ritual, who must die in order to fertilize the world with his sacrifice. He is culture bringer and hero, but he is also the penitent who transforms himself.

Quetzalcoatl's name combines *quetzalli*, 'tail feather,' and *coatl*, 'serpent.' He is the plumed serpent and also the serpent with head upraised; [121] in any case, he is a wind and rain god who brings fertility. As son of the primordial deities, Heaven and Earth, combining the lower character of the snakes with the upper character of the birds, he is a uniting symbol.[122] He belongs to the group of such dual gods as Xolotl, whose images [123] show him back to back with the god of death, i.e., in

[118] Vaillant, p. 170; Levy, pp. 184 f.
[119] Preuss, *Nayarit-Expedition*, Vol. I, pp. 193 f., according to Preuss, *Die Eingeborenen Amerikas*, p. 42.
[120] Danzel, Vol. I, p. 39.

[121] Ibid., p. 37.
[122] Jung, *Psychological Types*, s.v. "reconciling symbol."
[123] Danzel, Vol. I, Pls. 18 and 2.

FIG. *48.* QUETZALCOATL UNITED WITH MICTLANTECUHTLI,
GOD OF DEATH

Aztec, from a codex

the union of life and death typical for the gods of the moon, vegetation,
and transformation.

Thus Quetzalcoatl is also Xolotl Nanauatzin, who burns himself up
by way of atonement, and whose heart is turned into the rising morning
star.[124] Furthermore, his strange myth represents him as a beguiled,
vanquished, and fugitive god, whose downfall is connected with the loss

Fig. 49

[124] Ibid., Pls. *55, 56.*

FIG. 49. QUETZALCOATL'S HEART TRANSFORMED INTO THE
MORNING STAR

Aztec, from a codex

of paradise, of the ancient Toltec "golden age." [125] Quetzalcoatl is vanquished by primordial demonic powers with the help of an antigod, who plays the role of Set, the hostile brother of Isis. His sin, which among the Cora Indians is still imputed to the god of the morning star,[126] the sin that brought about the destruction of paradise and his own downfall, consisted of immoderate indulgence in intoxicating drink or sexual pleasure. Beguiled by liquor, the god is seized with uncontrollable yearning for death, to which he finally accedes, vanishing over the ocean on a raft formed by a sea serpent.

It is the sin of the son-lover, unable to resist the seductress who beguiles him in uroboric incest to self-destructive drunkenness.[127]

There is a beautiful tale relating how Quetzalcoatl succumbed to the terrible demonic power of the Great Mother.[128] Despite its late historicizing elaboration, it has preserved an abundance of primordial traits. Quetzalcoatl and also his sister, whom the demons bring to him, are made drunk. But the actual background of the crime, the full implications of which would otherwise be unintelligible, is illumined by a story relating that the demons brought him a "harlot" named Xochiquetzal.[129] This harlot is none other than the goddess of harlots and of love, identical with the Great Mother, and Quetzalcoatl, seduced by her, becomes Xochipilli, the prince of flowers; i.e., seduction by the Mother Goddess makes him regress into her son-lover.

Before the sin, the demons sing a lament over Quetzalcoatl:

> Of quetzal feathers is my house,
> Of yellow tropic bird's feathers,
> And of red shells.
> And now, it is said,
> I must leave it. Woe is me, woe.

And:

> My elder sister Quetzalpetlatl,
> Where is thy dwelling place?
> Let us now make ourselves drunk.
> Alas, alas, alas.

[125] Krickeberg, *Märchen*, p. 41.
[126] Ibid., pp. 337 f., with a reference to Preuss.
[127] My *Origins*, pp. 277 f.
[128] Krickeberg, p. 65.
[129] Ibid., p. 342.

But after the deed, Quetzalcoatl sings a lament for himself, in which he reveals the background of his downfall:

> A lament he made, a song
> About his going away, and sang:
> "Our mother
> The goddess with the mantle of snakes,
> Is taking me with her
> As her child.
> I weep."

Paradise, whose symbol is the yucca plant, is lost, and the others sing:

> The yucca is broken
> Let us behold it,
> Let us weep over it.[130]

Even Quetzalcoatl—in whom not only the lunar and astral quality but the solar quality as well was so strong that he nearly developed into the one supreme god of the Aztecs—could not withstand the power of the Terrible Mother. As land of origination, as mother, and as intoxicating sister-beloved, the Feminine proved stronger than the Masculine. True, the Feminine already appears here in its dual form; but since the transformative figure of the sister has not yet crystallized out of the elementary mother figure, the Feminine becomes the Terrible Mother who is doom.

[130] The four laments are from Krickeberg, pp. 66–68. After a long penitential wandering, in which Quetzalcoatl leaves his home and goes alone into foreign places, he at length transcends his doom by a heroic act of self-sacrifice and appears transformed as the morning star. How it was possible for Quetzalcoatl to combine the qualities not only of moon and stars but also of the sun, to such a degree that he almost became the supreme, unitary god of the Aztecs, cannot concern us here.

B
THE TRANSFORMATIVE
CHARACTER

Chapter Twelve

THE GREAT ROUND

WHILE in the elementary character the emphasis is almost entirely on the Archetypal Feminine and the individual is merely dependent, the center of gravity shifts when we come to the transformative character; for now what is transformed and transforms itself, i.e., the aspect of independence and individuality, moves into the foreground. But even in this phase the Feminine remains dominant; the Great Round stands at the beginning and end of the transformation that here takes place.

We shall attempt to describe the transformative character in phases rising from its containment in the totality of the Great Round to the natural plane and finally to the cultural level. The resultant development leads from the Great Goddess as Great Round to the natural plane and the bond between the Great Goddess and the world of plant and animal life, thence ascends to the cultural plane and the primordial mysteries of the Feminine, and finally reaches its climax and turning point in spiritual transformation.

In its entire phenomenology, the elementary character of the Feminine appears as the Great Round, which is and contains the universe. Its positive and negative aspects encompass the upper and the lower, the nearest and the remotest.

Night sky, earth, underworld, and primordial ocean are correlated with this feminine principle, which originally appears as dark and darkly embracing. The uroboric goddess of the beginning is the Great Goddess of the Night, although she is seldom worshiped directly as such.

It is self-evident that the early phase of man's existence, the matriarchal world of the beginning with which we are here concerned, could not be reflected in a discursive consciousness; for this was the time before the genesis of human consciousness, before the birth of the sun.[1] Its archetypal reality is to be found in the symbols, myths, and figures by which men speak of it; but all these are image and metaphor, never knowledge or the direct, reasoned statement by which the later, patriarchal world, rooted in consciousness, knows itself and seeks to formulate itself in religion, philosophy, and science. Moreover, because the patriarchal world strives to deny its dark and "lowly" lineage, its origin in this primordial world, it does everything in its power to conceal its own descent from the Dark Mother and—both rightly and wrongly at once—considers it necessary to forge a "higher genealogy," tracing its descent from heaven, the god of heaven,[2] and the luminous aspect.[3] But nearly all the early and primitive documents trace the origin of the world and of man to the darkness, the Great Round, the goddess.

Whether, as in countless myths, the source of all life is the primordial ocean or whether it is earth or heaven, these sources have one thing in common: *darkness*. It is this primordial darkness which bears the light as moon, stars, and sun, and almost everywhere these luminaries are looked upon as the offspring of the Nocturnal Mother.

It is this common factor, the darkness of the primordial night as the symbol of the unconscious, which accounts for the identity of night sky, earth, underworld, and the primeval water that preceded the light. For the unconscious is the mother of all things, and all things that stand in the light of consciousness are childlike in relation to the darkness—as is consciousness, which is also a child of these primordial depths.

We have designated this original psychic situation, which embraces opposites and contains male and female, conscious and anticonscious,

---

[1] My *Origins and History of Consciousness,* pp. 106 f.

[2] Characteristically, the Chinese ideogram for the god of heaven signifies "man with big head" (cf. the note in Rousselle's translation of Lao-tzu: *Lau-Dse, Führung und Kraft aus der Ewigkeit,* p. 64).

[3] My *Origins,* pp. 147 f.

elements in mixture, as "uroboric." [4] In Babylonia the male-female unity of the uroboros is constituted by Tiamat and Apsu,[5] who are the primordial chaos of the water. But Tiamat is the actual principle of origination: mother of the gods and possessor of the table of fate. Thus it is written: "Apsu, the oldest of beings, their progenitor, 'Mummu' Tiamat, who bare each and all of them"; [6] and it is taken for granted that Apsu and Mummu should submit their decisions to Tiamat.[7]

Tiamat survives the death of Apsu,[8] and when she is finally defeated by Marduk, the patriarchal sun god, the upper vault of heaven and the lower vault of the underworld are fashioned from her body. Thus, even after her defeat, she remains the all-containing Great Round. She is the "belly as such," and when the later gods disturbed her, it was said: "Tiamat was troubled . . . Her belly was stirred up." [9]

In primitive psychology, which can be followed down to the psychology of modern man,[10] this "belly," with which Tiamat is in a sense identical, is the seat of the unconscious and particularly of the emotions, which rise up "from below" and becloud or exclude the upper region, the head. Thus in connection with a passage that he translates as "Tiamat's feelings were outraged," Budge remarks: "Literally 'she put evil into her belly,' the internal organs being regarded as the seat of the affections." [11]

But Tiamat, whose open gullet seeks to devour Marduk, the solar hero, is not only evil; she is also the generative cave-womb of the Great Mother. Thus when Marduk fought with her, "he looked upon the 'middle' or 'inside' or 'womb' of Tiamat [or perhaps the belly of Tiamat] and divined the plan of Kingu who had taken up his place therein." [12] Similarly the relation of Tiamat to Kingu shows Tiamat to be the Great

[4] Part I, p. 20.

[5] The tohu bohu of the Biblical narrative of creation (Gen. 1:2).

[6] The Seven Tablets of Creation, I: 3, 4, in Budge and Smith, *The Babylon Legends of the Creation*.

[7] Budge and Smith, I: 32.

[8] The interpretation of Apsu as "fresh water" contradicts his identification with the "evil aspect," which represents an overlaying of the matriarchal stratum in which Tiamat ruled over heaven, earth, and underworld, while Apsu symbolized the earth-fructifying aspect of the male partner. In accordance with the law that decrees the negativization of surpassed powers and gods, both he and Tiamat were regarded in later times as solely "evil and abysmal."

[9] Budge and Smith, I, 22, 23.

[10] My *Origins*, pp. 25 ff.

[11] Budge and Smith, p. 37.

[12] Ibid., p. 20.

Mother. Kingu, identical with Tammuz, is the son-lover [13] whom Tiamat calls her husband but who is also the child sitting in her "womb."

Thus we repeatedly find the engendering male principle "in" the Feminine. The psychic equation of the unconscious is seed = phallus = son. All three are variants of the masculine procreative principle that remains subordinated to the Feminine in which it operates. This fundamental constellation forms the basis of the relation between the Great Mother and the son-lover.

Psychologically, this means that as long as the creative elements of the unconscious, those elements which strive toward the light, have not established their own luminous realm of the spirit and of consciousness, they are and remain dependent parts of the unconscious. But Tiamat's helpers are not only the evil powers that this "Ummu-Khubur" spawns.[14] The star gods, the gods of the night sky, which she created, are also her allies; and the tables of fate, which she, as great mistress of the magic incantation, handed down, are the constellations of the night sky.

Therefore Tiamat is far from being only the abysmal, nocturnal monster that the later patriarchal world of the victorious Marduk saw in her. She is not only the genetrix but also the true mother of her creatures. She is filled with wrath when Apsu and Mummu decide to kill the gods, her children; and it is only when the gods have slain Apsu, her husband, the primordial father, that she takes up the battle of vengeance against them and becomes destructive.

The question of how far Tiamat nevertheless succumbed to Marduk, the solar hero, need not concern us here. In any event she is an arbitrary ruler; the star gods and all destiny are the products of her caprice. Tiamat is the irrational power of the primordial age and of the creative unconscious. Even in her death she remains the upper and lower

---

[13] My *Origins*, index, s.v. "Great Mother, and son-lover."

[14] Budge and Smith, I: 113 ff. The dominant role of Tiamat can still be seen in the late record of the Babylonian priest Berossus: ". . . over all these (creatures) ruled a woman named Omorka. This in Chaldean is *thamte*, meaning in Greek 'the sea,' but in numerical value it is equal to 'moon' " [quoted from Heidel, *The Babylonian Genesis*, p. 67, who remarks that Omorka is a title of Tiamat]. It is in keeping with the same context when Damascius, in his listing of the first gods, mentions the goddess before the gods. Ibid., p. 65.

world into which she is split:[15] the Great Round that is primordial water, primordial parent, heaven, earth, and underworld, merciful and avenging in one. Marduk, on the other hand, is a lawgiver: to each of the celestial powers he assigns a fixed place, and like the God of the Biblical narrative of creation he orders the world according to rational laws that correspond to consciousness and its solar nature.

In Tiamat the numinous character of the Great Goddess still takes the form of a monster, but more frequently the early Goddess, when her fecundity and sexual character are stressed, appears nude with accentuated sexual characteristics. Yet in the representations of the clothed Great Goddess, which we likewise encounter at a very early date, the goddess as the Great Round of the beginning has not only assumed human form, but reveals, side by side with archaic elements, transformative and spiritual forms of the Feminine that become distinct only in later stages of development.[16]

The alabaster figure of the goddess of Mari and the seated funerary *Pl. 87* figure from Tell Halaf come from entirely different periods.[16a] In spite *Pl. 88* of their fundamental diversity, they resemble one another in the predominance of this spiritual expression. In the one it is manifested in the overaccentuation of the head with its towerlike headdress and large black eye craters; in the other by the magical chthonic quality of the self-contained, enthroned form, in relation to which the birdlike and almost expressionless head, bound firmly to the body by the hair hanging down from it, claims no independent existence. An intermediary link between the two is a veiled sphinx of Tell Halaf. "What is different *Pl. 89* from all the other Tell Halaf statues is the eyes. Instead of a big white inset, in which a small flat polished center of black stone is inlaid as the pupil, we have here an oval black stone center, markedly standing out, filling almost the whole eye-socket, and with a narrow white ring round it." [17]

We find the same eyes in our alabaster goddess, who like the sphinx *Pl. 87*

---

[15] My *Origins:* "The Separation of the World Parents."

[16] Since the "Astarte type," holding flowers or a flower and a snake at her breast, is the most familiar, I have accorded it the least attention in my selection of reproductions.

[16a] Cf. Frankfort, *Ancient Orient*, p. 256, n. 42

[17] Oppenheim, *Tell Halaf*, p. 109.

of Tell Halaf may be presumed to have originally been a night goddess, or rather a goddess of the night sky.

The death-underworld aspect of the goddess generally known as Ishtar is often symbolized by scorpions. The giant griffins with the scorpion's tail may be dominant beasts of a Great Goddess of Tell Halaf, who encompasses the darkness of the heavens and the underworld. Between the legs of the giant griffins we thus find a relief representing them as victorious over frightened lions,[18] the beasts of the sun.[19]

The Tell Halaf griffin hewn from black basalt, with telescopelike eyes formed of white limestone disks with great black pupils, has been regarded—incorrectly it seems to us—as a "bird of the sun." We believe it to be primarily a symbol of the night sky, like the eagle that Preuss (in writing of the Indians) tells us "symbolized the night sky and was later identified with the sun." It is associated with the great nocturnal goddess, the veiled sphinx.[20] The fourteen-sided basalt pillar on which the bird sits indicates a connection with the moon and shows (like the half-moon banners found there and the half-moon-shaped ornaments worn both by men and women) that the Great Goddess was worshiped as a goddess of the night.

Whereas many figures of the Great Goddess disclose either one or the other, either the elementary or the transformative, character of the Feminine, these early plastics reveal the unity of the two characters, the Great Round. Although they manifest a new aspect—the spiritual transformative character of Sophia, which transcends the earth-night-unconscious aspect of the Feminine—still the archaic self-contained form expresses the uroboric self-containment of the psychic situation of origination.

We also find this primordial uroboric situation of the Great Round in the religion and mythology of Egypt, the earliest seat of a highly developed culture; and the Great Goddesses, which for this reason are all

[18] Ibid., p. 170.
[19] See below, pp. 272 f.
[20] The occurrence of the same patterns on the sphinx and on the wings of the griffins indicates a connection between them.

identified with one another, are different expressions of the archetypal picture of the Great Mother. The unity of the primordial waters is male-female. Though later the god Nu or Nun, the oldest of the gods, was identified with the primordial ocean, Moret rightly says of him: "But he was a purely intellectual creation. In essence, the Nun is unorganized chaos, nothingness." [21]

The uroboric, male-female anonymity of the beginning [22] is best expressed by the mythology of Hermopolis,[23] whose eight original gods—Nun and Naunet, Huh and Hauhet, Kuk and Kauket, Amun and Amaunet—symbolize the primordial water,[24] spatial infinity, the darkness before the creation of the heavenly bodies, and impenetrable mystery.[25] The primordial ocean is a uroboric snake encompassing the earth that is born of it, and at the end of the world taking everything born of it back into its primordial waters:

> And I shall destroy everything I created. The earth will again appear as primordial ocean [Nun], as endlessness [Huh] as in the beginning. I [then] am everything that remains . . . after I have turned myself back into a snake that no man knows.[26]

In the official Egyptian religion and mythology the patriarchal re-working of a primary matriarchal symbolism is already clearly discernible. A case in point is the birth of the sun from the cosmic egg laid by the Nile goose, which is worshiped as the "great chatterer," the creator of the world.[27] Even if Bachofen had not informed us of the cosmogonic significance of the swamp birds,[28] it would be evident that the layer of the cosmic egg, from which the sun-chick emerged, must

---

[21] Moret, *The Nile and Egyptian Civilization*, p. 374.

[22] My *Origins*, p. 118.

[23] Criteria derived from experience in depth psychology almost always enable us to state what is original and what is secondary in a mythology. It is true that the Hermopolis formulation is conceptual and hence late, but it is the most perfect formulation of elements otherwise represented only in pictorial symbols.

[24] In a primitive form we find the goddess of the primordial waters as the frog-shaped Heqet, who is equated with Nekhbet, the vulture goddess. In Hermopolis she is the primordial mother of all existence, which she generates and protects.

[25] Kees, *Der Götterglaube im alten Aegypten*, p. 307.

[26] Kees, p. 216.

[27] Kees, p. 309.

[28] Bachofen, *Mutterrecht*, pp. 233 f.

originally have been a female. Thus the cosmic personification of the primordial water as Methyer, "the great flood," and as cow, which already appears in the Pyramid Texts,[29] is unquestionably an original and primitive symbol of the primordial age: "Methyer represents a feminine nature-myth variant of the Heliopolitan [male] primordial water Nun, while the cow as goddess of heaven is a variant of the Heliopolitan Nut [Lady of Heaven]." [30]

As we know, the Heliopolitan recension of the Egyptian religion is emphatically patriarchal. The priests of Heliopolis, the city of the sun, did their best, though not always successfully, to obliterate and overlay the old matriarchal religion.

The primordial flood as cow, or the cow as the first living creature rising from the primordial flood, is an authentic symbol of world-creating motherhood.[31] It accords with the other cow figures of Egyptian myth: Hathor, the great, cow-headed mother goddess, and Nut, the heavenly cow goddess who waters the earth with her rain-milk and carries the sun god on her back. To this context belong the cow and calf on the ancient seal of the twelfth Egyptian nome, from which Isis came and which was called the Divine Calf,[32] and the same is true of the well-known Cretan pottery images of cow and calf, goat and kid.

The great Egyptian cow goddess is "the watery abyss of heaven"; Mehurt, one of her variants, gives birth to the sun god.[33] In reality the unity of Hathor, Nut, and Isis encompasses all goddesses. Mehurt is sometimes represented as a "pregnant woman with protruding breasts" [34] and "sometimes she has the body of a woman and the head of a cow, and then she holds in her right hand a scepter round which is twined the stalk of a lotus flower, which she appears to be smelling; the flower itself is between the symbol of the South and the North and is supposed to represent the great world lotus flower, out of which rose the sun for the first time at the creation." [35]

[29] Pyramid Texts, 508, 1131, according to Kees, p. 75, n. 6.
[30] Kees, p. 75, n. 6.
[31] The same symbolism is found in India down to our own time.
[32] Kees, p. 76.
[33] Book of the Dead, Ch. XVII.
[34] Budge, The Gods of the Egyptians, Vol. I, p. 422.
[35] Ibid., p. 423.

If we recall the Egyptian forms of the Terrible Mother—Am-mit, the devourer of souls at the judgment of the dead, Ta-urt, and the goddesses of the gates of the underworld—it will not surprise us that the judgment of the dead should take place in the hall of Mehurt—one more indication of the original universality of the Egyptian Great Goddess, who also encompasses the underworld and the watery abyss. For in her character of Hathor, the Great Goddess is not only the "house of Horus," i.e., goddess of the eastern sky, where Horus, the sun, is born, but also the cow of the western mountain, the goddess of the dead.

Like all primordial mothers, she is, in the mythical paradox, her father's mother and her son's daughter; that is to say, she bears the male by whom she is begotten.[36] She is the vulture Mother Goddess of the south, Nekhbet, the white-crowned Great Goddess of Upper Egypt, who is worshiped as a "form of the primeval abyss which brought forth the light," and whose name means "the father of fathers, the mother of mothers, who hath existed from the beginning and is the creatrix of the world." [37] Heaven and vulture are the Mother's upper aspect as underworld and the serpent is her lower aspect. In her character of serpent she is Uadjet, who like Nekhbet was identified with Isis and all other goddesses. And just as the cow was both upper and lower, the serpent was also twofold: heavenly and subterranean.

But the goddess is not merely the vessel of the Great Round; she is also the dynamic of the life contained in it. In Egypt as in India [38] and in alchemy this dynamic is manifested as fire and heat. This fire can be consuming and destructive, but it can also be the positive fire of transformation. A chapter of the Book of the Dead, which was characteristically recited over the image of a cow, is called "The Chapter of Making Heat to Be Under the Head of the Deceased." [39] The chapter is attributed to the heavenly cow goddess, who was said to have composed it for the benefit of her endangered son Ra. Concerning this recitation it is written: "This is a composition of exceedingly great mystery. Let not the eye of any man whatsoever see it, for it is an abominable thing

---

[36] My *Origins*, p. 52.
[37] Budge, *The Gods*, Vol. I, p. 440.

[38] My *Origins*, pp. 21 f.
[39] (Tr. Budge), Ch. CLXII.

for (every man) to know it; therefore hide it. 'Book of the mistress of the hidden temple' is its name."

In Egypt, fire symbolism is usually associated with another form oᶜ the Great Goddess, the cat-bodied or cat-headed Bast, and the lion goddess Sekmet. The lion goddess symbolizes the devouring, negative aspect of the sun-desert-fire, the solar eye that burns and judges; while Bast, although she is a goddess of the east, is goddess not of the sun but of the moon. For the moon as well as the sun is born in the east and dies in the west.

The nocturnal cat with eyes that are believed to become roundest at the full moon is an animal of the moon; consequently it is green and associated with pregnant women. Its son is the moon, whose function it is "to make the woman fruitful and to make the human germ grow in his mother's womb," and who "was supposed to do this especially in his character of the 'moon the light bearer.' " [40]

This conception of the moon, which totally overlooks the earthly man, is clearly matriarchal.[41] Thus in Egypt the vulture was thought to be solely female and fertilized by the wind; in their aspect of vulture goddesses, Nekhbet and Nut are "daughter and mother who created their begettor." [42] And the snake symbolized the self-renewing character of the Great Egyptian Goddess.

Through her kinship with the moon, Bast takes her place in the unitary world of the Archetypal Feminine, as does Net or Neith, the lady of the West, one of the oldest and most widely distributed Egyptian deities, going back to the predynastic era. She is the goddess of Saïs, of whom Plutarch wrote: "I am all that has been, and is, and shall be, and my robe no mortal has yet uncovered." [43] Her cult was already ancient in the first dynasty. She too is male-female, belonging to the era of psychic origination, and her matriarchal character is more distinct than that of any other Egyptian goddess. Goddess of magic and weaving, unborn goddess, originating in herself, she was worshiped with mysteries and lantern processions. She is the personification "of the

[40] Budge, *The Gods*, Vol. I, p. 448.
[41] Briffault, *The Mothers*, index, s.v. "moon."
[42] Kees, p. 353.
[43] *De Iside et Osiride*, IX (tr. Babbitt).

great, inert, primeval watery mass." [44] In her character of cow with eighteen stars, she is the night sky, and—like the later Hecate—she is the "opener of the way," holding the key of the fertility goddesses, the key to the gates of the womb and the underworld, the gates of death and rebirth.

Budge sums up her significance in words that describe the Great Goddess in her full scope. "The statements of Greek writers, taken together with the evidence derived from the hieroglyphic texts, prove that in very early times Net was the personification of the eternal female principle of life which was self-sustaining and self-existent and was secret and unknown and all-pervading; the more material thinkers, whilst admitting that she brought forth her son Ra without the aid of a husband, were unable to divorce from their minds the idea that a male germ was necessary for this production, and finding it impossible to derive it from a power or being external to the goddess, assumed that she herself provided not only the substance which was to form the body of Ra but also the male germ which fecundated it. Thus Net was the prototype of parthenogenesis." [45]

Only now are we in a position to understand the significance of the Goddess Hathor's identification with the four cardinal points and four quarters of the world characterized by the goddesses Nekhbet, Uadjet, Bast, and Neith.[46] Since, as Jung has repeatedly shown, the quaternary is the archetypal symbol of wholeness, this quaternary of Hathor [47] is the symbol of the Archetypal Feminine as the world-governing totality in all its aspects.

The goddess Neith is identified with the heaven goddess Nut, the feminine form of the primeval ocean that we have already encountered as Nu or Nun. While in another symbolic order Nut rises as vault of *Pl. 92* heaven over the earth conceived as a flat disk, the male deity Geb, she is, in her character of celestial cow, the feminine principle, identical with the primeval water and genetrix of the sun, whose rays, in con- *Pl. 36* junction with the rain-milk flowing from her breast, nourish the earth.

[44] Budge, *The Gods*, Vol. I, p. 451. [46] Ibid., p. 438.
[45] Ibid., p. 462. [47] Kees, p. 220.

To Nut as the upper vault corresponds Naunet as the lower vault, the counterheaven lying "under" the disk of the earth, the two together forming the Great Round of the feminine vessel. But Naunet, the counterheaven, through which the sun passes at night, is identical with *Pl. 91a* Nut; for Nut is not only the daytime sky but also the western devourer of the sun that passes back to the east through her body, which is the upper night sky.

Thus Nut is water above and below, vault above and below, life and death, east and west, generating and killing, in one. For she is not only the lady "with the thousand souls," [48] who "causes the stars to manifest their souls," [49] but also the sow, who devours her own children, sun, moon, and stars in the west.

The Great Goddess is the flowing unity of subterranean and celestial primordial water,[50] the sea of heaven on which sail the barks of the gods of light, the circular life-generating ocean above and below the earth. To her belong all waters, streams, fountains, ponds, and springs, as well as the rain. She is the ocean of life with its life- and death-bringing seasons, and life is her child, a fish eternally swimming inside her, like the stars in the celestial ocean of the Mexican Mayauel [51] and like men in the fishpool of Mother Church—a late manifestation of the same archetype.

As vault of heaven she covers her creatures on earth like a hen sheltering her chicks, and accordingly she is named not only "Door" but also "Coverer of the Sky." [52] In innumerable representations, the outstretched wings of Isis, a fundamental form of the Great Mother, embrace, cover, and shelter Osiris and with him all the dead.

Pls. 90b, 91b The goddess Nut, represented· on the top of the sarcophagus as taking the dead man into her arms, is the same mother of death as the Christian Pietà, the Madonna, holding in her lap the dead Jesus, the *Pl. 94* child of death, who has returned to her.[53] And she is identical with the primitive vessel and urn that shelter both child and adult.[54]

---

[48] Ibid., p. 147, n. 1.
[49] Ibid., p. 226.
[50] Ibid., pp. 72 and 226, n. 4.
[51] See below, p. 301.
[52] Budge, *The Gods*, p. 106.

[53] We find a last modern manifestation of this archetype in Epstein's magnificent sculpture, *The Night* (Pl. 95), above the doorway to the headquarters of London Transport.
[54] See above, p. 134.

Already in the Rig-Veda the earth is invoked as the coverer who takes the dead man to herself: "As a mother covers her son with the hem of her cloak, so cover him thou, O earth." [55]

Here as everywhere the Great Mother encompasses and "is" heaven and earth, and water as night sky. Only later, with the separation of the primordial parents,[56] are light, sun, and consciousness born, and with them differentiation. Now, but only now, there is an upper and a lower heaven, Nut and Naunet, and between them lie Geb, the disk of the earth; Shu, the airy space; and Ra, the sun, son of the primeval water and the cow.[57]

In the matriarchal sphere, the daytime sky is the realm where the sun is born and dies, not, as later, the realm over which it rules. It is the light span of life, beginning and ending in night; within it the luminous son must describe his arc of light, which always ends in death.

The night sky is a reflection of the earth; [58] the two together form the primordial cave from which men, plants, and the luminous godhead arise. This is most evident in Mexico, where Huitzilopochtli, the Aztec sun god, shares the fate of the moon god and all the other gods of light. Over and over again he must "become bones"; i.e., die through and in the Terrible Mother of earthly and nocturnal darkness. The gods of light, however, are indistinguishable from the youthful gods of vegetation, of the corn and the flowers; for the stars are the flowers and cornstalks of heaven, and the flowers and cornstalks are the stars of the earth.[59] These Mexican dying youthful gods of vegetation correspond in every respect, and especially in their fatal dependency on the Great Mother, to Adonis, Tammuz, and other dying gods of the flowers and grain in the Old World.

It was only with the dominance of the patriarchal, solar world that the morning achieved its importance as the time of the sun's birth. Yet even then, it is interesting to note, time was not reckoned from sunrise but at the earliest from midnight.[60] In the matriarchal sphere, i.e.,

---

[55] Rig-Veda, X, 18, 45; cf. Geldner, *Vedismus und Brahmanismus*.

[56] My *Origins*, p. 102.

[57] See above, pp. 218 f.

[58] Krickeberg, *Märchen*, p. 312.

[59] My *Origins*, pp. 49 f.

[60] Solar mythology, with its conception of the full day, i.e., a unity of day and night, is a late abstraction. The original form was a unity of the night with its lunar process and a unity of the day with its solar arc, beginning with birth and ending in death. In the myth of the night

wherever the lunar mythology predominates, the reckoning of time begins and ends with nightfall.[61] Even in Egypt the evening is the time of birth,[62] because for early man the appearance of the stars and the moon is the visible "birth"; and the morning, when the luminous world of the stars vanishes, is a time of death, in which the daytime sky devours the children of the night.

This conception, which was universal among early mankind, becomes understandable if we free ourselves from the correlation day = sun. The sun is a son of the female daytime sky, just as the moon is a son of the night sky. The female sky is the fixed and enduring element; the luminaries—sun, moon, and stars—that rise and fall within the black-and-white cosmic egg of the Great Goddess are transient and perishable.

The correlation of the starry firmament with the Feminine determines the whole early view of the world, whether we speak of a Milky Way or whether this portion of the heavens is assigned to Hel,[63] the northern ruler of the night, and is called the "Path of Hel" or "of Hilda." [64]

Pl. 93   Thus in the zodiac of Dendera, a late representation of the Egyptian view of the heavens, Ta-urt, the matriarchal Great Mother, and the bull's thigh as symbol of the North Pole [65] occupy the center of the spiral in which the star gods and animal signs are ordered. Here we have a projection upon the heavens of the matriarchal situation of the Great Mother with her sacrificed son-lover. The bull's thigh, originally the thigh of a hippopotamus,[66] is Set's phallic "leg," [67] from which the Nile flows, but it is also the moon that is damaged and must be made whole again.[68]

Accordingly Set in his character of red hippopotamus is not only the enemy; he is not only red, evil, sin, desert, dark moon, and the de-

---

sea voyage, we already have an integration of the opposites: day-night, conscious-unconscious, male-female.
    [61] Cf. Bachofen, *Mutterrecht*, index, s.v. "Mond"; "Nacht."
    [62] Kees, p. 225.
    [63] See above, p. 170.

[64] Ninck, *Wodan und germanischer Schicksalsglaube*, pp. 177 f.
    [65] Kees, p. 321.
    [66] Ibid., p. 321, n., and p. 331, n. 1.
    [67] Ibid., p. 321.
    [68] Ibid., p. 424.

vouring darkness that swallows up the Osiris-moon [69]—originally, he is a "great god," having also the function of the good god, Osiris. And before the patriarchal Isis-Osiris relation, over against which Set is the evil one, there existed between Isis and Set a relationship that was by no means in keeping with the schema of a "good Isis." [70]

The chopped-off thigh is a symbol of castration, while thigh, leg, and moon are also phallic symbols of the procreative principle. Set, however, was connected originally with Ta-urt, the mother sow, and with the hippopotamus; he was the engendering boar and the male hippopotamus. His sacrifice was later replaced by the sacrifice of Osiris.

This matriarchal symbolism of the heavens survived in Egypt for thousands of years after the patriarchal solar theology had become the official world view. We find a corresponding situation in Mexico, where the celestial pole was looked upon as the "hole" in which the drill is inserted in firemaking.[71] Long after the patriarchate has become dominant in every sphere, we still encounter the matriarchal conception according to which the heavens and worlds revolve around the "hole," that is to say, the Great Mother, out of which life is drilled. And in India (on a higher plane), immortality is "whipped" from the female milk sea, of which it is said: "Water is the life milk of the world body, and the cosmic space is a sea of milk." [72]

Now that we have gained some idea of the full scope of the Great Mother, who in truth encompasses almost everything—heaven, water, and earth, while even fire is her son—it becomes evident that the Feminine cannot be identified with the telluric-chthonic, the lower, earthly principle, as the later patriarchal world and its religions and philosophies would have it. The totality of the Archetypal Feminine goes far beyond the projection in which she unites the elements of earth, water, air, and fire.

---

[69] Briffault, *The Mothers*, Vol. II, p. 768.
[70] Cf. my *Origins*, pp. 64–68.

[71] Krickeberg, "Das mittelamerikanische Ballspiel und seine religiöse Symbolik," p. 153, n.
[72] Zimmer, *Maya*, p. 101.

THE GODDESS OF FATE

After all that has been said, it is not hard to see that space is one of the most important projections of the Feminine as a totality; if there were no other indications of this, it would follow from her character of containing vessel and cosmic egg. But the Feminine is also the goddess of time, and thus of fate. The symbol in which space and time are archetypally connected is the starry firmament, which since the primordial era has been filled with human projections. Here it is a matter of indifference whether—as in Egypt, Babylonia, Arabia, India, China, and America—the heavens are interpreted as originally, according to the primordial twenty-eight stations of the moon, or as later, according to the twelve stations of the sun; and whether animal or plant, stream or ocean, are the dominant projections.[1] The essential point is that each one of these projections was experienced as a part of the life of the Great Goddess, who bears and encompasses all things.

The dependency of all the luminous bodies, of all the heavenly powers and gods, on the Great Mother, their rise and fall, their birth and death, their transformation and renewal, are among the most profound experiences of mankind. Not only the alternation of day and night but also the changes of the months, seasons, and years are subordinated to the all-powerful will of the Great Mother. And that is why, not only as the Mesopotamian Tiamat, but throughout the world, she holds the tables of fate, the all-determining constellations of heaven, which is herself. And accordingly the Great Mother, adorned with the moon and the starry cloak of night, is the goddess of destiny, weaving life as she weaves fate.

Since she governs growth, the Great Mother is goddess of time. That is why she is a moon goddess, for moon and night sky are the visible manifestations of the temporal process in the cosmos, and the moon, not the sun, is the true chronometer of the primordial era. From menstruation, with its supposed relation to the moon, pregnancy, and beyond, the woman is regulated by and dependent on time; so it is

[1] See above, p. 41.

she who determines time—to a far greater extent than the male, with his tendency toward the conquest of time, toward timelessness and eternity.[2] And this temporal quality of the Feminine is bound up with the moon. The temporal quality as well as the element of water are to be correlated with the Feminine, and this connection is made plain in the symbol "stream of time."

The primordial mystery [3] of weaving and spinning has also been experienced in projection upon the Great Mother who weaves the web of life and spins the threads of fate, regardless whether she appears as one Great Spinstress or, as so frequently, in a lunar triad. It is not by accident that we speak of the body's "tissues," for the tissue woven by the Feminine in the cosmos and in the uterus of woman is life and destiny. And astrology, the study of a destiny governed by the stars, teaches that both begin at once, at the temporal moment of birth.

Thus the Great Goddesses are weavers, in Egypt as in Greece, among the Germanic peoples and the Mayans. And because "reality" is wrought [4] by the Great Weavers, all such activities as plaiting, weaving, and knotting belong to the fate-governing activity of the woman, who, as Bachofen discovered,[5] is a spinner and weaver in her natural aspect.

The crossing of the threads is the symbol of sexual union—we still speak of a crossing of animals and plants—and the crossing of the sexes is the basic form in which the Archetypal Feminine "weaves" life.[6] Thus the Great Round is the world-containing and world-creating uterus, in which the real, the corporeal, and the material are formed by the Great Mother herself. The temporal moment of our birth (the epoch) and the body (the constitution) are the fated components of the individual existence, which everyone who seeks a fundamental understanding of the contingency of the individual life must accept.

[2] Cf. my "Über den Mond und das matriarchale Bewusstsein."

[3] See below, Ch. 15.

[4] 'To work' (OE. *wircan* = G. *wirken;* cf. ME. *wreak, wrought*) = 'to weave' is the restricted form of 'to work' = 'to perform an opus' = 'to perform a sacred action.' In all the actions, the goddess is the Maya, the great weaver of life.

[5] Bachofen, *Versuch über die Gräbersymbolik der Alten*, index, s.v. "Weben."

[6] Here we cannot go into the symbolism of the cross.

In line with its archetypal character, weaving has its positive as well as its negative significance, and all the Great Mothers—Neith, Netet, and Isis; Eileithyia or Athene; Urth, Holda, Percht, or Ixchel; and even the witch in the fairy tales—are spinners of destiny.

"Thus," writes Ninck, "in the beginning of the 'Song of Helgi,' the poet, by way of indicating the greatness of his hero, speaks of the weavers of fate, who are busily engaged in marking off the field of each man's future activity as he enters into life. The spinning, weaving women of fate survive to this day in fairy tales. Their presence at birth points to the knowledge born of experience that man 'comes into the world' with certain 'gifts' and 'aptitudes.' The reason for their appearance in threes or nines, or more seldom in twelves, is to be sought in the threefold articulation underlying all created things; but here it refers most particularly to the three temporal stages of all growth (beginning-middle-end, birth-life-death, past-present-future). Two of the Norns spin and twist the thread, the third breaks it off; two of the women are kindly and gracious, but the third lays a curse on their gifts. Later generations sought to create a connection between the three stages of time, past, present, and future, and the three names of the Norns: Urth, Verthandi, and Skuld; only the name of Urth is old:

> "It was the olden time, eagles screamed,
> From the mountains of heaven fell holy dew.
> It was then that Borghild bare the joyous Helgi
> In the castle of Bralund.

> It was night in the court, the Norns came,
> They created the fate of the treasure-bestower:
> Noblest of rulers, most glorious of warriors
> Was he to be.

> Firmly they fastened the threads of fate
> For the breacher of fortresses in Bralund's castle;
> They spun out golden thread,
> Fastening it in the middle beneath the hall of the moon.

They secured the ends in the East and West,
The Prince's land lay in between;
To Northward Neri's daughter cast
One of the bands, unbreakable." [7]

The oldest known representation of the great feminine triad, accompanied by the moon and perhaps the planet Venus, is to be found on *Pl. 101a* an Akkadian cylinder seal; its correspondences are the numerous Greek goddesses who appear in threes,[8] the Roman weaving goddesses of fate, *Fig. 50; Pl. 101b*

FIG. *50.* GODDESSES OF FATE
Coin of Diocletian, c. A.D. 300

and the many other threefold mother goddesses, including the three-headed Hecate, goddess of the crossroads.

But in her character of spinstress, the Great Mother not only spins human life but also the fate of the world, its darkness as well as its light. An old Swedish song runs:

> Mistress Sun sat on a bare stone
> And spun on her golden distaff
> For three hours before the sun rose.

And in an Estonian song:

[7] Ninck, *Götter- und Jenseitsglaube der Germanen*, pp. 145–146. [The "Song of Helgi" is from the Poetic Edda; cf. H. A. Bellows (tr.), *The Poetic Edda*, pp. 291–92—ED.] [8] Harrison, *Prolegomena to the Study of Greek Religion*.

The warp was woven at noon,
The woof in the house of dawn,
The rest in the hall of the sun. . .

Wrought on the loom,
Danced on the treads. . . .

Golden gown woven for the moon,
Shimmering veil for the little sun.

These spinstresses are originally the Great Women of Fate, the three-fold form of the Great Mother, for everywhere spinning is the business of women. And the attribution of weaving to the male creator god in the Estonian song is merely a typical patriarchal usurpation.[9] Where the material is adequately interpreted, it becomes evident that the spin-stresses are the mothers and not the daughters of the sun.

Thus the Moirai, the Greek goddesses of fate, who stand over the gods of Olympus, are in Homer also called Klothes, the Spinstresses. The Moirai, who survive in the popular beliefs of modern Greece,[10] have incorrectly been interpreted by Nilsson as post-Homeric. This they may be in their character of configured goddesses, but not as undefined powers spinning destiny. Nilsson himself intimates as much in speaking of the phrase "wound on the spindle": "The term means that man is clad in something, 'entwined,' one might say, if this did not suggest a different image, the net or noose." [11] But precisely this "different" image belongs, along with that of the clothier, to the character of the spinners of fate; for the woman must not only provide the clothing of man in the literal sense but also clothes him with the body she spins and weaves, and for this reason it is said of the Great Goddess: "Clother is her name." [12]

Thus Kerényi says of the Klothes, the Spinstresses: "That 'weaving' can be an expression for the creation of the human life or body is shown by the appearance of weaving woman in symbolic paintings in

[9] Kerényi, Töchter der Sonne, pp. 81 f.
[10] Nilsson, Geschichte der griechischen Religion, Vol. I, p. 340, n. 3.
[11] Ibid., p. 340.

[12] See above, p. 162. Book of the Dead (tr. Budge), Ch. CXLVI, "The Chapters of the Secret Pylons."

Roman tombs, and by the Greek word *mitos*, which designates the male seed as a woven thread, and which is the name of the primeval bridegroom of the Cabiri." [13]

The Aegean goddess of birth, Eileithyia, is a spinstress,[14] as are the Moirai, the Greek goddesses of fate.[15] "The domain in which these dark beings are at home," writes Otto, "is unmistakably indicated by another genealogy, also given by Hesiod (*Theogony*, 211 ff.): they are daughters of the primal goddess Night, who also gave birth to Moros and the Erinyes, whom Aeschylus (*Eumenides*, 960) too designates as sisters of the Moirai by their mother. The fifty-ninth Orphic hymn also calls them daughters of Night. . . . Aphrodite Urania is designated as 'the eldest of the Moirai' (Pausanias, 1, 19, 2). Their kinship with the Erinyes appears in the cult also: in the grove of the Eumenides at Sicyon the Moirai had an altar where they received sacrifices like those offered to the Eumenides, namely such as were characteristic of the earth deities and the deities of the netherworld (Pausanias, 2, 11, 14)." [16]

We again encounter the unity of the Feminine and the nocturnal when Otto points to the connection between the name of the Krataië and Krataiis, the mother of Scylla, "whose connection with the netherworld is plain to see and whose descent is sometimes derived from Hecate. This is clearly a parallel to Moira's connection with Night, the Erinyes, and other beings of the murky realm." [17]

The great triad of the Moirai is correlated with the three decisive moments of life: "Beginning and end, birth and death, are the great seasons of the Moirai, and along with these marriage is a third." [18]

That these points of crisis are not those of human life in general, but those of feminine life, becomes apparent when we find that the god-

[13] Kerényi, *Töchter*, p. 84.

[14] Thomson, *The Prehistoric Aegean*, p. 335.

[15] Particularly for the concept of fate, the exclusively sociological standpoint taken by Thomson in his excellent book proves inadequate. "The sharing of game, the sharing of booty, the sharing of land, the sharing of labor between the clans" (p. 33), does not adequately explain why the Moirai preside most particularly over initiation, marriage, and death. When Thomson follows Jane Harrison in relating them to the demon and genius, the *ka*, i.e., precisely the individual guardian spirit, we are, as we have elsewhere shown, brought up against the fact that the individual destiny coincides with the self and its first form, the body-self, in which the psychobiological elements of the constitution conditioned by the ancestors become the personal destiny of the individual.

[16] W. F. Otto, *The Homeric Gods*, pp. 266 f.

[17] Ibid., p. 269.

[18] Ibid., p. 267.

desses of destiny are always goddesses of birth, and that for woman there is an essential connection between childbearing and death as well as between marriage and death. In other words, the figures of the Moirai do not manifest any general philosophical considerations regarding the beginning and end of life, but represent numinous situations on which the life of woman but not of man depends.

But when the Moirai exert their power upon men, it is upon them first and foremost as warriors, for whom they weave a bloody death, and similarly the primordial Mexican symbolism links the destinies of the warriors and the childbearing woman seen as a hero. Here the weaving goddess of fate merges with the bloody goddess of war and death. The Valkyries, whose primary importance for Germanic mythology has been made clear by Ninck,[19] are also weavers. An Eddic lay relates the vision of a Scotsman who beholds twelve riding figures. When they vanish into a house, he looks in through a peephole. Twelve women are working a spectral loom and singing to the spectral refrain "Weave, weave, the web of spears." This is the song of these Valkyries:

> Widestretched is the warp presaging the slaughter, the hanging cloud of the beam; it is raining blood. The gray web of the hosts is raised up on the spears, the web that we the friends of Woden are filling with red weft.
>
> This web is warped with the guts of men, and heavily weighted with human heads; blood-stained darts are the shafts, iron-bound are the stays; it is shuttled with arrows. Let us strike with our swords this web of victory!

And the last lines:

> Tidings of devastation shall spread over the land. Now the web is woven and the field made red. Now it is awful to look around, for gory clouds are gathering over the sky, and the air shall be dyed with the blood of men. . . .[20]

This weaving of fate out of blood is characteristic of Germanic mythology with its gloomy and cruel orientation toward death. In most mythologies the natural life-creating aspect of the Great Goddess as weaver predominates over the negative aspect.

[19] Ninck, *Wodan*.
[20] "Darraðar-lióð" or "The Lay of Darts

[i.e., Spears]," tr. Vigfusson and Powell, *Corpus Poeticum Boreale*, Vol. I, pp. 281–83 (modified).

This aspect of the Feminine as a spinner of fate can be followed down to the late configuration of the Christian Madonna. Although the artist's conscious intention was probably no more than to represent the Madonna engaged in an everyday womanly activity, unconscious forces produced a work of archetypal grandeur. In this early Catalan An- *Pl. 96* nunciation, the Madonna is still the Great Goddess who spins destiny— though here destiny is the redemption of the world. The uplifted hand of the announcing angel and the lowered hands of onlooking mankind, embodied in the maidservant, stress the central position of the Madonna.

In another painting, a South German Madonna, the spinning might *Pl. 97* at first sight seem to be merely an idyllic domestic activity. But here again the archetypal structure has broken through. Whether intentionally or unintentionally, the oblique thread runs through the center of the Madonna where the radiant child is growing, and thus the act of spinning regains its true and original meaning: the mother becomes the spinning goddess of destiny; the child becomes the fabric of her body.

But in this connection, we again encounter a negative aspect, for the spider is also a symbol of the Terrible Mother.[21] Similarly net and noose are typical weapons of the Feminine's terrible power to bind and fetter, and the knot is a dire instrument of the enchantress.

Wherever the antivital fanaticism of the male spiritual principle predominates,[22] the Feminine is looked upon as negative and evil, precisely in its character of creator, sustainer, and increaser of life. Now life—and the Feminine is its archetype—is said to fascinate and hold fast, to lure and enchant. The natural drives and instincts overpower the human and the male principle of light and consciousness by means of the web of life, the veil of Maya, the "ensnaring" illusion of life in this world. And consequently this male principle of consciousness, which desires permanence and not change, eternity and not transformation, law and not creative spontaneity, "discriminates" against the Great Goddess and turns her into a demon.

But in so doing the male consciousness totally overlooks the hidden

[21] See above, Ch. 11.   [22] My *Origins*, p. 290.

spiritual aspect of the feminine principle, which through spiritual transformation exalts earthly man to a higher meaning.[23]

Rather surprisingly, the mill stands side by side with the loom as a symbol of fate and death. Baking, like weaving, is one of the primeval mysteries of the Feminine. The woman is a giver and transformer of nourishment, but at the same time we find the negative meaning of the symbol in the death mill as an attribute of the Terrible Mother. The death of the grain god in the mill was later transferred to Christ, and it still survives in the English ballad "John Barleycorn." Thus the mill becomes a goddess of death;[24] its relation to fate has come down to us in the familiar proverb, "The mills of the gods grind slowly," whose mythical origin is still discernible in the Germanic sphere.

In the Eddic poem known as "The Song of the Mill,"[25] the giant's daughters are at work in the wishing mill, seeking to create peace and riches by magic. "Playing under the earth, nine winters long, we grew mightily." But these imprisoned virgins and warrior maidens become powers of fate, who turn the blessing into a curse; and as formerly they magically milled life and happiness, now they mill death and doom. Thus the mill becomes a symbol of the negative wheel of life, the Indian samsara, the aimless cycle.[26] But this aimless cycle is a form of the

Fig. 51
Pl. 134
Pls. 177–78

Great Round, whose positive form, in India as elsewhere, is the great containing World Mother who, like the Boeotian goddess, the Vierge Ouvrante, and the Madonna of Mercy, raises her outstretched arms shelteringly. They too belong to the archetype of the goddesses with upraised arms.

Pl. 98

As the Tibetan wheel of life, the Great Round is held by a female demon of death, the witch Srinmo.[27] Concerning a painting of the same type as our reproduction, Bleichsteiner writes:

"The picture shows the demonic servant of the spirit of death, the red Mangus, as the Mongols call him, holding the wheel of the worlds

[23] Spiritual transformation is discussed in Ch. 15, pp. 281 ff.
[24] Jacob, *Six Thousand Years of Bread*, p. 58.
[25] Cf. A. G. Brodeur, *The Prose Edda by Snorri Sturluson*, p. 163; Vigfusson and Powell, Vol. I, p. 186.

[26] Cf. the same symbolism in alchemy, e.g., "Ein güldener Tractat vom philosophischen Stein," p. 60, in Lucas Jennis, *Dyas chymica tripartita*.
[27] Bleichsteiner, *Die gelbe Kirche*, p. 220.

between his long teeth and claws. A similar conception underlay the ancient Babylonian amulets showing the world held in the claws of a winged demonic beast; according to Grünwedel,[28] Manichaean monuments in Turkestan and Jaina works in India show the cosmic woman, a

FIG. *51.* BHAVANI-TRIMURTI-MOTHER

Hindu, XIX *century or earlier*

beautiful, richly ornamented girl with her body open in such a way as to disclose the stylized entrails, representing the disk of the world. Other correspondences, into which we cannot enter here, would carry us into the world of the European Middle Ages. The Tibetans also regard the demon of the cosmic wheel as a woman, the witch Srinmo. This is due in part to the antifeminine influence of Buddhism, which, because woman

[28] Albert Grünwedel, source not indicated.

creates new life, looks upon her as the chief obstacle to redemption, as an instrument of the passion beneath which the world moans. Among the legends of the *Padmasambhava* we find the following passage (translated by Grünwedel): 'Women are the unremitting stream of samsara. They are the black-faced ogresses incarnate. Their flesh is a copper witches' caldron, in which are enacted all the torments of purification by fire. . . .'

"In this copper caldron good and evil are differentiated. Woman is the name of this copper caldron; woman is the name of the prison of Mara (death); woman is the name of the death god's noose. [In this strange symbolism the witches' caldron within the female body may be equated with the cosmic wheel between whose spokes the creatures suffer every conceivable torment under the pressure of their passions.]

"The symbols of the wheel are arranged in three concentric rings. The innermost and smallest circle, the hub of the wheel, contains three animal figures, which originally no doubt were conceived as representatives of the three realms—earth, water, and air—for as such we encounter them in the legends of the most diverse peoples. In the religious view these animals—a pig,[29] a cock, and a snake—symbolize the three evils or mortal sins, in whose power the world and its creatures moan, since they engender sinful action and perpetuate the cycle of births. The pig signifies ignorance, the cock carnal passion, the serpent anger. In a parallelism with the hymns of the Veda, where the godhead who guides the worlds sits in the center of the universe, in the hub of the wheel, here the three cardinal sins sit in the innermost circle; regents of the cosmos, they fetter man to the world of the senses, rob him of the sound knowledge of their unreality, and prevent him from achieving redemption, nirvana; they are the axis around which turns the cosmic wheel with its realms and their inhabitants.[30]

"Moving outward from this innermost circle, we see between the six

[29] In our painting, a fantastic animal with the same significance corresponds to the pig. Characteristically, the uroboros formed of the three animals constitutes the black center.

[30] We find an analogous conception in a painting, the *Creation*, by Hieronymus Bosch (c. 1500), where the owl, always a symbol of evil in his work, sits in the middle of the central spring of life.

spokes of the wheel the six zones of the world, the realms of the gods, the Titans (Skr. *asuras*), of men, animals, and spirits, and lastly hell. In some representations, hell occupies the whole lower half of the central ring. Each separate zone of the world is dominated by a mortal sin in keeping with the character of its inhabitants.

"In the middle of our picture is the world of the gods, to the right that of the Titans or *asuras*, opposite the latter that of men. Under the world of men is the world of spirits; under that of the Titans is that of the animals. Below, opposite the world of the gods, is hell.

"On the thin outermost rim of the wheel, simple symbols indicate the twelve nidanas (Skr. *nidana*, 'band,' 'fetter,' 'foundation cause'), which lie at the heart of the Buddhist philosophy and embody the woeful causality of birth, old age, death, and rebirth—the eternal cycle, which can be halted only through the knowledge that the sensuous world is illusion and 'emptiness.' The nidanas are often explained astrologically.

"If we begin our interpretation of the nidanas at the lower rim of the wheel and proceed clockwise, we observe the following symbols: [31]

"1. Blind old woman leaning on a staff: she represents the ignorance or blindness of the creature.

"2. Potter shaping a vessel: suggests the formless products that arise in this way.

"3. Ape climbing a tree and plucking a fruit: a symbol of how man comes to know the objects of the world by consciousness and activity.

"4. Ship with mariners: the conscious is differentiated from the unconscious.

"5. Empty, masterless house (man): there is no one inside the cloak.

"6. Mother with child: symbol of attachment to the world (?).

"7. Man struck in the eye by an arrow: sense perception communicates pleasant and unpleasant impressions.

"8. Wine drinker: thirst for life; passionate yearning creates the purposive striving that becomes more and more avid.

"9. Man picking fruit: symbol of the enjoyment of life.

[31] The description is abbreviated and rearranged in accordance with the somewhat different content of the painting we reproduce in Pl. 98.

"10. Lovers in sexual embrace: the symbol of the perpetuation of life achieved in this manner.

"11. Birth: more and more life is created and the cycle is perpetuated.

"12. Corpse carried off in a bundle: suffering and death continue in conjunction with eternally renewed life." [32]

The mandala of the cycle rests on the world of the lower elements—water, earth, and air—and above, to the right and left, hover the redeeming contrary powers of the Buddhas and the "contrary wheel," the positive wheel of the doctrine, which annuls the negative feminine wheel of life.

And here Mephistopheles, that "strange son of chaos," seems almost the shadow of Buddha:

> Gone, and sheer Nothing left, flat null complete!
> What matters our creative endless toil,
> When, at a snatch, oblivion ends the coil?
> "It is bygone!"—How shall this riddle run?
> As if Existence never had begun,
> Yet claims a known careering none the less.
> I'd rather have Eternal Emptiness.[33]

In the Western Middle Ages we find a symbol corresponding exactly to the Tibetan wheel of life; this is the wheel of life in its negative aspect
Pl. 99 as "Wheel of Mother Nature," on which the ascending and descending cycle of human life is represented. Below, the wheel is held by the Earth Goddess; above, on a throne, sits three-headed Time, whose wings are the months and who makes life revolve with the alternations of day and night. On the tenth card of the tarot pack, the crowned sphinx, a familiar symbol of the Great Mother Goddess, sits similarly enthroned above the wheel of fortune with its rising and falling configurations.[34]

Our last representation of the Feminine in its character of Great

---

[32] Bleichsteiner, pp. 224–25.
[33] *Faust*, Part Two, Act V, tr. by Philip Wayne, from:
Vorbei und reines Nichts, vollkommenes Einerlei!
Was soll uns denn das ewige Schaffen!
Geschaffenes zu nichts hinwegzuraffen!

"Da ists vorbei!" was ist daran zu lesen?
Es ist so gut, als wär es nicht gewesen,
Und treibt sich doch im Kreis, als wenn es wäre.
Ich liebte mir dafür das Ewig-Leere.
[34] Bernoulli, "Die Zahlensymbolik des Tarotsystems," pp. 407 f.

Round is a bronze Etruscan lamp,[35] in the center of which the Gorgon's   *Pl. 100*
head is surrounded by an intricate wreath of figures. Leisegang has given
us a penetrating interpretation of this piece.[36] The *gorgoneion* is the midnight sun of the underworld—the terrible face of the Great Mother.
Around this center lies a first circle, on which a griffin and a lion each
rend to pieces an animal that is mortal life predestined to death. The
second circle, the watery region with its wreath of twenty-eight waves
(the lunar number), is inhabited by eight dolphins. The number eight
forms the transition to the region of air and fire, dominated by eight
sirens with birds' wings and human faces, "squatting on a three-stepped
base, covered with fine lines that I should interpret as rain falling from
the clouds of the air. Beside each siren squats a flute-playing silenus
with erect phallus; he symbolizes the rain that falls from heaven to
fertilize the earth. . . . Over the head of each of the sixteen figures we
see a sun and ten stars, indicating the stellar realm, which extends to the
real fire and light of the sixteen flames on the upper side of the bowl,
directly over the heads of the sirens and sileni, presumably representing
the luminous supracelestial realm to which the soul attains when it has
passed the outermost sphere of heaven." [37]

Thus the lamp represents the ascending structure of the world,
whose base and center is the *gorgoneion*. Leisegang relates this representation to a significant passage in Plato's *Republic*. According to Plato's
myth, the eight spheres of heaven are fastened to a spindle that "turns
on the knees of Necessity." [38] Here again the goddess of destiny sits enthroned above the whole cosmos, and the axis of the world—as in
Mexico and India—revolves in her womb that governs all things.[39]

---

[35] Here we are concerned with the underside
of the lamp.
[36] Leisegang, "The Mystery of the Serpent,"
pp. 245 ff.
[37] Ibid., pp. 246 f.
[38] Plato, *Republic*, 617B (tr. Jowett).
[39] See above, pp. 39, 211.

Chapter Thirteen

THE LADY OF THE PLANTS

THE Great Round is the universe, the primeval darkness, and the generative night sky, but above all it is water and earth, the life-bearing chthonic powers of the world; and even though Egyptian theology opposes the male godhead of the telluric disk to Nut, the goddess of heaven, the Feminine is nevertheless the black earth in need of fecundation, and the queen is the goddess of the land.

But this generative earth is itself generated; it arose from the watery primeval ocean. For the primeval ocean, whose character of night and origination we have already described, gives birth to the primeval hill, which cosmologically signifies the earth and psychologically is consciousness rising up out of the unconscious, the foundation of the diurnal ego. Thus the primeval hill is an "island" in the sea, as consciousness is in the unconscious.

The primeval hill is identical with the obelisklike benben stone and is related to the sacred heron, the Benu (phoenix).

"Both names are derived from a verbal stem signifying 'rise up.' [1] Thus the conical stone was interpreted as the first place to emerge from the primordial flood, and the bird as the first living creature to alight on this place where the world began." [2] Hence the phoenix, or Benu, is a rising principle of the higher plane, connected with the mythology of Osiris and Ra.

The association of the primeval hill with Heliopolis and the sun

[1] On the connection between "rising up" and the male spiritual principle, cf. above, p. 174.   [2] Kees, *Der Götterglaube*, pp. 217 f.

points to a relationship between the sun as the creative male principle and the luminous world of consciousness: "The Egyptian hieroglyph which means the primeval 'hillock of appearance' means also 'to appear in glory.' It shows a rounded mound with the rays of the sun streaming upward from it (⊖), graphically portraying this miracle of the first appearance of the creator-god." [3]

Because the benben stone is a manifestation of the creative principle, the holy of holies in all Egyptian temples was identified with this primeval hill. "The equation with the primeval hill received architectural expression also.[4] One mounted a few steps or followed a ramp at every entrance from court or hall to the Holy of Holies, which was thus situated at a level noticeably higher than the entrance." [5]

It is true that the creative principle of the spirit, as of consciousness, is also "eternal existence" and is experienced by the patriarchal world as "self-generated"; but before this it was viewed genealogically as derived from the chaos or primeval ocean of the unconscious, as a son-principle, born of the Feminine.

Like the primeval hill, the uroboric primeval serpent, the lotus blossom, and Horus, the sun-child, rise up from the primeval ocean as births and rebirths of the luminous principle. Ocean and earth as generative principles stand close together, and, like the ocean, blossom and tree are archetypal places of mythical birth.

The goddess as the tree that confers nourishment on souls, as the sycamore or date palm,[6] is one of the central figures of Egyptian art. *Fig. 52; Pl. 102* But the motherhood of the tree consists not only in nourishing; it also comprises generation, and the tree goddess gives birth to the sun.[7] *Fig. 53; Pl. 103* Hathor, the sycamore goddess, who is the "house of Horus" and as such gives birth to Horus, bears the sun on her head; the top of the tree is the place of the sun's birth, the nest from which the phoenix-heron arises.[8]

---

[3] John A. Wilson, "Egypt," p. 60.
[4] The most perfect architectural example of this symbolism of ascent is the stupa of Borobudur, whose ascending spiral leads from the lowest stage of the world to the invisible Buddha.
[5] H. and H. A. Frankfort, in *Before Philosophy*, p. 31.

[6] Cf., e.g., *The Cambridge Ancient History*, Plates Vol. I, p. 63 b.
[7] Cf. Bachofen, *Mutterrecht*, and Klages, *Der Geist als Widersacher der Seele*, 3, 2.
[8] My *Origins and History of Consciousness*, pp. 23 f.

Thus the "tall sycamore on the eastern horizon," the tree of the worlds on which "the gods sit," is linked with the birth of the sun god, and in the Book of the Dead [9] "two sycamores of turquoise" stand at the eastern gate of heaven, whence Ra goes forth each morning.[10] This sycamore is identical with the goddess of heaven, who, as we see in an illustration from the Book of the Dead, is likewise experienced as a tree;

FIG. 52. THE DATE-PALM GODDESS, DISPENSING NOURISHMENT

Egypt, from a relief, xviii *Dynasty*

and Hathor, as the tree goddess who gives birth to the sun, is identified with Nut, the goddess of heaven, the coffin goddess of rebirth. To both corresponds the *djed* pillar of Osiris, from which the sun, as Ra and soul, rises up in the morning. For Osiris is also a tree god and a god contained in a tree. His coffin hidden in a cedar of Lebanon is discovered by Isis,[11] and as the *djed* pillar he is the sun-generating principle, identical with the Great Tree Goddess. Here, as in Mexico, we find that the figures

[9] Ch. CIX (tr. Budge).
[10] Kees; cf. my *Origins:* "Transformation, or

Osiris," pp. 220–56.
[11] Ibid., pp. 229 f.

242

of the Great Mother Goddess and of her son merge with one another. Like the *djed* pillar, the sycamore, the "wood of life, from which the gods   *Fig. 54* live," [12] is she "who embraces the god." [13] And the half-buried *djed* pillar, with the life symbol whose arms are the *ka* that causes the sun to rise, corresponds to Nut, girded in the life symbol and saluted by the

FIG. *53.*   WORSHIP OF THE SUN TREE

Egypt, from a papyrus, XVIII *Dynasty*

worshiping baboons of morning, making the sun rise to a higher birth with her uplifted arms.[14]

The tree birth of Osiris recurs in Adonis; both are "vegetation   *Pl. 104* gods," as is the infant Jesus, the Babylonian grain god, the virgin-born ear of wheat, lying in his wooden manger.

In the symbolic equations of a Feminine that nourishes, generates, and transforms, tree, *djed* pillar, tree of heaven, and cosmic tree belong together. And the childbearing tree may be further differentiated into treetop and nest, crib and cradle. That is why the New Year's festival in Egypt is also called the "day of the child in the nest," [15] while the birth of the day, as time of the sun's little birth, is essentially identical with the birth of the year as the sun's great birth.

The wood, the *hyle*, which as crib and cradle represents the child-bearing maternal significance of the tree, is also the mother of death,

[12] Sethe, *Die alt-aegyptischen Pyramiden-texte*, Vol. II.

[13] Van der Leeuw, *Phänomenologie der Religion*, p. 37.

[14] The Babylonian moon tree and sun tree   *Pl. 108a* are corresponding symbols for the light's character of growth, transformation, and generation.

[15] Erman, *Die Religion der Ägypter*, p. 370.

Pls. 91–92 the "sarco-phagus," devourer of flesh, the coffin that in the form of tree and pillar encloses Osiris in its wood, just as Nut in her character of coffin encloses the dead. The original sheltering of the dead in the belly

FIG. *54.* *DJED* PILLAR, WITH LIFE SYMBOL AND RISING SUN,
IN THE MOUNTAIN OF MORNING

Egypt, from a papyrus, XVIII *Dynasty*

Pl. 105 of the maternal giant tree appears in our ethnological sketch from East Africa.[16]

But Nut, as tree of heaven, is also the mistress of the celestial *Pl. 35* beasts of the zodiac, as is Diana of Ephesus, whose robe and crown are adorned with numerous animal symbols. The earthly tree with its roots

[16] Becker, *La Vie en Afrique*, Vol. I, facing p. 156; Becker calls the tribe the Wagogo, of present-day Tanganyika, and the tree a baobab.

in the depths, and the astral tree of the heights, are symbols of time. The recurrence of the unity of day and night in the unity of the year is also found in the celestial year tree of China, beneath whose branches the beasts of the twelve heavenly constellations gather. Each one of these beasts of the months formerly ruled over a two-hour watch of the day, which as in our reckoning began at midnight. Each watch bears the name of one of the "twelve earthly branches" and that of the corresponding beasts; [17] the tree of time with its twelve branches is the tree of night-day-night and of the year as well.

Pl. 108b

The image of the tree,[18] firmly implanted in the earth that feeds it, but rising up into the air where it unfolds its crown, has stirred man's imagination from time immemorial.[19] It shades and shelters all living things,[20] and feeds them with its fruit, which hang on it like stars. In its branches nest the birds, the denizens of heaven who, rising up from it with their unfolded wings, hover in the middle space between the tree's branches below and the world-covering wing-branches of the tree or bird of heaven above.

The image of the tree of heaven derives not from the sun-generating eastern sky nor from the daytime sky, but from the night sky. In its shadow the world is sheltered and the astral beasts gather; in its branches the star fruits glitter, and from the nocturnal dew the thirsting world is nourished.

This heavenly tree that shines by night is also the soul tree of rebirth, in which every creature who dies becomes a celestial light and returns as a star to the eternity of the Great Round. Hence the archetypal connection between the candle and the lamp, for example, and the feast of the dead.

This connection is exemplified in the Christian-Germanic winter-solstice symbolism of the Christmas tree. Another fine example is the

---

[17] Bredon and Mitrophanow, *Das Mondjahr*, p. 37.

[18] The feminine significance of the date palm is made evident by the ritual harvest represented on numerous Babylonian cylinders; it is enacted at the new moon and only women participate in it.

[19] Cf. the role of the tree, of fruit gathering, etc., in early Indian seals and in the Cretan religion.

[20] Cf. also the vision in the Book of Daniel, Ch. 4, where the Great King, the original representative of heaven, is identified with the Great Tree.

Pl. 109 Buddhist tree,[21] which was bedecked with candles at the feasts of the dead. To every candle of the seven-terraced tree, whose summit is a lotus with many petals, belongs a flower of light, a soul illumined and redeemed, enthroned on a lotus blossom.

The Great Goddess of the night sky, "who causeth her souls to appear," nourishes and slakes the weary soul of the living creature in the somnolent darkness of the unconscious, the land of the dead, so that in the morning it is born fresh and strengthened into the eastern day, like the sun. As tree of life, the great Tree Goddess of the night sky and the underworld feeds the dead, and as the "suckling's tree" of the Aztecs she feeds the dead in the underworld with her milk.[22]

The identity of sea and night sky, the symbols of childbearing motherhood, recurs in the symbol of the Shekinah, the sea of the godhead, which renews by night. And here too the tree of birth, rebirth, and fate is related to these symbols.[23]

Thus in the thirteenth-century *Zohar*, the cabalistic Bible, we read:

> New every morning—this applies to men, who are each day renewed, why? Because, as the verse continues: "Thy fidelity is great." Thy "fidelity" (that is) the Shekinah, that consuming fire, by which they are renewed at night. It is in truth "great" and not small, for it takes all (the souls of men) the higher and the lower up into itself and encloses them in itself. It is the great wide place which contains everything in itself and yet is not overfilled, as is indicated in the verse: "All rivers flow into the sea and the sea is not full"—all (souls) go into this "sea," and the "sea" takes them in and consumes them without becoming full; it brings them forth new and they go their way, and that is why it is said (of the Shekinah): Great is thy "fidelity." [24]

The tree plays an important role in the cabala as tree of life and of the *sephiroth*. This symbolism goes back to the symbolism of the tree in the ancient Orient, where, as tree of life, of knowledge—and of death—

[21] Mensching, *Buddhistische Symbolik*, p. 32.
[22] Krickeberg, *Märchen der Azteken und Inkaperuaner, Maya und Muisca*, p. 30.
[23] It goes without saying that the symbol of the tree, which originally belonged to the matri-archal image world, was interpolated into the domain of the patriarchal god.
[24] Scholem, *Die Geheimnisse der Schöpfung*, p. 75.

it stands at the center of the events in paradise that decided human destiny. Thus in the *Book of Bahir*, a relatively early cabalistic text, we read:

> It is I who planted this "tree" that all the world might delight in it, and made it an arch over all things and named it "universe," for on it hangs the universe and from it the universe emanates; all things have need of it and behold it and tremble for it; it is thence that the souls emanate.[25]

And a similar passage:

> God hath a tree and on it there are twelve radii: northeast, southeast, east-above, east-below, northwest, southwest, west-above, west-below, north-above, north-below, south-above, south-below, and they stretch forth and extend to the unfathomable, and they are the arms of the world. And in their center is the tree. . . .[26]

And still another:

> And what is [this] "tree," of which thou hast spoken? He said to him: All the powers of God are situated one above the other, and they are like unto a tree: as the tree through water brings forth its fruit, so doth God through water increase the powers of the "tree." And what is God's water? It is Hokhma [wisdom], and that is the soul of the righteous, who fly from the "source" to the "great channel," and it rises up and clings to the "tree." [27]

As though reflecting one another, the heavens appear as a tree and the summit of the cosmic tree towers into the heavens. But this does not exhaust the relationship between them. Precisely because the tree is rooted in the depths, it has profound meaning. Its roots in the darkness of the unconscious are identical with its roots in the night sky. The stellar constellations of its "branches" are the manifestation of a profound destiny for which above and below are one. Thus the cabalistic tree, like the Hindu tree or Christian tree, is said to have its roots in heaven among the higher powers, and its summit, its unfolding, in the world below:

> Upward the roots, downward the branches, so grows the eternal fig tree; it is called seed, Brahman, immortal; in it rest the worlds, over it rises none.[28]

[25] Scholem, *Das Buch Bahir*, §14, p. 17.
[26] Ibid., §64, p. 64.
[27] Ibid., §85, p. 91.
[28] Katha Upanishad, VI, 1.

Pl. 110   To this context belongs the tree symbolism of alchemy, which C. G. Jung has discussed in detail [29] and which we shall therefore only mention in passing. The *arbor philosophica* of psychic development that took form in the alchemistic process is the female tree of destiny, whose summit is identical with the starry firmament in which the phoenix or pelican has made its nest of undying transformation—like the Benu-heron, which in the Egyptian tree of transformation becomes the upper soul of Ra.[30]

In alchemy, the psychological significance of birth from tree or flowers is particularly evident. A birth of this sort is always the ultimate result of processes of development and transformation, which cannot be assigned to the sphere of animal instinct. It arises from psychic strata in which—as in the plant—the elements are synthesized and achieve a new unity and form through a transformation governed by the unconscious. They belong to the "matriarchal consciousness" [31] whose nature and symbolism are as intimately bound up with the plant world as with the world of the Feminine. Its psychic processes—which are in large part independent of the ego and consciousness—are, like the fruit, the emergence of a luminous quality of consciousness, specifically related to time and the phenomenon of destiny. This relation of the tree to destiny is particularly evident in Germanic mythology. Ninck writes: "The tree is a symbol of destiny because it is rooted in the depths. But what is more important is that it grows into time, ramifies its branches like a family tree, and year after year takes on another ring,

Fig. 55   so manifesting its age. All-dominating stands Yggdrasill, the 'greatest and best of all trees' in the mythical world picture of the Edda, putting forth its crown aloft, so that 'its branches tower over the heavens,' reaching deep down into the depths with its three roots, which embrace Niflheim, Asgard, and Jotunnheim, the realm of the frost giants." [32]

---

[29] Cf. *Psychology and Alchemy*, index, s.v. "tree," both text and illustrations.
[30] Cf. my *Origins*, p. 237.
[31] My "Über den Mond und das matriarchale Bewusstsein."

[32] Ninck, *Wodan und germanischer Schicksalsglaube*, p. 215. (The picture we reproduce of the tree is, of course, a modern [eighteenth-century] man's conception of it. No ancient representation has been located.)

FIG. 55. YGGDRASILL, THE WORLD TREE OF THE EDDA

From Finnur Magnusson's edition of the Elder Edda, XVIII *century*

This writer remarks further: "Fate grows slowly out of them like a tree rooted in the depths, like the tall and mighty ash that reaches back to a stone age and in the depths embraces nine realms of the world with its three mighty roots.

"Fate is the sacred center of life. From its womb flow wealth and want (*auþr* and *nauþr*), happiness and unhappiness, life and death. ON. *skop*, used in the plural, means 'fate' and also means genitals; [33] it is related to Goth. *gaskapjan*, OE. *scyppan*, OS. *skeppian*, OHG. *scaffon*, 'to create, order, determine,' which survive in such words as *Schöffe*, 'magistrate'; *Beschaffenheit*, 'quality'; and in the ending *-schaft* (Eng. *-ship*). Thus the working of fate is an eternal becoming (whence Urth and Verthandi take their names), a weaving and creating, and to everything that is, fate assigns its part in life and its peculiar character.

"Cruelly the third of the three sisters cuts the thread, and Urth herself is called deadly wrath; but the Norns also lead into life and their womb is overflowing abundance. On the Roman-Germanic 'matron

Pl. 112   stones' they are represented holding baskets of fruit; they live by the well of Urth, from which day after day they draw water to pour on the tree and prevent it from rotting." [34]

But for the present the feminine character of destiny as tree and as night stands in the foreground. As Ninck writes:

"Always and everywhere fate was regarded among the Germanic peoples as a feminine power. The womb of the primeval mother bears all things. The Norns hold destiny in their hands; they spin the thread, tear it off, and determine what is to come. Something of the Norns is at work in women; each of them, as place of conception, growth, and birth, can be the voice of the primordial mother. More than the man, the woman is able to foresee the course of events and give such advice as will bring human action into harmony with destiny. Hence their immunity, their priestly sanctity, as attested among the Cimbri. There is no need to repeat Tacitus' much-quoted words about the *sanctum et providum* of Germanic women. . . . This state of affairs continued in

[33] The Norns are midwives: "Tell me then, Fafnir . . . Who are the Norns who are so helpful in need, And the babe from the mother bring?"—Bellows, *The Poetic Edda*, p. 375.
[34] Ninck, p. 191.

the North until the Christians began to persecute the seeresses as witches. In the Edda, Frigg and Gefjon foresee the destinies of the world, Groa sings magic songs over Thor, and Odin takes his wisdom from the volvas. In the sagas, the seeresses are highly honored in their wanderings among the peasants, and there is even confirmation of the statement that 'some were exalted to the rank of goddesses' (Tacitus, *History*, IV, 61), for Jarl Haakon ordered a special temple to be built for the seeress Thorgerd.

"However, not only the seeress, but the element itself can become a mediating voice between man and the primordial decree of fate (and this is an indication that the woman comes to her high calling not as a person but as a representative of the universal). Everything that dwells in the depths, close to the Norns, is fraught with destiny, and most of all the water that rises up from the depths and the tree rooted in them. Water and tree are for this reason the most important elementary symbols, and they were endowed with a primordial sacredness by all Germanic tribes." [35]

In another place Ninck writes: "Odin's relation to Mimir reflects his relation to the primordially sacred water of destiny, and the myth of his hanging from Yggdrasill reflects his relation to the tree of fate. So close was his bond with the spring that Odin here set up his judgment seat, and the name of the world ash tree points to the great significance attached to the hanging myth; for Yggdrasill is the 'steed of Uggr, of him who frightened Odin.' The importance of this myth follows also from the previously mentioned sacrifices by hanging, offered up to the god in connection with the act of initiation performed by himself, and of the scaldic names for Odin: Hangaguþ, 'Hanging God'; Geiguþr, 'the Dangling One'; Galgagramr, 'Lord of the Gallows'; and Hangi, 'the Hanged One.' Scarcely any aspect of their religion so facilitated the conversion of the Germans to Christianity as the apparent similarity of their hanged god to the crucified Christ, and here it is characteristic that the Goths and Anglo-Saxons rendered the word 'cross' in their language as 'gallows' (Goth. *galga*, OE. *gealga*). The myth is found in the

[35] Ibid., p. 203.

south as well, and throughout the Middle Ages, though in characteristically modified forms." [36]

The essential lines from the myth of Odin's hanging are these:

> I ween that I hung / on the windy tree,
> Hung there for nights full nine;
> With the spear I was wounded, / and offered I was
> To Odin, myself to myself,
> On the tree that none / may never know
> What root beneath it runs.[37]

Here, it is evident, sacrifice, death, rebirth, and wisdom are intertwined on a new plane. Thus tree of life, cross, and gallows tree are ambivalent forms of the maternal tree. What hangs on the tree, the child of the tree mother, suffers death but receives immortality from her, who causes him to rise to her immortal heaven, where he partakes in her essence as giver of wisdom, as Sophia. Sacrifice and suffering are the prerequisites of the transformation conferred by her, and this law of dying and becoming is an essential part of the wisdom of the Great Goddess of living things, the goddess of all growth, psychic as well as physical.

Regardless of theological superstructures, the archetypal symbolism of the tree reaches deep down into the mythical world of Christianity and Judaism. Christ, hanging from the tree of death, is the fruit of suffering and hence the pledge of the promised land, the beatitude to come; and at the same time He is the tree of life as the god of the grape. Like Dionysus, He is *endendros*, the life at work in the tree, and fulfills the mysterious twofold and contradictory nature of the tree. And the

Pl. 114

Pl. 115

---

[36] Ninck, pp. 299 ff. Just as Odin attains wisdom in falling from the tree, so in the medieval "Farce of the Turnip" the hanged man boasts that as he hung on the tree the course of the stars around the pole and the nature of all things, of plants, animals, stones, elements, was revealed to him (Grimm's tale 146, from a Latin poem, the oldest MS. of which goes back to the beginning of the 14th century, reprinted in Bolte and Polívka, *Anmerkungen*, Vol. III, pp. 170 ff.). It is inconceivable that a scribe at that period could have been familiar with the *Clouds* of Aristophanes, and moreover there is no analogy to the tree in the Greek comedy. To this context belongs the popular belief that a particular magic power resides in the relics of a hanged man: the rope, his last emission of semen, and the mandrake that sprouts from it (concerning the mandrake, cf. Hovorka and Kronfeld, *Volksmedizin*, Vol. I, pp. 14 ff.). The English "gallows tree" preserves the memory of the fact that the gallows was originally a tree.

[37] *Hovamol*, 139 (tr. Bellows, *The Poetic Edda*, p. 60).

tree of knowledge is identified with the tree of life and death that is the Cross. According to the Christian myth, the Cross was set up on the site where the tree of knowledge had stood, and Christ, as "mystical fruit" of the redeeming tree of life, replaced the fruit of the tree of knowledge, whereby sin came into the world.

The mythical twofold nature of the tree of knowledge, its opposition of "good" and "evil," appears in a Swiss manuscript. Its double *Fig. 56* aspects are Judaism and Christianity, Synagogue and Church, and it goes without saying that death and the devil are correlated with Judaism, redemption and life with Christianity. For the sake of mythical justice—which is paradox and ambiguity—life and death are joined in the Jewish, life-affirming aspect, the naked Eve. Her belly is life, symbolized by the grape, but in her hand she holds a skull, the fruit of the tree. The Church is the other, the life-negating aspect. It shows, though perhaps unbeknown to the artist, the womb of death, characterized by the Crucifixion, for the Church is the tree of death and the bride of death. But the fruit she holds is the Host, the bread of life. This twofold tree of good and evil culminates in the Cross, whose ambiguity is often brought out by the presence of the good and the bad thief at either side of it.

This late, theological womanhood is still the symbolic vessel of initiation, bound up with nurture and birth. The Church with the chalice is the vessel of salvation; Eve with the apple is the vessel of sin. In the transformative vessel of baptism,[38] the Feminine in its character *Pl. 113* of west, hell and underworld, still discloses its negative aspect; while in its character of east, of heaven and paradise, it reveals its positive aspect. And the snake-entwined tree of doom, whose leaves are human sins, has its roots in the head of the Babylonian harlot with the golden *Pl. 111* cup and is crowned with the image of Luxuria holding her naked bosom —a figure resembling Eve, Astarte, and Gaea.

In the next illustration, Christ is the third, the new element, tower- *Pl. 116* ing over the ambivalent maternal tree. Here again the two aspects are represented by Eve and by the Church, which looks up to Christ as the

[38] See below, Ch. 15.

FIG. *56*. THE TREE OF KNOWLEDGE: CHURCH AND SYNAGOGUE

From a Swiss manuscript, xv *century*

new Adam. But the essential line of the picture is the vertical, in which Christ hangs not on the Cross but on the tree of life, which towers over the old bifurcate tree of the knowledge of good and evil just as Christ, the "serpent of salvation," rises over the old serpent of doom.

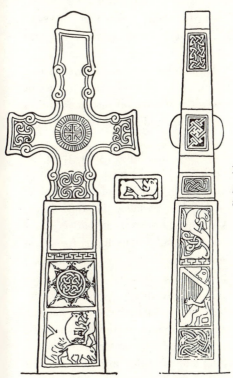

FIG. 57. STONE CROSS

Scotland, before XII *century (front, top, and side views)*

The two mother figures together, Eve and the Church, the earthly and the transcendent, good and evil, form the unity of the feminine tree, of womanhood, yielding both sin and redemption.

The features of the Cross-Mother stand out with striking clarity in Ireland and Scotland. The plastic execution of the Scottish cross en- *Fig. 57; Pl. 117a, b* hances the resemblance with the Diana of Ephesus and the Cretan god- dess—a resemblance extending to the coil of snakes in the belly region. *Pl. 56*

Pl. 117 The third cross symbolizes the clinging of childlike man to the Great Mother of Death; here again the Mother holds the child in her arms, embracing him in death as in birth.

The meaning of the cross as a tree of life and death is further amplified by the symbolism of the cross as a bed. "The Cross has become his marriage bed; the day . . . of his bitter death bears thee to sweet life," sings Ephraem Syrus.[39] The feminine wood, *materia*, the maternal substance of the tree, appears as a symbolic foundation in the marriage bed, the bed of birth and death. This *mater-materia* is the bed of the *hieros gamos;* it is the sacral scene of the fertility ritual, just as, in its character of crib, cradle, and nest, it is the bed of birth and, in its character of death tree, cross, gallows, coffin, and ship of the dead, it is the deathbed.

Pl. 118 The cradle and crib symbolism of the ship, known to us from the myths of the exposed hero child,[40] belongs, like the birth symbolism of the life-preserving ark of Noah, to the vessel symbolism of the Feminine. This is borne out by language: "In the older parlance the word *Schiff*, 'ship,' also meant vessel or dish. A remnant of this usage is *Schiff* as a water container built into the stove or oven." [41] The terms for vessel and ship are the same in many languages. Thus the roots of *Kanne*, 'pot,' and *Kahn*, 'boat,' are identical. On the other hand, the relationship between *Schiff–Nachen*, 'ship'–'skiff,' and *Baum*, 'tree,' is evident; cf. the term *Einbaum*, 'single-master.' And to this same sphere belongs the use of ON. *luþr* both for Bergelmir's ship and for the old-fashioned handmill [42] and the child's bed, the cradle.[43] The cradle is a copy of the uterus ship, in which the sleeping embryo rides into life, rocking on the primeval ocean, like the gods crossing the celestial ocean of the Great Mother in their cosmic bark.

The moon, the ship of the sea of night, is the great lamp, the vessel of light, of the female godhead, who is also seen as a container of souls in

[39] Rahner, *Mater Ecclesia*, p. 118.
[40] Cf. Rank, *The Myth of the Birth of the Hero*, and my *Origins*, p. 175.
[41] Kluge, *Etymologisches Wörterbuch der deutschen Sprache.*
[42] On the mill, cf. above, p. 234, and below, p. 285. Cf. *The Prose Edda*, p. 19.
[43] Ninck, *Wodan*, p. 218.

which the souls rising up from the earth like vapor are gathered and conveyed onward in their ascent to the Great Round.

But the ship is also a ship of the dead, "which leads back to the swaying, gliding, somnolent rhythm of earliest childhood, of the primordial ocean and the night. Over thousands of years we see this burial custom preserved, and for still another thousand years the cradle has endured. In it survives a primeval idea of mankind, to which the northern group of the Indo-Germanic peoples clings with particular tenacity. It is only in this light that we can fully understand what impelled the Germanic peoples, down to the introduction of Christianity and in part beyond it, to build their houses and temples exclusively of wood (originally around the tree of destiny); why for so long they did their best work in shipbuilding and woodcarving, and even developed the late Gothic architectural style in large part on the basis of symbols from the tree and plant world, of shipbuilding motifs and woodcarving patterns." [44]

Burial in ships can be traced back to the Bronze Age among the Germanic peoples,[45] and down to the Norman period the great ship tombs bear witness to the connection between the ship and the "great journey" to the land of the dead; [46] but the Indians of northwestern America also send out corpses in boats.[47] The ocean is experienced archetypally not only as a mother but also as the devouring primeval water who takes her children back into herself.

The fertility rite in which the ship in the form of a boat-shaped cart is drawn over the land is also bound up with the feminine symbolism of the ship, which for the mariner combines the protective character of womb, cave, and house with the character of the "beloved." That is why ancient ships are always "conceived of as feminine," [48] and why their names stress the saving function of womanhood. Thus Greek ships

[44] Ibid., pp. 218 f.
[45] *Miniaturen des frühen Mittelalters*, Pl. 12, p. 19. Our Pl. 119 shows Christ sleeping in the storm, but the ship recalls Germanic associations and the quiet mood recalls a burial.
[46] With regard to ship, yearning for death, and so on, in modern times, cf. my *Origins*, p. 279, the poem of D. H. Lawrence and its interpretation.
[47] See the illustration in Frobenius, *The Childhood of Man*, fig. 167, p. 145.
[48] Rahner, *Das Schiff aus Holz*.

bore such names as *Salvation, Grace, Bearer of Light, Blessed One, Victorious One, Virgin, Dove, Savioress, Providence,* and *Peace.*[49]

Even Christ the Saviour is seen as a ship. "And this Cross became a ship, bearing them safely through the floods of the worlds," [50] or the *Pl. 120* Cross with Christ becomes the mast of a ship, whose maternal significance is taken over by the Church and then the Son on the Cross becomes her male counterpart, like the man with the spear on the Norse ritual images of ships.[51] In Christian symbolism the ship signifies "beatitude and the means of attaining it—i.e., the Church, man's defense against the deluge of temptation. This ship's mast is the Cross, sometimes with a dove sitting on it." [52] The Cross as the mast of the Church —even today we call a part of the church the "nave"—is a variant of the tree of life and the ship of light. Christ is the sun-fruit of the Cross-Tree and rides in the Christian ship as the sun god Ra rides in the Egyptian ship.

Pls. 118–20 As place of birth, as way of salvation, and as ship of the dead, the ship is the wood of the beginning, the middle, and the end. It is the threefold goddess as mistress of fate and tree mother, who shelters the life of man and leads him from earth to earth, from wood to wood, but always back to herself.

Everywhere we encounter the ship as a symbol of salvation. "The lesser" and "the great" boat or vehicle are symbols of the Buddhist doctrine of salvation; and Tara, the Great Good Goddess,[53] is also the "mistress of the boats . . . capable of pacifying the watery flood. She has in her service countless boatwomen, like herself, who go out in barks to rescue the shipwrecked." Of herself she says: "From the world ocean of many terrors I will save the creatures, and therefore the bulls among the wise worship me as Tara." [54] And in her character of savioress she resembles the Madonna as *Stella Maris,* to whom Christian mariners pray for aid and succor.

[49] Boeckh, *Urkunden über das Seewesen des attischen Staates,* cited in Rahner, *Das Schiff.*
[50] Rahner, *Mater,* p. 69.
[51] Cf. Ninck, *Wodan.*
[52] W. Spemann, *Kunstlexikon,* p. 841.

[53] See below, p. 332. [Cf. Zimmer, *Philosophies of India,* index, s.v. "ferryboat."—ED.]
[54] Zimmer, "The Indian World Mother," p. 85.

Since the investigations of Mannhardt and Frazer, the central role of the Maypole and Christmas tree in vegetation rites has been so well known that we need merely mention it in passing. The numinous-feminine character of the tree speaks to us in the manticism not only of Greece and the Germanic countries but also of the Old Testament.[55] We know of the veneration in which the tree was held among the Semites —the tree cult on the heights; the worship of the cult pole of Asherah, the goddess of heaven; and the ritual dance around the tree—from the polemics against it in the Old Testament.

The tree, however, has not only feminine characteristics; in accordance with its uroboric nature it has masculine ones as well. The "spirit" of the tree is not necessarily of a female, dryad type; there may be a male principle, the serpent, dwelling in its branches, as, for example, in the myth of Medea or of Adam and Eve. The switch, wand, and bough, phallic symbols with which the Female is beaten in certain fertility rituals, are the most familiar expression of these relationships. We have elsewhere dealt at length with the youthful lover as plant and tree.[56]

But in his character of tree and tendril, the male is "contained"; he retains his dependency on the feminine earth-womb character. Though the "family tree" often takes the form of a phallus, the earth in which this masculinity is rooted, and which lives in the depths behind the phallic male principle, is the Great Goddess.

Bachofen quotes the solemn oath of the women of Priene—"In the darkness of the oak . . ."—and comments: "The women invoke the primordial mother of dark matter, not her product that has shot up into the light, the nocturnal oak. Higher than the tree of the gods stands the primordial shadow, the dark womb whence the tree sprang, to which the dead return, and which the women therefore invoke in their most ardent oath." [57] In this aspect the tree belongs to that stratum of life and growth which is most directly attached to the earth. Older than this stratum is only that of the sacred stones and mountains,

---

[55] II Samuel 5:24.
[56] Cf. my *Origins*, pp. 58 f., and Kerényi's
essay, "Arbor intrat," in *Niobe*.
[57] Bachofen, *Mutterrecht*, p. 427.

which along with water are direct incarnations of the Great Earth Mother, part of herself.

For this reason the female powers dwell not only in ponds, springs, streams, and swamps but also in the earth, in mountains, hills, cliffs, and—along with the dead and unborn—in the underworld. And above all, the mixture of the elements water and earth is primordially feminine; it is the swamp, the fertile muck, in whose uroboric nature the water may equally well be experienced as male and engendering or as female and birthgiving. The territory of the swamp has been so thoroughly explored by Bachofen [58] that there is no need of discussing it here in detail.[59] Among the Germanic peoples, the water lady is the primordial mother and the linguistic connection between *Mutter*, 'mother'; *Moder*, 'bog'; *Moor*, 'fen'; *Marsch*, 'marsh'; and *Meer*, 'ocean,' is still evident.[60]

Numinous sites of a preorganic life, which were experienced in *participation mystique* with the Great Mother, are mountain, cave, stone pillar, and rock—including the childbearing rock—as throne, seat, dwelling place, and incarnation of the Great Mother. As the Kagaba Indians [61] say: "She is the mother of the older brother stones." It is no accident that "stones" are among the oldest symbols of the Great Mother Goddess, from Cybele and the stone of Pessinus (moved to Rome) [62] to the Islamic Kaaba and the stone of the temple in Jerusalem, not to mention the *omphaloi*, the navel stones, which we find in so many parts of the world.[63]

The Great Earth Mother is the mother of the stones, of stone imple-
Fig. 33 ments, and of fire. In the Aztec "obsidian religion," a vestige of this view still survives. The sacral significance of the stone sacrificial knife, which we find among peoples who for other purposes have long since replaced the stone knife with a metal one, is a strong indication of a connection between the stone implement—particularly when it deals
Fig. 38 death—and the cult of the Great Mother.

---

[58] Ibid.
[59] My *Origins*, p. 27.
[60] Ninck, *Götter- und Jenseitsglaube*, p. 115.
[61] Preuss, *Forschungsreise zu den Kagaba-Indianern*, pp. 133 f., in Preuss, *Die Eingeborenen*

Amerikas, p. 39. See above, p. 88.
[62] Livy, XXIX, 10.
[63] For example in Cuzco, Delphi, Delhi, Jerusalem, and Peiping.

Chaos and night, primordial water of primordial sky, earth, mountain, and stone—and then living things begin to grow. Everywhere
vegetative life is born out of this depth and darkness of the nocturnal
beginning—as plant and tree, as star and herb. In the earliest stage of
human life, the gathering of plants, roots, and tubers was among the
main tasks of women, just as hunting belonged to the province of men.
Through this intimacy with the plant world, the woman of the primordial period possessed a wealth of knowledge concerning this sphere
of life which plays so essential a role in the primordial mysteries of the
Feminine.

This "division of labor" among early mankind is always archetypally conditioned and cannot be explained "from outside," i.e., sociologically.[64] There is no such thing as a sexual fitness or unfitness for this
or that task. We find inactive men and warrior women just as we find
inactive women and warrior men, and the relation of the group to the
powers may be the affair either of men or of women.

For the life of the group, the "psychic means of production" are at
least of equal importance with the economic. While outward life depends on the one, the equally important inner life, which at the primitive level expresses itself as a relation to the powers, depends on the
other. The distribution of these tasks between the sexes and the shifts
in correlation are among the essential problems of human history.

As goddess of earth and fertility, of sky and rain, whose priestess
was originally the repository of rain magic, the Great Goddess is everywhere the ruler over the food that springs from the earth, and all the
usages connected with man's nourishment are subordinated to her. She
is the goddess of agriculture, whether its product be rice, corn or wheat,
barley, tapioca, or any other fruit of the soil. For this reason the Great
Goddess is frequently associated with a vegetable symbol: in India and
Egypt with the lotus; as Isis, Demeter, or later the Madonna with the
rose. Flower and fruit are among the typical symbols the Greek Mother-

Pl. 121

---

[64] Where, for example, as among the
Tchambuli of New Guinea (Margaret Mead, *Sex
and Temperament in Three Primitive Societies*)
the archetypal character of the Feminine as
nourisher is accented, the women may mo-
nopolize the activity of fishing on which the
population depends for its food, while the men
do nothing for the economic "production" of the
group, although as a general rule it is uncommon
for women to engage in fishing.

Pl. 123; Fig. 68;
Pl. 60
Fig. 58
Fig. 59

Daughter Goddess [65] holds in her hands; the ear of grain is the symbol of the goddess of Ras Shamra, of Ishtar and Demeter,[66] of Ceres and Spes, and of the Madonna, who in her character of Earth Mother is the "Madonna of the sheaves."

Figs. 67–68

Apples, pomegranates, poppy seeds, and other fruits or boughs may be symbols of fertility. Branch and sprout were already related to the Great Goddess in Sumer, and in innumerable images of Ishtar and the Cretan goddess branches and flowers appear as cult objects of the Great Mother. And we still encounter such tree worship in the cult of

Fig. 60

Dionysus, as well as later in Rome and in the pagan rites of medieval peasants. And to this day offerings, gifts, and so on are attached to the branches of trees.

Because originally human life was so strongly affected by its *participation mystique* with the outside world that stone, plant and man, animal and star, were bound together in a single stream, one could always transform itself into another. Men and gods are born of trees and buried in trees; men can turn into plants; the two realms are so close together that one can merge with the other at any time. Man has achieved little independence and is still close to the maternal womb. This proximity to the womb is not only the cause of the frequent mythical transformations of men into plants but also of the magic by which human beings—and at first precisely women—attempted to influence the growth of plants.

Pl. 152
Pl. 128b

The bond between woman and plant can be followed through all the stages of human symbolism. The psyche as flower, as lotus, lily, and rose, the virgin as flower in Eleusis, symbolize the flowerlike unfolding of the highest psychic and spiritual developments.[67] Thus birth from the female blossom is an archetypal form of divine birth,[68] whether we think

Fig. 61

of Ra or Nefertem in Egypt, of the Buddhist "divine treasure in the lotus," or, in China and the modern West, of the birth of the self in the Golden Flower.[69]

On the boundary between the plant and animal realms, both gov-

[65] See below, p. 307.
[66] See below, p. 317.
[67] See below, p. 325.

[68] See below, Ch. 13.
[69] Jung and Wilhelm, *The Secret of the Golden Flower.*

FIG. *58*. SPES, WITH SHEAVES AND HIVE

After a Roman original

FIG. *59.* THE MADONNA OF THE SHEAVES

Woodcut, perhaps Bavarian, c. 1450

erned by the Great Mother, lives the bee. Along with milk, its honey was sacrificed in the oldest times to the earth goddesses. A contrast to the bloody death symbolism of the animal world, a kind of intermediary between plant and animal, it is a favorite with the Great Mother.

FIG. *60*. TREE HUNG WITH BACCHUS MASKS

Engraved gem, Roman

Bachofen describes the bond between the beehive and the one Queen Mother[70] in opposition to the many and "alien" father drones, and goes on to sum up the symbolic significance of the bee:

"This makes the beehive a perfect prototype of the first human society, based on the gynocracy of motherhood, as we find it among the peoples named. Aristotle goes so far as to place the bees higher than the men of that first period, because in them the great law of nature is expressed far more perfectly and firmly than among men. The bee was rightly looked upon as a symbol of the feminine potency of nature. It was associated above all with Demeter, Artemis, and Persephone. Here it symbolized the earth, its motherliness, its never-resting, artfully formative busy-ness, and reflected the Demetrian earth soul in its supreme purity. Its relationship with all physically conceived mother-hood was expressed in a custom recorded by Heraclides. In the Syra-

[70] The correlation of the bee with the Great Mother Goddess can only thus be explained. Evidently the conception—found in ancient documents—of a "bee king" is secondary.

cusan Thesmophoria, the participants carried *mylloi,* cakes made of honey and sesame in the shape of the female sex organ. In his monograph on bees, Menzel draws an apt parallel between this custom and the Hindu usage of daubing the woman's genitals with honey at the marriage feast. In Germany the honeyflower melissa is called *Mutter-*

FIG. *61.* THE SUN GOD'S
BIRTH FROM A FLOWER

Egypt

kraut, 'mother weed,' and is regarded as a specific for feminine sexual ailments. The bees express their motherhood also as nurses and feed the newborn infant Zeus with honey. The purest product of organic nature, in which animal and vegetable production seem so intimately intertwined, is also the purest food for mothers. It was used by earliest mankind, and priestly men, the Pythagoreans, Melchizedek, John the Baptist, reverted to it. Honey and milk belong to motherhood, wine to the male Dionysian principle." [71]

[71] Bachofen, pp. 114 f.

The "virginity" of the Great Mother, i.e., her independence of the male, becomes particularly evident in the Amazonian bee state, where only the queen is fecundated by the male, and she only once. For this reason, and because of the food she eats, the bee is pure; Demeter is the "pure mother bee," [72] and the bee priestesses of Demeter must, like the Vestals and many other priestesses of the Great Mother, be virgins. And among the bees, as so often among beasts and men, matriarchal womanhood assumes a character of the "terrible" in its relation to the males; for after mating, the drone mate and all other drones are slain like aliens by the female group inhabiting the hive.

The beehive is an attribute of the Great Goddess as Demeter-Ceres-Spes. But the bee is also associated with the moon: the priestesses *Fig. 58* of the moon goddess were called "bees," and it was believed that all honey came from the moon, the hive whose bees were the stars.[73]

Honey is the vital essence, the supreme nutriment of the plant mother, but it also has its death symbolism. Bachofen pointed to the connection between Glaucus' burial in honey and the matriarchal principle of Lycia, and this theme has been developed by a recent writer.[74] The vessel of death with its maternally nourishing honey is the instrument of a honeyed death, embalmment in honey. " 'To fall into a jar of honey' is to be identified with 'to die.' " [75] The custom of burying the dead in a great jar is known to us from pre-Hellenic Asia Minor (3500–1750 B.C.), while the use of honey in the cult of the dead and in embalming was also widely distributed.

[72] Ibid., pp. 584, 879.
[73] Briffault, *The Mothers*, Vol. III, p. 179.
[74] Persson, *The Religion of Greece in Prehistoric Times*, pp. 9 ff.
[75] Ibid., p. 12.

Chapter Fourteen

THE LADY OF THE BEASTS

ANOTHER essential aspect of the Great Goddess is her relation to the world of animals. As "Lady of the Beasts" she was worshiped at the matriarchal stage from India to the Mediterranean—in Asia Minor, Crete, Greece, Syria, Mesopotamia, Egypt, Africa, and westward to Malta, Sicily, and southern Spain. What makes this aspect particularly significant is that the sociological school of anthropologists correlates the Great Mother with agriculture and the economic dominance it gave to woman.

There is no doubt that the development leading from the group psyche to ego consciousness and individuality, and from the matriarchal to the patriarchal dominance in psychic life, has its correspondence in the social process. The development to the ego brings with it not only the acquisition of an individual "soul," of an individual name and a personal ancestry, but also of private property.

Whether the social process is the foundation and the psychic process an epiphenomenon, or whether conversely the psychic development is the base and the social evolution one of its manifestations, is a question that today must be re-evaluated. The materialist view of history is pre-psychological; the depth psychology of man was unknown to its founders and is still largely unknown to sociologists. The relating of all ideologies to their foundations in human nature is one of the decisive intellectual gains of our time, but any true reduction must culminate in the unconscious psychic reality of mankind, and not merely in an outward reality that is largely an expression of the human psyche. There are well-nigh unlimited data arguing that the decisive configurations of the primitive psyche—religion, art, social order—are symbolic expressions of unconscious processes. Despite its inadequacy, Freud's psycho-analytical derivation of these forms of expression from the human psyche was epoch-making. But just as social science starts from the group and not from the later social structure of the individual, so depth psychology must also start from the collective psychology of the un-conscious and not from the psychic situation of modern man, the family constellation and its personal unconscious.

In the early situation of human culture, the group psyche was dominant. A relation of *participation mystique* prevailed between the in-dividual and his group, and between the group and its environment, particularly the world of plants and animals.[1] The clearest expression of this situation is totemism: almost everywhere the original group ex-perienced itself as descended from an animal or a plant with which it stood in a relation of kinship. What made this phenomenon possible was that the differences between man, animal, plant, and the inorganic world were not perceived as in modern consciousness.

Here a few words must be said, if only in passing, about the con-nection between the origin of totemism and the psychology of the Femi-nine. In her character of Great Mother, the Feminine is a "virgin":[2] a creative principle independent of the personal man.[3] For many good reasons, the basic matriarchal view saw no relation between the sexual act and the bearing of children. Pregnancy and sexuality were dissoci-ated both in the inner and outward experience of woman. This may be readily understood when we consider that these early societies were characterized by a promiscuous sex life that began far before sexual maturity. The continuity of this personal sex life was just as mysteri-ously interrupted by the inception of menstruation as by its cessation and the wonder of pregnancy. Both phenomena occur in the inner femi-nine-matriarchal sphere and are not connected either with sexual love

[1] My *Origins and History of Consciousness,* pp. 105 f.

[2] Briffault, *The Mothers,* Vol. III, pp. 168-71.

[3] See above, p. 221.

play or with the profounder experience of love for a personal man, if, as is more than doubtful, the latter existed at the primitive stage.

In the primordial phase, therefore, the woman always conceived by an extrahuman, transpersonal power. The myths and fairy tales of all times and peoples teach us that she was usually impregnated by contact with numinous animals, e.g., bird and serpent, bull and ram, but also by the eating of fruit, by the wind, the moon, ancestral spirits, demons, gods, and so on. And the totem was an impersonal fecundating spirit of this sort.

Fecundation makes the woman into a numinous being for herself and for the male. This matriarchal significance of the Feminine is far older than the "agricultural phase," from which the sociological school has attempted to derive the matriarchate. It was not only the agricultural age with its ritual of sacred marriage and rain magic, but also and especially the primordial era and the hunting magic pertaining to it, which served to shape the matriarchal world whose later offshoots we encounter in early and primitive cultures.[4] The totem's connection with fertility and with food and food taboos indicates that it originally belonged to the domain of the woman, the repository of the fertility mystery as well as the mystery of food. Considered in this context, exogamy falls into the psychologically meaningful context to which Briffault has already assigned it.[5]

Exogamy reveals two essential characteristics: first the cohesion of the female group of grandmother, mother, daughter, and children, vehicles of the matriarchal psychology and of the mysteries characterized by the primordial relation between mother and daughter;[6] second the "expulsion" of the males, of the sons, who live on the margin of the female group with which they are sexually associated.[7] Thus exogamy constellates not only the power of the female group but—equally important—also the specifically male quality of the men, and leads to the historically necessary differentiation and specialization of the males.

---

[4] The matriarchal mentality, in which a male principle appears numinous and transpersonal in contrast to the merely personal reality of the man as sexual partner, corresponds to a level of the feminine psyche that we still encounter among modern women.

[5] Cf. all the relevant material in Briffault, The Mothers.

[6] My "Die Urbeziehung der Mutter."

[7] Cf. my Origins, p. 139.

For woman containment in the primordial relation to the mother means a certain intensification of womanhood, but the male's incestuous bond with the maternal and female group, his continuance in the primordial relation, means a weakening of his manliness.[8] On the other hand, all the processes that lead to the expulsion of the male by the female group and the formation of a male group strengthen and develop the masculine side of the male. Consequently the Great Goddess as a goddess of the hunt and of war is for the males a goddess of death. She magically dehumanizes the men and transforms them into wild beasts, which go to their doom as satellites of the Goddess. In this aspect, too, she is the Lady of the Beasts, and the orgiastic form of her cult arouses the beast of prey and the warrior in the male:

> She is well-pleased with the sound of rattles and of timbrels, with the voice of flutes and the outcry of wolves and bright-eyed lions.[9]

This one-sided masculine development brings with it the prowess in battle and the hunt necessary for the protection and sustenance of the female group, and by the polarity it creates between male and female enhances the mutual attraction of the sexes. Thus the tension between contradictories gives rise to the first form of social structure: exogamy prohibits the pairing of symbolic similars, and only antithetical groups, e.g., clans bearing the symbols of sun and moon, day and night, black and white, may intermarry.

But it is not only into bloodshed that the Goddess drives the male group. Along with the warriors and hunters, the chieftains and leaders, the sacrificial priests and seers are also her followers. If only indirectly, the Great Goddess favors the development of will and action among men, and she also promotes spiritual growth. For the spirit, as it first emerges from the unconscious, is fed from the primordial underground springs in the realm of the Great Mother.

How this matriarchal situation is experienced by the male, how he surpasses it and why the male group and the patriarchate must inevitably achieve predominance, has elsewhere been shown in detail.[10]

[8] My "Die Urbeziehung."
[9] "Homeric Hymn to the Mother of the Gods" (tr. Evelyn-White), p. 439.
[10] My *Origins*, index, s.v. "patriarchate: transition from matriarchate."

Once the male frees himself from the domination of the female group, he turns against the Feminine through that very quality which it led him to develop. The totem ancestor, the transpersonal male principle, which for the women had originally been antagonistic to the earthly male of the male group, is now usurped by the men and set up in opposition to the Great Mother as the source of the male spirit.

The animal form of the gods and goddesses is only a late expression of something that is self-evident to the totemistic psychology of early man. For early man it is just as natural that the numinous progenitor should have animal form as that the Great Goddess should be endowed with all sorts of animal attributes and appear as an animal, or accompanied by animals.

At first sight there seems to be no difference between male and female gods. Both can assume animal form. But there is a difference. Whereas the male god in myth, like the male hero, usually appears in opposition to the animal that he fights and defeats, the Great Goddess, as Lady of the Beasts, dominates them but seldom fights them. Between her and the animal world there is no hostility or antagonism, although she deals with wild as well as gentle and tame beasts.

Pls. 17, 122   A snake-headed or bird-headed goddess, a goddess with the wings
Pl. 126   or the feet of a bird, is known to us from early Mesopotamia and
Pl. 124   Boeotia, while in Sumer and in Egypt she appears as a cow goddess and mistress of the herd.[11] And we find the same character in the goddess of
Pl. 123   Ras Shamra, who, bearing sheaves and surrounded by leaping rams, rules over the fertility of vegetation and cattle.

Pl. 124b   The pillar of the Great Goddess evinces her rule over the bull and
Pl. 124a   the lions. And for millenniums she stands or sits enthroned upon lions, as the Mesopotamian goddess Lilith of night, evil, and death, winged,
Pl. 37   bird-footed, and accompanied by owls; as the Hittite goddess clasping the child to her breast; on the gate in Mycenae, where she is symbolized by a tree or pillar standing between lions; or in Crete, playing with a
Fig. 62   pair of lions, or standing upon the lion-flanked mountain before a worshiping youth. It is the same goddess who in Phrygia appears with

[11] See above, pp. 158, 213.

272

Attis between two lions,[12] who was worshiped in Lycia, Lydia, Thrace, Syria,[13] Phoenicia, and other places. At a later period, she stood on a lion in Sparta; held lions in the character of Capuan winged Artemis; strangled them as Gorgon, as Cybele; or—thousands of years later—as

Pl. 127

Pl. 125

Pls. 80, 128a

FIG. *62*. THE GODDESS, STANDING ON MOUNTAIN

Seal impression, Crete, late Palace period

Fortuna sat in a chariot drawn by lions. In India or as the Tibetan Tara, she rode on a lion and held the sun in her hand; and as the Christian Madonna, she still sits on a throne adorned with lions.

Pl. 129

Pl. 130

Pl. 131a

The Aphroditelike Circe of the *Odyssey* is also the Lady of the Beasts:

> They found in a dell the house of Circe, well built with shaped stones, and set in a clearing. All round it were wolves and lions of the mountains, really men whom she had bewitched by giving them poisonous drugs. They did not attack the men, but ramped up fawning on them and wagged their long tails, just like a lot of dogs playing about their master when he comes out after dinner because they know he has always something nice for them in his pocket. So these wolves and lions with their sharp claws played about and

[12] Hoenn, *Artemis*, p. 55.

[13] Cf., particularly, the pictures of the Kedesha, e.g., in Gressmann, *Altorientalische Texte und Bilder zum Alten Testamente*.

pawed my men, who were frightened out of their wits by the terrible creatures.[14]

And to the same group of goddesses belongs the Aphrodite of the Homeric hymn:

> After her came gray wolves, fawning on her, and grim-eyed lions, and bears, and fleet leopards, ravenous for deer; and she was glad in heart to see them, and put desire in their breasts, so that they all mated, two together, about the shadowy vales.[15]

FIG. *63*. ARTEMIS ORTHIA

Ivory plaque, Sparta, c. *740* B.C.

Pls. 132–33   As Lady of the voracious beasts and the deer; as the bird-strangling
Pl. 134   Gorgon; as Boeotian ruler over the three realms of water, earth, and air,
Fig. 63   symbolized by fish, wolf, and bird; as the Spartan Orthia [16] (of Ana-

[14] *Odyssey*, X (tr. W. H. D. Rouse).   p. 411.
[15] "Hymn to Aphrodite" (tr. Evelyn-White),   [16] Thomson, *The Prehistoric Aegean*, p. 271 f.

tolian origin); and as the Hallstatt goddess on the bronze hydria—as the   *Pl. 135*
Great Artemis and Diana—she is queen of the animal world.

What interests us here is not the forms assumed by this Great
Goddess in the different parts of the world. Her names are innumerable
—Britomartis and Dictynna, Cybele and Mâ, Dindymene and Hecate,
Pheraia and Artemis, Baubo and Aphaia, Orthia and Nemesis, Demeter,
Persephone, and Selene, Medusa and Eleuthera, Taeit and Leto,
Aphrodite and Bendis. And Hathor and Isis, and all other Great Goddesses who appear in animal form, are in reality the Lady of the Beasts.
All beasts are their subjects: the serpent and scorpion, the fishes of river
and sea, the womblike bivalves and the ill-omened kraken, the wild
beasts of wood and mountain, hunting and hunted, peaceful and
voracious, the swamp birds—goose, duck, and heron—the nocturnal   *Pl. 136–37*
owl and the dove, the domesticated beasts—cow and bull, goat, pig,
and sheep—the bee, and even such phantasms as griffin and sphinx.[17]

In naming all these, we are practicing an age-old rite. Such lists
as we find in Apuleius, who identifies Isis with innumerable kindred
goddesses,[18] are a form of ritual worship. The abundance of manifestations is a characteristic of the archetype, and the plethora of names by
which the powers are invoked among all peoples is an expression of their
numinous ineffability.

As our illustrations show, the Lady of the Beasts is often winged;
that is to say, she is a heavenly and not a chthonic goddess. As goddess
of opposites, she is the Whole, containing in herself the three realms that
in Greek mythology were later shared by her sons Zeus, Poseidon, and
Hades.

An example of the Lady of the Beasts in a non-Mediterranean
sphere is the goddess with the wild beasts from Jutland.   *Pl. 133*

On the bronze jar (found in Switzerland) the goddess, who at the   *Pl. 135*
same time is always the ruler over twins,[19] i.e., over the principle of op-   *Pl. 45*
posites, holds one hare upward, the other downward. This is no acci-
dent, as is shown by the Boeotian goddess flanked by wolves, one hold-   *Pl. 134*

---

[17] Cf. Hoenn, *Artemis.*

[18] Apuleius, *Metamorphoses* (*The Golden Ass*).
[19] My *Origins*, pp. 95 f.

275

Pl. 6

ing his spiral tail up, the other down, in a correspondence to the spiral on the belly of the Primordial Mother. On the Boeotian amphora, the opposition of life and death, represented by the goddess, is expressed by the life-giving swastikas and by the bull's loins and bull's head as symbols of death, castration, and sacrifice.

Pl. 93

Mutilated beasts, from which "a member was cut off," [20] were sacrificed to Artemis not only in Boeotia but also in Euboea and Attica, and her name has—quite plausibly—been derived from the verb *artamein*, 'to slaughter.' The bull's or hippopotamus's thigh as an attribute of Ta-urt,[21] the castrated priests of Cybele and Diana of Ephesus, fit into this context.

But what does it mean that the Lady of the Beasts—even when her deadly character is accented; even when, for example, she becomes Gorgon, the strangler of animals—not only dominates but also protects the animal kingdom? It does not suffice to interpret this figure as the Aphroditian ruling principle of nature, to which the whole world, including the world of beasts, is subordinated. And why, precisely here, does the Great Mother appear in human and not in animal form?

We know how often the goddess appears as an animal, as cow and swamp bird, as ewe and lioness. She also "is" a fish. She bears the fish's tail of the mermaids; in her character of Artemis, Aphaia, Dictynna, Britomartis, and Atargatis, she is associated with sacred fishpools, and the lower part of the Boeotian Great Goddess consists of a fish and waves.

Pl. 134

Later, however, she ceases to "be" the goose itself, but rides on it or wears its symbol on her cloak; and she ceases to "be" the lioness, but stands on it. She no longer "is" the serpent but is accompanied by it. At this higher stage, she becomes a goddess in human form, ruling over the animal kingdom; and in alchemy she was still represented as Earth Mother with upraised arms, feeding the beasts.

Artemis has been characterized as a goddess of the "outside," of the free wild life in which as huntress she dominates the animal world. This is a symbolic projection of her role as ruler over the unconscious

---

[20] Hoenn, p. 24.   [21] See above, p. 224.

powers that still take on animal form in our dreams—the "outside" of the world of culture and consciousness.

The Lady of the Beasts is not a goddess of the cultural and agricultural stage; she is not the Demeter of the wheat, bringing culture and manners. She is close to the wild, early nature of man, i.e., to the savage instinct-governed being who lived with the beasts and the free-growing plants.

While the plant is a symbol of "vegetative life," of a life without consciousness and without urgent drives, consisting essentially of reaction to the world and the barest minimum of independent motion, the animal is the symbol of the next higher stage. Here the prevailing factors are drive and activity, movement within and without. In this stage, the dominent elements are the sensory consciousness of the individual and the community sense that holds together and directs the group; these, on the human level, are the foundation of all culture. Yet all this impulse and activity are blindly subordinated to the life and purpose of the species, and individuals, equipped with numerous organs for perceiving and ordering the world, remain unconscious victims of their own existence in life and in death.

What then is the meaning of this divine principle in human form, of this woman who governs the animal world and dominates instincts and drives, who gathers the beasts beneath her spirit wings as beneath the branches of a tree?

Long before a consciousness centered in the ego takes cognizance of the self as the center of psychophysical totality, the self appears as a body-self, i.e., as a totality directing the body and all its functions.[22]

The purposive ordering of inherently independent impulses and instincts, for which the human body is the prototype, is experienced as "nature," that is, projected outward as the world of plants and animals. The history of the natural sciences shows that man's view of nature develops parallel to his experience of his own nature. When in a later phase of development man seems to be centered in consciousness, ego, and will, a patriarchal god of heaven "governs" nature. But in the

[22] My *Origins*, pp. 288–90.

matriarchal unconscious phase, a feminine self creates an inner hierarchy of powers. Her image in the human psyche manifests the unconscious and unwilled, but purposive, order of nature. Cruelty, death, and caprice stand side by side with supreme planning, perfect purposiveness, and immortal life. Precisely where man is a creature of instinct living in the image of the beast or half-beast, i.e., where he is wholly or in large part dominated by the drives of the unconscious, the guiding purpose, the unconscious spiritual order of the whole, appears as a goddess in human form, as a Lady of the Beasts.

Man's experience of this goddess in human form is the first indication that he now knows the multiplicity of his own instinctual drives, which he had experienced in projection upon animals, to be inferior to the human principle that is specific to him. He experiences the authority that conditions and orders the instinctual drive. The Great Goddess is an embodiment of all those psychic structures that are superior to instinct. In this phase the male ego, with its independent will, its consciousness, and its patriarchal values, is not yet dominant; but it has become clear that the nature of man contains spiritual forces superior to instinct, even though they are not yet freely available to the ego but must be experienced by the ego as a numinous godhead outside it.[23]

This feminine divine spirit orders the world hierarchically; it knows levels of strength and vitality, of purposiveness and unpurposiveness, but—unlike the male godhead—it shines mercifully and maternally on good and evil, righteous and unrighteous, alike. This Great Goddess has favorites whom she showers with gifts and stepchildren, whom she seemingly sends out ill-equipped and as though half-finished; she is playful and cruel in her experiments and often—it would seem— arbitrary and unjust. But a deeper initiation into her secrets often re-

---

[23] It is because such cultural situations as ritual projections of a psychic reality are preserved long after the underlying reality has disappeared that it is so hard to date the psychic development of mankind. The decisive date is the *first* appearance among mankind and in the particular cultural spheres. Whether the duration of a culture or of one of its rituals corresponds to a living psychic reality, or is merely a consequence of the conservative tendency of mankind to cling to rituals that have long become atavistic, can only be shown by specialized investigation.

veals meaning beneath the meaningless. As in the fairy tale, the maternal tree, whose roots go down to the underworld, suddenly shakes its riches down upon a Cinderella, and a celestial growth, whose hidden powers come from the world of the ancestors and primordial images, unexpectedly unfolds the richest flowers of psychic life. But it is inherent in the mysteries of the Great Goddess and in her spiritual character that she grants life only through death, and development toward new birth only through suffering—that as Lady of Beasts and Men she confers no birth and no life without pain.

The culture-bearing significance of the Archetypal Feminine is exemplified by the goddess who in human form rules among and over the animal powers. Many of the phenomena that Bachofen's intuition led him to associate with the blessings of the Demetrian stage belong to this context, although he was too one-sided in relating them to the social matriarchate. Just as the hierarchical order of the body subordinates the individual organs and requires them to sacrifice their independence in favor of the whole, so the Great Goddess everywhere demands sacrifices. But here sacrifice implies purposive renunciation in favor of a larger context embracing the whole of life and therefore of human existence.

Thus the concept of sacrifice is a basic symbol in the life of primitive man. Because the unity of life is the central phenomenon of the situation of psychic origination, every disturbance of this unity—the felling of a tree, the killing or eating of an animal, and so on—must be compensated by a ritual offering, a sacrifice. For early man all growth and development depend on man's sacrifices and ritual activity, precisely because man's living bond with the world and the human group is projected upon nature as a whole.

Because the decisive moments in the life of the female—menstruation, deflowering, conception, and childbearing—are intimately bound up with a sacrifice of blood, the goddess perpetuates life by exacting bloody sacrifices that will assure the fertility of game, women, and fields, the rising of the sun, and success in warfare. But the male like the female is impelled by his very nature to sacrifice. Sacrifice stimulates the development of male aggression—e.g., in the warrior—but it also compels the male to sacrifice his aggressiveness.

Here castration, one of the essential symbols of the Terrible Mother, appears in a new light. As a symbol of man's domination over the animal world, bullfighting and games with bulls are among the great rituals of the Feminine. This ritual, rooted in the magical domination of animals, in the fertility and hunting magic of the primordial age, runs through the Cretan culture, Mithraism, the Roman gladiatorial fights, down to the bullfights of Spain.

In Crete, the goddess herself played victoriously with the bull, and the youthful lovers and ephebes were her priests and helpers. The Great Goddess Tauropolos is the Lady of the Bull; as Pheraia or Europa, riding on a bull, she tames the masculine and bestial.

Woman was entrusted with the care of the captive young animals; she was the tamer of domestic beasts and the founder of cattle breeding. What is more, she domesticated the male through the taboos that she imposed on him, and so created the first human culture. In exacting the domination, curtailment, and sacrifice of the instinctual drives, the Lady of the Beasts represented more than the principle of natural order. She was more than a protectress and breeder of beasts.

Thus the formative power of the Feminine that is realized in this connection starts from the narrowest confines of the family, tribe, or clan. But here it does not remain; in the course of human development it achieves transformations that show why the supreme embodiments of the Great Goddess always reflect woman's ability and willingness to love. For neither the exaction of sacrifice nor domination over the world of plants and animals, the instinctual world of the unconscious, is the central concern of the Great Goddess. Over both these stands the law of transformation in which she sublimates all life and raises it to a development where, without losing its bond with the root and foundation, it achieves the highest forms of psychic reality.

Chapter Fifteen

SPIRITUAL TRANSFORMATION

W E HAVE already spoken of the primordial mysteries of the Feminine. Although an exposition of these mysteries belongs properly to a "psychology of the Feminine," we must here attempt at least a brief summary.

It was Briffault who discovered the fact (which is still insufficiently recognized) that early culture is in very high degree the product of the female group,[1] and that the relative sedentariness of the matriarchal community of mothers and children was bound to provide a biological, psychological, and sociological force for the "ennoblement" of the original natural state.

Man's rise to consciousness operated at first through an unconscious process that appeared significant to the group as well as the individual: this process we call ritual.[2] Every important activity of primitive man is in this sense a ritual: hunting, food preparation, eating, weaving, pottery making, the brewing of intoxicants, the fashioning of weapons for the hunt, and so on. One expression of this fact is that these activities were often handed down secretly and that originally those engaging in them had to undergo a special ritual preparation. The ramifications of such ritual acts extend deep into the Western world. Not only the guilds and corporations, with their special costumes, customs,

---

[1] Cf. Briffault on women as hunters and fishers, as warriors, on primitive industries, pottery, building, primitive trade, medicine, and surgery, in *The Mothers*, Vol. I, pp. 447–90.

[2] Cf. my "Zur psychologischen Bedeutung des Ritus."

and codices, but also the prayers and symbols that accompany the various phases of life—the solemnities, gatherings, and processions of groups, associations, and societies—are vestiges of such rites.

But while the male mysteries, in so far as they are not mere usurpations of originally female mysteries, are largely enacted in an abstract spiritual space, the primordial mysteries of the Feminine are connected more with the proximate realities of everyday life. It is only later, for example, in the Eleusinian mysteries, the mysteries of Isis, and so on, that the mysteries are concerned with the consciousness and self-consciousness of the woman; in accordance with an essential trait of feminine psychology, the earlier mysteries take place on the level of direct but unconscious experience. In her molding of a fragment of reality into "symbolic life," the woman undergoes an inner experience of which she need not necessarily be conscious. Only the intensity and emotional accent of the action, and often the secrecy in which it is cloaked, reveal its character of mystery.

In the primordial mysteries, the Feminine—whose nature we have attempted to discern in the symbols and functions of its elementary and transformative character—assumes a creative role and so becomes the determining factor in early human culture. Whereas the instinctual mysteries revolve around the central elements in the life of woman—birth, menstruation, conception, pregnancy, sexuality, climacteric, and death—the primordial mysteries project a psychic symbolism upon the real world and so transform it.

The mysteries of the Feminine may be divided into mysteries of preservation, formation, nourishment, and transformation.

As we have shown, the vessel lies at the core of the elementary character of the Feminine. At all stages of the primordial mysteries it is the central symbol of their realization. In the mysteries of preservation this symbol is projected upon the cave [3] as sacral precinct and temple and also upon its development as dwelling, tent, house, storeroom, and temple. That is why the building and preparation of the dwelling are so often the prerogative of women.[4] The "sheltering struc-

---

[3] Cf. Levy, *The Gate of Horn*, p. 62.   [4] Briffault, Vol. I, pp. 477–83.

ture" of the vessel gives its form to the grave, the underworld dwelling, as it does to the dwelling house on earth and the temple, the house of the powers, the upper world. In Lycia and Asia Minor, houses are "the exact counterpart of the ancient tombs and temples the ruins of which are found in that ancient land of matriarchy." [5]

Not only temple, tomb, and house but also the central pillar supporting the structure of the house is a symbol of the Great Mother. The earliest houses, in Mesopotamia, for example, consisted of mats supported by pillars, from which Levy [6] derived the pillar symbol of the Great Mother.

Like gate, enclosure, and cattle pen,[7] the collective of village and city is a symbol of the Feminine. Their establishment originally began with the marking of a circle, the conjuring of the Great Round, which reveals its female nature equally well as containing periphery or as womb and center. The latest ramifications of this symbolism are the goddesses crowned with walls and the feminine names of cities. The Roman lares and penates, the gods of the household and fields, are companions of the *Mater larum* who in her character of Mania is connected with *mundus* and wall, and with the center of the city that lies deep in the earth. Thus not only house, pillar, door, threshold, and tomb (so often situated beneath the house) belong to the Feminine sphere but also the *penus*, 'storeroom,' whose tutelary gods are the penates.

The woman is the natural nourishing principle and hence mistress of everything that implies nourishment.[8] The finding, composition, and preparation of food, as well as the fruit and nut gathering of the early cultures, are the concern of the female group. Only the killing of large animals falls to the males, but the life and fertility of the animals were subordinated to the Feminine, since hunting magic, the magical guarantee of success in the hunt, lay in her province, although it was later taken over by the male hunting group.[9] This rule over food was largely based on the fact that the female group formed the center of the dwell-

[5] Briffault, Vol. I, p. 482.
[6] Levy, pp. 99 f.
[7] See above, p. 158.
[8] See Ch. 10, "The Positive Elementary Character."
[9] This is the beginning of the emancipation of the male group, which later led to the patriarchate; see my *Origins*, pp. 432 ff.

ing, i.e., the actual home to which the nomadic males again and again returned.

The function of shelter and preservation, which was incumbent on woman and which in general led to the creation of the "dwelling," was embodied in the activities of plaiting, weaving, binding, and knotting required for the fashioning of mat and screen, the original instruments of shelter.

The same function of the elementary Feminine character includes the clothing of the body, which in fact lies almost entirely in the province of the female group. This process begins with the preparation of the skins and the fashioning of leather, which, as the vast numbers of "scrapers" show, played an important role in prehistoric cultures. It continues with the preparation of thread from bast, bark, and leaves; with the weaving and sewing, waterproofing, dying, and painting of the cloth.

To the primordial mysteries of the Feminine belongs also the making of the vessels [10] used for gathering food, transporting water, and so on from fruit rinds, bladders, and clay. These instruments of preservation are important for another aspect of feminine domination that is of critical importance for the development of culture, namely, the storing of food. This first measure to stave off hunger from the group when the hunt failed proved to be the foundation of property. The "stores" belonged beyond any question to the women, whose domination was thus enhanced. At first accidentally (when the stored grains or tubers sprouted and took root), later by conscious direction, this storing of food led to the development of agriculture among the relatively sedentary female group.

But at the center of the mysteries over which the female group presided stood the guarding and tending of the fire. As in the house round about, female domination is symbolized in its center, the fireplace, the seat of warmth and food preparation, the "hearth," which is also the original altar. In ancient Rome this basic matriarchal element was most

[10] See above, pp. 123, 133.

conspicuously preserved in the cult of Vesta [11] and its round temple. This is the "old round house or tent with a fireplace in the middle. Models of these prehistoric houses were found in the form of cinerary urns in the Roman Forum." [12]

The third central symbol of female domination is the couch, or "bed," the place of sexuality and of the related fertility ritual. Up to our own time the existence of the family rests on these central symbols, which constellate female domination inside the family: the house, the table—or hearth—and the bed.

With the use of fire as the symbol and instrument of transformation, the vessel, too, is transformed; this is the origin of ceramics. And now food begins to be improved by frying, roasting, and boiling. A later development is the bake oven, intimately bound up with the mysteries of agriculture: grain and bread.[13] Thus the Feminine becomes the repository of transformation and in the primordial mysteries lays the foundations of human culture, which is transformed nature.

We have already referred to the deathly significance of the mill and the fertility significance of cakes and cakelike symbols. In Greece and Rome and in the European Middle Ages, mills and bakeries were often connected with brothels,[14] and another reminder of this context is the "fair miller-girl" of the song. This whole symbolism is based on the profound identity between the food-giving and food-transforming Feminine, not only with the mill but in a positive sense with the oven, particularly the baking oven, and with bread itself.

Here we are concerned only with the transformative aspect of the oven, in which it appears as sacral, life-transforming vessel, as the mystery of the uterus. In Roman mythology, the oven goddess and her festival, the Fornacalia, play an important role in connection with the archaic national bread, the *far*. So evident is the connection between transformation, birth of the bread, nourishment, and the Feminine that

---

[11] See also the works of Brelich: *Vesta* and *Die geheime Schutzgottheit von Rom.*
[12] Van der Leeuw, *Phänomenologie der Reli-gion*, p. 374.
[13] Cf., in this regard, Jacob, *Six Thousand Years of Bread.*
[14] Bloch, *Die Prostitution*, p. 277.

an old proverb says: "The oven is the mother." Of a woman about to give birth it is said: "The oven will soon cave in," and among many peoples invalids and cripples are said to be in need of "rebaking." [15] Another indication of this thoroughgoing identification of the oven with the Feminine is that the oven is looked upon as "prophetic" and is questioned about destiny and other matters.

In these primordial mysteries of the Feminine, all of which lie on the natural plane, woman is already the Lady of Transformation. The transformation of matter and of life is subordinated to her, whether as goddess of the water, as "she who promiseth torrents," [16] she commands the magic of rain; whether as goddess of the earth she commands the fertility of the soil; whether as Lady of the Beasts she governs the fecundity of the animals; or whether as goddess of the blood she ordains the transformation of blood into milk or rain.[17]

But beyond this, she transforms nature into a higher, spiritual principle, which she has power to distill from the natural substrate of matter. As goddess of the food-giving plants, herbs, and fruits, she numinously transforms these basic elements into intoxicants and poisons. It is quite evident that the preparation and storage of food taught woman the process of fermentation and the manufacture of intoxicants, and that, as a gatherer and later preparer of herbs, plants, and fruits, she was the inventor and guardian of the first healing potions, medicines, and poi-

---

[15] A passage in a story by the Czech writer Čapek shows that these mysteries can still be experienced as such: " 'You wouldn't believe what a fine job it is to bake rolls, and especially to bake bread. My poor old dad had a bakery, so I know all about it. You see, in making bread, you've got two or three important secrets which are practically holy. The first secret is how to make the yeast; you have to leave it in the trough and then there's a sort of mysterious change takes place under the lid; you have to wait until the flour and water turn into live yeast. Then the dough is made and mixed with what they call a mash-ladle; and that's a job that looks like a religious dance or something of that sort. Then they cover it with a cloth and let the dough rise; that's another mysterious change, when the dough grandly rises and bulges, and you mustn't lift the cloth to peep underneath—I tell you, it's as fine and strange as the process of birth. I've always had a feeling that there was something of a woman about that trough. And the third secret is the actual baking, the thing that happens to the soft and pale dough in the oven. Ye gods, when you take out the loaf, all golden and russet, and it smells more delicious than a baby, it's such a marvel—why, I think that when these three changes are going on, they ought to ring a bell in the bakeries, the same as they do in church at the elevation of the host.' " —Karel Čapek, "The Needle" (from *Tales from Two Pockets*, pp. 264–65).

[16] Cf. Pietschmann, *Geschichte der Phönizier.*, p. 235 n.

[17] Spence, *The Religion of Ancient Mexico*, p. 27.

sons.[18] Among the Sumerians, Inanna, the "celestial Mother Goddess of the wine," was already the grain goddess and both correspond astronomically and astrologically to the virgin with the ear of grain.[19] The goddess is therefore not only the queen of the ennobled fruit of the soil but also of the spirit matter of transformation that is embodied in the wine. Thus the transformative character of the Feminine rises from the natural to the spiritual plane. The culture-bringing primordial mysteries culminate in a spiritual reality that completes the mystery character of the Feminine.

THE WOMAN AS MANA FIGURE

Thus there unfolds before us a magnificent world of feminine cultural development, which is at the same time an unfolding of feminine power. In ever new circles of numinous fascination it takes form around the Archetypal Feminine, which as goddess represents the center of the female group and the self of the individual psyche. At first the image of the Feminine as goddess and as Great Round has filled the human horizon. But now, as the development progresses, the earthly-human vehicle of this numinous principle, the woman as a figure endowed with mana, enters the foreground of human consciousness. The Feminine, at first worshiped as an animal—lioness, she-bear, bird, snake—has become a human goddess, beside which the animal stands as an attribute. And now, by a corresponding development, the vessel, the central symbol of the Feminine, becomes at length her attribute and instrument. Here, as so often, psychic-symbolic and objective sociological factors work together. The vessel on the one hand is the form within which matter is transformed, whether it be cooked or allowed to ferment; whether it be made into medicine, poison, or intoxicant. But on the other hand—and this is fundamental—this transformation, which is viewed as magical, can only be effected by the woman because she

---

[18] Among nearly all primitive peoples intoxicants are consequently prepared by the female group; the old woman as repository of medicinal and poisonous herbs has survived in belief and fact down to our own day.

[19] Cf. Langdon, *Tammuz and Ishtar*, pp. 43, 44.

herself, in her body that corresponds to the Great Goddess, is the caldron of incarnation, birth, and rebirth. And that is why the magical caldron or pot is always in the hand of the female mana figure, the

Pl. 138 priestess or, later, the witch.[1] Helios rides through the heavens in the vessel of transformation, in which he was originally renewed in the dark region whither he returned each evening. And just as Pelops, after be-

Pl. 139 ing boiled in a sacred kettle, was renewed by Clotho the goddess of destiny or Rhea the Mother Goddess, so Dionysus also became "whole and perfect" after being "cooked over" in a magical kettle of transformation.[2]

The ancient mana figure that most clearly represents this principle of transformation is Medea. But in her the declining matriarchate is already devaluated by the patriarchal principle, and the mythical reality she represents is personalized,[3] that is, reduced to a mere personal level and so negativized. Like Circe, she was originally a goddess, but has become a "witch" in the patriarchally colored myth.

The kettle of transformation is identical with the sacrificial blood bowl whose content the priestess requires in order to achieve her magical purpose. Here the blood has not yet the later "spiritual" significance of a sacrificial offering, but a magical significance; it "contains" the soul, as the Bible still teaches. The necessity of its use rests on the matriarchal belief that even in the womb no life can be built up without

Pl. 76 blood.[4] For this reason the kettles of Mexico, the blood bowls,[5] like the

Fig. 46 caldrons of the underworld,[6] are vessels of transformation on which depend fertility, light, and transformation.

We find the same in the ancient North of Europe. Strabo reports concerning the Cimbri:

> Their women who traveled with them were accompanied by sacred priestesses, gray-haired, white-robed, with a linen scarf buckled over their shoulder and a girdle of brass, and walking barefooted. These priestesses, with a sword in their hand, met the prisoners of war when they were brought

[1] On the godhead as vessel, see above, pp. 132 f.
[2] Briffault, *The Mothers*, Vol. III, p. 451, n. 3.
[3] My *Origins and History of Consciousness*,

p. 201.
[4] See above, p. 32.
[5] See above, p. 191, n. 59.
[6] See above, p. 192.

to the camp; and having crowned them, they led them to a brass basin as large as thirty amphorae. They had a ladder which the priestess mounted, and, standing over the basin, she cut the throat of each prisoner as he was handed up to her. With the blood that gushed into the basin they made a prophecy.[7]

A silver vessel of this kind, the so-called Gundestrap caldron, with   *Pl. 140* a sacrificial scene represented on it, has been found in Jutland. The goddess depicted on it, whom Briffault describes as a moon goddess,[8] is already known to us as the Lady of the Beasts. In the present reproductions two types are clearly differentiated: first, the old priestesses, whose hair is worn like that of the Great Goddess of the Beasts, toward whom they turn; these evidently are the actual priestesses of fertility and prophecy. Beside them we see two "hovering" young female figures resembling the young witches who later rode on broomsticks. They are Artemislike, Amazonian goddesses of the hunt. One battles with a wild beast; the other appears to be slaying an aurochs. We shall have more to say of the relation between the young and old priestess or deity.

The magic caldron is originally a symbol of fertility belonging to the elementary character of the Feminine. As such it yields food, it is the cornucopia, for example; and even its latest form, the Christian, sublimated Grail, which has almost lost its original significance as the magical kettle of the cult priestess, retains its food-giving aspect. This food-giving quality is imputed to many magical vessels in Irish legend; [9] the Grail itself, as the legend has it, nourished Joseph of Arimathea during his imprisonment, and in the Castle of the Grail it still fulfills this function: "It proceeded to every place in the hall, and as it came before the tables, it filled them with every kind of meal that a man could desire." [10]

Beside the elementary character of the magical vessel its transformative character is at work from the very outset. A sublimated spiritual "conception" did not merely gain acceptance in the course of

[7] Strabo, VII, 2, quoted from Briffault, Vol. II, p. 542.

[8] Briffault, Vol. II, p. 542.
[9] Ibid., Vol. III, p. 452.
[10] Cf. ibid., Vol. III, p. 452.

time; rather, the transformative character is from the very beginning bound up with the magical significance of the woman as mana figure, for it would seem to be fundamental to the magical world view as such that for unknown, that is, numinous, reasons the Feminine can create life within it.

As Briffault has shown, all taboos originated in the menstruation taboo that the women imposed on themselves and the men. The matriarchal epoch was the source of totemism, and exogamy and taboo as well as the principle of initiation seem to have belonged originally to the central institutions of the female group. One indication of this is that many female mysteries were taken over by the men,[11] and that in some the men still wore the more primordial woman's dress.[12] We even have traditions—among the primitive aborigines of Tierra del Fuego, for example—to the effect that the earliest mysteries were mysteries of the moon goddess, against which the men rebelled under the leadership of the sun, slaying all the grown women and only permitting ignorant and uninitiated little girls to survive.[13]

When we look for the psychological conditions that must have given rise to the initiation of adolescents, to the various secret rites, and to segregation, we find nothing of the sort in the normal male development; while the mysterious occurrence of menstruation or pregnancy and the dangerous episode of childbearing make it necessary for the inexperienced woman to be initiated by those who are informed in these matters. The monthly "segregation" in the closed (i.e., taboo) sacral female precinct is only a logical continuation of the initiation that has occurred in this place at the first menstruation. Childbearing occurs in this same precinct, which is the natural, social, and psychological center of the female group, ruled over by the old, experienced women. And it is perfectly natural that the knowledge of the effect of herbs, fruits, and so on should here have led to the first blood stanching, healing of wounds, and soothing of pain.

In the beginning, at the height of the matriarchal epoch, the col-

---

[11] Ibid., Vol. II, pp. 543–55.
[12] Ibid., Vol. II, pp. 543 ff.
[13] Ibid., Vol. II, p. 543. Also cf. Koppers, "Zum Ursprung des Mysterienwesens."

lective existence of the group stood in the foreground; individuality and individual relations between men and women were relatively undeveloped. In this period the female mysteries consisted largely in fertility rituals oriented toward the community as a whole. Later the primordial mysteries were traditionalized into cults, which, as we know, were kept secret by the women.[14] Still later, rules governing sexual intercourse, methods of preventing conception, and finally love magic were added to these original secrets of feminine initiation.

It is important for the basic understanding of the magical efficacy of woman and of woman as a mana figure to bear in mind that woman necessarily experienced herself as subject and object of mysterious processes and as a vessel of transformation. The mysterious occurrences in her body, the instinctual mysteries of her existence, are exclusively the possession of woman. Apart from his strength and technical dexterity, the male had no corresponding secret to offer. This situation changed only with the development of the characteristic masculine consciousness.

But the magical efficacy of the Feminine is not confined to the elementary character and the fertility ritual; in a sphere transcending the fertility of animals and men, of the earth and heaven, the goddess as Great Round becomes a force for sublimation and rebirth. Not only does the night, leading through death and sleep to healing and birth, renew the cycle of life; but, transcending earthly darkness, it sublimates the very essence of life through the eruption from the depths of those powers that, in drunkenness and ecstasy, poetry and illumination, manticism and wisdom, enable man to achieve a new dimension of spirit and light. *Pl. 141*

We have repeatedly referred to the spiritual aspect of the feminine transformative character, which leads through suffering and death, sacrifice and annihilation, to renewal, rebirth, and immortality. But such transformation is possible only when what is to be transformed enters wholly into the Feminine principle; that is to say, dies in re-

---

[14] Such tendencies may be followed down to modern life, where recipes, etc., become a secret family tradition.

turning to the Mother Vessel, whether this be earth, water, underworld, urn, coffin, cave, mountain, ship, or magic caldron. Usually several of these containing symbols are combined; but all of them in turn are encompassed in the all-embracing psychic reality, the womb of night or of the unconscious. In other words, rebirth can occur through sleep in the nocturnal cave, through a descent to the underworld realm of the spirits and ancestors, through a journey over the night sea, or through a stupor induced by whatever means—but in every case, renewal is possible only through the death of the old personality. Whether, as in Malta long before the days of healing in the Greek shrines of Asclepius, the sick man undergoes a slumber of "incubation," in the course of which he encounters the healing godhead in the form of a serpent; or whether he is drawn through a dolmen or an ancient stone gate, or in some other way brought to rebirth—in every case, we have a recurrence of the same archetypal constellation.

And later, in the ancient Orient, for example, when the renewal of the divine kingdom had become an institution of vital importance for the collectivity, the rebirth of the king was bound up with the old symbols and rites: he mounted the throne representing the Great Mother; he was drawn through an animal's pelt; a death ritual was enacted in which the king, in Egypt for example, was identified with the dead Osiris and like him awakened by the Great Goddess Isis.

But every magical process presupposes a ritual, and every ritual presupposes a transformation of the human personality, which makes it receptive to ritual and endows it with powers not normally at its command.[15]

Here we need not ask whether this ritual of rebirth was originally performed by the female group, by individual priestesses, or by the whole community. One thing is certain: everywhere a particular magical and mantic power was attributed to the woman. Psychologically this is readily understandable; for while the specific achievement of the male world lies in the development of the masculine consciousness and the rational mind, the female psyche is in far greater degree dependent on

[15] Cf. my "Zur psychologischen Bedeutung des Ritus."

the productivity of the unconscious, which is closely bound up with what we accordingly designate as the matriarchal consciousness.[16]

But precisely this matriarchal consciousness which rests in large part on man's *participation mystique* with his environment,[17] and in which the human psyche and the extrahuman world are still largely undivided, forms the foundation of the magical-mantic power of the human personality. Originally the matriarchal consciousness, with its greater proximity to this reality and its great receptivity toward the powers of the unconscious, is stronger in woman and less overlaid by the abstracting form of the patriarchal consciousness.

Here we cannot undertake to cite the material that proves how vast a role was performed by the woman as a mana figure, as repository of positive as well as negative magic, as priestess and witch. It suffices to point out that she originally played this role in Sumer, Assyria, Babylonia, Egypt, Greece, Rome; among the Celtic and Germanic peoples; in Africa, Asia, the Americas, Indonesia, Polynesia, Australia; in short throughout the uncivilized and civilized world.[18] We shall rather seek to explain the psychological causes that led to this function of woman as a mana figure.

Here again, Bachofen, in writing on the nature of woman, was first to formulate a very fundamental insight, even though there is a certain one-sidedness in his moralizing evaluation.

"That Bacchic *mania* which Euripides portrays and whose physical manifestation is represented in so many works of art is rooted in the depths of woman's emotional life, and the indissoluble bond between those two mightiest of forces, religious emotion and sensual desire, raised it to that frenzy of enthusiasm, that reeling drunkenness, which was bound to be looked upon as an immediate revelation of the glorious gods. Smitten in the core of her being, the woman rages over the silent mountain heights, everywhere seeking the manifest god who also loves best to walk in the heights. . . . The intensity of the orgiastic passion compounded of religion and sensuality shows how the woman, though

---

[16] My "Über den Mond und das matriarchale Bewusstsein."

[17] My "Die Psyche und die Wandlung der Wirklichkeitsebenen."

[18] See the material in Briffault, Vol. II, pp. 502–70.

weaker than the man, is able at times to rise to greater heights than he. Through his mystery, Dionysus captured the woman's soul with its penchant for everything that is supernatural, everything that defies natural law; by his blinding sensuous epiphany, he works on the imagination that for the woman is the starting point of all inner emotion, and on her erotic feeling without which she can do nothing, but to which under the protection of religion she gives an expression that surpasses all barriers." [19]

We have repeatedly mentioned the significance of the "transpersonal male principle," of the paternal uroboros,[20] the deeper stratum of what Jung has described as the "animus" [21] aspect, the masculine spiritual aspect of the Feminine. The spiritual aspect of the unconscious confronts woman as an invisibly stimulating, fructifying, and inspiring male spirit,[22] whether it appear as totem or demon, as ancestral spirit or god.[23] In the woman, every psychic situation that leads to an animation of the unconscious, or to an *abaissement du niveau mental*, sets in motion the unconscious patriarchal structures of the animus, and behind them the world of the paternal uroboros. Here it is a matter of indifference whether we have in mind constitutional gifts, abilities developed by initiation or by a natural debilitation (menstruation, childbearing, sickness, hunger), or changes in the normal personality, provoked by age, hardship, or special measures of any sort whatever.

We know that such measures form a part of the preparation for magic and manticism. They may consist in isolation, hunger, the infliction of pain, the consumption of intoxicants, the drinking of blood, poisoning with laurel, ivy, opium, tobacco, or innumerable other vege-

[19] Bachofen, *Mutterrecht*, Vol. I, pp. 587 f.

[20] My *Amor and Psyche*, pp. 104 ff., 130, 132.

[21] Jung, "The Relations between the Ego and the Unconscious."

[22] My "Über den Mond."

[23] It is no accident that the oldest of the Egyptian goddesses, the vulture goddess Nekhbet and the snake goddess Uto of Buto, are called "those who are rich in magic." The vulture, believed to occur only as a female, fertilized by the wind, is like Mut, the vulture goddess, the protecting and nurturing celestial mother of the king's child. The child's father is the godhead, which in the matriarchal stage is experienced as paternal uroboros, as an anonymous transpersonal principle, here, for example as "spirit-wind," and later in the patriarchate as "spirit-sun." With regard to the snake, see many passages above. The "magic" arises from the union of the Feminine with the transpersonal principle.

table substances gained from fruits, leaves, tubers, and seeds. The manipulation of these substances has formed part of the woman's primordial knowledge from her earliest domination, through the ritual of growth, down to the witch and herb woman of the matriarchal decadence.

All these aids merely set in motion a natural potency of the female psyche, through which from time immemorial woman, in her character of shaman, sibyl, priestess, and wise woman, has influenced mankind. And this psychological situation is intensified by the circumstance that the male projects the anima figure [24] living within him upon the woman, or experiences it through her. This anima figure, as we can still see in the psychology of modern man, is in large part formed by the woman as young priestess, as Sophia, or as young witch. The more unconscious a man is, the more the anima figure remains fused or connected with the mana figure of the mother or of the old woman. In other words, the unconscious psyche of the man is directed by a magical unity of old and young women. We find a constellation of this sort in the magical-mantic dominance of the female group in the life of primitive mankind. The psychological consequence of this is a hierarchy of "spiritual-magical" potencies and planes of power, with the Great Mother at the summit and beside her, as an effective male principle, the animus of the transpersonal male. On this world of the animus, which has its focus in the figure of the moon as "Lord of the Women," depends the magical-spiritual reality of the female group. But in the matriarchal phase of which we are speaking, this female group, whose practical importance is further increased by the projection of the male principle, dominates the whole world of the males, who have not yet come to identify themselves with the transpersonal male principle experienced by the woman.

But when consciousness and reason cannot, as in a later human development, be drawn upon to decide a situation, the male falls back on the wisdom of the unconscious, by which the female is inspired; and thus the unconscious is invoked and set in motion in rite and cult. It is

[24] See above, Ch. 3.

evident that in this phase the woman's pre-eminence—quite aside from her sociological position—is firmly entrenched; for the less developed the consciousness of mankind, the more it is in need of orientation by the unconscious, that is, by the transpersonal powers. Even in a later period the male shaman or seer is in high degree "feminine," since he is dependent on his anima aspect. And for this reason he often appears in woman's dress.[25]

Thus the woman is the original seeress, the lady of the wisdom-bringing waters of the depths, of the murmuring springs and fountains, for the "original utterance of seerdom is the language of water." [26] But the woman also understands the rustling of the trees and all the signs of nature, with whose life she is so closely bound up. The murmuring of the waters in the depths is only the "outside" of the speech of her own unconscious, which rises up in her like the water of a geyser.

Because the ecstatic situation of the seeress results from her being overpowered by a spirit that erupts in her, that speaks from her, or rather chants rhythmically from her, she is the center of magic, of magical song, and finally of poetry. She is the source from which Odin received the runes of wisdom; she is the Muse, the source of the words that stream upward from the depths; and she is the inspiring anima of the poets.[27]

As a power of inspiration she may appear singly, in the triad with which we are familiar, or in an indeterminate plural. The Graces, nymphs, wood sprites, Muses, Fates, and innumerable corresponding figures are the singing, dancing, and prophetic forces of this inspired and inspiring woman to whom, in time of need, the male, farther removed as he is from the origin, appeals for wisdom. And over and over again we find this mantic woman connected with the symbols of caldron and cave, of

Pl. 141   night and moon.

For the caldron is not only a vessel of life and death, renewal and

[25] In this sense the psychologically significant factor is for us the archetypal aspect of the Feminine as it lives in both sexes. Even where later the male mantic becomes dominant —or stands at least on an equal footing with the female—it is with the help of his feminine aspect, of the anima in him, that he penetrates the depths of the unconscious.

[26] Ninck, *Wodan*, p. 305.

[27] In this regard, cf. not only Graves, *The White Goddess*, but also Briffault's and Thomson's works cited above.

rebirth, but also of inspiration and magic. Its transformative character leads through dissolution and death to the ecstatic intensification and birth of the eloquent spirit that, as symptom of rebirth, leads in ecstatic inspiration to vision and word, to song and prophecy.

But the word is also fate, for it proclaims what the powers have decreed, and curse as well as blessing are dependent on the magical rituals that rest in the hands of the women. What we later designate as poetry originated in magical incantation and song, rising spontaneously from the unconscious and bringing its own form, its own rhythm, and its own sensuous images up with it from the depths.

In his fine chapter on "The Art of Poetry" [28] and particularly in the section on "Improvisation and Inspiration," Thomson follows the psychic reality of poetry back to the prophets and thence to the "possession" that in the primitive phase was identical with inspiration. But today our insight into depth psychology gives us a better understanding of this "possession." It is possession by what analytical psychology calls a "partial soul," by an unconscious component of the human psyche, which sets itself in the place of an ego that is still relatively weak and not yet fixated in consciousness.

How it is possible that not meaningless or "wishful" products but integrated contents, which are even superior to the consciousness of the time, are manifested in this possession cannot concern us here. In any event, the fundamental phenomenon, the fact that the transpersonal unconscious is culture-creating and enriches the consciousness of the individual and the group (for all primitive culture and almost all culture of any kind originate in the incursions of the unconscious)—precisely this makes the repository of the "unconscious word" a mana figure, a "Great Individual," the exalted instrument of the powers.

The universal relationship between seizure, rage, spirit, and poetry has been illustrated by the example of Wotan-Odin.[29] The derivation of his name is in reality an extension of the root *Wut*, 'fury': "*Wut*, OHG. *wuot*, 'fury.' Beside it the adjective OHG. *wuot*, OE. *wöd*, ON. *öör*, 'furious'; Go. *wöds*, 'possessed,' 'insane.' Related to this family stands

[28] *The Prehistoric Aegean*, pp. 454 ff.   [29] Ninck, *Wodan*, index, s.v. "Wodan."

OE. *wōþ*, 'voice song'; ON. *ōōr*, 'passion,' 'poetry.' The meaning is conveyed by the unrelated L. *vātēs*, 'god-inspired singer' (OIr. *fáith*, 'poet'); cf. OIran. *api-vatāgáti*, 'stimulates spiritually,' 'makes to understand'; Avestan *aipi-vat-*, 'to understand.' Probably the god's name Wodan . . . belongs to the same family." [30]

To this stem, as Ninck adds, also belongs the signification *Brunst*, 'passion,' 'ardor'; MD. 'furious,' 'raving,' 'violently desiring,' 'burning with love.' The etymological relation of fury, storm, excitement, drunkenness, ardor, seerdom, and poetry must also be brought into connection with the spirit-moon root,[31] to which Mimir, the wise man of the well, also belongs, and with the significations of the word *Geist*, 'spirit': "As its fundamental meaning we deduce *Aufgeregtheit*, 'agitation,' from ON. *geisa*, 'to rage' (of fire and passion), and Gothic *us-gaisjan*, 'to bring [someone] out of himself,' E. 'aghast.' " [32]

And with this we must further relate the group of significations related to "sing": "The Germanic root *sengw* from Indo-Germanic *sengᵘh* seems to have a relative only in Greek ὀμφή (from *songᵘha*) 'divine voice,' 'oracle.' " [33]

All these etymological relations between seizure, fury, passion, spirit, song, ardor, being-outside-oneself, poetry, and oracle characterize the creative aspect of the unconscious, whose activity sets man in motion, overpowers him, and makes him its instrument. The superiority of the irrupting powers of the unconscious, when they appear spontaneously, more or less excludes the ego and consciousness; that is to say, men are seized and possessed by these powers. But since this possession causes higher, supraconscious powers to appear in man, it is methodically sought after in cult and ritual.

In this connection the dance plays a crucial role, as expression of the natural seizure of early man. Originally all ritual was a dance, in which the whole of the corporeal psyche was literally "set in motion." [34]

---

[30] Cf. Kluge and Götze, *Etymologisches Wörterbuch der deutschen Sprache*, p. 700.
[31] Cf. my "Über den Mond," pp. 342 f.
[32] Cf. Kluge and Götze, *Wörterbuch*, p. 194.

[33] Cf. ibid, p. 564.
[34] Cf. my "Zur psychologischen Bedeutung des Ritus."

Thus the Great Goddess was worshiped in dance, and most of all in orgiastic dance.

We find the oldest example of such a dance in an Ice Age cave *Fig. 64* painting, which seems to show a group of women dancing around the phallic figure of a boy. A Mexican example shows women dancing *Pl. 143* around men with staffs. The archaic goddess of Boeotia stands in the *Pl. 144*

FIG. 64. DANCE GROUP

Rock painting, Cogul, Spain, paleolithic

center of the ring of dancing women. And on the headdress of the Cyprian goddess, adorned with heads of Hathor and floral rosettes, *Pl. 145* fauns and women are engaged in an orgiastic round dance.

Because seizure in large part presupposes an exclusion of the normal daytime consciousness, the Great Goddess of the night, as ruler of the unconscious, is the goddess not only of poisons and intoxicants but also of stupor and sleep. Her priestess is the original giver of incubation, the sleep of healing, transformation, and awakening; and her intervention is necessary wherever intercourse with the powers demands liberation from the body in dream or ecstasy. In the pile dwellings of the Stone Age we already find evidence of the growing of poppies, the typical plant *Fig. 58; Pl. 60* of the Cretan Great Goddess, of Demeter, Ceres, and Spes.[35] The efficacy of the poppy as a magic potion of forgetfulness is recorded by Homer. And it is precisely in matriarchal Sparta that Telemachus is introduced to this nepenthe. Helen of Troy, who pours him the potion, and the land of its origin, Egypt, also belong to the matriarchal sphere: [36]

> She lost no time, but put something into the wine they were drinking, a drug potent against pain and quarrels and charged with forgetfulness of all trouble; whoever drank this mingled in the bowl, not one tear would he let fall the whole day long, not if mother and father should die, not if they should slay a brother or a dear son before his face and he should see it with his own eyes. That was one of the wonderful drugs which the noble Queen possessed, which was given her by Polydamna, the daughter of Thon, an Egyptian.[37]

The magical efficacy of the poppy is a secret of the woman; thus the priestess puts the dragon guarding the temple of the Hesperides to sleep with opium.[38]

In Mexico, a region that is entirely apart from Mediterranean culture, we find the same archetypal correlations with the Feminine. Mayauel, goddess of the intoxicant made from the maguey, possessed the secret of the plant that made the juice ferment and possessed also "the wort, or 'medicine,' which gave a narcotic quality to the *octli* drink and which was thought of as 'strangling' or choking the drunkard. The plant in question has the appearance of a rope . . ." [39] She is the Strangling One, and all males have succumbed to the pleasure, magic, and in-

[35] Lewin, *Phantastica*, p. 41.
[36] Thomson, p. 416.
[37] *Odyssey*, IV, 220 ff. (tr. W. H. D. Rouse).
[38] Virgil, *Aeneid*, IV, 486. Not only Troy, Sparta, and Egypt but the whole ancient Mediterranean region, and particularly Malta with its incubation cult, form a cohesive unit. This cult (Levy, pp. 134 ff.) embraces a territory including the western Mediterranean, Africa, Sicily, Sardinia, and extending to Ireland, Scotland, southern England, northern France, Portugal, and the Canary Islands. See Hefel, "Der unterirdische Vielkammerbau in Afrika und im Mittelmeergebiet."
[39] Spence, *The Religion of Ancient Mexico*, p. 117.

toxication that she communicates; but she is also the Healing One, and her husband is "he from the land of medicine." Like Tlazolteotl, who is goddess of pleasure and death, with medicine men, physicians, fortune-tellers, and magicians in her train, Mayauel, too, is a bringer both of intoxication and death.

Here again the goddess of intoxicating liquor is the Great Goddess, the Mother, goddess of the earth and the night. It is therefore no accident that Mayauel is the earth monster, the goddess of the earth and the corn, and the night sky.[40] As the goddess with the "four hundred"—i.e., innumerable—breasts, she is the heavenly mother nourishing the stars who are the fish swimming in the heavenly ocean, and with whom the four hundred gods of the octli or pulque, her sons, are identical.[41]

Pulque was forbidden to the young, and a drunkard showing himself in public was punished by death. It was taken in moderation at many festivals, but its true importance was that warriors drank it before going into battle and prisoners before being sacrificed.[42] The magical power of the pulque was a means employed by the war goddess to make the men braver in battle, but it was also the symbol of the deadly power of the Feminine itself, in which intoxication and death are mysteriously interwoven. The Mexicans also believed that a man born under the sign of the pulque-medicine plant would be a brave warrior.[43] Everywhere and in all times we find this use of alcohol as a battle stimulant.[44] But warlike frenzy is not always the consequence of poison-

[40] Ibid.

[41] Because she is related to the moon, for the moon feeds on the wine of the maguey (Krickeberg, *Märchen*, p. 324), Mayauel often sits on a tortoise, the maternal beast of the moon and the earth, which withdraws into the darkness like the moon (p. 368). This again is archetypal, for in Egypt, too, the tortoise stands in opposition to the sun (Book of the Dead [tr. Budge], Ch. CXLI) and as an oracular beast in China fits into the same context.

[42] It is characteristic that even today, in connection with the ritually accented preparation of the pulque, the Mexicans speak of "cutting out the heart," or "castrating" the plant (Toor, *Mexican Folkways*, p. 16). Here again, in

other words, we encounter the relation between castration, sacrifice, and fertility, of which we have given numerous examples in Ch. 11, "The Negative Elementary Character."

[43] Spence, *Religion*, p. 117.

[44] This significance of alcohol is evident in our own culture. And the same function was once imputed to opium. "There is no Turk," it was reported by the French traveler, Pierre Belon, in the sixteenth century, "who does not spend his last penny on opium, which he carries with him both in peace and war. The reason for this opium eating is to be found in the conviction that it makes men braver and less afraid of the dangers of war" (Lewin, *Phantastica*, p. 45). Nepenthe had the same significance.

ing by intoxicants, although such "aids" were no doubt widespread in the secret societies.

We have several times referred to the warlike figures accompanying the Great Mother, the male followers representing her destructive aspect. Battle frenzy is known to us particularly among the Germanic peoples with their berserkers who were transformed into bears or wolves.

A psychological analysis of the warlike ecstasy of the berserkers, "whom iron bit not," [45] is not yet possible today. It was characterized by attacks of uncontrollable rage.[46] As an example we may cite the story of twelve seafaring berserkers: "And it was their custom when they were alone to go ashore when they found that the madness was coming over them. And then they flung themselves against forests and huge rocks; for there were times when they had slain their own people and emptied their ships." [47] Another berserker was said to have swallowed live coals and walked through fire in his rages, as members of certain primitive peoples are recorded to have done after initiation.[48]

The same kind of trance occurs in the amok of the Malays, and we find related phenomena in the "invulnerability" of the Balinese dancers; in the madness of the great warrior Ajax, who in one of his attacks slaughtered a herd of cattle, mistaking them for his enemies; and in the madness that made Herakles kill his own wife and children. Characteristically, there are numerous reports that these berserker trances end in total exhaustion and depression.[49]

It is possible that the battles of Oriental heroes and kings with wild animals belong to the same psychological sphere. Mastery of the beast in single combat is among the heroic deeds that accredit the king as such, and battle rage may have been an original hallmark of the warrior chieftain. Among the Germanic peoples this was unquestionably so. The teeth-gnashing rage of the berserkers made them princes, that is, leaders in battle, for *Grim*, 'rage,' is closely related to *Gram*, 'prince.'

---

[45] *Egils Saga Skallagrímssonar*, Ch. 9, in *Thule*, Vol. 3, p. 44.
[46] Ninck, *Wodan*, pp. 34 ff.
[47] Ibid., p. 37.
[48] For example, Buschan, *Die Sitten der*

Völker, Vol. I, pp. 46–47, on the firewalkers of the Beqa, with photographs.
[49] Regarding such other symptoms as barking, frothing at the mouth, blood lust, insensibility, etc., cf. Ninck.

To the same stem belongs 'grimace,' the face distorted by passion, for those seized with battle rage became beasts. They turned into wolves, bears, wild boars, and bulls. But such a change of form is characteristic also for the magical transformation of souls, which is the work of the Great Mother.

We now understand why, on the caldron from Jutland, warriors on foot and on horseback are represented along with the Lady of the Beasts and the sacrifice scene. Here again we clearly have battle magic connected with blood sacrifice and bloody prophecy.

"The Norse rock pictures, these oldest records of the Germanic nature, are full of battles," writes Altheim. "A granite slab near Litsleberg shows a spearsman of more than average size, surrounded by animals and ships. The erected member of this warrior (who may have been either a god or a human hero) is a symbol of his warlike ecstasy, not of his fertility, as has been supposed. It is precisely this ecstatic principle, this demonic, unfathomable character, that makes the god Odin [Wodan] what he is; it is even expressed in his name." [50] Actually there is no contradiction between warlike ecstasy and fertility. The masculine-phallic principle is necessary for the preservation of life as experienced by the matriarchate. The woman is dependent both on the hunting, warring, killing, and sacrificing male—the "knife of the Great Goddess," the phallus that bloodily opens the female—and on the plow that tears open the earth. For she is identical with the thrice-plowed field on which she gives herself for fecundation to the male, of whom she indifferently makes use.[51] Precisely in the primordial god-king, identical with the male's phallic power, who was sacrificed or had to prove his power in battle, we see this twofold, warlike and generative, quality of the Masculine and its essential function in the community.

The male remains inferior to, and at the mercy of, the Feminine that confronts him as a power of destiny. Thus the king was deposed and killed when he was forsaken by the fortunes of war, or when the

---

[50] Altheim, *Die Soldatenkaiser*, pp. 87 f.

[51] The sexual union with the soil that is a constant feature of agricultural fertility rituals is based on the identity of the woman with earth and furrow, of the man with the plow. The nude recumbent goddess is the earth itself.

earth withheld the harvest for which he was responsible. Like all males, he was merely the "bondsman" of the powers, on whose favor he depended.

The symbol of Odin hanging on the tree of fate is typical for this phase (particularly evident in the Germanic sphere), in which the king-hero was characterized merely by an acceptance of fate. The male, who in this stage is largely unconscious, lives in a fatalistic world, driven by the wind of destiny: "One more proof that fate is experienced only passively is offered by the universal Germanic word *werden:* it provides the stem of the names of the two elder Norns (Urth and Verthandi) and in Old Norse it was still employed in the sense of 'must,' and it is in widespread use as an auxiliary for the formation of the passive." [52]

This Fate may appear as a maternal old woman, presiding over the past and the future; or in a young, fascinating form, as the soul. As Valkyrie, as "following spirit," as the emotion-dominating battle fury, it seems to follow the masculine ego. But in reality it is the directing force that the masculine ego obeys.

Dependency on the powers and on the unconscious is an unalterable truth; only man's relation to it changes. In the matriarchal phase, the accent for the male is on being dominated, invaded, violated. The male experiences this force that violates him not as something of his own, but as something "other," alien, and therefore feminine. This is true in all the transformations that the male undergoes, whether he is transformed into an animal, i.e., into a lower but in its own way perfect and homogeneous form of life; whether he loses his "specific principle" and is castrated; or whether, dressed as a woman and identified with the Feminine, the Great Goddess, the anima, the priestess, he fulfills the function of the Feminine.

Accordingly, Ninck has written of Odin: "Like his runic lore and magic power, his gift of poetry comes from water, from the tree, from the Norn, the volva, from the dead. This gift also has a feminine source, as the ancients fully recognized. Gunnlöd holds out the cup to him after three nights of marriage in the darkness of the mountain; the volva

[52] Ninck, p. 198.

sings the principal poem of the Edda at Odin's bidding—poetry is a weaving, spinning, lacing, binding, fastening, as evidenced by numerous terms in the Germanic language, hence a feminine, Norns' activity, yet even in the hands of the volva the male staff is needed to 'awaken' and 'arouse' the song." [53]

The staff is the male symbol in the hand of the woman, the goblet, the vessel, the Feminine. The magic philter, the love potion, the poet's elixir, the intoxicant, soma, and nectar poured by this woman are vehicles of transformation, forms of the water of life, which the Feminine itself is. Through them the male rises to a sublimated, intoxicated, enthusiastic, and spiritualized existence of vision, ecstasy, and creativity, and to a state of "out-of-himselfness" in which he is the instrument of higher powers, whether "good" or "evil."

The ambivalent female mana figure may guide the male or beguile him. Side by side with sublimation stands abasement, as, for example, where man is transformed into an animal, where the human is lost to a superior bestial power. And how close ecstasy is to madness, enthusiasm to death, creativeness to psychosis, is shown by mythology, by the history of religions, and by the lives of innumerable great men for whom the gift from the depths has spelled doom.

THE WOMAN'S EXPERIENCE OF HERSELF
AND THE ELEUSINIAN MYSTERIES

In our exposition of the transformative character, we have thus far stressed the reaction of the male object of transformation. But this must not blind us to the importance of the woman's experience of her own transformative character for her understanding of herself.[1]

The woman experiences herself first and foremost as the source of life. Fashioned in the likeness of the Great Goddess, she is bound up with the all-generating life principle, which is creative nature and a culture-creating principle in one. The close connection between mother

[53] Ibid., p. 328.
[1] Here, again, as in connection with the primordial mysteries, we can only give a brief intimation of a vast field that it would require a "psychology of the Feminine" to consider in full.

and daughter, who form the nucleus of the female group, is reflected in the preservation of the "primordial relationship" between them. In the eyes of this female group, the male is an alien, who comes from without and by violence takes the daughter from the mother. This is true even if he remains in the place of the female group, but much more so if he carries the woman off to his own group.

Abduction, rape, marriage of death, and separation are the great motifs underlying the Eleusinian mysteries. Although these are late mysteries that in a certain sense were usurped by the males, it is to them that we owe much of our knowledge of the matriarchal mysteries. Unquestionably the patriarchal development, which began very early, effaced or at least overlaid many elements of the old matriarchal culture, so that, as in studying a palimpsest, we must first remove the upper layer before we can see the matriarchal culture beneath. The Creto-Mycenaean culture and the Greek culture based on it disclose unmistakable vestiges of the older matriarchate, but we do not know the Cretan ritual.

We know that the Great Goddess was worshiped by priestesses who enacted the bullfights and the games with bulls, and by ephebes who often appeared in woman's dress. And we know that the double ax, the central symbol of the cult, was borne only by women.

The son-lovers and ephebes are familiar to us not only from mythology [2] but also from the frescoes and seals of Crete, in which "men" appear almost exclusively as warriors. Characteristically, these warriors are equipped with the extraordinary shield that symbolizes the protective character of the Great Mother and is worshiped as the Great Mother. The shield-idol is a symbol of the sheltering, protective power of the elementary character of the Feminine; its form is an archaic "abbreviation" of the Primordial Goddess, as is proved by our "violin" figures and the corresponding primitive idol from another cultural sphere.

Pl. 131b

Pl. 24
Pl. 157a

Pl. 54

In Syria, as we have mentioned above,[3] the goddess also appears accompanied by a little girl—her daughter, as we assume—and the

---

[2] My *Origins and History of Consciousness*, index, s.v. "Great Mother, and son-lover."
[3] See above, p. 142.

Cycladean "genealogical" figure of the mother with the daughter on   *Fig. 26*
her head belongs to the same context. The goddess accompanied by one
or two maidens is so frequent in Mycenaean seals that there can be no   *Pl. 146a, b*
doubt of a ritual significance. This motif is perpetuated in the Boeotian
sculpture of Demeter and Kore, which confirms the mother-child re-   *Pl. 147*
lationship between the two. The well-known reliefs, finally, show Kore
full grown and almost identical with her virgin-mother Demeter. Virgin
and mother stand to one another as flower and fruit, and essentially   *Pl. 148*
belong together in their transformation from one to the other.

The goddesses with the flower and the fruit are scarcely distin-
guishable from one another. Demeter and Kore are worshiped in one as
"the Goddesses," and in the pictures where the two appear together one
cannot make out at first which is mother and which is daughter—it is
only their attributes that make the distinction possible. One is often
characterized as a maiden only by the flower she bears, the other as
the mature goddess by the fruit. In the wonderful relief in which the
two look smilingly and knowingly into each other's eyes, both hold   *Pl. 149*
flowers. The early form of Kore holds a flower and the later-enthroned   *Pl. 150b*
youthful Aphrodite bears a fruit, but precisely this goddess enthroned on   *Pl. 153*
sphinxes and adorned with flowers manifests the unity of the two goddesses. Whereas the background of the figure of Aphrodite always discloses the figure of the Great Mother as Lady of Plants and Animals, in
the foreground she always remains the young and seductive goddess.
But even as such she represents not so much the transformative anima
character of the Feminine as the world-governing unindividual love
principle and sexual principle of life.

In the unique relief of a feminine cult both enthroned goddesses   *Pl. 150a*
appear as the twofold aspect of the mother-daughter unity. Their significance is made clear by the representation of cow and calf suggestive
of Crete, and by the abundance of familiar symbols that belong to this
context: flower, fruit, egg, and vessel. The whole is permeated by the
self-contained transformative unity of mother and daughter, Demeter
and Kore. This unity of Demeter and Kore is the central content of the
Eleusinian mysteries.

The one essential motif in the Eleusinian mysteries and hence in all matriarchal mysteries [4] is the *heuresis* of the daughter by the mother, the "finding again" of Kore by Demeter, the reunion of mother and daughter.

Psychologically, this "finding again" signifies the annulment of the male rape and incursion, the restoration after marriage of the matriarchal unity of mother and daughter. In other words, the nuclear situation of the matriarchal group, the primordial relation of daughter to mother, which has been endangered by the incursion of the male into the female world, is renewed and secured in the mystery. And here Kore's sojourn in Hades signifies not only rape by the male—for originally Kore-Persephone was herself the Queen of the Underworld—but fascination by the male earth aspect, that is to say, by sexuality.

In the myth this is reflected by two symbols, the pomegranate and the narcissus. The redness of the pomegranate symbolizes the woman's womb, the abundance of seeds its fertility. Outwitted by Hades, persuaded to taste of the "sweet morsel," the pomegranate seeds, she consummates her marriage with him and belongs to him for at least part of the year. With regard to the other symbol, the seductive narcissus, "which beguiled the maiden," we read in the Homeric "Hymn to Demeter":

> It was a thing of awe whether for deathless gods or mortal men to see; from its root grew a hundred blooms and it smelled most sweetly, so that all wide heaven above and the whole earth and the sea's salt swell laughed for joy. And the girl was amazed and reached out with both hands to take the lovely toy; but the wide-pathed earth yawned . . .[5]

Through this embodiment of the seduction that fills the whole world, through desire to seize the phallus, she "succumbs" to Hades and is carried off by the male from "Mycone," the moon country of virginal dreams.

Figs. 65–66
Pl. 154   Kore's resurrection from the earth—the archetypal spring motif—signifies her finding by Demeter, for whom Kore had "died," and her reunion with her. But the true mystery, through which the primordial

[4] Cf. my *Amor and Psyche.*
[5] Tr. Evelyn-White, p. 289.

situation is restored on a new plane, is this: the daughter becomes identical with the mother; she becomes a mother and is so transformed into Demeter. Precisely because Demeter and Kore are archetypal poles of the Eternal Womanly, the mature woman and the virgin, the mystery of the Feminine is susceptible of endless renewal. Within the female group, the old are always Demeter, the Mother; the young are always Kore, the Maiden.

The second element of the mystery is the birth of the son. Here the woman experiences an authentic miracle that is essential to the orienta-

FIG. *65.* RESURRECTION OF KORE

Seal impression, Boeotia, late Helladic period

tion of the matriarchate: not only is the female, her image, born of woman, but the male as well. The miracle of the male's containment in the female is expressed at the primitive level by the self-evident subordination of the male to the female: even as lover and husband, he remains her son. But he is also the fecundating phallus, which on the most spiritual plane is experienced as the instrument of a transpersonal and suprapersonal male principle. Thus, at the lowest level of the matriarchate, the male offspring remains merely that which is necessary for fertility.

But at the mystery level, where the Kore who reappears is not only she who was raped and vanished but also a Kore transformed in every respect, her childbearing too is transfigured, and the son is a very special son, namely, the luminous son, the "divine child." [6]

FIG. *66.* RESURRECTION OF KORE

Vase design, Attic, IV century B.C.

The luminous male principle is experienced by woman in two forms, as fire and as higher light. In this connection the fire that is everywhere tended by woman is lower fire, earth fire and fire contained in the woman, which the male need only "drill" out of her. The libido that flames up in sexuality, the inner fire that leads to orgasm, and which has its higher correspondence in the orgasm of ecstasy, is in this sense a fire resting "in" the Feminine, which need only be set in motion by the Masculine.[7]

This association is probably as old as the making of fire, which is

[6] Cf. Jung and Kerényi, *Essays on a Science of Mythology.*
[7] See above, p. 294.

often interpreted as a sexual act, with the fire arising, or rather being born, in the feminine wood. For primitive mankind, friction does not "make" fire, but merely calls it forth. Thus archetypally, the "heat," the "ardor," of the woman can also appear as a ruinous diabolical power that burns the male.

Agni, the Indian fire god, is called "he who swells in the mother (the fire board)." [8] And everywhere the meaning of light and fire is attributed to the divine son, down to Christ, who says: "He that is near to me is near the fire" and "Cleave the wood and I am there." [9]

Another expression of this relation between fire and son, wood and the Feminine-Motherly, is that Demeter, like Hecate and many other goddesses, bears a torch as her symbol. The fire of the torch, the lower fire-light son of the wood, corresponds to the upper luminous sons—the stars, moon, and sun—which are the children of the night.

Pls. 156, 161–62

Thus the winged figure of Tanith, the Carthaginian goddess of heaven, standing beneath the vault of heaven and the zodiac, holds the sun and moon in her hands, and is surrounded by pillars, the symbols of the Great Mother Goddess. But on the lower plane of the stele, we find the same goddess stylized with upraised arms, possibly as a tree assimilated to the Egyptian life symbol. Her head is the sun, an illusion to the tree birth of the sun, and she is accompanied by two doves, the typical bird symbols of the Great Goddess.[10]

Pl. 157b

The sons—light and fire—fecundate the maternal darkness from which they were born. But the matriarchal mother-son incest is enacted not only on the lower plane of fertility but also on a higher plane. Torch and light are also fecundating spiritual symbols, and in the Catholic rite of the consecration of the font—the maternal generative principle—when the burning candle is about to be dropped into the water, the celebrant says: "*Ab immaculato divini fontis utero in novam renata creaturam progenies coelestis emergat.*" [11] Through the *hieros gamos* with light and

[8] Deussen, *Geschichte der Philosophie*, Vol. I, pp. 88 f.

[9] From Origen, *Homily on Jeremiah*, 3, 3, and from an Oxyrhynchus papyrus, tr. in James, *The Apocryphal New Testament*, pp. 35, 27.

[10] The right hand above the stele is the symbol of the male godhead.

[11] "May a heavenly offspring, conceived in holiness and reborn into a new creation, come forth from the stainless womb of this divine font."—*The Missal*, ed. O'Connell and Finberg.

fire, the upper and lower feminine principles are kindled, and Mary is still *"igne sacro inflammata."* [12] Over and over again, the darkness of the nocturnal Feminine is kindled and fecundated by fire and light; and even when the luminous embrace means a marriage of death for the woman, it is a death transfigured in new birth.

The mysterious aspect of this process is that the woman always recognizes the fecundating light within her as a son born of her, and that mother-son incest forms the secret background of this spiritual experience. Christ, too, is the bridegroom of Mary—Mother Church, who is and remains his mother. This ancient matriarchal mystery of the birth of the luminous son lives in the words: "The Virgin has given birth; the light grows." [13]

FIG. 67. MOTHER GODDESS WITH SON

Akkadian, basalt seal

The birth of the divine child, whether he bears the name of Horus, Osiris, Helios, Dionysus, or Aeon, was celebrated in the Koreion in Alexandria, in the temple dedicated to Kore, on the day of the winter solstice, when the new divine light is born.

Pl. 157c   One of the oldest representations of the Mother Goddess with son is an Akkadian relief from the middle of the third millennium.[14] Related
Fig. 67 to it are two others, one of which shows the son sitting on the lap of the
Fig. 68 goddess beside a tree, the other the goddess with (apparently) her daughter standing behind her. Both are characterized by sprouting

[12] Buonaiuti, "Maria und die jungfräuliche Geburt Jesu," p. 359.
[13] Gressmann, "Tod und Auferstehung des Osiris," p. 24.
[14] Jeremias, *Handbuch*, p. 255.

tendrils symbolizing tree or earth. With these works we may group the Cretan ring showing the adoration of the divine son—here too the daughter stands behind the mother—and the Christian ring, approximately two thousand years later, showing the adoration of the kings. *Fig. 69*

Fig. 70

Another analogy may be found in the Hindu representation of *Fig. 71* mother and son sitting in the crescent moon, both contained in a uroboric ring with the signs of the zodiac inscribed on it. This picture represents the domination of the moon goddess in the constellation of

FIG. *68*. GODDESS WITH DAUGHTER (?) BEHIND HER

Akkadian, cylinder seal

the year, and it represents also the birth of the luminous son. The bird [15] standing on the sun-lion is probably a symbol of the heavenly mother whose enthronement on the lion *always*, in all likelihood, signifies the domination of the mother-moon over the sun.[16]

The winter solstice, when the Great Mother gives birth to the sun, stands at the center of the matriarchal mysteries. At the winter solstice, the moon is full and occupies the highest point in its cycle, the sun is at its nadir, and the constellation of Virgo rises in the east.[17] "From this position the first month in the oldest known Semitic-Babylonian

[15] See above, pp. 272 ff.
[16] See above reference to the Hindu picture of the goddess riding on a lion and holding the

sun. (I cannot accept Müller's interpretation that fig. 71 represents husband and wife.)
[17] Jeremias, p. 74.

Pl. 130

calendar, which begins with the winter solstice, takes its name: *muhur ilê*, the confrontation of the gods. From this basic position it follows that in astral mythology the moon has an upper-world character and the sun an underworld character. The moon signifies life; the sun signifies death." [18]

But the birth of the sun-child and the related mythological conception of the year are relatively late and abstract. They are preceded by the lunar mythology with its visible and manifest phases of the

FIG. *69*. ADORATION OF THE DIVINE SON

Boeotia, Minoan, impression of a signet ring

moon. To the joyful birth of the annual sun there corresponds in an earlier phase the joy of the true matriarchal childbirth, the birth of the "new light," that is, of the new moon. And records of this have come down to us from all parts of the world.

In an early matriarchal phase the moon was looked upon as the son, the son-lover, the lord of women, and also as he who was sacrificed

[18] Ibid., p. 74.

and torn to pieces. The maternal principle was the light-bearing goddess of the night. Later the conflict between the matriarchate and the masculine principle began to be reflected in the opposition between sun and moon. But in this phase the orientation is still matriarchal: the moon signifies life and the sun death. The death of the feminine moon, the dark moon, is identical with its rape by the male death-sun (Hades),

FIG. *70.* ADORATION OF THE THREE KINGS

Impression of a stone ring, found at Naples, vi *century* A.D.

which is the underworld.

The moon cloaks itself in its dying and is carried off to the underworld, where it suffers a marriage of death with the sun, the negative male principle that rapes and kills the Feminine. From this marriage of death, in which the paternal uroboros is manifested as the sun's deadly embrace, a son is born. The primordial self-fecundation of the Feminine gives way to fecundation by the transpersonal male within the female. Then in the patriarchate, the next stage of development, the sun becomes a dominant and positive symbol.[19]

FIG. 71. QUEEN OF HEAVEN, WITH HER SON

Hindu

The mythological figure of the suffering moon woman plays a role in Christianity, though here of course it undergoes a patriarchal re-

[19] We do not mean to imply that the astral process brought about this mythology or was represented in it; rather, as always, a psychic process is projected upon an "objective" reality that is assimilated to this psychic process. In the "mythological apperception" of early man, these two factors—psyche and object—which we ex- perience as separate conditions, are combined in a single process. What is here projected is the typical segment of female-matriarchal psy- chology, in which the negative Masculine prin- ciple forces the Feminine into a marriage of death, but the Feminine gives birth, so that Kore, the virgin, becomes a mother.

evaluation. Here she becomes *luna patiens;* [20] of her, as of the dying mother in Mexico, who gives birth to a warrior,[21] it is said: "Dying, she will give birth." [22]

But the conjugal *synodos* of sun and moon, in which Selene, Queen of the Night, dies in the new moon, was a familiar motif in antiquity. Hence this conjuncture was regarded as especially favorable for the conclusion of marriages; [23] for as Ambrose still wrote: "The moon wanes to give things their fullness." [24]

The childbearing virgin, the Great Mother as a unity of mother and virgin, appears in a very early period as the virgin with the ear of grain, the heavenly gold of the stars, which corresponds to the earthly gold of the wheat. This golden ear is a symbol of the luminous son who on the lower plane is borne as grain in the earth and in the crib, and on the higher plane appears in the heavens as the immortal luminous son of night. Thus the virgin with the spica, the ear of grain, and the torch-bearer, Phosphora, are identical to the virgin with the child.

Because the upper, spiritual side is contained in the luminous son, the motif of "supernatural birth," i.e., of a conception or birth that is not effected in the lower, earthly manner, belongs to the archetypal sphere of the Virgin–Mother Goddess. The Virgin conceives, as always in the original matriarchal notion, by the Holy Ghost, the transpersonal male of the paternal uroboros; the "seed" is conveyed by food, touch, a kiss; it enters through the ear; and so on. It follows that the birth itself is "unnatural"; the child springs from a rock, a tree,[25] the earth, the mouth, the flank. And this is the symbolic expression of a spiritual-pneumatic reality, not of an antiphysical "purity."

A number of these motifs of matriarchal psychology recur in the Eleusinian mysteries. Some of them have been richly interpreted in the work of Jung and Kerényi,[26] which, however, does not fit them into the context of matriarchal psychology. Otto [27] and Kerényi have pointed

[20] Rahner, "Das Christliche Mysterium von Sonne und Mond."

[21] See above, pp. 195 f.

[22] Rahner, p. 399.

[23] Proclus, scholium on Hesiod, according to Rahner, "Mysterium lunae."

[24] Ambrose, *Hexaemeron* IV, 8, 31, according to Rahner.

[25] See above, Ch. 13.

[26] *Essays on a Science of Mythology.*

[27] Otto, "The Meaning of the Eleusinian Mysteries."

out the correspondence (extending even to such details as the torchlight dance) between the Greek myth of the rape of Kore and the Ceramese myth of Hainuwele,[28] in which the rape and slaying of the maiden are similarly connected with her ascent to the heavens as moon and a pledge of fertility for the world. The belief that "a mythical woman had to die, in order that the fruits of the field might spring from her dead limbs," [29] was, it seems to us, the foundation of the original, matriarchal form of the "queen's ritual," [30] in which woman had to sacrifice herself for the fertility of the world. From all we know of it this queen's ritual was a symbolic marriage of death, in which the royal pair of the year were killed together.[31]

In Eleusis "the community expected its salvation from what took place in the subterranean hall." It is believed that this central event was a forced marriage, ritually enacted by the hierophant, the priestess of Demeter, and those who were to be initiated. This *hieros gamos* was also experienced as a death situation, for the Eleusinian mysteries were compared to a "gruesome celebration of the death night."

Our interpretation is further supported by the circumstance that the Lesser Mysteries preceding the Great Mysteries at Eleusis represented the descent, death, and veiling of Persephone, that is to say, the abduction of Kore, leading up to the Great Mysteries with their forced marriage.[32]

After Demeter's search and sorrowful wanderings, after the period of anxious waiting in the darkness of death, the central action begins. Amid total darkness the gong is struck, summoning Kore from the underworld; the realm of the dead bursts open. There follows the *heuresis*. Suddenly the torches create a sea of light and fire, and the cry is heard:

---

[28] Jensen and Niggemeyer, eds., *Hainuwele: Volkserzählungen von der Molukken-Insel Ceram.*
[29] Otto, p. 94.
[30] See above, pp. 194 f.
[31] See Lord Raglan, *Jocasta's Crime*, p. 123. Just as in later times the god-king of the year was no longer slain as formerly but replaced by a substitute victim, it seems probable and would also be symbolically meaningful that the matriarchal queen, representing the Great Mother and the principle of permanence, was no longer slain, but only her male partner, who changed with the moon and the year. But as the matriarchal position grew weaker and the "negative masculine" principle grew stronger, the motif of the marriage of death, in which the moon maiden dies, gained prominence.

[32] Cf. Kerényi, "The Mysteries of the Kabeiroi."

"The noble goddess has borne a sacred child. Brimo has borne Brimos." This child, whether he be Iacchus, Plutus, Dionysus, Zeus-Zagreus, or Phanes-Eros, is the divine child, identical with the center of the vision, the *epoptia*, the ear of grain shown in silence, which according to a late but essentially correct interpretation is "the perfect great light that comes from the ineffable." [33]

In connection with the *heuresis*, the finding again of Kore by Demeter, or rather their reunion, the mystery of the marriage of death expresses the transformative character of the Feminine as manifested in the experience of growing from girlhood to womanhood. Rape, victimization, downfall as a girl, death, and sacrifice stand at the center of these events, whether they are experienced through the impersonal god, the paternal uroboros, or, as later, personalized and placed in relation to a male who is in every sense "alien."

But Kore is not merely overcome by the male; her adventure is in the profoundest sense a self-sacrifice, a being-given-to-womanhood, to the Great Goddess as the female self. Only when this has been perceived, or emotionally suffered and experienced in the mystery, has the *heuresis*, the reunion of the young Kore turned woman, with Demeter, the Great Mother, been fulfilled. Only then has the Feminine undergone a central transformation, not so much by becoming a woman and a mother, and thus guaranteeing earthly fertility and the survival of life, as by achieving union on a higher plane with the spiritual aspect of the Feminine, the Sophia aspect of the Great Mother, and thus becoming a moon goddess.

For the renascent Kore no longer dwells as before on the earth, or only in the underworld as Persephone, but in conjunction with Demeter becomes the Olympian Kore, the immortal and divine principle, the beatific light. Like Demeter herself she becomes the goddess of the three worlds: the earth, the underworld, and the heavens.

This transformation presents a typical opposition to the Masculine, whose transfiguration appears as an illumination of the head—solification, coronation, and halo. True to her feminine nature, Kore becomes a

[33] Hippolytus, V, 9.

"bearer" of light. Her luminous aspect, the fruit of her transformative process, becomes the luminous son, the divine spirit-son, spiritually conceived and spiritually born, whom she holds on her lap, or who is
Pl. 158 handed up to her by her creative Earth Mother aspect.

With the birth of her son, the woman accomplishes the miracle of nature, which gives birth to something different from itself and anti- thetical to itself. Moreover, the divine son is totally new, not only as to sex but also in quality. Not only does he engender, while she conceives and bears; he is also light in contrast to her natural darkness, motion in contrast to her static character. Thus the woman experiences her power to bring forth light and spirit, to generate a luminous spirit that despite all changes and catastrophes is enduring and immortal.

Her delight at being able to bear a living creature, a son who complements her by his otherness, is increased by the greater delight of creating spirit, light, and immortality, the divine son, through the transformation of her own nature. For in the mystery, she who gives birth renews herself. No doubt the Eleusinian cry, "The noble goddess has borne a sacred child. Brimo has borne Brimos," preserves the name of an ancient and presumably "primitive" goddess. But the mystery action teaches that the resurrected Kore is no longer a Kore who can be abducted by Hades. In the mystery the late psychological insight that matriarchal consciousness was the true native soil of the processes of spiritual growth [34] becomes the "knowledge" of woman, and it is no accident that she experiences Brimos, the male, as a mere variant of her own self as Brimo.

The woman gives birth to this divine son, this unconscious spiritual aspect of herself; she thrusts it out of herself not in order that she her- self may become spirit or go the way of this spirit, but in order that she herself may be fructified by it, may receive it and let it grow within her, and then send it forth once more in a new birth, never totally trans- forming herself into it.

For even if the Feminine has given birth to the moon, the luminous son, or even if it is itself the moon, it remains the nocturnal Great

[34] My "Über den Mond und das matriarchale Bewusstsein."

Round, and the luminous aspect is only one of its aspects, just as Sophia is only *one* aspect of the Great Goddess. In accordance with its masculine nature, masculine psychology will look upon Sophia and worship her as the "highest" aspect of the Womanly. But the Great Mother remains true to her essential and eternal and mysterious darkness, in which she is the center of the mystery of existence.

Only this filial relation of male to female makes intelligible the higher mystery function of the Feminine for the Masculine. In the Eleusinian mysteries the Feminine teacher of Triptolemus invests him *Fig. 72* with the ear of grain to distribute throughout the world. Very significantly, the subservience of the boy Triptolemus to the two Great *Pl. 148* Goddesses is evident in all representations.

This investiture is not an "agricultural" rite, although in the earliest primordial age it was probably bound up with such a rite. In the mysteries at least, it has a far more profound significance. It is the investiture of the male with his chthonic and spiritual fecundating function, which is transmitted to him by woman.

The invested son is himself the golden wheat of this seed, and it is the Great Earth Mother, from whom he has grown, who has endowed him with his true being as a lower and higher god and son of fertility.[35] For this reason his chariot is drawn by the dragons, the power of the Great Mother, and the gold of the grain that he distributes is not only the gold of the earthly grain whose seed is sowed in the earth-womb of the Great Mother, where it dies and whence, transformed, it is resurrected.

Triptolemus on his celestial chariot is also the bearer of the spiritual gold, the supraterrestrial grain, whose mystery seed leads through death in the Great Mother to transformation and resurrection in the celestial meadows of the night sky, where the earthly male rises as an immortal gold-seed-star.

---

[35] We find the same constellation in Egypt, where the moon god Khonsu is the child of Mut, the great vulture Mother Goddess of Heaven, who in her protective character is, like Nekhbet, the king's mother (Kees, p. 355). The spring of this moon-son god is called Benent, which may be interpreted both as "place of rising" and as "seed grain." Thus the son-light-moon-grain symbolism of the matriarchal phase is already evident in Egypt.

A song of the Aztec god Xipe runs:

> It may be that I shall fade, fade and die,
> I the young corn stalk.
> A green jewel is my heart,[36] but I will see gold,
> I will be content once it has grown ripe;
> The warrior chief is born.[37]

FIG. 72. TRIPTOLEMUS IN HIS CHARIOT

Greece, design from an amphora

The transformations of Xipe are those of the corn and also those of the light, both of which rise upward to maturity from the depths of earthly darkness. Here the green Xipe, the god of the young sun and

[36] A green stone was set into the breast of many Aztec statues of gods.
[37] Preuss, *Die Eingeborenen Amerikas*, p. 52.

322

the corn, is transformed into Huitzilopochtli, the war god; for Xipe, the corn, the gold, the sun, has grown ripe.[38] The elementary sentence "A green jewel is my heart, but I will see gold" contains a transformation symbolism that recurs in the transformation of the green Osiris into the sun-golden Ra [39] and in the alchemical transformation of the "green stone" into gold. Thus, in the *Rosarium philosophorum*, we read:

> Our gold is not the common gold. But thou hast inquired concerning the greenness [*viriditas*, presumably verdigris], deeming the bronze to be a leprous body on account of the greenness it hath upon it. Therefore, I say unto thee that whatever is perfect in the bronze is that greenness only, because tha greenness is straightway changed by our magistery into our most true gold.[40]

And the "green lion" of alchemy is the youthful form of the corn god, as also of the sun, the light.

This brings us to the question of why *men* were initiated into the Eleusinian mysteries and what these mysteries, which deal exclusively with the central events in the mysterious life of woman, could mean to men. For in the Homeric "Hymn to Demeter" we read:

> Happy is he among men upon earth who has seen these mysteries; but he who is uninitiate and who has no part in them, never has lot of like good things once he is dead, down in the darkness and gloom.[41]

And if we consider the awe in which all antiquity stood of these mysteries, it is clear that they must have constituted a genuine mystery experience for men as well as women.

The nature of the experience was this: the male initiate, as we can see from many particulars in the accounts, sought to identify himself with Demeter, i.e., with his own feminine aspect. Here it should be stressed that in Eleusis, as in all mysteries, the experience was predominantly emotional and unconscious, so that even in a late epoch, when

---

[38] This transformation into gold and light is characteristic of Mexican mythology, and Preuss declares that "the transformation of nocturnal figures into sun gods is a trait running through the whole Mexican religion; without it the annual cult festivals would be incomprehensible" (Preuss, cited in Danzel, *Magie und Geheimwissenschaft*).

[39] My *Origins:* "Transformation, or Osiris."

[40] Cited in Jung, *Psychology and Alchemy*, p. 152.

[41] Tr. Evelyn-White, p. 322.

the male consciousness had long become patriarchal, such a pre-patriarchal experience was possible in a mystery.

And another essential factor seems to be that in the mysteries the male was enabled, through his experience of the creatively transforming and rebearing power of the Great Mother, to experience himself as her son—i.e., to identify himself both with the newborn, divine spirit son, as child of the Great Goddess, and with Triptolemus, the son invested by her with the golden ear of grain.[42]

The Eleusinian mysteries, in which both men and women partici-pated, stood in this respect between the older, matriarchal mysteries intended only for women (preserved in Rome, for example, in the cult of the Bona Dea) and the male mysteries (such as those of Mith-ras) with their purely patriarchal foundation. This development is illustrated by three works of art, representing a fertility ritual in which the fructifying liquid was poured from a little pot (in the Eleusinian mysteries the men carried such pots) into a large standing jar, the Feminine Vessel.

Pl. 159a In Crete and Boeotia this ritual was enacted only by women; the mother-daughter figures stand on the right; the pouring figure to the left
Pl. 159b also wears woman's dress. In the Eleusinian relief we see the mother-daughter goddess; beside her stands a boy holding the pot, from which
Pl. 159c he pours into the large vessel. On the vase painting in the Cabirion we again have the boy pouring from the pot into the large jar. But behind him sits a father figure. Since Kerényi's work on Hermes,[43] we know of the unity of the Cabirian male principle, of father, boy, and seed. And the phallic significance of the "pouring boy" is unquestionable. Al-though Kerényi here speaks of the "masculine source of life" (and in this late sense we too call these reproductions "patriarchal"), he himself pointed to their ancient matriarchal foundation. "The classical mytho-graphic tradition, which purposely avoids clarity in its statements about mystery gods, calls the primordial mother of the Cabiri Cabiro and also

---

[42] A study of the development of the mys-teries, aimed at determining to what extent changes, additions, etc., were psychologically conditioned by the changes in the people par-taking in the mysteries, is today much to be de-sired.

[43] Kerényi, "Hermes der Seelenführer: Das Mythologem vom männlichen Lebensursprung."

speaks of three 'Cabirian nymphs.' It thus dissolves her triformity in the familiar classical way: it is as though one sculptor were to surround a statue of Hecate with three dancing girls and another were to represent her as three separate smaller goddesses endowed with the attributes of the Great Goddess. Such is the relation of the 'Cabirian nymphs' to the Cabirian Mother. In Thebes the Great Goddess is named Demeter Cabiria, which betokens her relation to the realm of the dead and also to the Cabiri. In all these manifestations she is the primordial feminine source of the absolute male principle of the Cabiri, known to us from the myth of the primordial herma." [44]

But even more clearly than the Mycenaean ring, the representation of Theseus, the patriarchal hero of Greece, being led by Athene to Amphitrite, to obtain the golden ring from her,[45] shows to what degree this "investiture" of the boylike male by the woman was taken for granted. Here we see no man and warrior who already has a great number of heroic deeds behind him, but a boy favored by the goddesses and receiving a gift from them.

Pl. 160

Pl. 146c

Fig. 62

SOPHIA

The dual Great Goddess as mother and daughter can so far transform her original bond with the elementary character as to become a pure feminine spirit, a kind of Sophia, a spiritual whole in which all heaviness and materiality are transcended. Then she not only forms the earth and heaven of the retort that we call life, and is not only the whirling wheel revolving within it, but is also the supreme essence and distillation to which life in this world can be transformed.

Sophia, who achieves her supreme visible form as a flower,[1] does not vanish in the nirvanalike abstraction of a masculine spirit; like the scent of a blossom, her spirit always remains attached to the earthly foundation of reality. Vessel of transformation, blossom, the unity of Demeter reunited with Kore, Isis, Ceres, the moon goddesses, whose

[44] Ibid., p. 90.
[45] Rose, *Handbook of Greek Mythology*, p. 265.
[1] See above, Ch. 13.

luminous aspect overcomes their own nocturnal darkness, are all expressions of this Sophia, the highest feminine wisdom.

In the patriarchal Christian sphere Sophia is reduced to an inferior position by the male god,[2] but here too the female archetype of spiritual transformation makes itself felt. Thus in Dante's poem the sacred *Pl. 163* white rose belonging to the Madonna is the ultimate flower of light, which is revealed above the starry night sky as the supreme spiritual *Pl. 164* unfolding of the earthly. In the Crescent Madonna the Feminine stands again at the center of the earthly and heavenly spheres. And the same is *Pl. 165* true of the medieval painting of Philosophia, one of the medieval forms of Sophia, gathering the arts around her, teaching the philosophers, and inspiring the poets. In our twelfth-century work, the Feminine still, strangely enough, has three heads, like Hecate. She remains the Great *Pl. 166* Mother even when as Philosophia she bears within her the world disk, zodiac, planets, sun, and moon (an exact counterpart to the negative Tibetan cosmic wheel). And the queen sitting with her child in her lap, *Pl. 167* enthroned in the center of paradise, surrounded by the Evangelists and the virtues, is again the feminine self as the creative center of the mandala.

The symbolism of the vessel appears even at the highest level as the vessel of spiritual transformation. Although Christianity did its best to suppress it, this matriarchal symbolism has survived, and not only in the cup of the Last Supper or in the mythical Grail.

The pre-Christian plunge bath signifies return to the mysterious uterus of the Great Mother and its water of life. The plunge bath, which in Judaism has retained its ritual significance down to the present day, became in Christianity the baptismal bath of transformation that, *Fig. 73* as a late work of art still shows, is a return to the primordial egg of the *Pl. 168* beginning. For this reason the baptismal font is a vessel of transformation;[3] it is not only the crown of the tree of life but also the spring of *Pl. 173* life, which, through the descending upper water of the Holy Ghost, becomes an alchemistic vessel of renewal.

[2] Correspondingly, in patriarchal Greece, Athene, whose relation to the Cretan Great Mother, the earth serpent, and to weaving, and whose autochthony, her self-begottenness, are indubitable, becomes the daughter of Zeus, sprung from his head.
[3] Cf. also the baptismal font in Pl. 179.

Paradise, too, is taken as a transformative situation "in the vessel."   *Pl. 169*
Yet because the "fall from grace" is connected, not with the tree of life,
but with the death tree of knowledge, the life vessel of paradise becomes
through it a death vessel of negative transformation, leading downward
to the underworld, into the gaping jaws of hell. In this Christian sphere

FIG. 73. BAPTISM

Illustration from the Roda Bible, xi century

the vessel remains, to be sure, the container of opposites;[4] but as a
recipient of the lower power, it confronts a higher power that as Holy
Ghost, as dove, and as upper water flows down upon it and fructifies it.   *Pl. 173*

[4] Cf. Jung, *Psychology and Alchemy*, index, s.v. "opposites"; and his "The Spirit Mercurius."

In contrast to this, we find later in alchemy a revival of the original matriarchal symbolism of the vessel that contains the whole. This important aspect of alchemy must be discussed at length elsewhere; here a reference to the symbolism of a single picture may suffice. It is a *Pl. 170* representation of the old cosmic egg, the universally known symbol of the primordial matriarchal world, which as Great Round contains the universe. At the base lies the chaos dragon of matter; the uppermost level, also theriomorphic, is the spirit, which as dove, i.e., as "holy spirit-bird," is the quintessence of what must issue from the spirit. Development to it is suggested by two symbols of growth. The trees of sun and moon signify the male and female principles of the polar tension that is to be synthesized; the intertwined and yet hierarchically arranged three figures of body, soul, and spirit are also symbols of the ascending transformation in the womb of the Archetypal Feminine. Over the figure of the spirit with its outspread arms flies the upper bird of the Great Mother, the dove of the Holy Ghost—the supreme spiritual principle.

In many other pictures the alchemistic principle of growth is also symbolized by the ascending snake. The snake is often—and not only in the Biblical story of paradise—the "spirit" of the tree as well as the vessel.[5] The connection between staff and snake, already found in predynastic Egypt, appears in many myths as the often ambiguous but always numinous and divine spirit of a process of growth whose purpose is inaccessible to the intelligence.[6] This phenomenon dominates the symbolism of the "fall from grace" that leads to consciousness, and also the symbolism of alchemy.[7]

In our illustration the transformative process rising from the *Pl. 171* vessel is represented by the pillar-tree, round which is twined the double snake of the opposites that are to be united.[8] This tree is crowned by a Mercury-Queen with a scepter in her hand. The scepter is a combination of the snake-entwined healing staff of Hermes and Asclepius and of the

[5] Cf. Zimmer, *Myths and Symbols in Indian Art and Civilization*, fig. 70.
[6] Cf. the rising Kundalini serpent of Tantric Yoga and the body symbolism of the spinal cord serpent in Chinese alchemy, the Talmud, etc.
[7] Cf. Jung, *Psychology and Alchemy*.
[8] Cf. the sun-moon snakes of the spinal cord in Indian psychology, which are likewise united by alchemy.

lily scepter, which in Crete was already the symbol of goddess and queen. Mercury's bisexuality points here to the corresponding male-female uroboric nature of the Archetypal Feminine, which combines the form of the virgin goddess (lily) with the character of engendering transformation and cure (the caduceus).

Both symbols recur in a late painting of the Annunciation. Here *Pl. 172* the angel bears the staff of saving fecundation, which is at the same time a staff of transformation and healing. But beside Mary stands the vessel that is herself. The body of this vessel bears the host with the name of the divine son, and above it towers the lily of the Cretan virgin goddess. This means that this vessel is the goddess herself bearing the divine sun-child, and Mary—without any conscious intention on the part of the artist—becomes once more the goddess of the beginning.

The feminine vessel as vessel of rebirth and higher transformation becomes Sophia and the Holy Ghost. It not only, like the Gnostic *krater*, receives that which is to be transformed, in order to spiritualize and deify it, but is also the power that nourishes what has been transformed and reborn.

Just as in the elementary phase the nourishing stream of the earth [9] flows into the animal and the phallic power of the breast flows into the *Pl. 29* receiving child,[10] so on the level of spiritual transformation the adult human being receives the "virgin's milk" of Sophia. This Sophia is also *Pl. 174* the "spirit and the bride" of the Apocalypse, of whom it is written: *Pl. 173* "And let him that is athirst come. And whosoever will, let him take the water of life freely."[11]

And at this highest level there appears a new symbol in which the elementary character and the transformative character of nourishment achieve their highest spiritual stage: the heart spring of Sophia, the nourishment of the middle. This central stream flows from Sophia in our *Pls. 165 175*

[9] See above, pp. 47 f.
[10] See above, p. 130.
[11] See Jung, *Psychology and Alchemy* (which was published after the completion of the original MS. of the present work), fig. 7, "A maternal figure presiding over the goddesses of fate," and fig. 26, "The Virgin Mary surrounded by her attributes." Both illustrate the highest feminine figure, the Sophia.

Philosophia, in the Ecclesia, and also in the representation of the Indian
Fig. 51 World Mother. A new "organ" becomes visible, the heart that sends
forth the spirit-nourishing "central" wisdom of feeling, not the "upper"
wisdom of the head.

At this highest level the Feminine more and more loses her original
archetypal character as goddess and seems to become concept and
allegory. Sophia, like Philosophia and in the Jewish sphere Torah, "the
law," and Hokhma, "wisdom" (a central symbol of the cabala), tends
in this direction; while in the Shekinah, the glory of God in exile, and
its personification, Rachel weeping for her children, the personal
character is still preserved, or else reasserts itself.

Here, however, it should be borne in mind that conceptual symbols,
as, for example, the Egyptian Maat, need not necessarily be products of
a late epoch. They seem on the contrary to stand at the beginning of
the development of the human spirit, which starts with an accent on the
visionary symbolic figure and ends with the abstract concept.

In psychological terms, we speak of the law of compensation by
which the unconscious, through dreams and visions, through its reactions and its action-determining mechanisms, equalizes the one-sided
deviations of the centroverted conscious personality. In other words, the
unconscious not only endangers the ego through the superior power of
instincts and drives but also helps and redeems it.

The study of depth psychology has shown that consciousness with
its acquisitions is a late "son" of the unconscious, and that the development of mankind in general and of the human personality in particular
has always been and must be dependent on the spiritual forces dormant
in the subconscious. Thus modern man, on a different plane, discovers
what primordial man experienced through an overpowering intuition;
namely, that in the generating and nourishing, protective and transformative, feminine power of the unconscious, a wisdom is at work
that is infinitely superior to the wisdom of man's waking consciousness,
and that, as source of vision and symbol, of ritual and law, poetry and
vision, intervenes, summoned or unsummoned, to save man and give
direction to his life.

This feminine-maternal wisdom is no abstract, disinterested knowledge, but a wisdom of loving participation. Just as the unconscious reacts and responds, just as the body "reacts" to healthful food or poison, so Sophia is living and present and near, a godhead that can always be summoned and is always ready to intervene, and not a deity living inaccessible to man in numinous remoteness and alienated seclusion.

Thus the spiritual power of Sophia is living and saving; her over-flowing heart is wisdom and food at once. The nourishing life that she communicates is a life of the spirit and of transformation, not one of earthbound materiality. As spirit mother, she is not, like the Great Mother of the lower phase, interested primarily in the infant, the child, and the immature man, who cling to her in these stages. She is rather a goddess of the Whole, who governs the transformation from the elementary to the spiritual level; who desires whole men knowing life in all its breadth, from the elementary phase to the phase of spiritual transformation.

In the patriarchal development of the Judaeo-Christian West, with its masculine, monotheistic trend toward abstraction, the goddess, as a feminine figure of wisdom, was disenthroned and repressed. She survived only secretly, for the most part on heretical and revolutionary bypaths. To follow these pathways lies beyond the scope of our undertaking. Here we can deal neither with the survival of the Great Mother as a witch nor with her return in the Renaissance and her reascent in modern times.[12] We must content ourselves with illustrating the archetypal and irrespressible vitality of the Great Mother with a few pictures from the Christian sphere.

Seen from outside, the "Vierge Ouvrante" is the familiar and un- *Pls. 176–77* assuming mother with child. But when opened she reveals the heretical secret within her. God the Father and God the Son, usually represented as heavenly lords who in an act of pure grace raise up the humble, earth-bound mother to abide with them, prove to be contained in her; prove to be "contents" of her all-sheltering body.

But it is not only in her and in the numerous "mantle" Madonnas *Pl. 178* sheltering needy mankind beneath their outstretched cloaks that the

[12] See my "Die Bedeutung des Erdarchetyp für die Neuzeit."

Great Mother still lives. She may be discerned in still another Christian figure, though this circumstance has passed almost unnoticed.[13] In the

Pl. 180 representations of "St. Anne with Virgin and Child," [14] the unity of the female group of mother-daughter-child, of Demeter, Kore, and the divine son, reappears in all its mythical grandeur. And often in these paintings the Kore-daughter character of the Madonna in relation to Anne as the Great Mother is emphasized even outwardly: here the

Pl. 181 Madonna with Christ sits in Anne's lap, herself like a small child. The childlike quality of the Virgin is even more marked in certain examples of Christian folk sculpture from the Latin countries.

In contrast with this Western development, in which the patriarchal element nearly always overlays and often quite submerges the matriarchal, the fundamental matriarchal structure has proved so strong in the Orient that in the course of time the patriarchal stratum overlaying it has either been annulled or very much relativized. This can be shown not only in Hinduism but also in Buddhism, which was at first so patriarchally abstract and hostile to nature. Here Kwan-yin is the goddess who "hears the cry of the world" and sacrifices her Buddhahood for the sake of the suffering world; she is the Great Mother in her character of loving Sophia.

In India the old matriarchal Goddess has reasserted herself and reconquered her place as Great Mother and Great Round. We have not

Pl. 182 only the Tantric Shakti in mind. Kali herself, in her positive and nonterrible aspect, is a spiritual figure that for freedom and independence has no equal in the West. And on a still higher level stands the "white

Pl. 183 Tara" symbolizing the highest form of spiritual transformation through womanhood.

Pl. 184 Tara is revered as "she who in the mind of all Yogis leads out (*tarani*) beyond the darkness of bondage, [as] the primordial force of self-mastery and redemption." [15] Whereas on the lower plane she is a

---

[13] It may have been noted first in the Eranos Archive.

[14] A particularly strange and significant example of "St. Anne with Virgin and Child" by Joos van Cleve, and the celebrated picture of the same subject by Leonardo, merit a special treatment (see my "Leonardo da Vinci and the Mother Archetype").

[15] Zimmer, "The Indian World Mother," p. 84.

protectress and redemptress, *tarati iti Tara* ('she leads happily across,' hence she is called Tara),[16] on the higher plane it is she who leads out of the world involvement of samsara, which she herself created in her character of Maya. Thus Tara came into being when the sea of knowledge, of which she is the quintessence, was churned.[17]

"In her eternal, loving embrace the great Maya, in her aspect as the 'redeeming one' (Tarini), holds Shiva, the 'imperturbable,' who in the crystal unapproachability of his Yogi immersion is the divine representation of the attitude of the redeemed one. . . .

"As 'perfection of knowledge'—Prajnaparamita—which confers illumination and nirvana, Tara is sublime womanhood in the circle of the Buddhas and Bodhisattvas—especially revered in matriarchal Tibet. . . . In Tantric Buddhism she rises to the very zenith of the pantheon: as Prajnaparamita, she is the mother of all Buddhas—she signifies nothing other than the illumination that makes one into a Buddha, *Paramita*, i.e., gone (*ita*) to the other shore (*param*); she leads the soul across the river of samsara to the far shore which is nirvana. Her emblem as the wisdom of illumination is the book resting on a lotus blossom beside her shoulder, and her hands form a circle signifying the inner contemplation of the true doctrine (*dharma-chakra-mudra*). . . .[18]

"The enchantress, the Great Maya, who delights in imprisoning all creatures in the terrors of samsara, cannot be pronounced guilty in her role of temptress who lures souls into multiform all-embracing existence, into the ocean of life (from the horrors of which she unceasingly saves individuals in her aspect as 'boat woman'), for the whole sea of life is the glittering, surging play of her shakti. From this flood of life caught in its own toils, individuals ripe for redemption rise up at all times, in Buddha's metaphor like lotus blossoms that rise from the water's surface and open their petals to the unbroken light of heaven." [19]

She is not only the power of the godhead as the whirling wheel of life in its birth-bringing and death-bringing totality; she is also the

---

[16] Cf. the Tara Upanishad in *Kaula and Other Upanishads*, ed. by Sîtârâma Shâstrî; and Zimmer, p. 85.

[17] Ibid.

[18] Ibid., pp. 85–86.

[19] Ibid., p. 87.

force of the center, which, within this cycle, presses toward consciousness and knowledge, transformation and illumination.

Thus Brahma prays to the Great Goddess: "Thou art the pristine
spirit, the nature of which is bliss; thou art the ultimate nature and the
clear light of heaven, which illuminates and breaks the self-hypnotism
of the terrible round of rebirth, and thou art the one that muffles the
universe, for all time in thine own very darkness." [20]

But this illumination is no gift or flash of light fallen from heaven;
it is a living growth, which has taken root in the moldering depths of
the earth, which has grown slowly, fed by the numinous water of life,
and put forth a closed bud that only in the end will open up a lotus
blossom "in the unbroken light of heaven."

FIG. 74. TRIMURTI

From a Hindu painting

The Archetypal Feminine in man unfolds like mankind itself. At
the beginning stands the primeval goddess, resting in the materiality
of her elementary character, knowing nothing but the secret of her
womb; at the end is Tara, in her left hand the opening lotus blossom of
psychic flowering, her right hand held out toward the world in a gesture
of giving. Her eyes are half closed and in her meditation she turns to-

[20] Zimmer, *The King and the Corpse*, p. 264.

ward the outward as well as the inner world: an eternal image of the redeeming female spirit. Both together form the unity of the Great Goddess who, in the totality of her unfolding, fills the world from its lowest elementary phase to its supreme spiritual transformation.

In the Indian Trimurti we find at the lowest level the earth symbol, *Fig. 74* the maternal tortoise; on it rests the Great Mother in her terrible character, the death's head with the two antithetical flames spurting from it; and above it the Great Mother as Lotus-Sophia. Concerning this work, Jung writes: "The whole picture corresponds to the alchemical *opus*, the tortoise symbolizing the *massa confusa*, the skull the *vas* of transformation, and the flower the 'self' or wholeness." [21]

Tortoise, vessel of death, and flower are matriarchal transformative symbols of the Great Mother. Slightly modified, they appear as such in our representation of Tara, which encompasses all the stages of feminine transformation.

Each stage of transformation rests on the foundation of a unity of lotus and cobra, of life-giving and deadly power. The base consists of the material world of the tortoise, the lunar world of earth and water; it supports the tree of life with the antagonistic dragons to either side of it: [22] the world of life in the opposites. The crown of this tree is the second lotus upon which stands, strong and powerful, the sun lion of the masculine spirit born of it. But above this lion rises the goddess, Tara-Sophia, no longer riding upon him but enthroned on her own lotus chair. Around her shines a halo of spirit in which the animal principle of the lower world, beginning with the lion, is transformed into a vegetal light, into the grown and growing illumination characteristic of her being. In her hands she holds flowers and above her is spread the fiery canopy of light, strewn with silver star blossoms. And this canopy is herself: moon, lotus, and Tara of the highest knowledge.

If now, in conclusion, we look back over the archetypal world of the Feminine with all the richness of its symbolism and all its interwoven

---

[21] Jung, *Psychology and Alchemy*, fig. 75, p. 147.
[22] Cf. our alchemical illustration, Pl. 171.

constellations and images, we may at first be more impressed by its diversity than by its order and unity. It is to be hoped, however, that the axial structure outlined in Part I has asserted itself in the material, so enabling the image of the Archetypal Feminine to crystallize out in all its grandeur.

The stages of the self-revelation of the Feminine Self, objectivized in the world of archetypes, symbols, images, and rites, present us with a world that may be said to be both historical and eternal. The ascending realms of symbols in which the Feminine with its elementary and transformative character becomes visible as Great Round, as Lady of the Plants and Animals, and finally as genetrix of the spirit, as nurturing Sophia, correspond to stages in the self-unfolding of the feminine nature. In the woman this nature is revealed as the Eternal Feminine, which infinitely transcends all its earthly incarnations—every woman and every individual symbol. But these manifestations of the Archetypal Feminine in all times and all cultures, that is, among all human beings of the prehistoric and historical worlds, appear also in the living reality of the modern woman, in her dreams and visions, compulsions and fantasies, projections and relationships, fixations and transformations.[23]

The Great Goddess—if under this name we sum up everything we have attempted to represent as the archetypal unity and multiplicity of the feminine nature—is the incarnation of the Feminine Self that unfolds in the history of mankind as in the history of every individual woman; its reality determines individual as well as collective life. This archetypal psychical world which is encompassed in the multiple forms of the Great Goddess is the underlying power that even today—partly with the same symbols and in the same order of unfolding, partly in dynamic modulations and variations—determines the psychic history of modern man and of modern woman.

[23] Whereas the world of the Great Goddess is, even more so, eternal and hence can be described in its pure form, independent of the psychic process of the individual, its living reality is based on the individuality of the modern man. For this reason an exposition of the psychic phases of feminine transformation exceeds the scope of this work. We hope that we may be able to submit such a study in the future.

BIBLIOGRAPHY

BIBLIOGRAPHY

(P/B = Princeton/Bollingen paperback)

Albright, William Foxwell. *From the Stone Age to Christianity.* Baltimore and London, 1940.

Allen, John R. *The Early Christian Monuments of Scotland.* (Rhind Lectures for 1892.) Edinburgh, 1903.

Altheim, Franz. *Die Soldatenkaiser.* Frankfort on the Main, 1939.

Aristotle. *Parts of Animals* [*De partibus animalium*]. Translated by A. L. Peck. (Loeb Classical Library.) London and Cambridge, Mass., 1937.

Bachofen, Johann Jakob. *Das Mutterrecht.* (Gesammelte Werke, Vols. II and III.) Basel, 1948. 2 vols.

———. *Die Sage von Tanaquil.* (Ibid., Vol. VI.) 1951.

———. *Versuch über die Gräbersymbolik der Alten.* (Ibid., Vol. IV.) 1954.

———. *Myth, Religion, and Mother Right. Selected Writings of J. J. Bachofen.* Translated by Ralph Manheim. Princeton (Bollingen Series LXXXIV) and London, 1967.

Becker, Jerome. *La Vie en Afrique.* Paris and Brussels, 1887. 2 vols.

Bellows, Henry Adams (tr.). *The Poetic Edda.* New York, 1923.

Benzinger, Immanuel. *Hebraeische Archäologie.* (Angelos Lehrbücher, Vol. I.) 3rd revised edition, Leipzig, 1927.

Bernoulli, Rudolf. "Die Zahlensymbolik des Tarotsystems." *Eranos-Jahrbuch 1934* (Zurich, 1935).

Bleichsteiner, Robert. *Die gelbe Kirche.* Vienna, 1937.

Bloch, Iwan. *Die Prostitution.* Berlin, 1912.

Boeckh, August. *Urkunden über das Seewesen des attischen Staates hergestellt und erläutert.* Berlin, 1840.

Bohmers, A. *Die Aurignac Gruppe.* Berlin, 1942.

Bolte, Johannes, and Polívka, Georg. *Anmerkungen zu den Kinder- und Hausmärchen der Brüder Grimm.* Leipzig, 1912–32. 5 vols.

Breasted, James Henry, Jr. *Egyptian Servant Statues.* (Bollingen Series XIII.) New York, 1948.

Bredon, Juliet, and Mitrophanow, Igor. *Das Mondjahr; chinesische Sitten, Bräuche, und Feste.* Translated from the English by Richard Hoffmann. Vienna, 1937.

BRELICH, ANGELO. *Die geheime Schutzgottheit von Rom.* (Albae Vigiliae, new series, No. 6.) Zurich, 1949.

——. *Vesta.* (Albae Vigiliae, new series, No. 7.) Zurich, 1949.

BRIFFAULT, ROBERT. *The Mothers.* London and New York, 1927. 3 vols.

BRODEUR, ARTHUR GILCHRIST (tr.). *The Prose Edda by Snorri Sturluson.* (Scandinavian Classics, Vol. V.) New York, 1916.

BUDGE, SIR E. A. WALLIS (ed. and tr.). *The Book of the Dead; An English Translation of . . . the Theban Recension.* 2nd edition, revised, London, 1949.

——. *A General Introductory Guide to the Egyptian Collection in the British Museum.* London, 1904.

——. *The Gods of the Egyptians.* London, 1904. 2 vols.

—— and SMITH, SIDNEY. *The Babylon Legends of the Creation.* London, 1931.

BUONAIUTI, ERNESTO. "Maria und die jungfräuliche Geburt Jesu." *Eranos-Jahrbuch 1938* (Zurich, 1939).

BURLAND, C. A. *Art and Life in Ancient Mexico.* Oxford, 1948.

BUSCHAN, GEORG. *Die Sitten der Völker,* Vol. I. Stuttgart, Berlin, Leipzig, 1914–22. 4 vols.

CAIRNS, HUNTINGTON (ed.). *The Limits of Art; Poetry and Prose Chosen by Ancient and Modern Critics.* (Bollingen Series XII.) New York, 1948. (P/B, 3 vols., 1969–70.)

Cambridge Ancient History, The. Cambridge and New York, 1923–39. 12 vols. and 5 vols. of plates.

CAMPBELL, JOSEPH. *The Hero with a Thousand Faces.* New York, 1949; London, 1950. 2nd edn., Princeton, 1968. (P/B, 1972.)

ČAPEK, KAREL. "The Needle." In: *Tales from Two Pockets.* Translated by Paul Selver. London, 1932.

CASSIRER, ERNST. *The Philosophy of Symbolic Forms.* Translated by Ralph Manheim. Vol. III: *The Phenomenology of Knowledge.* New Haven and London, 1957.

CHILDE, V. GORDON. *New Light on the Most Ancient Near East.* London, 1934.

CUSHING, F. H. *A Study of Pueblo Pottery.* (Fourth Annual Report of the Bureau of Ethnology.) Washington, 1886.

DANZEL, THEODOR-WILHELM. *Magie und Geheimwissenschaft.* Stuttgart, 1924.

——. *Mexiko.* (Kulturen der Erde, Vols. XI–XIII.) Hagen and Darmstadt, 1922–23. 3 vols. (Vol. 3 by Ernst Fuhrmann.)

DEUBNER, LUDWIG. *Attische Feste.* Berlin, 1932.

Bibliography

DEUSSEN, PAUL. *Allgemeine Geschichte der Philosophie*. Leipzig, 1899–1920. 7 vols.

DIETERICH, ALBRECHT. *Eine Mithrasliturgie*. Leipzig, 1903; 2nd edn., 1910.

DREWS, ARTHUR. *Die Marienmythe*. Jena, 1928.

DUNBOYNE, LORD (ed.). *The Trial of John George Haigh* (The Acid Bath Murder). (Notable British Trials Series.) London, Edinburgh, Glasgow, 1953.

EBERT, MAX. *Reallexikon der Vorgeschichte*. Berlin, 1924–32. 15 vols.

ERMAN, ADOLF. *Die Religion der Ägypter*. Berlin, 1934.

EVANS, SIR ARTHUR J. *The Earlier Religions of Greece in the Light of Cretan Discoveries*. (The Frazer Lecture, 1931.) London, 1931.

——. "The Palace of Knossos." *Annual of the British School at Athens*, VII (1900–01), 1–120.

——. *The Palace of Minos at Knossos*. London, 1921–36. 4 vols.

——. "The Ring of Nestor: A Glimpse into the Roman After-World." *Journal of Hellenic Studies* (London), XLV (1925), 1–75.

EVELYN-WHITE, HUGH G. (tr.). *Hesiod, the Homeric Hymns and Homerica*. (Loeb Classical Library.) London and Cambridge, Mass., 1920.

FERGUSSON, JAMES. *A History of Indian and Eastern Architecture*. London, 1899.

FOLKARD, RICHARD, JR. *Plant Lore, Legends, and Lyrics*. London, 1884.

FRANKFORT, HENRI. *The Art and Architecture of the Ancient Orient*. (Pelican History of Art.) Harmondsworth, 1954.

——. *Kingship and the Gods*. Chicago, 1948.

——; FRANKFORT, H. A.; WILSON, JOHN A.; and JACOBSEN, THORKILD. *Before Philosophy: The Intellectual Adventure of Ancient Man*. (Penguin Books.) Harmondsworth, 1949.

FRAZER, SIR JAMES GEORGE. *The Golden Bough*. Abridged edn. New York, 1951.

——. *The Worship of Nature*. (The Gifford Lectures, University of Edinburgh, 1924–25.) New York, 1926.

FROBENIUS, LEO. *The Childhood of Man*. Translated by A. H. Keane, Philadelphia, 1909. (Translation of *Völkerkunde in Charakterbildern*, Hanover, 1902.)

——. *Das sterbende Afrika, die Seele eines Erdteils*. (Veröffentlichung des Forschungsinstituts für Kulturmorphologie.) Frankfort on the Main, 1928.

—— and OBERMAIER, HUGO. *Hádschra Máktuba; urzeitliche Felsbilder Kleinafrikas*. (Veröffentlichung des Forschungsinstituts für Kulturmorphologie.) Munich, 1925. 2 vols.

FUCHS, E., and KIND, A. *Die Weiberherrschaft.* In: *Der Geschichte der Menschheit.* Munich, 1913. 3 vols.

FUHRMANN, ERNST. *Reich der Inka.* (Kulturen der Erde, Vol. I.) Hagen and Darmstadt, 1922.

———. *Peru II.* (Kulturen der Erde, Vol. II.) Hagen and Darmstadt, 1923.

———. *See also* DANZEL, *Mexiko.*

FURTWÄNGLER, ADOLF, and REICHHOLD, KARL. *Griechische Vasenmalerei.* Munich, 1904.

"GALAHAD, SIR" (pseud. of Berta Eckstein-Diener). *Mütter und Amazonen.* Munich, 1932.

GELDNER, KARL F. *Vedismus und Brahmanismus.* (Religionsgeschichtliches Lesebuch, edited by Alfred Bertholet, No. 9.) Tubingen, 1928.

GERHARD, EDUARD. *Auserlesene griechische Vasenbilder hauptsächlich etruskischen Fundorts.* Berlin, 1840–47. 3 vols.

GLASER, CURT. *Gotische Holzschnitte.* Berlin, 1923.

GLOTZ, GUSTAVE. *The Aegean Civilization.* Translated by M. R. Dobie and E. M. Riley. London and New York, 1925.

GRAVES, ROBERT. *The White Goddess.* New York and London, 1948.

GRESSMANN, HUGO. *Altorientalische Texte und Bilder zum Alten Testament.* Tübingen, 1909.

———. "Tod und Auferstehung des Osiris nach Festbräuchen und Umzügen." *Der Alte Orient* (Leipzig), XXIII (1923): 3.

GRIFFITH, FRANCIS L. *A Collection of Hieroglyphs.* (Egypt Exploration Society, Memoir No. 6.) London, 1898.

Grimm's Fairy Tales. Translated by Margaret Hunt, revised, corrected, and completed by James Stern, with a folkloristic commentary by Joseph Campbell. New York and London, 1944.

HALL, H. R., and WOOLLEY, C. L. *Ur Excavations.* London, 1927.

HARRIS, FRANK. *Contemporary Portraits* [First Series]. New York, 1915.

HARRISON, JANE E. *Prolegomena to the Study of Greek Religion.* 3rd edition, Cambridge, 1922.

———. *Themis; A Study of the Social Origins of Greek Religion.* Cambridge, 1912.

HEFEL, A. "Der unterirdische Vielkammerbau in Afrika und im Mittelmeergebiet." *Archiv für Völkerkunde* (Vienna), I (1946).

HEIDEL, ALEXANDER. *The Babylonian Genesis.* Revised edition. Chicago, 1951.

HEILER, FRIEDRICH. *Das Gebet.* Munich, 1923.

HOCART, ARTHUR MAURICE. *Kingship.* London, 1927.

HOENN, KARL. *Artemis: Gestaltwandel einer Göttin.* Zurich, 1946.

HOERNES, MORITZ. *Urgeschichte der bildenden Kunst in Europa.* Completed by Oswald Menghin. Vienna, 1925.

HOLLÄNDER, E. *Aeskulap und Venus.* Berlin, 1928.

HOLLIS, SIR CLAUD. *The Nandi: Their Language and Folk-Lore.* Oxford, 1909.

Homeric Hymns. *See* EVELYN-WHITE.

HOVORKA, OSKAR VON, and KRONFELD, ADAM. *Vergleichende Volksmedizin.* Stuttgart, 1908–9. 2 vols.

JACOB, HEINRICH EDUARD. *Six Thousand Years of Bread.* Translated by Richard and Clara Winston. New York, 1944.

JACOBI, JOLANDE. *Complex/Archetype/Symbol in the Psychology of C. G. Jung.* Translated by Ralph Manheim. New York (Bollingen Series LVII) and London, 1959. (P/B, 1971.)

JAMES, M. R. (tr.). *The Apocryphal New Testament.* Oxford, 1924.

JENNIS, LUCAS. *Dyas chymica tripartita.* Frankfort on the Main, 1625.

JENSEN, AD. E., and NIGGEMEYER, H. (eds.). *Hainuwele: Volkserzählungen von der Molukken-Insel Ceram.* Frankfort on the Main, 1939.

JEREMIAS, ALFRED. *Handbuch der altorientalischen Geisteskultur.* Leipzig, 1913.

JUNG, C. G. *Alchemy. See* JUNG, *Psychology and Alchemy.*

——. "Archetypes of the Collective Unconscious." In: *The Archetypes and the Collective Unconscious.* Translated by R. F. C. Hull. (Coll. Works, Vol. 9, i.*) New York and London, 1959. An earlier version (from which the passage quoted in this book is taken) in: *The Integration of the Personality.* Translated by S. M. Dell. New York, 1939; London, 1940.

* References are given in this way to the published volumes of the edition of the Collected Works of C. G. Jung, translated by R. F. C. Hull, now in course of publication in London and Princeton. All have been issued in revised editions. Titles of volumes are as follows:

1. Psychiatric Studies.
2. Experimental Researches.
3. The Psychogenesis of Mental Disease.
4. Freud and Psychoanalysis.
5. Symbols of Transformation.
6. Psychological Types.

7. Two Essays on Analytical Psychology.
8. The Structure and Dynamics of the Psyche.
9, i. The Archetypes and the Collective Unconscious.
9, ii. Aion.
10. Civilization in Transition.
11. Psychology and Religion: West and East.
12. Psychology and Alchemy.
13. Alchemical Studies.
14. Mysterium Coniunctionis.
15. The Spirit in Man, Art, and Literature.
16. The Practice of Psychotherapy.
17. The Development of Personality.
Final Volumes: Miscellaneous.

——. "Instinct and the Unconscious." In: *The Structure and Dynamics of the Psyche.* (Coll. Works, Vol. 8.*) New York and London, 1960.

——. "On the Nature of the Psyche." In: *The Structure and Dynamics of the Psyche.* (Coll. Works, Vol. 8.*) New York and London, 1960. (P/B, 1969.)

——. "On Psychic Energy." In: *The Structure and Dynamics of the Psyche.* (Coll. Works, Vol. 8.*) New York and London, 1960.

——. "A Psychological Approach to the Dogma of the Trinity." In: *Psychology and Religion: West and East.* (Coll. Works, Vol. 11.*) New York and London, 1958; 2nd edn., 1963.

——. *Psychological Types.* (Coll. Works, Vol. 6.*) London and Princeton, 1971.

——. *Psychology and Alchemy.* Translated by R. F. C. Hull. (Coll. Works, Vol. 12.*) New York and London, 1953.

——. "Psychology and Religion." In: *Psychology and Religion: West and East.* (Coll. Works, Vol. 11.*) New York and London, 1958; 2nd edn., 1963.

——. "The Psychology of the Child Archetype." In: *The Archetypes and the Collective Unconscious.* (Coll. Works, Vol. 9, i.*) New York and London, 1959.

——. *Psychology of the Unconscious.* Translated by Beatrice M. Hinkle. New York, 1916; London, 1917. (For revision, see Jung, *Symbols of Transformation.*)

——. "The Relations between the Ego and the Unconscious." In: *Two Essays on Analytical Psychology.* (Coll. Works, Vol. 7.*) New York and London, 1953.

——. "Spirit and Life." In: *The Structure and Dynamics of the Psyche.* (Coll. Works, Vol. 8.*) New York and London, 1960.

——. "The Spirit Mercurius." In: *Alchemical Studies.* (Coll. Works, Vol. 13.*) Princeton and London, 1967.

——. "The Structure of the Psyche." In: *The Structure and Dynamics of the Psyche.* (Coll. Works, Vol. 8.*) New York and London, 1960.

——. *Symbolik des Geistes.* Zurich, 1953.

* See footnote on p. 343.

——. *Symbols of Transformation.* 4th revised edition of *Wandlungen und Symbole der Libido* (*Psychology of the Unconscious*). (Coll. Works, Vol. 5.*) New York and London, 1956.

——. "Trinity." See his "A Psychological Approach to the Dogma of the Trinity."

——. *Wandlungen und Symbole der Libido.* Ein Beitrag zur Entwicklungsgeschichte des Denkens. Leipzig and Vienna, 1912. (First published 1911–12 in the *Jahrbuch für psychoanalytische und psychopathologische Forschungen,* III–IV.) For translation, see Jung, *Psychology of the Unconscious.* For revision, see his *Symbols of Transformation.*

—— and KERÉNYI, C. *Essays on a Science of Mythology.* Translated by R. F. C. Hull. New York, 1950; London (entitled *Introduction to a . . .*), 1951. (Jung's essays in Coll. Works, Vol. 9, i.*) (P/B, 1969.)

—— and WILHELM, RICHARD. *The Secret of the Golden Flower.* Translated by Cary F. Baynes. New York and London, 1931; revised edition, 1962. [Jung's commentary in Coll. Works, Vol. 13.*]

KARSTEN, RAFAEL. *Blood Revenge, War, and Victory Feasts among the Jibaro Indians of Eastern Ecuador.* Washington, 1923.

KEES, HERMANN. *Der Götterglaube im alten Aegypten.* (Mitteilungen der Vorderasiatisch-Ägyptischen Gesellschaft, Vol. 45.) Leipzig, 1941.

KELLER, GUSTAVE, and STRAUB, AUGUST (eds.). *Herrad von Landsberg: Hortus deliciarum.* Strassburg, 1879–99 (1901).

KERÉNYI, C. "Arbor intrat." In: *Niobe.* Zurich, 1949.

——. "Hermes der Seelenführer: Das Mythologem vom männlichen Lebensursprung." *Eranos-Jahrbuch 1942* (Zurich, 1943).

——. "The Mysteries of the Kabeiroi." In: *The Mysteries.* (Papers from the Eranos Yearbooks, 2.) New York and London, 1955.

——. *Töchter der Sonne.* Zurich, 1944.

—— and JUNG, C. G. *See* JUNG and KERÉNYI.

KLAGES, LUDWIG. *Der Geist als Widersacher der Seele.* Leipzig, 1929–32. 3 vols.

* See footnote on p. 343.

KLUGE, FRIEDRICH. *Etymologisches Wörterbuch der deutschen Sprache.* 12th and 13th editions, revised by Alfred Götze. Berlin, 1948.

KOHLBRUGGE, J. H. F. *Tier- und Menschenantlitz als Abwehrzauber.* Bonn, 1926.

KOPPERS, WILHELM. "Zum Ursprung des Mysterienwesens im Lichte von Völkerkunde und Indologie." *Eranos-Jahrbuch 1944* (Zurich, 1945).

KRAUSE, WOLFGANG. *Die Kelten.* (Religionsgeschichtliches Lesebuch, edited by Alfred Bertholet, No. 13.) Tübingen, 1929.

KRICKEBERG, WALTER. "Ballspiel." *See* "Das mittelamerikanische Ballspiel und seine religiöse Symbolik."

——. *Märchen der Azteken und Inkaperuaner, Maya und Muisca.* (Märchen der Weltliteratur.) Jena, 1928.

——. "Das mittelamerikanische Ballspiel und seine religiöse Symbolik." *Paideuma* (Frankfort on the Main), October, 1948.

KÜHN, HERBERT. *Die Kunst der Primitiven.* Munich, 1923.

LANGDON, STEPHEN HERBERT. *Tammuz and Ishtar.* Oxford, 1914.

LAYARD, JOHN W. *The Lady of the Hare.* London, 1944.

——. "The Making of Man in Malekula." *Eranos-Jahrbuch 1948* (Zurich, 1949).

——. *Stone Men of Malekula: Vao.* London, 1942.

LEENHARDT, MAURICE. *Arts of the Oceanic Peoples.* Paris, 1947; London, 1950.

LEEUW, GERARDUS VAN DER. *Phänomenologie der Religion.* Tübingen, 1933.

LEHMANN, WALTER. *Mexikanische Kunst.* (Orbis Pictus, Vol. VIII.) Berlin, 1921.

LEICHT, HERMANN. *Indianische Kunst und Kultur.* Zurich, 1944.

LEISEGANG, HANS. "The Mystery of the Serpent." In: *The Mysteries.* (Papers from the Eranos Yearbooks, 2.) New York, 1955.

LENORMANT, CHARLES, and WITTE, J. J. A. M. *Élite des monuments céramographiques.* Paris, 1844–61. 4 text vols., 4 atlas vols.

LEVY, G. RACHEL. *The Gate of Horn.* London, 1948.

LEWIN, LOUIS. *Phantastica: die betäubenden und erregenden Genussmittel.* Berlin, 1924.

LÖWENFELD, VIKTOR. *The Nature of Creative Activity.* London and New York, 1939.

LUSCHAN, FELIX VON. "Entstehung und Herkunft der ionischen Säule." *Der Alte Orient* (Leipzig), XIII (1912): 4, 1–43.

Bibliography

MAGNÚSSON, FINNUR. *Eddalaeren og dens Oprindelse.* Book III. Copenhagen, 1824–26. 4 vols.

MASPERO, GASTON. *The Dawn of Civilization.* London, 1922.

MEAD, MARGARET. *Sex and Temperament in Three Primitive Societies.* New York, 1935.

MÉNANT, JOACHIM. *Les Pierres gravées de la Haute-Asie.* Paris, 1883–86. 2 vols.

MENSCHING, GUSTAVE. *Buddhistische Symbolik.* Gotha, 1929.

MEREDITH, GEORGE. *A Reading of Earth.* London and New York, 1888.

Miniaturen des frühen Mittelalters. Intro. by Hanns Swarzenski. Bern, 1951.

MODE, HEINZ. *Indische Frühkulturen und ihre Beziehungen zum Westen.* Basel, 1944.

Monumenti inediti, pubblicati dall' Instituto di corrispondenza archeologica (Rome), XII (1884–85).

MORET, ALEXANDRE. *The Nile and Egyptian Civilization.* Translated by M. R. Dobie. London, 1927.

MORLEY, SYLVANUS G. *The Ancient Maya.* Palo Alto, Calif., 1946.

MÜLLER, NIKLAS. *Glauben, Wissen und Kunst der alten Hindus.* Mainz, 1822.

NEUMANN, ERICH. *Amor and Psyche: The Cultural Development of the Feminine— A Commentary on the Tale by Apuleius.* Translated by Ralph Manheim. New York (Bollingen Series LIV) and London, 1960. (P/B, 1971.)

——. "Die Bedeutung des Erdarchetyp für die Neuzeit." *Eranos-Jahrbuch 1954* (Zurich, 1955).

——. *Kulturentwicklung und Religion.* (Umkreisung der Mitte, Vol. I.) Zurich, 1953.

——. "Leonardo da Vinci and the Mother Archetype." In: *Art and the Creative Unconscious.* Translated by Ralph Manheim. New York (Bollingen Series LXI) and London, 1959. (P/B, 1971.)

——. "Mystic Man." In: *The Mystic Vision.* (Papers from the Eranos Yearbooks, 6.) Princeton (Bollingen Series XXX) and London, 1968.

——. *The Origins and History of Consciousness.* Translated by R. F. C. Hull. New York (Bollingen Series XLII) and London, 1954. (P/B, 1970.)

——. "Die Psyche und die Wandlung der Wirklichkeitsebenen." *Eranos-Jahrbuch 1952* (Zurich, 1953).

——. "Über den Mond und das matriarchale Bewusstsein." *Eranos-Jahrbuch*, Sonderband, Vol. XVIII (Zurich, 1950). Also in: *Zur Psychologie des Weiblichen*, q.v.

——. "Die Urbeziehung der Mutter." *Psychologie* (Bern), III (1951): 7 and 8.

——. *Zur Psychologie des Weiblichen*. (Umkreisung der Mitte, Vol. II.) Zurich, 1953.

——. "Zur psychologischen Bedeutung des Ritus." *Eranos-Jahrbuch 1950* (Zurich, 1951). Also in: *Kulturentwicklung und Religion*, q.v.

NIEDNER, FELIX. *See Thule.*

NILSSON, MARTIN P. *Geschichte der griechischen Religion.* (Handbuch der Altertumswissenschaft, Vol. I.) Munich, 1941–50.

——. *Die Religion der Griechen.* (Religionsgeschichtliches Lesebuch, edited by Alfred Bertholet, No. 4.) Tübingen, 1927.

NINCK, MARTIN. *Götter- und Jenseitsglaube der Germanen.* Jena, 1937.

——. *Wodan und germanischer Schicksalsglaube.* Jena, 1935.

O'CONNELL, J. O., and FINBERG, H. P. R. (eds.). *The Missal in Latin and English.* London, 1949.

OPPENHEIM, MAX, BARON VON. *Tell Halaf: A New Culture in Oldest Mesopotamia.* Translated by Gerald Wheeler. London, 1933.

OTTO, RUDOLF. *The Idea of the Holy.* Translated by John W. Harvey. London, 1923.

OTTO, WALTER F. *The Homeric Gods.* Translated by Moses Hadas (from *Die Götter Griechenlands*). New York, 1954.

——. "The Meaning of the Eleusinian Mysteries." In: *The Mysteries.* (Papers from the Eranos Yearbooks, 2.) New York and London, 1955.

PATAI, RAPHAEL. *Man and Temple.* London, 1947.

PERSSON, A. W. *The Religion of Greece in Prehistoric Times.* (Sather Classical Lectures, No. 17.) Berkeley and Los Angeles, 1942.

PETRIE, FLINDERS. *The Making of Egypt.* London and New York, 1939.

PICARD, CHARLES. "Die Ephesia von Anatolien." *Eranos-Jahrbuch 1938* (Zurich, 1939).

——. "Die Grosse Mutter von Kreta bis Eleusis." *Eranos-Jahrbuch 1938* (Zurich, 1939).

PIETSCHMANN, RICHARD. *Geschichte der Phönizier.* (Allgemeine Geschichte in Einzeldarstellungen, Vol. I, 4, 2nd half.) Berlin, 1889.

PIGGOTT, STUART. *Prehistoric India.* (Penguin Books.) Harmondsworth, 1950.

PLATO. *Dialogues of Plato*. Translated by Benjamin Jowett. 3rd edition, London, 1892.

PLUTARCH. *De Iside et Osiride*. In: *Moralia*, Vol. V. Translated by F. C. Babbitt. (Loeb Classical Library.) Cambridge, Mass., and London, 1936.

PORADA, EDITH, and BUCHANAN, BRIGGS (eds.). *Corpus of Ancient Near Eastern Seals in North American Collections*, Vol. I: *The Collection of the Pierpont Morgan Library*. (Bollingen Series XIV.) New York, 1948.

PORTMANN, ADOLF. *Biologische Fragmente zu einer Lehre vom Menschen*. Basel, 1944.

——. "Mythisches in der Naturforschung." *Eranos-Jahrbuch 1949* (Zurich, 1950).

PREUSS, KONRAD T. *Die Eingeborenen Amerikas*. (Religionsgeschichtliches Lesebuch, edited by Alfred Bertholet, No. 2) Tübingen, 1926.

——. *Forschungsreise zu den Kagaba-Indianern*. Vienna, 1926–27.

——. *Die geistige Kultur der Naturvölker*. Leipzig, 1923.

——. *Die Nayarit-Expedition*, Vol. I: *Die Religion der Cora-Indianer* (no more pub.). Leipzig, 1912.

PRINZHORN, HANS. *Bildnerei der Geisteskranken*. Berlin, 1922.

PRITCHARD, JAMES B. (ed.). *Ancient Near Eastern Texts relating to the Old Testament*. Translated by E. A. Speiser et al. Princeton, 1950.

RAGLAN, LORD [Fitzroy Richard Somerset, 4th Baron Raglan]. *Jocasta's Crime*. (Thinker's Library, 80.) London, 1940.

RAHNER, HUGO. "Das christliche Mysterium von Sonne und Mond." *Eranos-Jahrbuch 1943* (Zurich, 1944).

——. "Mysterium lunae." *Zeitschrift für katholische Theologie* (Innsbruck), LXIV (1940).

——. "Das Schiff aus Holz." *Zeitschrift für katholische Theologie* (Innsbruck), LXVII (1943).

—— (ed.). *Mater Ecclesia: Lobpreis der Kirche aus dem ersten Jahrtausend christlicher Literatur*. Einsiedeln and Cologne, 1944.

RANK, OTTO. *The Myth of the Birth of the Hero*. Translated by F. Robins and Smith Ely Jelliffe. (Nervous and Mental Disease Monograph Series, No. 18.) New York, 1941.

RAPHAEL, MAX. *Prehistoric Pottery and Civilization in Egypt*. Translated by Norbert Guterman. (Bollingen Series VII.) New York, 1947.

READ, HERBERT. *The Meaning of Art.* (Penguin Books.) Harmondsworth, 1949.

REICHEL, WOLFGANG. *Über vorhellenische Götterkulte.* Vienna, 1897.

REITLER, RUDOLPH. "A Theriomorphic Representation of Hecate-Artemis." *American Journal of Archaeology* (Cambridge, Mass.), LIII (1949): 29–31.

ROEDER, GÜNTHER. *Die Religion der Babylonier und Assyrer.* Jena, 1915.

ROOSVAL, J. A. H. *Die Steinmeister Gotlands.* (Kungliga vitterhetshistorie och antikvites akademia, Monografiserie, 11.) Stockholm, 1918.

ROSCHER, WILHELM HEINRICH (ed.). *Ausführliches Lexikon der griechischen und römischen Mythologie.* Leipzig, 1884–1937. 6 vols.

ROSE, HERBERT J. *A Handbook of Greek Mythology.* London, 1950.

ROUSE, W. H. D. (tr.). *The Story of Achilles; A Translation of Homer's "Iliad" into Plain English.* London and New York, 1938.

—— (tr.). *The Story of Odysseus.* New York and London, 1937.

ROUSSELLE, ERWIN. *Lau-Dse, Führung und Kraft aus der Ewigkeit.* Wiesbaden, 1950.

SARZEC, ERNEST DE. *Découvertes en Chaldée.* Edited by Léon Heuzey. Paris, 1884–1912. 2 vols.

SCHÄFER, HEINRICH, and ANDRAE, WALTER (eds.). *Die Kunst des alten Orients.* (Propyläen Kunstgeschichte, II.) Berlin, 1925.

SCHARFF, A. "Ägypten." In: W. Otto. *Handbuch der Archäologie,* Part 6, Vol. 1 (Munich, 1939).

SCHMIDT, HUBERT (ed.). *Heinrich Schliemann's Sammlung trojanischer Altertümer.* Berlin, 1902.

SCHOLEM, GERSHOM GERHARD. *Das Buch Bahir.* Leipzig, 1923.

——. *Die Geheimnisse der Schöpfung: Ein Kapitel aus dem Sohar.* Berlin, 1935.

SCHREIBER, THEODOR. *Die Hellenistischen Reliefbilder.* Leipzig, 1890.

SCHUMACHER, GUSTAV. *Tell el-Mutesellim.* Leipzig, 1908–29. 2 vols. in 3.

SELER, EDUARD (ed.). *Codex Borgia, eine altmexikanische Bilderschrift.* Berlin, 1904–8. 3 vols.

SELIGMANN, SIEGFRIED. *Der böse Blick und Verwandtes.* Berlin, 1910. 2 vols.

SETHE, KURT HEINRICH (ed.). *Die alt-aegyptischen Pyramidentexte, nach den Papierabdrücken und Photographien des Berliner Museums.* Leipzig, 1908–22. 4 vols.

SHĀSTRĪ, SĪTĀRĀMA. *Kaula and Other Upanishads.* (Tantrik Texts, edited by Arthur Avalon, XI.) London, 1922.

SMITH, SIR GRAFTON ELLIOT. *The Evolution of the Dragon.* Manchester, 1919.

SPEISER, E. A. *See* PRITCHARD.

SPEISER, FELIX. *Südsee-Urwald Kannibalen.* Leipzig, 1913.

SPEMANN, WILHELM. *Kunstlexikon.* Berlin, 1905.

SPENCE, LEWIS. *The Myths of Mexico and Peru.* London, 1927.

——. *The Outlines of Mythology.* (Thinker's Library, 99.) London, 1949.

——. *The Religion of Ancient Mexico.* (Thinker's Library, 107.) London, 1945.

Standard Dictionary of Folklore, Mythology, and Legend. Edited by Maria Leach. New York, 1949–50. 2 vols.

SYDOW, ECKART VON. *Die Kunst der Naturvölker und der Vorzeit.* Oldenburg, 1926.

THOMSON, GEORGE. *The Prehistoric Aegean.* London, 1949.

Thule: Altnordische Dichtung und Prosa. Edited by Felix Niedner. Vol. 3: *Egils Saga Skallagrímssonar.* Jena, 1923.

THURNWALD, RICHARD. "Primitive Initiations- und Wiedergeburtsriten." *Eranos-Jahrbuch 1939* (Zurich, 1940).

TOOR, FRANCES. *A Treasury of Mexican Folkways.* New York, 1950.

UNDERWOOD, LEON. *Bronzes of West Africa.* London, 1949.

VAILLANT, GEORGE C. *The Aztecs of Mexico.* (Penguin Books.) Harmondsworth, 1950.

VAN DER LEEUW. *See* LEEUW.

VIGFUSSON, GUDBRAND, and POWELL, F. YORK (trs. and eds.). *Corpus Poeticum Boreale: The Poetry of the Old Northern Tongue.* Oxford, 1883. 2 vols.

VIRGIL. *Bucolica, Georgica, Aeneis, illustrata, ornata, et accuratissime impressa.* London, 1750. 2 vols.

WHITEHEAD, H. *The Village Gods of South India.* Calcutta, 1916.

Wiener Vorlegeblätter für archäologische Übungen, 4th series (1872).

WILHELM II [ex-Kaiser of Germany]. *Studien zur Gorgo.* Berlin, 1936.

WILSON, JOHN A. "Egypt." In: Henri Frankfort, H. A. Frankfort, John A. Wilson, and Thorkild Jacobsen. *Before Philosophy: The Intellectual Adventure of Ancient Man.* (Penguin Books.) Harmondsworth, 1949.

ZERVOS, CHRISTIAN. *L'Art en Grèce.* (Editions "Cahiers d'Art.") Paris, 1946.

——. *La Civilization de la Sardaigne.* (Editions "Cahiers d'Art.") Paris, 1954.

ZIMMER, HEINRICH. *The Art of Indian Asia: Its Mythology and Transformations.* Completed and edited by Joseph Campbell. (Bollingen Series XXXIX.) New York, 1955. 2 vols.

——. "The Indian World Mother." In: *The Mystic Vision.* (Papers from the Eranos Yearbooks, 6.) Princeton (Bollingen Series XXX) and London, 1968.

——. *The King and the Corpse.* Edited by Joseph Campbell. New York and London, 1948. (P/B, 1971.)

——. *Maya, der Indische Mythos.* (Gesammelte Werke, Vol. II.) Zurich, 1952.

——. *Myths and Symbols in Indian Art and Civilization.* Edited by Joseph Campbell. New York and London, 1946.

——. *Philosophies of India.* Edited by Joseph Campbell. New York and London, 1951. (P/B, 1969.)

INDEX

INDEX

An asterisk following a page number indicates an illustration on that page. Plate references are indicated in italic.

lion/lioness, 17, 128, 153, 155*, 156*, 183*n*,
216, 220, 239, 272, 273*, 274, 313&*n*,
316*, 323, 335; *Pls. 37, 72, 80, 100, 125,
127, 128a, 129–30, 131a*
lips, 168
liquor, *see* intoxicants
Litsleberg, Norway, 303
Livy, 260*n*
logos, 61, 168
Lombard School, *Pl. 104*
London, England, 222*n*; *Pl. 95*
loneliness, 67–68, 76
Lorelei, 81
lotus, 218, 241, 246, 261, 262, 333–35, 334*
Lovatelli urn, 139
love, withdrawal of, 67–68
love magic, 172, 291
lower aspects, 81, 103–4, 123–28, 138, 211–
12, 214–15
Loyalty Islands, 170
Ludovisi Throne of Venus, *Pl. 155*
Luini, Bernardino, *Pl. 104*
luminosity, 127*n*
luna patiens, 317
lunar consciousness, 54*n*, 56–59; *see also*
moon
Lusatia, 124*n*
luþr, 256
Luxuria, 253
Lycia, 267, 273, 283; *Pl. 150a*
Lydia, 99*n*, 275
Lysimachides, *Pl. 159b*

M

Mâ, 275
Maat, 80
madness, 34*n*, 69, 71, 72–73, 74, 76, 78, 79,
305; *see also* frenzy
Madonna, 168*n*, 222, 223, 234, 261–62,
264*, 273, 326; *Pls. 5, 94, 96–97, 118,
131a, 163–64, 167, 172, 176–78, 180–81*
magic, 16, 30*n*, 41&*n*, 61, 72, 74, 114–15,
116, 136–37, 172–73; hunting, 44*n*, 115,
283; *see also* mana
magic papyrus, Paris, 14
magical anatomy, 42*n*
Magna Mater, 11
Magnússon, Finnur, 249*
maguey, 195, 300, 301*n*
maize, 190, 199
"Majestatis," *Pl. 113*

Malaya, 134, 302
male group, *see* patriarchy
Malekula, New Hebrides, 157, 159, 168*n*,
203; Terrible Goddess in, 173–79, 176*
Mallia, Crete, 125; *Pl. 28b*
Malta, 268, 292, 300*n*; *Pl. 3*
Mama/Mami, 135–36
mana, 106; and woman, 193*, 287–305,
299*, *Pls. 76, 138–41, 143–45*
mandala, 60, 200
mandorla, 145; *Pl. 62*
mandrake, 252*n*
Mangus, 234
Mania, 283
mania, Bacchic, 293
manic and depressive states, 3
Mannhardt, Wilhelm, 259
manticism, 70, 72&*n*, 73, 259, 291, 292–94,
296*n*
mantle, 331; *Pl. 178*
Manyema tribe, *Pl. 78*
Mara, 236
Marduk, 213–15
Mari, Syria, 215; *Pl. 87*
Mars, 41&*n*
Marquesas Islands, *Pl. 75b*
marriage, 317; *see also hieros gamos*
Mary, Virgin, 14, 80, 312, 329; *Pls. 94, 96–
97, 118, 131a, 163–64, 167, 172, 176–78,
180–81*
Masaccio, *Pl. 180*
masks, 107, 168, 195, 265*
massa confusa, 335
mast, 258; *Pl. 120*
Mater larum, 283
materia, 49
maternal uroboros, 19, 21, 34, 37
matriarchal incest, 198
matriarchy, 24*n*, 25&*n*, 28, 43, 48, 50, 52–
54, 72*n*, 94–95, 97, 100, 213*n*, 218, 220,
223–24, 290–91, 304, 328, 332; in America, 179–208; consciousness of, 25*n*, 78–
79; and Eleusinian mysteries, 306, 308,
309, 311, 313–18; in Melanesia, 173–79;
and psychohistorical development, 91–
92; psychology of, 268–72; and transformation mysteries, 55–63
matron stones, 250; *Pl. 112*
maw, 71
maw of the earth, 149*, 200, 201*
Maya, 175, 227*n*, 233, 333

ERICH NEUMANN

Born in Berlin in 1905, Erich Neumann earned his Ph.D. at the University of Berlin in 1927. He then began medical studies in Berlin and completed the examinations for the degree in 1933, after which he left Germany. He studied with C. G. Jung in 1934 and 1936, and from 1934 his permanent home was Tel Aviv, where he practiced as an analytical psychologist. For many years he returned regularly to Zurich to lecture at the C. G. Jung Institute. From 1948 until 1960 he was a regular contributor at the Eranos meetings in Ascona, Switzerland, and he also lectured frequently in England, France, and the Netherlands. He was a member of the International Association for Analytical Psychology and president of the Israel Association of Analytical Psychologists. He died in Tel Aviv on November 5, 1960.

Dr. Neumann had a theoretical and philosophical approach to analysis contrasting with the more clinical concern in England and the United States. His most valuable contribution to psychological theory is the empirical concept of "centroversion," a synthesis of extra- and introversion. His philosophical considerations of psychology are contained in *Tiefenpsychologie und neue Ethik* (1949), but he is best known for his statements of a coherent theory of feminine development. In *The Origins and History of Consciousness* (1949; tr. 1954), which illustrates by interpretations of basic mythologems the archetypal stages in the development of human consciousness, the emphasis on matriarchal symbolism foreshadowed his monumental work *The Great Mother* (first published in English, 1955), a study of the Magna Mater in the art of all times and in ethnological and mythological documents. Other works dealing with the idea of the feminine are *Amor and Psyche: The Psychic Development of the Feminine—A Commentary on the Tale by Apuleius* (1952; tr. 1956) and *The Archetypal World of Henry Moore* (first published in English, 1959). The extent of his interests and his penetrating comprehension of the fine arts are demonstrated by essays on Leonardo da Vinci, Marc Chagall, Mozart, Kafka, Georg Trakl, Jewish symbolism, and many other topics. Some of these are contained in his collected essays (*Umkreisung der Mitte*, 3 vols., 1953–54), four of which are translated in his *Art and the Creative Unconscious* (1959).

PLATES

A. VENUS OF WILLENDORF
Limestone, Austria

B. VENUS OF MENTON
Soapstone, Austria

C. VENUS OF LESPUGUE
Ivory, France

PALEOLITHIC FIGURES OF THE GODDESS

VENUS OF LAUSSEL
Stone relief, France, paleolithic

SLEEPING WOMAN
Clay, Malta, neolithic

ISIS WITH THE KING
Temple of Seti I, Abydos, XIX Dynasty

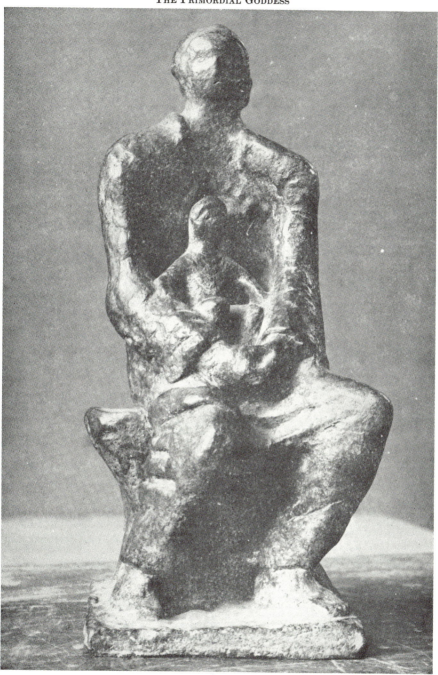

MADONNA AND CHILD
Sculpture by Henry Moore, 1943

GODDESS
Clay, Thrace, neolithic

A. FEMALE FIGURINE
Terra cotta, Peru, pre-Columbian

B. DRAWING BY A
PSYCHOTIC
Germany, xx century

GODDESSES
Clay, Cyprus, c. 2500 B.C.

FRAGMENTS OF FIGURES OF THE GODDESS BELTIS
Stone, Susa, VII *century* B.C.

GODDESSES
Terra cotta, Mesopotamia, c. XXIV *century* B.C.

GODDESSES
Terra cotta, Mesopotamia, c. XXIV *century* B.C.

A. GODDESS
Lead, Troy, iii *stratum (probably from Mesopotamia)*

B. ASTARTE
Gold plaque, Syria, c. xiii *century* b.c.

12

GODDESS
Terra cotta, Crete

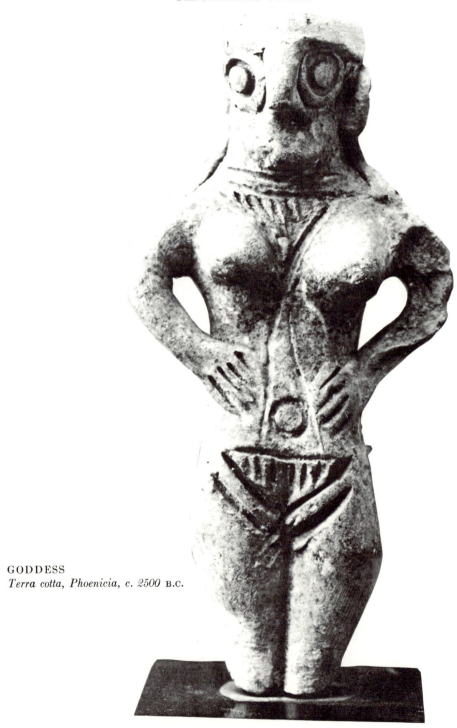

GODDESS
Terra cotta, Phoenicia, c. 2500 B.C.

MOTHER GODDESSES
Clay, India, 1000–300 B.C.

FEMALE FIGURINES
Terra cotta, Ur, c. 3000 B.C.

FEMALE FIGURINE
Terra cotta, perhaps Egypt, c. 2000 B.C.

HEAD
Bronze, Benin, Nigeria

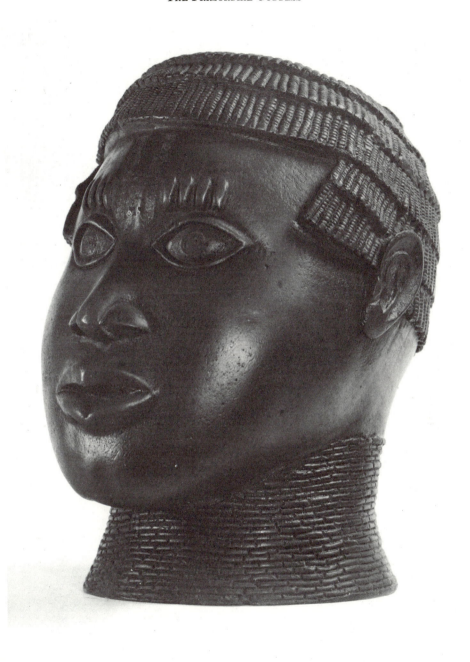

HEAD
Bronze, Benin, Nigeria

GODDESS
Clay, Yugoslavia, Bronze Age

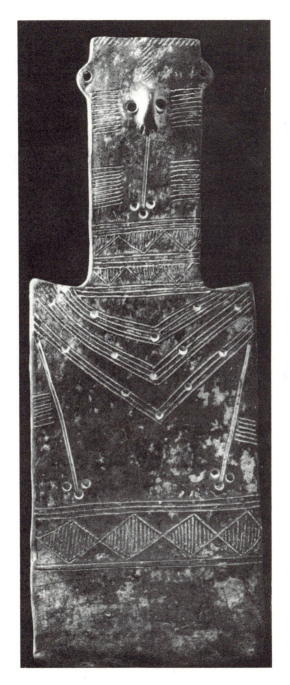

FERTILITY GODDESS
Clay, Cyprus, c. 2500–2000 B.C.

FEMALE FIGURE
Stone, southern France, late neolithic

FEMALE FIGURINES
Stone, Aegean Islands, c. 2500 B.C.

FEMALE FIGURINES
Marble, Cyclades, c. 2500 B.C.

FEMALE FIGURE
Clay, Egypt, predynastic

FEMALE FIGURINES WITH UPRAISED ARMS
Terra cotta, Egypt, predynastic

A. EFFIGY VESSEL
Terra cotta, Troy, IV *stratum*

B. MOTHER GODDESSES
Clay, Crete, Minoan period

A. GODDESS WITHIN UR
Terra cotta, Crete

B. EFFIGY VESSEL
Terra cotta, Crete, early Minoan III *period*

EARTH
From a manuscript, Abbey of Monte Cassino, XI *century*

A. PAINTING BY A PSYCHOTIC
Germany, xx century

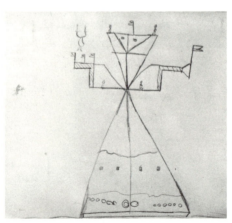

B. CHILD'S DRAWING
Israel, xx century

A. FEMALE CULT FIGURE
Clay, Prussia, IX–VII *century* B.C.

B. EFFIGY VESSEL
Clay, Prussia, VIII–IV *century* B.C.

MOTHER AND CHILD
Terra cotta, Cyprus, xx–xviii *century* B.C.

A. EFFIGY VESSELS: VASE WOMEN
Terra cotta, Cyprus, XII–VI *century* B.C.

B. RAIN GODDESS, WITH WEATHER GOD IN CHARIOT
Cylinder seal, Mesopotamia, Akkad period

FOUR-BREASTED VESSEL
Terra cotta, Peru, pre-Columbian

DIANA OF EPHESUS

Alabaster and bronze, Rome, II century A.D.

THE GODDESS NUT

Painted ceiling relief, Temple of Hathor, Dendera, Egypt, Roman period

GODDESS, HOLDING CHILD, ON LION
Bronze, Hittite, c. 1500 B.C.

ISIS WITH HORUS
Copper, Egypt, c. 2040–1700 B.C.

MOTHER AND CHILD
Wood, Belgian Congo

MOTHER AND CHILD
Effigy vessel, Peru, pre-Columbian

MOTHER AND CHILD
Effigy vessel, Peru, pre-Columbian

MOTHER AND CHILD
Wood, Yoruba, Nigeria

MOTHER AND CHILD
Wood, Yoruba, Nigeria

ISIS-HATHOR, SUCKLING HORUS
Bronze, Egypt, VIII–VI *century* B.C.

CELTIC MOTHER GODDESS
Stone, II *century* A.D.

GODDESS WITH YOUNG GOD
Bronze, Sardinia, prehistoric

GODDESS WITH DEAD YOUNG GOD
Bronze, Sardinia, prehistoric

BAUBO FIGURES
Terra cotta, Priene, Asia Minor, v *century* B.C.

)ESS
ter, Parthian, c. I–II *century* A.D.

THE EARTH GODDESS, TLAZOLTEOTL
From an Aztec codex

HECATE-ARTEMIS AS WHELPING BITCH
Scaraboid seal, archaic Ionian style

WINGED GODDESS
Terra cotta, Mexico, pre-Columbian

FEMALE FIGURE
Clay, Mexico, pre-Columbian

53

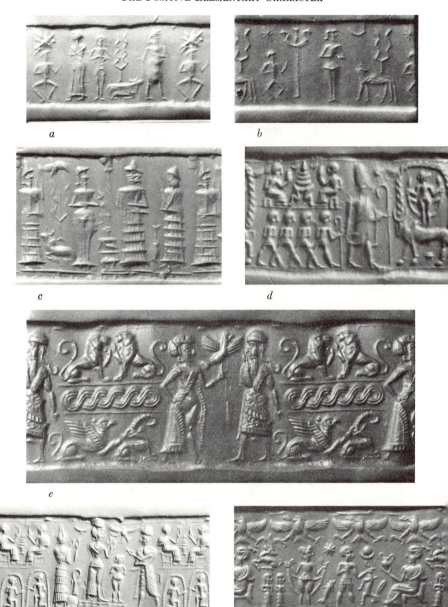

a

b

c

d

e

f

g

THE NUDE GODDESS
Cylinder seals, Babylon, I Dynasty, and Syria, XV century B.C.

A. ENTHRONED NUDE FIGURE
Terra cotta, Sanctuary of Delphi

VESSEL: FEMALE FIGURE AND
AKE
erra cotta, Crete, early Minoan II *period*

SNAKE GODDESS
Faïence, Crete, middle Minoan III *period*

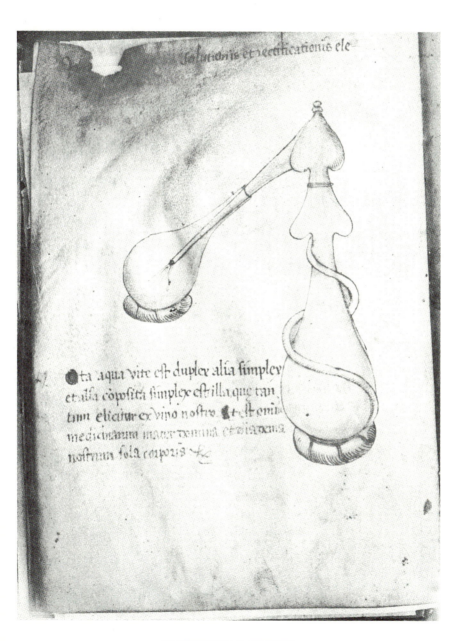

ALCHEMICAL VESSEL
From a Florentine codex, XIII *century*

SNAKE GODDESS
Terra cotta, Greece, VI *century* B.C.

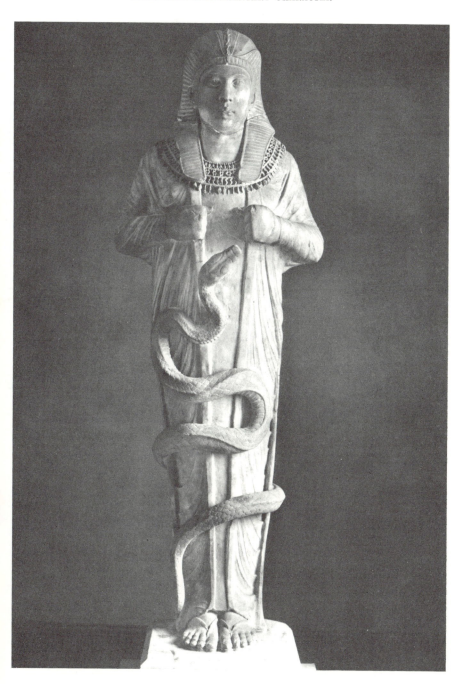

ATARGATIS, OR DEA SYRIA
Bronze, Rome

CERES
Terra-cotta relief, Hellenic

CEREMONY IN HONOR OF CERES
Fresco, Pompeii

THE TRIUMPH OF VENUS
Tray painting, School of Verona, early xv century

SIREN AS INCUBUS
Hellenistic relief

THE GODDESS RATI
Wood, Bali, XIX *century*

KALI DANCING ON SHIVA
Painted clay, India, XIX century

KALI THE DEVOURER
Copper, northern India, XVII–XVIII *century*

KALI
Copper, southern India, XIX *century*

THE EARTH GODDESS COATLICUE
Stone, Aztec

COATLICUE WITH SERPENT SKIRT
Stone, Aztec

GORGON
Marble relief, Corfu, c. VI *century* B.C.

RANGDA STEALING CHILDREN
Watercolor by a modern Balinese

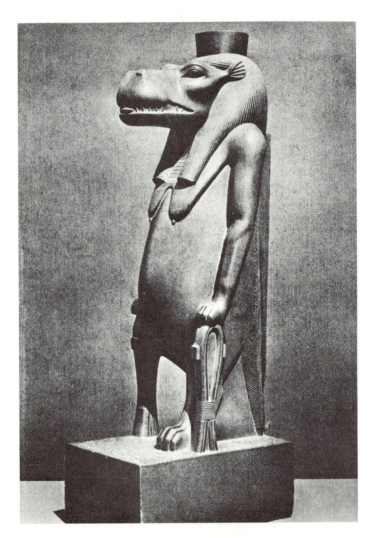

TA-URT
Green schist, Thebes, XXVI *Dynasty*

A. THE WINGED GATE

B. THE WINGED GATE

C. BYRE WITH EMERGING CALVES
Cylinder seals, Mesopotamia, c. 3000 B.C.

LIBATIONS BEFORE THE KING (*ABOVE*) AND
BEFORE THE DOOR OF THE SHRINE (*BELOW*)
Limestone relief, Ur, c. 3000 B.C.

A. HERMES AS PSYCHOPOMP, SUM-
MONING SOULS OF THE DEAD
From a terra-cotta vase, Attic

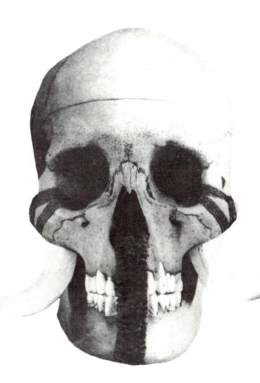

B. ANCESTRAL FIGURE
Decorated skull, Marquesas Islands

SACRIFICIAL BLOOD BOWL: EARTH TOAD
Stone, Mexico, pre-Columbian

THE LAND OF THE DEAD
From an Aztec codex

HEADREST
Wood, Belgian Congo

THE SKY GOD IN THE JAWS OF THE EARTH MONSTER
Sandstone, Mayan, VIII *century*

GORGON, FLANKED BY LIONS
Bronze relief, Perugia, VI *century* B.C.

SOULS IN THE JAWS OF HELL
Detail of wooden choir stall, France (?), medieval

a. Owl god

b. Snail God

CLAY VESSELS
Chimu Indians, Peru

a. Sea crab with star god

b. Sea crab with star god

CLAY VESSELS
Chimu Indians, Peru

a. Serpents strangling (?) the star god

b. Gorgon goddess with sn

c. Crab goddess giving birth

CLAY VESSELS
Chimu Indians, Peru

THE SOLAR BARGE PASSING INTO THE MOUNTAIN
OF THE WEST
From an Egyptian papyrus

FEMALE FIGURINES
Clay, Aztec, Lower Midd
Culture

GODDESS
Alabaster, Mari, Syria,
c. 2500 B.C.

FUNERARY FIGURE
Basalt, Tell Halaf, Mesopotamia, IX *century* B.C.

THE VEILED SPHINX
Stone, Tell Halaf, Mesopotamia, c. IX *century* B.C.

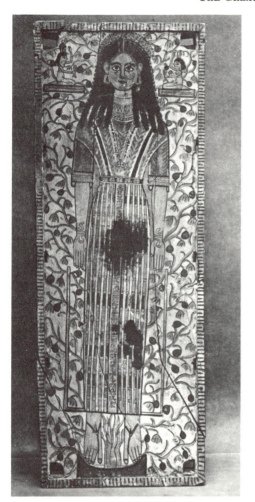

A. PORTRAIT OF THE DECEASED
Sarcophagus bottom, wood, Thebes, II century

B. THE GODDESS NUT
Vaulted cover of same

A. THE GODDESS NUT-NAUNET
Sarcophagus interior, Egypt,
XXI *Dynasty*

B. THE GODDESS NUT
Sarcophagus interior, Egypt

THE GODDESS NUT
Sarcophagus lid, stone, xxx *Dynasty*

ZODIAC
Sandstone relief, Dendera, Egypt, Ptolemaic period

PIETÀ
Italian, xiv century

THE NIGHT
Sculpture by Jacob Epstein, stone, London, 1929

ANNUNCIATION
Fragment of a fresco, Sorpe, Spain, XII *century*

THE VIRGIN MARY
Painting, Upper Rhenish Master, Germany, c. 1400

WHEEL OF LIFE
Painting, Tibet

THE WHEEL OF MOTHER NATURE
From a French manuscript

LAMP WITH GORGON HEAD
Bronze, Etruscan, v *century* B.C.

A. THREE GODDESSES
Cylinder seal, Mesopotamia,
Akkad period

B. THE EUMENIDES
Limestone relief, Argos, Greece

VENERATION OF THE TREE GODDESS
Limestone stele, Egypt, XVIII *Dynasty*

NUT AS TREE GODDESS WITH THE SUN DISK

Bronze vessel, Egypt, Saïte period, c. 600 B.C.

THE BIRTH OF ADONIS
Detail of fresco by Bernardino Luini, Lombard School, c. 1500

PRIMITIVE TREE BURIAL
East Africa (ethnological drawing)

"THE ORIGIN OF THE LINGAM"
Stone, South India, XIII *century*

LINGAM REVEALING THE GODDESS
Stone, Cambodia, XIV century

A. SUN AND MOON TREE
Cylinder seal, Assyria

B. YEAR TREE, WITH THE
TWELVE ZODIAC ANIMALS
Teak and porcelain, China

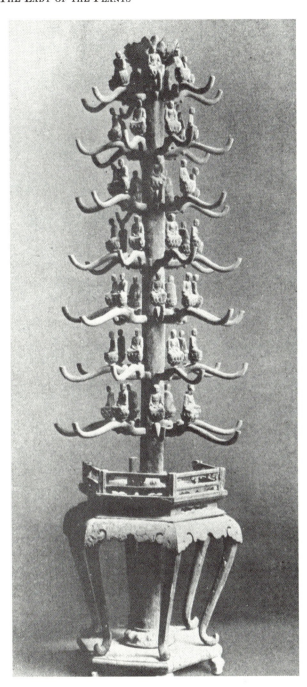

TREE OF THE DEAD
Wood, China

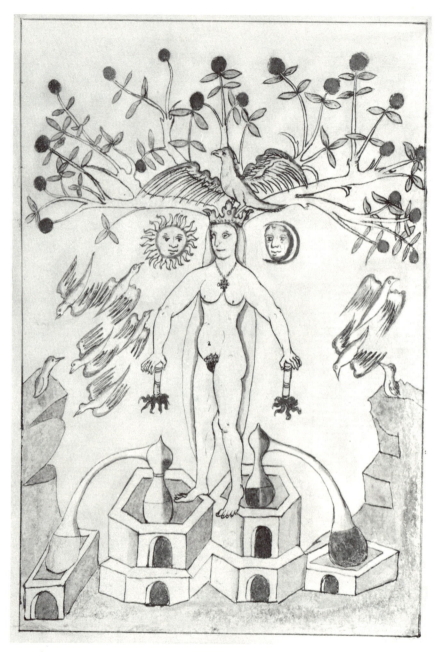

ALCHEMICAL TREE
From a Swiss manuscript, XVI *century*

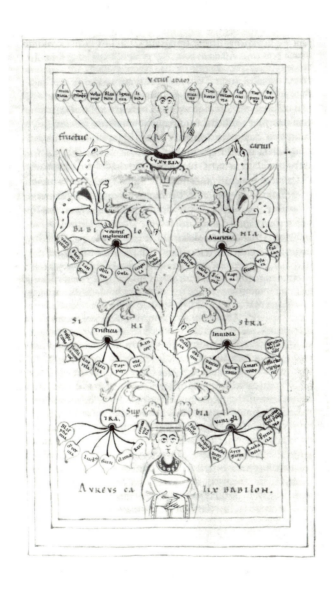

TREE OF VICE
From an Italian manuscript, XIII *century*

MATRON STONE
Roman relief, from Bonn

BAPTISMAL FONT
Sandstone, Gotland, XII century

CHRIST AS A CLUSTER OF GRAPES
Detail of church door, Sion, Switzerland, XIII *century*

THE CHALICE OF ANTIOCH
Silver with gold leaf, I–IV century

115

THE RESTITUTION OF THE MYSTIC APPLE TO THE TREE OF KNOWLEDG
Fresco by Giovanni da Modena, Bologna, xv *century*

SS OF STS. PATRICK AND COLUMBA
'ells, County Meath, Ireland, x century

B. CROSS OF GRAIGUENAMANAGH
County Kilkenny, Ireland, IX century

117

MADONNA AS SHIP
Miniature from a Yugoslav psalter

comminatuʃeʃt ei·ʃtatimq; eiecit
illum·&dixit ei· Uide nemini dixe
riʃ·ʃedua de oʃtende te principi ʃa
cer dotum·& offer pro emundatio
ne tua quae precepit moyʃeʃ in te
ʃtimonium illiʃ·7

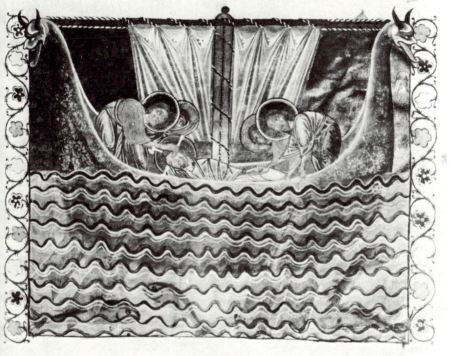

CHRIST ASLEEP IN A SHIP
Miniature from an Austrian lectionary, XI century

SHIP WITH THE CROSS AS MAST
From an Italian manuscript, xv century

LIBATION TO VESSEL WITH BRANCHES, AND SEATED GODDESS
Stone relief, Sumer, c. 3000 B.C.

GODDESS WITH CHILD
Terra cotta, Boeotia, archaic period

FERTILITY GODDESS

Lid of ivory box, Ras Shamra, Syria, Mycenaean, XIII *century* B.C.

a. Relief on a stone bowl

b. Fragment of relief on stone votive feeding trough.

SYMBOL OF THE GREAT MOTHER WITH ANIMALS
Stone reliefs, Sumer, c. 3000 B.C.

ARTEMIS
Stone, Italy, 500 B.C.

LILITH, GODDESS OF DEATH
Terra-cotta relief, Sumer, c. 2000 B.C.

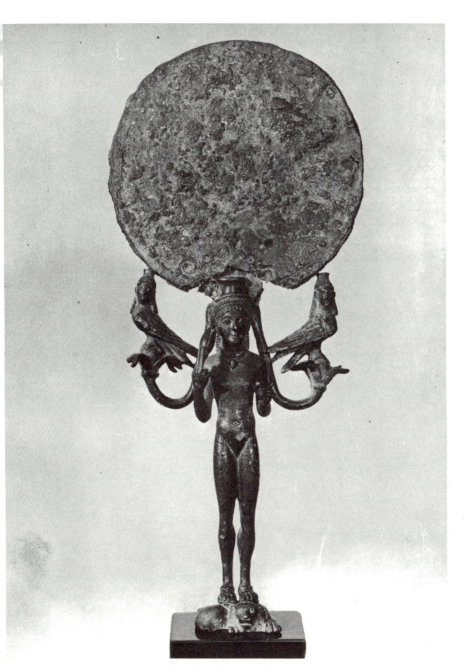

GODDESS WITH SOUL BIRDS, STANDING ON A LION
Bronze mirror, Hermione, Greece, c. 550 B.C.

A. CYBELE ON A LION-DRAWN PROCESSION CAR
Bronze, Rome, II *century* A.D.

B. ISIS OR DEMETER ON A ROSE-WHEELED PROCESSION CAR
Etruscan

FORTUNA
From an Italian manuscript, medieval

GODDESS ON THE COSMIC LION
Miniature, Delhi, India, XVII–XVIII *century*

A. MADONNA ON THE LION THRONE
Wall hanging, xiv *century*

B. ADORATION OF THE SHIELD GODDESS
Painted limestone tablet, Mycenae

a. Detail of vase painting, Etruscan, VI century B.C.

b. Detail of plate, Rhodes

LADY OF THE BEASTS

a. Interior plate: goddess with animals

b. Exterior plate: goddess

c. Bottom plate: hunting of the aurochs

THE GUNDESTRUP CALDRON
Silver, Jutland, III–II *century* B.C.

LADY OF THE BEASTS

Painting, terra-cotta amphora, Boeotian, VII *century* B.C.

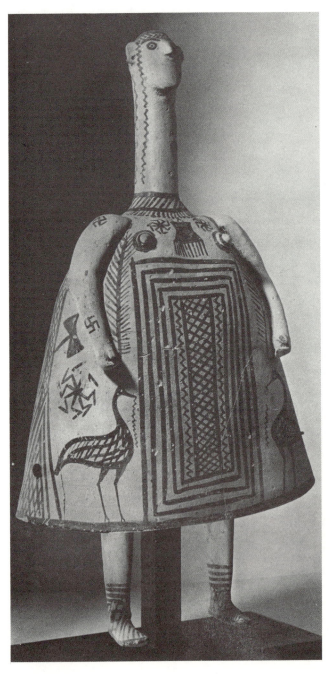

LADY OF THE BEASTS
Terra cotta, Boeotia, archaic period

APHRODITE ON A GOOSE
Terra cotta, Boeotia, classical period

137

HERCULES ON THE NIGHT SEA JOURNEY
Painting, terra-cotta vessel, Attic, c. 480 B.C.

a. Detail, black-figured amphora, Attic, vi *century* B.C.

b. Detail, red-figured vase, Attic, Vulci, v *century* B.C.

REVIVIFICATION OF THE SACRIFICED RAM

THE GUNDESTRUP CALDRON
Silver, Jutland, III–II *century* B.C.

THESSALIAN MOON OATH
Terra-cotta vessel, Greek

RECLINING NUDE GODDESS
Terra cotta, Megara (?), VI *century* B.C.

DANCE GROUP
Clay, Mexico, Tarascan culture, pre-Columbian

BELL-SHAPED GODDESS
Terra cotta, Boeotia, archaic period

GODDESS
Limestone, Cyprus, late VI *century* B.C.

a. Mycenae

b. Thisbe, Boeotia

c. Mycenae

THE GREAT MOTHER
Signet rings, c. 1500 B.C.

DEMETER AND KORE
Stone, Thebes, Boeotia

DEMETER AND KORE
Stone relief, Eleusis, v *century* B.C.

DEMETER AND KORE (?)
Marble stele, Pharsalus, Greece, early v *century* B.C.

A. HARPY TOMB
Marble relief, Xanthos, Lycia, c. 500 B.C.

B. GODDESS WITH FLOWER
Stone, Cyprus, V *century* B.C.

GODDESS WITH POMEGRANATE
Marble, perhaps Attica, VI *century* B.C.

GODDESS AS FLOWER MAIDEN
Stone, Eleusis, Roman period

APHRODITE WITH POMEGRANATE
Terra cotta, Cyprus, vi–v *century* B.C.

THE ASCENT OF KORE
Black-figured vase, Greek

THE BIRTH OF THE GODDESS
Marble relief, Rome (Greek style), v *century* B.C.

DEMETER, TRIPTOLEMUS, KORE
Marble relief, Eleusis, c. 450 B.C.

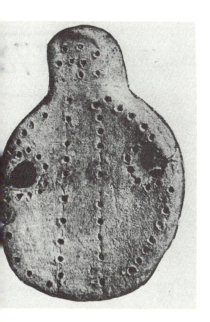

A. IDOL
Clay, Canaan, prehistoric

B. VOTIVE STELE
Stone relief, Carthage

C. MOTHER GODDESS
WITH SON
Cylinder seal, Mesopotamia,
Akkad period

BIRTH OF ERICHTHONIUS
Detail, terra-cotta vase, Attic, c. v century B.C.

A. GODDESS AND LIBATION
Gold seal, Boeotia

B. FUNERAL BANQUET
Votive relief, Eleusis

C. CABIRIAN GROUP
Detail, vessel, Thebes, IV century B.C.

THESEUS, ATHENE, AMPHITRITE
Detail, terra-cotta bowl, Attic, v century B.C.

DIANA LUCIFERA
Stone, Roman

CERES
Fresco, Pompeii

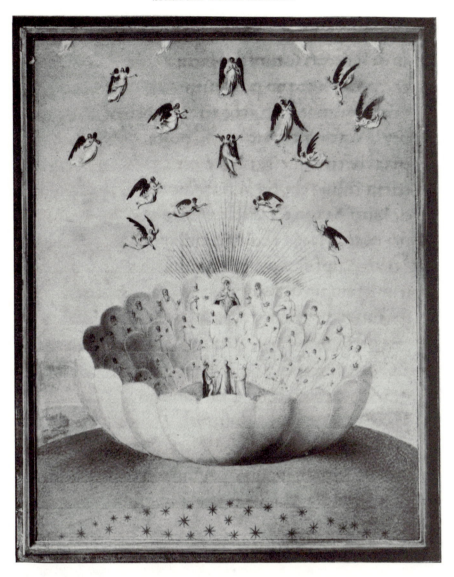

THE WHITE ROSE OF DANTE
Miniature, manuscript of the Divina Commedia, xv *century*

MADONNA
Detail of painting by Theodorus Poulakis, Crete, xvii century

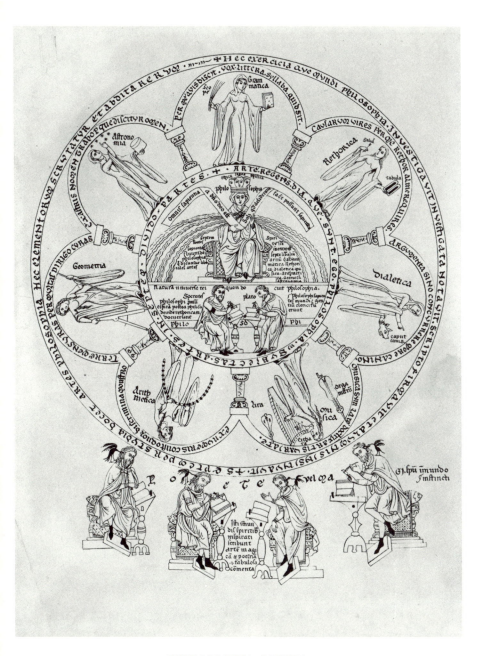

PHILOSOPHIA-SOPHIA

From the manuscript Hortus deliciarum *of Herrad of Landsberg,* XII *century*

PHILOSOPHIA WITH THE WORLD DISK
Miniature from a Flemish manuscript, c. 1420

MADONNA AS PARADISE
From a German manuscript, XIV *century*

BAPTISM
Miniature from the manuscript Les Grandes Heures du duc de Berry, *c. 1400*

PARADISE AS VESSEL
From an Italian manuscript, xv *century*

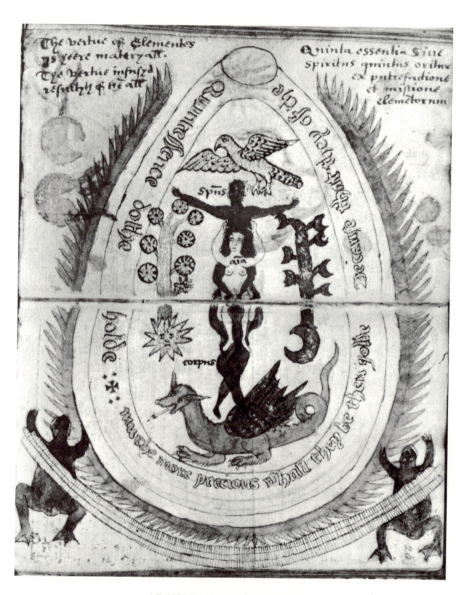

ALCHEMICAL EGG VESSEL
From the manuscript De lapide Philosophorum, *England,* xvi *century*

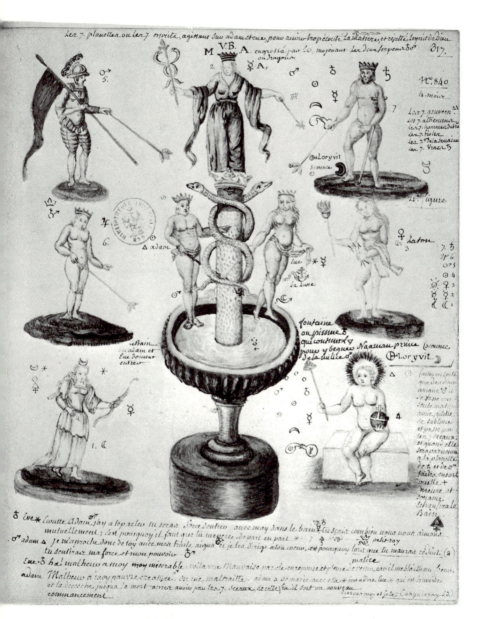

ALCHEMICAL VESSEL WITH TREE
From the manuscript Livre des figures hiéroglifiques, *France*, XVI *century*

ANNUNCIATION
Painting by Bartel Bruyn, Cologne, XVI century

THE OUTPOURING OF THE HOLY SPIRIT
Miniature from Beatus' Commentary on the Apocalypse, XII *century*

SOPHIA-SAPIENTIA
From an Italian manuscript, medieval

ECCLESIA
From a German manuscript, XII *century*

"VIERGE OUVRANTE" *CLOSED*
Painted wood, France, xv century

"VIERGE OUVRANTE" *OPEN*

THE MADONNA OF MERCY
Painting by Giovanni di Paolo, Siena, 1437

THE SPRING OF LIFE
Stone relief, Venice, IX–X century

ST. ANNE, THE VIRGIN, AND THE CHILD
Painting by Masaccio, Florentine School, xv *century*

ST. ANNE, THE VIRGIN, AND THE CHILD
Painted and gilded walnut, Spain, c. xiv *century*

KALI
Bronze, South India, XII–XV *century*

WHITE TARA
Stone, Java, XIII *century*

TARA
Bronze, Tibet

GREEN TARA
Bronze, Tibet

MYTHOS: The Princeton/Bollingen Series in World Mythology

DATE DUE

12-01-13			
			PRINTED IN U.S.A.